CEMETERY LAW

The Common Law of Burying Grounds in the United States

Tanya D. Marsh

Daniel Gibson

ISBN-13: 978-0692519080 (God's Acre Publishing)

ISBN-10: 0692519084

DEDICATIONS

For my grandmother and friend, Eunice Esther (Engelhardt) Marsh who first helped me realize that the grave is full of instruction.

—Tanya D. Marsh

For my wife, Lindsey, whose compassion, kindness, and wisdom comforted me through the anxiety of law school. Without you, I may have been the subject, rather than an author, of this book.

—Daniel Gibson

ACKNOWLEDGEMENTS

We are grateful to those who have contributed their scholarship and creativity to this volume.

Thank you to:

- ❖ Dub Lee for creating the painting that graces the cover of this book;
- ❖ Brett Becker, Al Brophy, Crissy Dixon, Tyler Gardner, Dana Horlick, Ryan Seidemann, and Shelby Roth for contributing their scholarship;
- ❖ Harold Lloyd for his photographs of Highgate Cemetery;
- ❖ Cass Pyatt for his photographs of Crown Hill Cemetery;
- ❖ Liam Sherman for his photograph of Salem Cemetery;
- ❖ Riley Sherman for his art direction; and
- ❖ Mark Clare for his careful editing.

As always, I am nothing short of thankful for my very patient husband, sons, sister, and parents for their cheerful support.

—Tanya D. Marsh

I would also like to thank my parents, John & Sharyn, whose boundless generosity helped get me here.

—Daniel Gibson

CONTENTS

CHAPTER 1

CEMETERY LAW: WHAT IT IS AND WHY IT MATTERS

Crown Hill Cemetery, Indianapolis, Indiana
Photo by Tanya D. Marsh

CHAPTER 1.1
THE GRAVE IS FULL OF INSTRUCTION

Tanya D. Marsh

Oh my love but we are bound to die.
—The Avett Brothers

Just remember that death is not the end.
—Bob Dylan

Cemetery Law: The Common Law of Burying Grounds in the United States is the first comprehensive examination of cemetery law in the United States since the second edition of Percival Jackson's *The Law of Cadavers* was published in 1950. The common law of cemeteries has not changed significantly in the past six and a half decades—or, for that matter, in the past two centuries. Why, then, devote the resources in 2015 to write this book?

Although the law has not changed significantly in 200 years, America has. Two centuries ago, the rules were made by those of European descent (primarily English) and of Christian faith (primarily Protestant). Even after the American Revolution, jurists and legislatures were strongly informed by the precedents set by English law and custom which were, in turn, informed by Roman law and Catholic (canon) law. In 1856, New York attorney Samuel B. Ruggles called the United States the "new, transplanted England of the Western continent" and explained that seventeenth century English ecclesiastical law was the starting point for U.S. cemetery law. However, that body of law depended upon an established Church of England. Even in colonial times, there was diversity among the largely Protestant population, with sometimes stark theological and cultural divides between Anglicans, Puritans, Quakers, Baptists, Anabaptists like Mennonites and the Amish, Moravians, Lutherans, Presbyterians, and Unitarians, among others. The first stumbling block, therefore, in adapting English cemetery law to America was the absence of a single church that would build a universal system of burying grounds and establish the theological and practical rules to govern them.

Instead, beginning in the colonial era, Americans were forced by necessity to innovate. Massachusetts established (and still retains) a law that each town must create a burying ground for the use of residents and strangers. In the Chesapeake, where the population was more widely dispersed, family burying grounds were established in addition to more traditional churchyards. Although the location of American burials differed from the uniform English precedent, other aspects of the process were the same during colonial times. Remains were wrapped in a shroud or encased in a wood coffin, then placed in the earth, a family tomb, or a mausoleum. Americans originally followed other European Christian customs—not all graves were individually memorialized and many contained the remains of more than one person. Early U.S. cemetery law was a rough application of English ecclesiastical law to the realities of the American experience. Jurisdiction over graves and cemeteries was given to courts of equity. As Samuel Ruggles artfully put it—"the dead will find protection, if at all, in the secular tribunals, succeeding, by fair inheritance, to the primeval authority of the ancient, uncorrupted common law." Other legal rules regarding burial and cemeteries essentially remained unchanged, after reflecting the lack of a single, established church.

American disposition practices and the law that governed them, next shifted after the Civil War. Embalming was rarely practiced before the war. During the war, a crude method of embalming was used to stabilize the remains of wealthier men, primarily on the Union side, so they could be sent home for burial. After the Civil War, undertakers trained in embalming evolved into funeral directors. Into the twentieth century, death moved from the home to the hospital; and the ceremonies surrounding death moved from the parlor to the funeral parlor. Undertaking had once been a complementary profession for carpenters—they could build the coffin and transport the remains to the cemetery. But the Industrial Revolution moved casket production from small workshops to factories, particularly after World War II. "Modern business principles" were applied to create modern cemeteries, owned by for-profit companies, larger in scale and designed to minimize the costs of maintenance. These companies benefited from laws that gave great deference to cemetery owners—traditionally families, religious organizations and municipalities—to establish their own rules and regulations. Modern cemeteries adopted rules that required concrete and/or steel vaults or grave liners that would encase the coffin and prevent the uneven terrain that follows grave collapse. These companies also adopted rules that limited graves to a single interment. The cumulative effect is a very different set of practices than existed before the Civil War. Nearly all modern graves in the United States are dedicated in perpetuity to the remains of a single individual, memorialized with a tombstone.

This "traditional" burial—embalming, encasement in a casket, and use of a vault or grave liner in a single, perpetual grave—is still the prevailing practice in the United States. However, Baby Boomers concerned about the cost and environmental consequences of this model have led the first significant change in American disposition practices since the Civil War. Practices that minimize consumption and cost—including "green" burial and cremation—have exploded in popularity in the past decade. Nearly half of all deaths in the United States now result in cremation, and that method of disposition is anticipated to overtake burial in the next few years.

Americans eager to innovate in the disposition of human remains find that the law—still heavily rooted in seventeenth century European assumptions, practices, and beliefs—is ill-equipped to adapt. Cemetery law in the United States has changed little in the past 200 years, but changes in our disposition practices are so widespread and significant that it will soon have no choice. It is unimaginable that we will start with a clean slate. Instead, the law will, as it always does in a common law system, slowly evolve from its current form. This book is therefore designed to help begin that process by illuminating the structure and history of the common law of burying grounds in the United States, including the foundational assumptions, beliefs, and doctrines.

One foundational document in U.S. cemetery law, excerpted in Chapter 6.3, is the 1831 address by Justice Joseph Story at the dedication of Mount Auburn cemetery in Boston, Massachusetts. Story, then an Associate Justice on the United States Supreme Court and a professor at Harvard, emphasized "the duty of the living" to "provide for the dead." He explained that although the obligation to provide "grounds ... for the repose of the dead" is a Christian duty, our "tender regard for the dead" is universal and "deeply founded in human affection." One of the hallmarks of humanity, Story suggested, is that we do not casually dispose of what remains after death.

Story referred to cultural and legal precedents in his speech at Mount Auburn including the stories contained in Genesis 23 and 49 and the practices of the "aboriginal Germans," ancient Egyptians, Greeks, and Romans.

In his address at Mount Auburn, Story suggested that the living are obligated to provide for the dead for several reasons. First, because we are ourselves comforted by the idea that we will be cared for after our own deaths. "We derive solace, nay pleasure, from the reflection, that when the hour of separation comes, these earthly remains will still retain the tender regard of those whom we leave behind." But, Story cautioned, "there are higher moral purposes" that lead us to establish and care for cemeteries—"[i]t should not be for the poor purpose of gratifying our vanity or pride, that we should erect columns, and obelisks, and monuments to the dead; but that we may read thereon much of our own destiny and duty."

> [T]he repositories of the dead bring home thoughts full of admonition, of instruction, and slowly but surely, of consolation also. They admonish us, but their very silence, of our own frail and transitory being. They instruct us in the true value of life, and in its noble purposes, its duties, and its destinations. ... We return to the world, and we feel ourselves purer, and better, and wiser, from this communion with the dead.

I am asked—quite often—why I have dedicated so much time and energy to the study of human remains and cemeteries. This question could be more generally re-framed—why are cemeteries important? I have long struggled to articulate a satisfactory answer. I have always been interested in history. I am a genealogist. I am a real estate lawyer and cemeteries are, after all, a land use. In the process of putting this book together, I have come to understand my true answer—the grave is full of instruction.

I do not remember my first visit to a cemetery, but I do remember my first meaningful visit. I was born and grew up in Indianapolis, but my parents are both from Nebraska. My grandparents were born in Nebraska. My great-grandparents were born in Nebraska. And so on. My interest in genealogy emerged to satisfy my curiosity regarding my paternal grandfather's family. My grandfather, Donald Marsh, died when I was three years old. His parents and one brother died before I was born. His younger brother lived in California. I knew next

Harris Cemetery, Barada, Nebraska

to nothing about the Marsh family or its history except that the Marsh family had been in Richardson County, Nebraska as long as any living person could remember. I asked my grandmother, Eunice (Engelhardt) Marsh question after question about my Marsh family. What were the names of my great-grandparents? Where was their farm? Where did they come from? Grandma was born in Cuming County, Nebraska and moved to Richardson County only after she married my grandfather. Grandma, the daughter of a German farmer and a committed pragmatist, thought that this romantic interest of mine was a waste of time, but she shared what little she knew. Grandma explained that most of the family was gone before she married my grandfather, but that she had often accompanied her mother-in-law and my great-grandmother, Inez (Ray) Marsh, in her annual visits to clean and place flowers on local graves. Grandma couldn't promise that she could remember where all the graves were specifically located, or how they were related to me, but she could take me to the cemeteries and point me in the right direction. After exploring the cemeteries in Richardson County, Grandma and I also visited the cemeteries in Cuming County where her parents, grandparents and other family members rested. In the years since, I've searched for my ancestors in cemeteries in a dozen states. And so, in a very personal way, the grave has been full of instruction for me because it has helped me develop my family tree.

Arborville Cemetery, Arborville, Nebraska

These early expeditions also sparked my eventual interest in the law of cemeteries. If Grandma thought that she'd end my badgering line of questions by taking me to a few cemeteries, she was wrong. Who owns this cemetery? Are there any spots left for me? Cousin Eleanor's grave is unmarked and that just seems wrong. Who do I need to talk to in order to install a tombstone? A tree limb fell on that tombstone and broke it. Is anyone required to fix it? Understandably, Grandma couldn't answer my questions, but it turned out that my Property professor in law school couldn't either. As I learned more about cemetery law, I realized that very few people understood it at all.

As Justice Story advised, the grave also instructs us "in the true value of life, and in its noble purposes, its duties, and its destinations." One of the first burying grounds that Grandma and I visited was Harris Cemetery in the community once known as Barada in Richardson County, Nebraska. The Marsh family plot there contains the remains of my great-great-great-grandparents—Elijah Marsh and Delilah (Horner) Marsh and many of their children. Elijah and Delilah were born in southwestern Ohio in the early 1830s. As a young couple, they headed west and stopped in Wisconsin and Missouri before finally settling in Nebraska Territory in the 1850s. Elijah and his two eldest sons, including my great-great-grandfather William S. Marsh, enlisted with the Missouri cavalry during the Civil War, leaving Delilah and a half-dozen children alone for months at a time to run a farm beyond the edge of settlement. One of the few true epiphanies that I have had occurred while standing in Harris Cemetery on a beautiful summer day, perfectly quiet save for the whistling of the wind and the songs of birds. Staring at their tombstone, I realized that there is nothing that I can ever attempt to do that could come close to the level of risk that Elijah and Delilah Marsh willingly accepted when they left their home in Ohio in order to give their children, their children's children, and, ultimately my children and myself, a better life. The grave is full of instruction.

My maternal grandmother—Pansy (Curren) Eschliman—also regularly visited graves to place flowers. Her parents are buried in Arborville Cemetery, in York County, Nebraska. Like so many small towns in the Great Plains, Arborville has disappeared, but the cemetery remains, the only tangible reminder of a thriving community and all who lived there. The cemetery contains the small tombstone of my aunt, Shirley Jean Eschliman, who was born January 17, 1938. "She lived to be just 17 days old," Grandma wrote, "so we didn't get to keep her." Shirley Jean's grandparents, Harvey Curren and Frances (Conrad) Curren, gave their daughter Pansy and son-in-law Harley Eschliman a portion of their lot at Arborville so that they could bury their baby. My grandparents now occupy the graves on one side of Shirley Jean and my great-grandparents are on the other side. They could not keep her in life, but ensured that they could watch over her in death. As Justice Story wrote, "[d]ust as we are, the frail tenements, which enclose our spirits but for a season, are dear, are inexpressibly dear to us."

The existence of cemeteries remind and comfort us about our own mortality, allow us to discover and remember the past, and grant us a place to grieve and find solace. The grave is full of instruction, but not all of the instruction is positive. After the shooting of Michael Brown in 2014, when the nation's attention was focused on Ferguson, Missouri, I received a phone call from a reporter in New York. He had visited Ferguson and stumbled across what he thought may be a story. The cemetery in Ferguson, the last resting place for generations of African-Americans, had been abandoned. It sat in the middle of a residential neighborhood but was overgrown, covered with trash, and a magnet for crime. The reporter viewed the neglected cemetery as a symbol of a broader abandonment of the African-American community in Ferguson. He wanted to know if African-American cemeteries were particularly vulnerable to neglect. I regretfully informed him that cemetery abandonment has been a problem since colonial days. And while, yes, African-American cemeteries are more likely to include unmarked graves, abandoned cemeteries are a broader problem. As Justice Story's address notes, Mount Auburn was established in 1831 by the "gentlemen" of Boston to solve a still-lingering problem.

> It is painful to reflect, that the Cemeteries in our cities, crowded on all sides by the overhanging habitations of the living, are walled in only to preserve them from violation. And that in our country towns they are left in a sad, neglected state, exposed to every sort of intrusion, with scarcely a tree to shelter their barrenness, or a shrub to spread a grateful shade over the new-made hillock.

The perpetual dedication of a grave to a single person is a deeply entrenched norm in the United States, even though it is of recent vintage. Common and statutory law protects graves from disinterment and desecration. Cemeteries are tangible memorials to the past, but the law does not force us to honor or even remember that past. One of the cemeteries that I most enjoy visiting is Cupola Cemetery in Richardson County, Nebraska. There are a dozen graves there, including my great-great-grandparents—William S. Marsh and Lillie (Calvert) Marsh—and her parents. Cupola Cemetery sits on a knoll overlooking a cross-roads about a mile north of the town of Verdon. The Marsh family farmhouse once stood on the opposite corner. William and Lillie lived in that house when they buried her parents. They could have sat on the front porch at twilight and seen the tombstone through the grass. I can't find records that establish Cupola Cemetery. As far as I can tell, it is merely a corner of another farm. Sometimes when I visit the graves, the cemetery has been newly mown. After we buried our grandmother in Verdon Cemetery, my cousin and I visited

Cupola Cemetery, near Verdon, Nebraska

the graves with our families and walked through the then-tall grass to pull weeds obscuring the tombstones.

One reason that cemeteries fall into a "sad, neglected state" is because people move away. The Marsh family lived in Richardson County, Nebraska for nearly 150 years. They came from Southeastern Ohio, where they lived for 50 years, and before that from New Jersey and Rhode Island. None of us live in any of those places anymore. I'm probably the only member of the family that even knows about those previous homes and my own visits to the Marsh graves in Highland County and Adams County, Ohio are intermittent. My aunt and uncle live in Kansas City and visit Richardson County often. Still, that isn't the same as sitting on the porch of the Marsh farmhouse, watching over the cemetery across the road.

Since the middle of the 20th century, cemeteries have been required to establish perpetual care funds for maintenance and repair. The Ferguson cemetery was supposed to have such a fund, but the law doesn't appear to have done any good. The cemeteries where my family are buried pre-date such requirements, and now largely depend upon the episodic benevolence of neighbors and those who still feel a connection to them.

The "traditional" American burial—each of us occupying a single grave, encased in metal and wood and concrete—provides graves full of instruction, but it also consumes a great deal of land and resources. In Western Europe, few deaths result in a single, perpetually dedicated grave. The vast majority of deaths result in cremation or temporary burial followed by deposit in a communal ossuary. As American social norms evolve closer to the modern Western European model, we stand to both gain and lose much.

Cemeteries are expensive and take land in our most densely populated areas out of service to the living, yet provide us with personal and communal reminders of the past. The texts and cases in this book agree that cemeteries are important, although sometimes for different reasons. The materials from the United States universally acknowledge the influence of English ecclesiastical law, but simultaneously reflect a view that America is entitled to its own unique cemetery law. What form that law shall take in the future remains to be seen. But the foundation for it can be found in these pages.

❖ ❖ ❖

Crown Hill Cemetery, Indianapolis, Indiana
Photo by Cass Pyatt

CHAPTER 1.2
EVERY GRAVE TELLS A STORY
Daniel Gibson

When I started working on funeral and cemetery law, my mum had the best response: "What?" Most of my friends have no idea this is a distinct area of law. Those that do (mainly from my own insistence and instruction) doubt its utility.

I will admit I have had my doubts. I began working on cemetery law because I liked Professor Marsh. "Any job is better than no job," my wife liked to remind me As I delved into the history and (for me) the theology of cemetery law, I became more and more engrossed. I liked cemetery law—even if I still doubted its utility. I couldn't, for all my passion, intellectually explain why cemetery law was important.

I still can't. What I can do is say why it is important to me and why it will be important to you.

My wife and I had been married six-months when her father was diagnosed with brain cancer. By another six months, he was gone. I'd studied funerals and burial. I felt I knew all the law, all the issues, and all my opinions. Nothing prepared me for death. I, a self-proclaimed expert, felt powerless to help. The week of the funeral blurred by us all. We were too busy grieving to make thought-out decisions about the funeral. Viewings, receptions, even the burial itself had a momentum of their own. We laid him to rest in an antebellum cemetery much like the one at Mount Auburn, and rested ourselves.

Death finds us all. Our culture's tendency is to run. Even after death we hide it with make-up, cosmetics, and dangerous chemicals. We stubbornly refuse to think, or plan, for it.

Joseph Story found "lessons of human morality" in cemeteries. Here we confront death. Planned or unplanned, we will all be buried.

I study cemetery law, not merely because I like the history and the theology, because of what I have learned from cemeteries. Every grave tells a story. It tells a story of lives lived. It shows you their connections. It tells a story of place and a people. To preach the resurrection, the Puritans drew souls ascending to heaven on their graves. Modern memorial parks offer organized, unobtrusive, standardized graves and so speak of our values. Our law and practices reflect those values. In studying the law we learn the story our graves try to tell. To my ear, the story goes something like "Run. Hide. Think of life instead." Many modern graves tell this story without even thinking about it.

I hope my grave will tell a different story.

This flesh and blood of mine will meet their end. But, even in this yet unresurrected world, that is not the end. I hope to be buried. I hope to be remembered. I hope that my grave can instruct my children like the graves of my fathers have instructed me: "This is where you came from; this is where you are; this is where you will go."

❖　❖　❖

Crown Hill Cemetery, Indianapolis, Indiana
Photo by Cass Pyatt

CHAPTER 1.3
KEY PRINCIPLES OF U.S. CEMETERY LAW
Tanya D. Marsh

The key principles of U.S. cemetery law can be divided into two categories. The first is the dedication of real property for cemetery purposes, which I contend is essentially an implied servitude burdening the real estate and benefitting the public. It is comparable to a public right of way. The second is the common law right of sepulcher, which is an easement in gross, benefiting the next of kin of the occupant of the grave.

DEDICATION OF LAND FOR CEMETERY PURPOSES

Principle #1
A parcel of real estate set apart for the burial of the dead, regardless of whether it has been used for such purpose, is a "cemetery."

Principle #2

Once land has been characterized, by dedication or use, as a cemetery, it may not be used for any other purpose (or inconsistent purposes – compare to railroad easements) **except as expressly permitted by law.**

Principle #3

A "cemetery" … used by the general community or neighborhood, or a church, is a "public cemetery", while one used by a family only, or by a small portion of community, is a "private cemetery". The owners of private cemeteries may freely discriminate based on any criteria other than the race of the decedent.

Principle #4

Cemeteries are not a "per se" nuisance

THE COMMON LAW RIGHT OF SEPULCHER

State and federal courts, including the U.S. Supreme Court, have emphasized that the Right of Sepulcher is well-established in our "case law and traditions." *See Nat'l Archives & Records Admin. v. Favish*, 541 U.S. 157, 168 (2004) ("th[e] well-established cultural tradition acknowledging a family's control over the body and death images of the deceased has long been recognized at common law.") In 2012, the Ninth Circuit Court of Appeals concluded that this right was protected by substantive due process. *Marsh v. Cnty. of San Diego*, 680 F.3d 1148, 1154-55 (9th Cir. 2012) ("[W]e find that the Constitution protects a parent's right to control the physical remains, memory and images of a deceased child against unwarranted public exploitation by the government.") State courts have long and consistently supported a common law Right of Sepulcher, although they do not always refer to it by name.

> The right to the next of kin to control and direct the burial of a corpse and arrange for its preservation is not only a natural right, embracing a high order of sentiment, but has become to be well recognized as a legal right.
> *Whitney v. Cervantes*, 328 P.3d 957, 960 (Wash. Ct. App. 2014).

Before interment, the Right of Sepulcher attaches to the remains themselves and exists for the purpose of preservation and disposition of the remains. After interment, the Right of Sepulcher attaches to the grave or tomb in which the remains have been interred and exists for the purpose of protecting the remains. If a third party interferes with the Right of Sepulcher, either before or after interment, the person holding the right may be entitled to damages or, more commonly, equitable relief.

Principle #1

The Right of Sepulcher is a perpetual easement in gross.

     a.   The Right of Sepulcher may be created by express agreement of the parties or, in the absence of such agreement, by the operation of law upon the interment of human remains in real estate.

b.   The burdened parcel is the cemetery or larger parcel in which the grave or tomb is located.

c.   A Right of Sepulcher may be created before interment if a person purchases such right from a cemetery.

Principle #2

At common law, in the absence of any testamentary disposition, the Right of Sepulcher initially belongs to the next of kin. (Most states have statutes that at least partially modify this common law rule.)

Principle #3

At common law, the Right of Sepulcher passes via intestate succession. It is neither devisable nor alienable. [If the decedent gave the Right of Sepulcher to a non-family member via testamentary disposition, the common law is unclear regarding who inherits that right]

Principle #4

The Right of Access, a perpetual easement in gross that arises by operation of law, permits the descendants of a decedent to cross private property to access a grave or tomb. The Right of Access is neither devisable nor alienable. The Right of Access is broader than the Right of Sepulcher and benefits a larger number of descendants.

Principle #5

Human remains are not property. After interment, human remains become a part of the real estate in which they have been interred.

Principle #6

There is a strong presumption at common law that once interred, human remains shall not be disinterred except with the consent of the holder of the Right of Sepulcher and a court of equity.

Principle #7

At common law, the holder of the Right of Sepulcher has the right (and sometimes the obligation) to protect the grave from desecration or interference.

Principle #8

Interference with interred human remains shall be remedied by courts of equity rather than courts of law.

Principle #9

If human remains are disturbed after interment:

a.   the holder of the Right of Sepulcher has equitable remedies at common law based on the common law tort of interference with the Right of Sepulcher; and

b.   the owner of the grave has equitable remedies at common law based on the common law claim of trespass *quare clausum fregit*.

Principle #10

The rights of the grave owner, the holder of the Right of Sepulcher (if different from the grave owner), and the cemetery owner must be balanced and disputes among them shall be resolved by courts of equity who shall consider, among other things, the wishes of the decedent.

❖   ❖   ❖

King's Chapel Burying Ground, Boston, Massachusetts
Photo by Tanya D. Marsh

CHAPTER 1.4
THE SOURCE OF U.S. CEMETERY LAW
Tanya D. Marsh

Article I, Section 14 of the Constitution of the State of New York provides:

> Such parts of the common law ... as ... did form the law ... on the nineteenth day of April, one thousand seven hundred seventy-five... shall be and continue the law of this state ... [b]ut all such parts of the common law ... as are repugnant to this constitution, are hereby abrogated.

Similar provisions are included in other state constitutions and statutes. As Justice Joseph Story stated in *Van Ness v. Pacard*:

> The common law of England is not to be taken in all respects to be that of America. Our ancestors brought with them its general principles, and claimed it as their birthright; but they brought with them and adopted only that portion which was applicable to their situation.

Van Ness v. Pacard, 27 U.S. 137, 143-44 (1829).

As both the New York Constitution and the United States Supreme Court reflect, English common law as it existed in the 1770s is the foundation as of U.S. common law, but the legal principles brought from England have been freely adapted to the American experience.

The story of cemetery law in the United States, however, is a little more complicated. As the readings in Chapter 5 explain, the common law did not govern cemeteries and graves in England in the 18th century. Instead, cemeteries were owned by the Church of England and subject to the jurisdiction and cognizance of English ecclesiastical law. The existence of an established church and a single system for the disposition of human remains were therefore central assumptions of 18th century English law. The presented a challenge for the adoption of English common law in the new United States. English common law was expressly adopted by state legislatures, while an established church and its ecclesiastical law were antithetical to the principles of the new Republic. But the disposition of human remains was a practical problem that needed to be addressed. Until the 20th century, and the creation of an occupational licensing scheme for funeral directors and embalmers, state legislatures asserted little authority over the law of human remains. Even though English common law, and therefore U.S. common law, offered no clear precedent or principles, disputes over the disposition of human remains and the competing interests in cemeteries were left to state courts to resolve.

As a result, state courts drew on shared principles and values. In 18th century and 19th century America, the principles and values of the descendants of English Protestants dominated the culture sphere. Those principles and values were shaped by the funerary practices imported from 17th and 18th century England. In other words, although state legislatures and courts did not expressly adopt English ecclesiastical law, and indeed often denounced its applicability in the United States, the doctrines of English ecclesiastical law found their way into U.S. cemetery law.

As discussed in Chapter 5, English ecclesiastical law and English common law both rely on similar sources, including civil law and canon law (the rules and doctrines of the Roman Catholic Church), both of which were derived from or heavily influenced by Roman law. The influence of Roman law, filtered through canon law, is much more clearly seen in English ecclesiastical law. Therefore, to understand U.S. cemetery law, we must:

First, identify the law and funerary customs of pre-Christian Roman (Chapter 2);

Second, observe the influence of Christian belief on Roman law, and of Roman customs on Christian practices (Chapters 3 and 4);

Third, examine how the Reformation shaped the funerary practices of Protestants and therefore English ecclesiastical law (Chapter 5); and

Fourth, understand the challenges encountered by U.S. courts in adapting the principles of English cemetery law to the United States (Chapters 6, 7, and 8).

❖ ❖ ❖

CHAPTER 2

ROMAN LAW

Remains of funerary structures along the Appian Way
Piranesi, Giovanni Battista, La Antichità Romane opera di Giambattista Piranesi
architetto veneziano divisa in quattro tomi…, vol. III, Rome, Angelo Rotilj *(1757)*

CHAPTER 2.1

ROMAN LAW

Tanya D. Marsh

Chapter 2 addresses the funerary practices and laws of pre-Christian Rome. The Romans practiced both cremation and interment, both of which were banished beyond the city limits in order to preserve public health. Those with means built family tombs that lined the roads leading into the cities, including the legendary Appian Way. The common people were interred in city cemeteries, often in common graves.

Roman law introduces an interesting concept regarding the legal status of cemeteries. Real property was divided into two categories—property subject to divine law (*divini juris*) and property subject to human law (*humani juris*). The first category included sacred places like temples…and cemeteries. Significantly, property subject to divine law was the property of no one. *Quod autem divini iuris est, id nullius in bonis est.* The words *nullius in bonis* appear later in this story, in the work of Lord Edward Coke, and have had lasting significance in U.S. cemetery law.

Many concepts established by Roman law survive in U.S. cemetery law, for example, the qualified irrevocability of the dedication of land for cemetery purposes. The concept that family burying grounds or tombs pass via intestate succession (then known as "hereditary rights") and cannot, at common law, be alienated or devised, is a curious doctrine rooted in Roman law. The rules of the Roman empire governing disinterment are virtually identical to modern U.S. law, as are the remedies available to a person whose rights of sepulcher have been violated by a third party.

NOTES

1.   As you read through Chapter 2, particularly Chapter 2.6, use the list of key principles set forth in Section 1.3 as a checklist. How many of the key principles of modern U.S. cemetery law can be found in Roman law?

2.   As you read through the next several chapters, consider how the Roman concept of *res divini juris*, the idea that property subject to divine law is not owned by the government or any living person—it is simply unowned because it has been dedicated to a religious or secular purpose—is reflected in later Christian practices and ultimately in modern U.S. law. Do we still feel the influence of this doctrine today?

❖   ❖   ❖

The Appian Way, Rome, Italy
James Harvey Robinson, Outline of European History Part I *(1914)*

CHAPTER 2.2
ROMAN BURIAL PRACTICES
Olinto L. Spadoni, TOMBS AND CATACOMBS OF THE APPIAN WAY (1891)

The custom of burying the Dead together in a common and enclosed cemetery is not an ancient one.

During the most remote epochs in the history of man, that is during that long period which preceeded the establishment of different communities, each family had its own tomb within the limits of the family estate, which estate, besides the tomb, contained also the temple and the family residence. ...

The State during these early periods of antiquity did not extend beyond the family boundary...

With the gradual advance of civilization this patriarchal state of society suffered an evolution; prompted by the advantages that cooperation offered over isolation and competition, and for the sake of more effectual defence, families united together, and formed communities and cities. These cities were built, as far as it was practicable, in places near the lands possessed by the families who entered such unions; and then also arose the necessity of burying the Dead in a common burial-ground.

Thus, from each family tomb, existing within the limits of the family property during the patriarchal period, after the establishment of Communities, we come to the city cemetery. Now whether for the sake of public health, or for other reasons which we are unable to ascertain, the localities selected for burial were not within the city walls but outside them, along the public roads beyond the city gates.

Such was the case with the Pelasgian and Etruscans, as demonstrated by their cities and cemeteries. Such was the case with Rome, which was the highest expression of Etruscan civilization; and such was the case with all other cities, which derived from Rome.

During the dark and middle ages, when ancient culture and civilization were lost or slumbered under the thick strata of religious fanaticism and ignorance, the hygienic laws which had reached the highest degree in Rome were altogether lost sight of; and we find the Dead buried in the cloisters of convents in the crypts of churches or in the graveyards adjoining churches.

Many a plague, during the middle ages, were caused by this promiscuity of the dead with the living.

In our present modern Italy a law was passed, which is the equivalent of the ancient Roman law of the twelve tables, prohibiting burials within the city limits; and every inhabitant, be he a layman or priest, prince, beggar, or Pope, must be buried outside the City walls.

As I have already stated, the public roads were the public cemeteries in ancient Rome. They were selected by the people for their public walks an resorts, offering a greater attraction than the narrow streets of the city, on account of the monumental tombs and gardens which lined them, tombs and monuments, for the building and decoration of which the skill of the architect and painter was tasked, as well as that of the sculptor, mosaic maker, and gardener. They were at times edifices of colossal dimensions, on whose decoration enormous sums of money were frequently lavished.

The noblest and wealthiest families had their mausoleums on the principal roads, along which property was more valuable than elsewhere. Poorer people had their tombs on roads of secondary importance.

In Rome the Via Latina and the Via Appia were amongst the most ancient roads and owing to the places to which they led as also to their antiquity, they were considered the most fashionable to be buried in. Here then, in preference to any other spot, the Roman aristocracy at the time of the Republic, as well as the aristocracy of the Empire buried their Dead. The Via Appia was the most important of all. Its importance was such, that its fame passed to tradition, and spread over the world. …

We have had in Italy, during antiquity, three distinct religious epochs. The very first the religion the Italians had, was the religion of their fathers or the worship of their ancestors.

After death, every man was considered as a God. The most respectful epithets they could think of, were bestowed upon the dead by the living. They were called good, holy, and happy. The living entertained for the dead all the veneration man could have for a God whom they loved and feared.

This apotheosis was not merely the privilege of great men; but every man, after death, was entitled to the veneration of his posterity, even if during his lifetime his life had been the reverse of virtuous and honourable. — Sinful men became Gods as well as good men; the only difference being, that the virtuous continued to be virtuous after death and the wicked retained their wickedness for all Eternity.

It is positive; as too many proofs have attested, that during the very earliest epochs, when the only religious sentiment Italians had, consisted in the worship of their dead, corpses were embalmed and buried.

The production of telluric motions and volcanism, in this land of fire, as Italy has been so appropriately called, and the fright they exercised upon the people, were considered holy punishments sent by the Dead for the faults committed by their posterity. It was customary, then, to propitiate the good-will of the Dead by sacrifices. When these cataclysms appeared and were considered as the tangible manifestations of the wrath of the departed ones, the terror and panic-stricken people gave themselves up to all sorts of propitiations and sacrifices so as to appease their angry ancestral deities and thus end their terrible vengeance. As fire was the predominating element of these telluric commotions, that never previously seen element was considered as a living and huge monster exacting thousands and thousands of animal and human victims; a monster who raged everywhere, multiplying itself everywhere, and which neither man nor thing could resist. A monster, who scorched the earth as he approached, and who brought desolation and death where he appeared. ...

Thus fire, the principal protagonist of volcanism and of the explosions of nature, was considered at first as the agent by which their ancestors and Gods, punished posterity for faults committed. Then, owing firstly to its own monstrosity, when its usefulness became known it was venerated as a new religion, the religion of nature's forces; nature in her good and evil influences.

Hence we have two religions, not one against the other, but rather completing themselves. The one, the worship of fire, was the adoration of nature; the second, the adoration of the human soul. — Consequently, on this religious innovation, the way by which bodies were disposed of, after death, underwent a change; entombment was replaced by cremation. ...

Cremation, as far as it can be ascertained, prevailed in Italy during the patriarchal period; that is before the establishment of communities.

When cities were founded, cremation ceased generally, if not altogether. ...

Burials lasted for the whole of the kingly period, and for the greater part of the time of Republic that followed.

In 78 B.C. Sylla, the dictator, died at Puteoli. His body was brought to Rome in a golden litter and a funeral, worthy a king's, was celebrated in the Campus Martius .... Here his body was cremated, and cremated in fulfillment of his express will, and by order of his relations. Historians state that Sylla wished to be cremated, according to the ancient custom, so that his corpse might not meet the fate of his antagonist's, Caius Marius, who was disinterred by his order, and after having been dragged through the streets, was thrown in the river Anio, as the corpse of a parricide.

From the example thus set by Sylla, the chief of the aristocratic party, cremation became again the fashion among the nobles, and few years later, it became generally adopted. During the whole time of the Empire, burial was seldom, if ever practiced.

The Hebrews seem to have always adhered to the system of burial and to have discarded cremation altogether. Thus Christ, according to the Jewish custom, was buried.

With the introduction and propagation of Christianity in Rome, the adherents to the new religion, in veneration of the Founder of their Faith again adopted burial, and after the complete triumph of the Church, cremation was again completely abandoned in the Roman Empire. ...

Thus ... we have three distinct epochs in Italy when burial prevails: The first, during the patriarchal state of the people, preceding the establishment of the worship of Fire; The second, from Saturn to Sylla, that is during the whole of the Roman epoch until 70 B.C.; the third, from the introduction of Christianity to the present day...

Before proceeding further to the explanation of the Catacombs, it is necessary to say how the Roman family was constituted. ...

The Roman family [during patriarchal times] was a regular clan, a complete institutions within itself, held by a special religion and governed by special laws; and its members were numbered by hundreds, sometimes by thousands. The Roman *gens*, or family, celebrated the same sacred ceremonies...

The whole *gens* answered for the debts of its members, redeemed their prisoners, paid the fines of their condemned. ...

We must make a distinction between the gens, and the family; as the word family has to-day quite a different meaning from the one it had during antiquity. *Gens* is the name which corresponds to the modern meaning of clan; whereas the Roman word *familia* meant, in its widest significance, the totality of that which belonged to a Roman citizen who was a *paterfamilias*.

Thus in certain cases of testamentary disposition the word *familia* is explained by the equivalent, *patrimonium*, patrimony. Thus *familia* was the estate or patrimony held by a paterfamilias and received by him in inheritance from his ancestors, and which he was obliged to transmit intact to posterity. Hence *paterfamilias* meant father or chief, or master, or administrator of the estate, goods, chattels and cattle belonging to a gens, or clan. By the laws that governed the gens, the *paterfamilias* was jointly their chief, treasurer, judge, priest, and military leader. ...

Each *gens* having originated from a common stock, they venerated the same deified ancestor; and their offerings and sacrifices were always deposited upon an altar, which was always the tomb of the venerated ancestor and founder of the *gens*. As the *gens* resided on the same estate, as they had a common ancestor, as they worshipped the same gods, as they helped each other, as they were mutually responsible for all their actions, as they formed a total whole, so were they also buried together in a common sepulchre.

Clients and slaves forming as they did part of a *gens*, were also buried in the same tomb.

...By law, if a patron had no children to whom to leave his patrimony, he was required to adopt one of his near relatives thus insuring the continuity of the family, with the constant worshippers to the Gods of the *gens*. Therefore, as tombs were inviolable, for they contained the bodies of the deified ancestors, and consequently inalienable, they required to be extensive places, sufficiently large enough to give shelter to the dead of a whole *gens*, whose members numbered thousands; and this not for a generation but for all times to come. ...

A Roman family tomb, especially during the Republic when ... the Dead were buried and not cremated, was required to be necessarily of very extensive dimensions so as to furnish accommodation for all the Dead of a family.

Land on the Via Appia was very valuable, and the Roman paterfamilias could not make a compromise by burying his direct and nearest relatives in the family tomb of the Via Appia and his clients and slaves elsewhere where land was not so valuable.

We have seen that all members of a *gens* were required to be buried together in their sepulchre; therefore to do otherwise would have been sacrilegious.

The problem of burying so many people in one sepulchre was solved by the Romans in a very simple way. They took advantage of the compact formation of the sandy soil of the Roman Campagna. Suppose a field owned by a gens for the purpose of burial along the Via Appia; in this field was erected the stone mausoleum capable of containing a large number of sarchopaghi, in which were placed the bodies of those belonging to the direct lineage of the family proper; at the back of the mausoleum was the forum or open space where the funeral orations in honour of the Dead were delivered, and where the funeral banquets were held …

Around the monument, the open area, and the other places adjoining the tomb, was a railing or a small ditch marked by boundary stones; which ditch formed the sacred limits of the abode of the Dead, which no one could trespass. In a word, it was a proper *pomerium*, similar to the one which surrounded as a sacred boundary of City.

Below the surface, in narrow passages excavated in tufa, loculi or niches were cut right and left for the reception of the bodies of the less important members of the gens, namely the clients and slaves. Steps led from the interior of the funeral chamber of the mausoleum where the sarcophagi were, down to the crypt; so that all those underground passages were nothing else but the supplement of the funeral chamber above.

These underground passages could not be excavated beyond the limits of the area above ground, as that would have been trespassing over the soil belonging to the tomb of a neighbouring gens. But by turnings, and by making the passages parallel, and by extending these passages to the same length as the area above, an infinite number of niches for depositing the dead could be obtained. For these passages were sufficiently deep, as to allow, in some cases, even twelve niche to be cut in them one above the other.

The niches were deep enough to allow from one to four bodies being placed in them. When the niches on the level of this first flooring had all been filled, a second excavation was made, and an additional series of passages were cut below the original one, and another stairway placed them in communication, the upper with the lower one. In many cases, when the family had large numbers of clients and slaves, these crypts were four, five, and even more stories deep.

The introduction of cremation, commencing as we have seen with Sylla, in 78 B.C., put an end to the custom of burying in these underground passages. …

[D]uring the Empire, owing to the revival of cremation, and owing to the discredit in which Gods and religion had fallen, it was possible to accomplish with impunity that which three, or even two hundred years before, would have ben considered as the greatest crime committed against all human and divine laws, I mean the burial of clients and slaves and even relatives, away from the tomb of their ancestors and patrons.

Already towards the latter end of the Republic, there were separate *columbaria* for the servants and clients of the nobles. With the Empire, the Caesars built others for depositing there the ashes of the members of their households; and even enterprises were not wanting, who built *columbaria* with the object of speculation by allowing the ashes of the dead to be deposited in them, on payment of a sum of money. …

Thus from the year 78 B.C. the crypts for slaves and clients, under the gorgeous mausoleums of the patricians of the Via Appia and other roads, commenced to be abandoned; and remained so, until they were used again by the Christians, that is, for over a century and a half. …

The noble Christian ladies of Rome and their families buried their relatives and their kindred in their ancient mausoleums an in the crypts extant below them. The crypt of one family was later, placed in communication with the crypt of that of a neighbor and thus catacombs were formed. I use the word catacombs with the significance of "general, early Christian cemeteries," the etymology of the word proper meaning underground tomb, or excavation, or subterranean place; the first to be called so being the one in which the bodies of Peter and Paul were deposited at the Cemetery of St. Sebastian.

Evidently, when the ancient pagan loculi became occupied by the Christians, the remains of those originally deposited there, had to be removed, in order to make room for the bodies of the brethren of the new faith.

❖ ❖ ❖

St. Louis Cemetery #1, New Orleans, Louisiana
Photo by Tanya D. Marsh

CHAPTER 2.3
CUSTOMS OF THE ROMANS
Stephen Wickes, SEPULTURE (1884)

"To bury a dead body, whether known before or not, is a debt I owe to humanity."

—SENECA

The Romans in their earlier days practised interment. ... It seemed to be an accepted fact that interment of the dead within the city and inhabited places was dangerous to the living, and the places of burial were removed to some distance. The law of the twelve tables expressly forbade the burning or burying of the dead within the city.

By the terms of that law it appears that from the 4th century of the republic, burning and burial were both practised. The outrages to the buried bones exposed to the barbarians in war, and their religious sentiments, led them to favor burning and to bring the funeral pile more and more into use.

The law appointed the open country for funeral rites and inhumations. The practice of these ceremonies was scarcely permitted contiguous to the suburbs of the city. It was ordained that the dead should be respected. "Their sanctuary was thus rendered inviolable and their sepulture sacred. In whatsoever place the dead was interred, all the ground which surrounded it was withdrawn from the purposes of trade or commerce." In the course of time tombs ceased to be constructed at the country seats, and those of the most illustrious families were transported to the highways. Thus the great roads and avenues were named the Aurelian, Flaminian, Lucinian, Appian, Lavinian and Julian way, after the families whose superb mausoleums and sarcophagi of marble adorned them.

The common people among the Romans had also their funeral piles and public tombs. Such were the small wells (*puteoli*) or deep cavities into which the dead bodies were cast. The places where the bodies were burned were called *ustrinae* or public funeral piles. ...

❖   ❖   ❖

Crown Hill Cemetery, Indianapolis, Indiana
Photo by Cass Pyatt

CHAPTER 2.4

THINGS SUBJECT TO DIVINE LAW

Charles Phineas Sherman, ROMAN LAW IN THE MODERN WORLD, VOLUME II (1917)

The Roman law of property was intelligently philosophized in the 2d century A.D. by the jurist Gaius, who indicated the fundamental differences between things, dividing them into various antithetical groups. His first and fundamental classification of things was into those subject to divine and those subject to human law. This distinction of things derived its importance from the peculiar relation existing—especially in pagan times—between the religious and civil (secular) law of Rome.

Things not subject to any ownership were described in Roman law as belonging to divine law. Instances of *res divini juris* were temples, burial places, holy things, and certain sanctioned or forbidden things, like city gates and walls. … Sir Henry Maine declares that "some part of the Roman rules as to this class of things still affects our law of churchyards" in England.

The Roman *res sacrae* correspond somewhat to the law of England, to consecrated buildings or churches. But ownership of the latter is always vested in some authority, like the bishop, dean, and chapter.

❖ ❖ ❖

Street of Tombs at Pompeii, Italy
A. Rosengarten, W. Collett-Sandars A Handbook of Architectural Styles *(1895)*

CHAPTER 2.5

RES DIVINI JURIS; RES HUMANI JURIS

J.D. Abdy (translator), *The Commentaries of Gaius* (1870)

[The Roman jurist Gaius lived around 130-180 AD. He authored several authoritative treatises on Roman law, including his *Commentaries on the Twelve Tables*, a translated excerpt of which is set forth below.]

The chief division of things, then, is reduced to two heads: for some things are *divini juris*, others *humani juris*. Of the *divine juris* class are things sacred or religious. Things sacred are those which are consecrated to the Gods above: things religious those which are given up to the Gods below. Now land is considered sacred when made so by authority of the Roman people: for it is consecrated by the passing of a *lex* or the making of a *senatusconsultum* in respect of it.

On the other hand, we make ground religious of our own free will by conveying a corpse into a place which is our own property, provided only that the burial of the corpse devolves on us. ...

Now that which is *divini juris* is the property of no one [*Quod autem divini iuris est, id nullius in bonis est...*]; whilst that which is *humani juris* is generally the property of some one, although it may be the property of no one.

❖ ❖ ❖

Highgate Cemetery, London, England
Photo by Harold Lloyd

CHAPTER 2.6
THE ROMAN LAW OF SEPULCHRE

Samuel Parsons Scott, *The Civil Law Including The Twelve Tables, The Institutes of Gaius, The Rules of Ulpian, The Opinions of Paulus, The Enactments of Justinian, and The Constitutions of Leo: Translated from the original Latin, edited, and compared with all accessible systems of jurisprudence ancient and modern, Volume IV* (1932)

CONCERNING RELIGIOUS PLACES, THE EXPENSES OF FUNERALS, AND THE RIGHT TO CONDUCT THE SAME

1. Ulpianus, On the Edict, Book X.

Where anyone expends anything on account of a funeral, he is considered to have made the contract with the deceased and not with his heir.

2. The Same, On the Edict, Book XXV.

Aristo says that a place in which a slave has been buried is religious.

(1) A party who has placed a dead body in the premises of another or caused this to be done, is liable to an action *in factum*. We must, however, understand "the premises of another" to mean either a field or a building; but these words grant the action to the owner, not to a possessor in good faith; for when the statement is made "In the premises of another," it is

apparent that the owner is meant, that is the party to whom the ground belongs. ... It is debatable whether a joint-owner is liable if he acted without the knowledge of his co-owner; but the better opinion is that he can be sued in an action for the partition of an estate, or in one for the division of common property.

(2) The Prætor says: "Where the body or bones of a dead man are said to have been taken to ordinary ground or to a burial place in which the party had no right, he who does this is liable to an action *in factum,* and will be subjected to a pecuniary penalty."

(3) The "taking" which the Prætor was thinking of is that which occurred for the purpose of burial.

(4) Ground is styled "ordinary" which is neither sacred, consecrated, nor religious, but is a locality to which none of these adjectives will apply.

(5) A burial-place is a spot where human bodies or bones are deposited. Celsus, however, says that a place which is destined for burial does not become religious entirely, but only that portion of it where the body is laid.

(6) A monument is whatever is erected for the purpose of preserving the memory of the deceased. ...

(8) No one can make a place religious which is subject to a servitude, unless the party entitled to the servitude consents. But if the party can make use of the servitude no less conveniently in some other place, it cannot be held that the burial was made for the purpose of interfering with the servitude, and therefore the place becomes religious; and indeed this is reasonable.

(9) Where a person has given his land in pledge and buries one of his own family therein, he will make it religious; and if he himself should be buried there, the same rule applies; but he cannot assign this right to another.

3. Paulus, On the Edict, Book XXVII.

It is more to the public advantage to say that a place can be made religious by the consent of all parties; and this was held by Pomponius.

4. Ulpianus, On the Edict, Book XXV.

Where a party who was appointed heir buries the body of the head of the family before he enters upon the estate, by doing so he makes the place religious, but no one should think that by this act he is conducting himself as heir; for let us suppose that he is still deliberating as to whether he will enter upon the estate. I, myself, am of the opinion that even though the heir did not bury the body but someone else did, and the heir either took no active part, or was merely absent, or feared that he might be considered as conducting himself as heir, still he makes the ground religious; for very often deceased persons are buried before their heirs appear. In this instance the ground becomes religious only when it was the property of the deceased, for it is but natural to hold that a place where a person is buried belonged to him; especially if he is buried in a spot which he himself had selected. To such an extent does this rule apply that, even where the body is buried by the heir in ground bequeathed by a legacy, still, the burial of the testator renders the place religious, provided that he could not have been buried as conveniently elsewhere.

5. Gaius, On the Provincial Edict, Book XIX.

"The family burying place" means one set apart by some one for himself and his household; but an "hereditary burial-place" is one which a man provides for himself and his heirs.

6. Ulpianus, On the Edict, Book XXV.

Or where the head of the household acquired it by hereditary right. In both instances, however, heirs and other successors of every description whatever may legally be buried, and may also bury others, although they may be heirs to a very small amount either by will or on intestacy, even if the other heirs do not consent.

The same privilege is granted to children of both sexes, and descendants of other degrees, as well as to emancipated persons, whether they have become heirs or have rejected the estate. With reference to disinherited relatives, however, they may be buried through motives of humanity, unless the testator, influenced by just hatred, has expressly forbidden it; but they cannot bury others except their own descendants. Freedmen can neither be buried, nor bury others under such circumstances, unless they become the heirs to their patron; although certain patrons have indicated by inscriptions that they have erected monuments for themselves and their freedmen. Papinianus also held this opinion, and it has repeatedly been established by decisions.

(1) So long as there is only a monument, anyone can sell it, or give it away; if, however, it becomes a cenotaph, it must be stated that it can be sold; as the Divine Brothers stated in a Rescript that a structure of this kind is not religious.

7. Gaius, On the Provincial Edict, Book XIX.

He who buries a dead body on land belonging to another can be compelled by an action *in factum* to either remove the body which he buried, or to pay the price of the land. This action can be brought by an heir as well as against one, and it is perpetual.

(1) Where a man placed a dead body in a stone chest which belongs to another, in which, as yet, no corpse has been laid; the proconsul grants an equitable action *in factum* against him, since it cannot be properly said that he placed the body in a burial-place, or on land belonging to another.

8. Ulpianus, On the Edict, Book XXV.

Where bones or a body have been buried by another party not a relative, it is a question whether the owner of the land can dig them up, or remove them without a decree of the pontiffs or the order of the Emperor; and Labeo says that the pontifical permission or the order of the Emperor must be obtained, otherwise an action for injury will lie against the person who removed the remains.

(1) Where a place that is religious is alleged to have been sold as profane, the Prætor grants an action *in factum* in favor of the party who is interested in the matter against the vendor; and this action can also be brought against the heir of the latter, since it resembles an action on a contract of sale.

(2) Where a man buried a dead body in a place intended for the use of the public, the Prætor will grant an action against him if he acted maliciously, and he should be punished by the extraordinary authority of the Court, although the penalty is a moderate one; but where he acted without malice he must be discharged.

(3) In this action the term "profane place" is also applicable to a building.

(4) This action can not only be brought by an owner but by anyone entitled to the usufruct in the land, or by one who is entitled to a servitude over the same; because these parties also have the right to prevent it being done.

(5) Where anyone is prevented from burying in a place where he has the right to do so, he is entitled to an action *in factum* as well as an interdict, even though he himself has not been hindered but his agent has been; since, under such circumstances, he himself is considered to have been prevented.

9. Gaius, On the Provincial Edict, Book XIX.

Where some one is prevented from burying the body or bones of a deceased person, he can at once make use of an interdict by which it is forbidden to employ force against him, or he can make the interment elsewhere, and afterwards bring an action *in factum*, by means of which, as plaintiff, he will recover damages to the amount of his interest in not having been prevented from making the interment; and in the calculation shall be included the price of the land which he purchases or the rent of any which he leases, or the value of his own land which no one would render religious unless compelled to do so. Therefore, I wonder why it should appear to be settled that this action cannot be granted either in favor of, or against an heir; as it is evident that it involves the account of a certain sum of money which forms the basis of the claim; at all events the suit can be brought at any time between the parties themselves.

10. Ulpianus, On the Edict, Book XXV.

Where the vendor of land reserves a burial-place for the interment of himself and his descendants, and he is prevented from using a road for the purpose of burying a member of his household, he can bring suit; for it has been decided that a right of way through the land for the purpose of burial was reserved in the agreement between the purchaser and the vendor.

11. Paulus, On the Edict, Book XXVII.

If, however, the site of a monument should be sold under the condition that no one should be buried there whom there was a right to bury; an agreement of this kind will not be sufficient, but it must be made secure by means of a stipulation.

12. Ulpianus, On the Edict, Book XXV.

Where anyone has a burial place but has no right of way to it, and is prevented from reaching it by his neighbor, the Emperor Antoninus and his father stated in a Rescript that it is customary to petition for a pathway to a burial place by sufferance, and it is usually granted; and, whenever there is no servitude, the privilege can be obtained from the party who owns the adjoining premises. This rescript, however, which gives the means of obtaining the right of way by petition, does not allow a civil action, but it may be applied for in extraordinary proceedings; for the governor is required to compel a pathway to be granted to the party where a reasonable price is paid, and the judge must also investigate whether the place is suitable so that the neighbor may not suffer serious injury.

(1) It is provided by a decree of the Senate that the use of a burial place is not to be contaminated by alterations, that is to say, it must not be used for other purposes.

(2) The Prætor says: "Where any expense is incurred on account of a funeral I will grant an action for its recovery against the party who is interested in the same."

(3) This Edict is issued for a good reason, namely, in order that a party who conducted the funeral may bring suit for what he expended; so that the result would be that bodies will not lie unburied, or that some stranger should conduct the funeral.

(4) He whom the deceased selected must conduct the funeral, but if he should not do so he will be liable to no penalty, unless something of value was left to him for this purpose; for then, if he does not comply with the will of the deceased, he will be excluded from the bequest. If, however, the deceased did not make any provision for this, and the duty has not been transferred to anyone, it will devolve upon the heirs who were appointed, and, if none were appointed, upon the heirs at law or the cognates who succeed in their regular order.

(5) The funeral expenses are to be regulated in accordance with the means or dignity and rank of the deceased.

(6) The Prætor, or the municipal magistrate, is required to order the funeral expenses to be paid out of the money belonging to the estate if there is any, and if there is none, he must order such property to be sold as would perish by lapse of time, and the retention of which would be a burden to the estate; and in case this cannot be done, he shall order any gold or silver which there may be, to be sold or pledged, in order to provide the necessary funds.

13. Gaius, On the Provincial Edict, Book XIX.

Or he may collect the money from debtors to the estate if he can easily do so.

14. Ulpianus, On the Edict, Book XXV.

And if anyone should interfere with the purchaser in order to prevent said property from being delivered to him, the Prætor must intervene and protect an act of this kind, where any obstacle is interposed.

(1) Where the deceased was either a tenant or a lodger, and left nothing to pay his funeral expenses; Pomponius says that they must be paid out of the proceeds of articles which have been brought into the lodging, and if there is anything in excess, this will be liable for unpaid rent.

Moreover, if any legacies have been bequeathed by the testator whose funeral is the subject of discussion, and there is nothing with which to bury him, the said legacies must also be utilized for this purpose; for it is better that the funeral expenses of a testator should be obtained from his own property than that others should receive their legacies. Where, however, the estate has been entered upon, any property sold must not be taken from the purchaser, because he who has brought anything under an order of court is a *bona fide* possessor, and has the ownership of the same. Nevertheless, a legatee should not be deprived of his legacy if he can be indemnified by the heir; but if he cannot, it is better for the legatee not to be benefited pecuniarily, than that the purchaser should sustain any loss.

(2) Mela says that if a testator directs anyone to attend to his funeral and he does not do so after having received money for that purpose, an action on the ground of fraud shall be granted against him; nevertheless, I think, that he can be compelled to conduct the funeral under the extraordinary authority of the Prætor.

(3) The only expense which can be incurred on account of a funeral is that without which the funeral could not be conducted; as, for instance, what is incurred by the removal of the body, and also where money is expended on the place where the body is to be buried. Labeo says it must be considered to be expended on account of the funeral, because a place must be prepared in which the body may be laid.

(4) The expenses of anyone who dies away from home and which are incurred for the purpose of bringing back the body, are included in the funeral expenses, although he is not yet buried; and the same rule applies where anything is done for the purpose of guarding the body, or for preparing it for burial, or where anything is expended in providing marble or clothing.

(5) It is not proper, however, that any ornaments nor other articles of this kind should be buried with the body, as persons of the lower class are accustomed to do.

(6) This action which is styled a funeral one, is based upon what is proper and reasonable, and includes only what has been expended with reference to the funeral, but no other outlay. The term "reasonable" must be understood to have reference to the rank of the party who was buried, to the circumstances of the case, to the time, and to good faith; so that no charge may be made for more than the actual amount disbursed, nor even for what was actually expended, if this was immoderate. Therefore the means of the party for whom the money was spent must be taken into consideration, as well as the property itself, where it is immoderately expended without good cause. But what must be done where the expense is provided for by the will of the testator? In reply to this it must be held that his will is not to be followed if the expense should be excessive, for it ought to be in proportion to the means of the deceased.

(7) Sometimes, however, where a man has assumed the payment of funeral expenses he cannot recover them if he was actuated by filial affection, and did not pay with the intention of recovering the amount which he incurred; and this our Emperor stated in a Rescript. Therefore an estimate will have to be made by an arbiter, and the motive with which the expense was incurred carefully considered; that is, whether the party attended to this matter for the deceased or for his heir, or whether he was induced by humanity, or compassion, or filial reverence, or affection? Nevertheless, the degree of compassion may be distinguished so as to conclude that the party who conducted the funeral at his own expense did so in order that the deceased should not remain unburied, and not that he did this gratuitously; and if this should be clear to the judge he ought not to discharge the defendant; for who is there that can bury the dead body of a stranger without being impelled by a sense of duty? Hence it is proper for the party to state whom he buried, and from what motive he did so, to avoid being afterwards interrogated with reference to the same.

(8) In the case of many sons who conduct the funerals of their parents, or other persons who could have been appointed heirs do so although on this account it is not to be presumed that they are acting as heirs, or entering on the estate, still, in order that necessary heirs may not be held to have interfered, or others to have acted as heirs; it is customary for them to state that they caused the funeral ceremonies to be conducted from motives of duty. If anything superfluous should have been done, it would be held that the parties protected themselves to avoid being thought to have intermeddled, and not for the purpose of recovering their expenses; since they have plainly stated that they acted from motives of duty, but they must go still farther in their allegations in order to be able to recover what they expended.

(9) Perhaps someone may say that there are instances where a certain share of the expense incurred can be recovered, so that the individual in question did this partly while transacting business for another, and partly because he was impelled by a sense of duty. This is true, and therefore he can recover a portion of the expense which he did not incur with the intention of donating.

(10) When a judge hears a case of this kind which is based on grounds of equity he should sometimes not allow a moderate expenditure where, for example, the expenses of his funeral had been small, with the intention of casting odium upon the character of the deceased, who had been a wealthy man; as the judge, in this instance, ought not to consider an account of this kind, since it is apparent that by burying him in this manner a premeditated insult was offered to his memory.

(11) Where anyone buries the head of a household while under the impression that he himself is his heir, he cannot bring an action to recover the funeral expenses; because he did not act with the intention of transacting the business of another; and this is also the opinion of Trebatius and Proculus. I think, however, that an action for the funeral expenses should be granted to him where proper cause is shown.

(12) Labeo says that whenever anyone has some other action for the purpose of recovering funeral expenses he cannot avail himself of a funeral action; and therefore, if he is entitled to an action for the partition of an estate, he cannot bring a funeral action; but it is clear that if an action for the partition of an estate has been already brought, he can bring one for the recovery of the funeral expenses.

(13) Labeo also says that if you conduct the funeral of a testator against the wishes of his heir, you can bring the funeral action if proper cause is shown; but what if the person whom the heir forbade to act was the son of the testator? In this instance it can be alleged against the plaintiff, "Therefore you have conducted the funeral through a sense of duty." But suppose that I have made the statement, I will then be entitled to bring the funeral action, for it is proper that deceased persons should be buried by means of funds obtained from their estates. What if a testator had directed you to make arrangements for the funeral, and the heir prohibits it, and you, nevertheless, conduct it; is it not just that you should have the right to bring an action for the recovery of the funeral expenses?"

Generally speaking, I am of the opinion that a just judge will not rigidly adhere to the mere action based on business transacted, but will construe the rules of equity more liberally, since this is something which the character of the proceeding enables him to do.

(14) The Divine Marcus, however, stated in a Rescript that any heir who prevents a funeral from being conducted by the party whom the testator selected, does not act honorably; although there is no penalty established by which he may be punished.

(15) If anyone conducts a funeral at the request of another, he is not entitled to a funeral action, but he certainly is who directed the funeral to take place, whether he paid the expense of the same to him whom he requested to conduct it, or whether he still owes it. Where, however, a ward makes such a request without the authority of his guardian, a prætorian action for the recovery of the funeral expenses should be granted against the heir in behalf of the party who incurred them; for it is unjust for the heir to profit in this way. Where, however, a ward orders a funeral which he himself ought to attend to be conducted without the authority of his guardian; I think that the action should be granted against him, if he himself is the actual heir to the party who was buried, and the estate is solvent.

On the other hand, where anyone conducts a funeral at the request of the heir, Labeo says he cannot bring the funeral action, because he is entitled to an action on mandate.

(16) If, however, he conducts the funeral as one transacting business for the heir, although the latter may not have ratified the act, Labeo said that he is, nevertheless, entitled to an action for the recovery of the funeral expenses.

(17) This action is granted against those who ought to conduct the funeral, for instance, against the heir, the possessor of the property of the estate, or any other successor.

...

33. Ulpianus, On the Edict, Book LXVIII.

Where a man was formerly heir, but the estate was subsequently taken from him as being unworthy; the better opinion is that the right of sepulture still remains with him.

34. Paulus, On the Edict, Book LXIV.

Where a place is bequeathed under a condition, and in the meantime the heir buries the deceased, this does not make the place religious.

...

37. Macer, On the Law of the Twentieth Relating to Successions, Book I.

... (1) The Divine Hadrian stated in a Rescript that a sepulchral monument is anything which is erected as a monument, that is to say, for the protection of the place where the body is laid; and therefore, if the testator ordered a large building to be constructed, for example, a number of porticos in a circular form, these expenses are not incurred on account of the funeral. ...

38. Ulpianus, On All Tribunals, Book IX.

It is the duty of the governor of a province to see that the bodies or bones of deceased persons are not detained, or maltreated, or prevented from being transported on the public highway, or buried.

39. Marcianus, Institutes, Book III.

The Divine Brothers decreed by an Edict that a body should not be disturbed after it had been lawfully interred, that is to say, placed in the ground; for a body is held to be placed in the ground where it is deposited in a chest with the intention that it shall not be removed elsewhere. It must not be denied, that it is lawful to remove the chest itself to a more convenient spot, if circumstances demand it.

40. Paulus, Questions, Book III.

For where anyone has interred a body with the intention of subsequently removing it to some other locality, and preferred to deposit it there for a time rather than to bury it permanently, or to provide, as it were, a last resting place for it; the place will remain profane.

41. Callistratus, Institutes, Book II.

Where several persons own the place where a body is brought for interment, all of them must give their consent if the remains are those of a stranger; for it is established that any one of the joint-owners themselves can properly be buried there, even without the consent of the others, especially when there is no other place in which he could be buried.

42. Florentinus, Institutes, Book VII.

Generally speaking, a monument is something which is handed down to posterity by way of a memorial; and in case a body or remains should be placed inside of it, it becomes a sepulchre; but if nothing of this kind is deposited therein, it becomes merely a monument erected as a memorial which is termed by the Greeks a cenotaph, that is to say an empty sepulchre.

43. Papinianus, Questions, Book VIII.

There are persons who, although they cannot make a place religious, still can very properly make application for an interdict with reference to the burial of a dead body; as, for instance, where the mere owner of property buries or wishes to bury a corpse in land of which the usufruct is held by another, since, if he buries it there he will not make the place a lawful sepulchre, but if he is prevented from doing so, he can very properly make application for an interdict by means of which an inquiry can be instituted as to the right of ownership.

The same rules apply to the case of a joint-owner who wishes to bury a dead body in ground held in common against the consent of his co-owner; for, on account of the public welfare, and in order that corpses may not lie unburied, we have ignored the strict rule which sometimes is dispensed with in doubtful questions relating to religious matters; for the highest rule of all is the one which is favorable to religion.

44. Paulus, Questions, Book III.

Where interment is made in different places, both of them do not become religious, for the reason that two sepulchres are not created by the burial of one person; but it seems to me that place should be religious where the principal part of the body is laid; that is to say, the head, whereof a likeness is made by means of which we are recognized.

(1) When, however, permission is obtained for remains to be removed, the place ceases to be religious.

...

46. Scævola, Questions, Book II.

Where a man had several tracts of land and bequeathed the usufruct of all of them separately, he can be buried in any one of them, and the heir shall have the right of selection, and the opportunity to favor the others. A prætorian action will, however, be granted the usufructuary against the heir, to enable him to recover damages to the amount that the value of his usufruct is diminished by the selection.

(1) Where the heir of a woman buries her body on land belonging to her estate, he can recover from her husband the amount which he should contribute towards the expense of the funeral, which depends upon the value of the land.

(2) Where clothing is bequeathed to anyone, and he sells it for the purpose of paying the funeral expenses, it is held that a prætorian action based on a prior claim should be granted against the heir.

CONCERNING RELIGIOUS PLACES, AND THE EXPENSES OF FUNERALS.

1. The Emperor Antoninus to Dorita.

If the remains of your son should be threatened by the waters of a river, or any other just and necessary cause should arise, you can transfer them to another place, with the consent of the Governor of the province.

Given on the eighth of the Kalends of November, during the Consulate of Antoninus, Consul for the fourth time, and Balbinus, 214.

2. The Same to Hilarianus.

When a dead body has been brought on land belonging to you, either against your consent or without your knowledge, or a stone is placed there, this does not make the place religious. If, however, anyone should bring a corpse upon your land with your consent, the place will thereby become religious, as there is no doubt that a monument cannot be erected, nor any place be rendered religious, if the owner forbids this to be done.

Given on the Kalends of May, under the Consulate of Acquilinus, Consul for the second time, and Anulinus, 217.

...

4. The Same to Lucian.

If by the term "monument" you mean a sepulchre, you are informed that no one can claim it by the right of ownership; but where it belongs to the family the title to it will be vested in all the heirs, and in a partition it cannot be allotted to any individual one. Profane places, however, which are near it, and have always been connected with buildings intended for the use of men, will belong to the person to whom the structures to which they appear to have been attached are granted by the partition.

Given on the sixth of the Nones of November, during the Consulate of Maximus, Consul for the second time, and aelianus, 224.

5. The Same to the Soldier Cassius.

A father and a mother who are the heirs of their son, who was a soldier, should not fail to comply with his will, in which he provided for the erection of a monument to himself, for although all complaints on this ground have been abolished by former constitutions, still, the parents cannot avoid experiencing regret, and being conscious that they have neglected their duty by failing to comply with the last will of the deceased.

Given on the eighth of the Kalends of May, during the Consulate of Julian and Crispinus, 225.

6. The Same to Primitivus and Others.

The inscriptions on monuments do not transfer to freedmen either the right of sepulture, or the ownership of a place which is not religious; but you can take advantage of prescription for a long time, if there was good ground for it in the beginning.

Given on the eighth of the Kalends of July, during the Consulate of Julian and Crispinus, 225.

7. The Emperor Gordian to Claudius.

You are not forbidden to place statues upon a tomb, or to decorate with ornaments a sepulchre which you allege that you have built, for everyone is perfectly free to avail himself of his right, provided that he does not do anything prohibited by law.

Given on the third of the Kalends of August, during the Consulate of Gordian, Consul for the second time, and Pompeianus, 242.

8. The Emperor Philip to Julia.

The right of sepulture in a family tomb does not extend to persons connected by affinity, or to mere blood-relatives who have not been appointed heirs.

Given on the sixteenth of the Kalends of July, during the Consulate of Peregrinus and Aemilianus, 245.

9. The Same, and the Caesar Philip, to Faustina.

It is evident that a religious place should not be sold; but it is none the less certain that a field which is not religious, and adjoins a monument, is subject to the law as profane property, and hence can legally be alienated.

> Given on the sixth of the Kalends of December, during the Consulate of Philip and Titian, 246.

10. The Emperors Diocletian and Maximian, and the Caesars, to Aquilina.

If the body was not permanently committed to the tomb, you will not be prevented from removing it.

> Given on the eighth of the Ides of February, during the Consulate of Diocletian, Consul for the fourth time, and Maximian, Consul for the third time, 290.

11. The Same, and the Caesars, to Gaudentius.

We do not forbid criminals to be buried who have suffered the punishment that they deserved.

> Given on the eighth of the Ides of April, during the Consulate of the above-mentioned Emperors; the first, Consul for the fourth time, and the second, Consul for the third time, 290.

12. The Same, and the Caesars, to Victorinus.

It was long since forbidden that the remains of deceased persons should be buried inside a city, lest the sacred right of citizens might be defiled.

> Given on the third of the Kalends of October, during the Consulate of the above-mentioned Emperors; the first, Consul for the fourth time, and the second, Consul for the third time, 290.

13. The Same, and the Caesars, to Dionysius.

The family, as well as the hereditary right of sepulture, extends also to foreign heirs. The family right, however, is vested in its members, even if none of them is an heir, but it is enjoyed by no one else who is not an heir.

> Given on the third of the Ides of November, during the Consulate of the Caesars, 294.

14. The Emperors Valentinian, Theodosius, and Arcadius to Cynegius, Praetorian Prefect.

No one can transfer a human corpse from one place to another without permission of the Emperor.

> Given at Constantinople, on the third of the Kalends of March, during the Consulate of the Noble Youth Honorius and Evodius, 386.

CONCERNING THE TRANSPORT OF A DEAD BODY, AND THE CONSTRUCTION OF A SEPULCHRE

1. Ulpianus, On the Edict, Book LXVIII.

The Prætor says: "Whither or howsoever anyone has a right to transport a dead body without your consent, I forbid force to be employed to prevent him from taking the said dead body thither and burying it there."

(1) Where anyone has the right to bury a corpse, he must not be prevented from doing so, and he is held to be prevented if he is hindered from conveying the body to the place or is interfered with on the way.

(2) The mere owner of the premises can make use of this interdict with reference to the transport of a dead body; and, indeed, it is applicable in the case of land which is not religious.

(3) Moreover, if I have a right of way to a tract of land to which I desire to take a corpse for burial, and I am prevented from using the said right of way, it has been held that I can proceed by means of this interdict; because, having been prevented from using the right of way, I am also prevented from transporting the corpse; and the same rule must be adopted where I am entitled to any other servitude.

(4) It is evident that this interdict is a prohibitory one.

(5) The Prætor says: "Wherever anyone has a right to take a dead body without your consent, I forbid force to be employed to prevent him from building a sepulchre on the land, if he does this without malicious intent."

(6) This Edict was promulgated because it is to the interest of religion that monuments should be erected and adorned.

(7) No one shall be prevented from building a sepulchre or a monument in a place where he has a right to do so.

(8) A person is held to be prevented when he is hindered in having material transported which is necessary for erecting a building; and hence if anyone prevents the workmen who are necessary from coming, there will be ground for an interdict; and if anyone prevents the placing of machinery the interdict will also be available, provided he does this in a place which is subject to the servitude; but if you try to set up your machinery on my land, I will not be liable to an interdict, if I have the right to prevent you from doing so.

(9) A person must be understood to "build" not only when he begins a new work, but also where he wishes to make repairs.

(10) When a man does something in such a way that a sepulchre falls down, he is liable to this interdict.

2. Marcellus, Digest, Book XXVIII.

The Royal Law refuses permission for a woman who died during pregnancy to be buried before her unborn child is removed from her; and anyone who violates this law is held to have destroyed the hope of a living child by the burial of the pregnant mother.

3. Pomponius, On Sabinus, Book IX.

Where anyone is building a sepulchre near your house you can serve notice of a new structure upon him; but after the work has been completed, you will have no right of action against him except by means of the interdict *Quod vi aut clam.*

(1) Where a body is buried near a house belonging to another but within the limits prescribed by law, the owner of the house cannot afterwards prevent the same party from burying another body there, or from erecting a monument; if he acted with the knowledge of the owner from the beginning.

4. Ulpianus, Opinions, Book II.

The right to a burial-place is not acquired by a party through long possession, if it does not lawfully belong to him.

5. The Same, Opinions, Book I.

Where human remains are deposited in a tomb which is said to be unfinished, this does not offer any hindrance to its completion.

(1) Where, however, the place has already been made religious, the pontiffs should determine to what extent the desire of repairing the structure may be indulged without violating the privileges of religion.

CONCERNING THE ACTION ON PARTNERSHIP

39. Pomponius, On Sabinus, Book XIII.

Where you and I own a field in common, and you bury a dead body therein, I can bring an action on partnership against you.

❖ ❖ ❖

CHAPTER 3

EARLY CHRISTIAN PRACTICES AND BELIEFS

Highgate Cemetery, London, England
Photo by Harold Lloyd

CHAPTER 3.1
EARLY CHRISTIAN PRACTICES AND BELIEFS
Daniel Gibson

For if the dead rise not, then Christ is not raised: and if Christ be not raised your faith is in vain; ye are yet in your sins. Then they also which are fallen asleep in Christ are perished. If in this life only we have hope in Christ, we are of all men most miserable.

—1 Corinthians 15:16-18

The resurrection of the dead is the Christian's confidence. By believing it we are what we claim to be.

—Tertullian, on the Resurrection of the Flesh

Christian doctrine and practice shaped the laws and customs of burial in England. Although the United States did not subject itself to the authority of the Church of England, English ecclesiastical law and Protestant Christian beliefs and customs heavily influenced the growth of American law and norms.

Several issues confronted the United States in applying English law. First, the United States was a Christian kaleidoscope. Instead of England's established Church, America had everything from New England Puritans to Pennsylvania Quakers to Appalachian Presbyterians to Southern Baptists. Simply adopting English ecclesiastical law would not answer in the United States because of this religious diversity. Second, Church teaching is not necessarily synonymous with Christian belief and practice. Clergy and laymen often have different understanding of the same doctrines and rites, particularly where there are large educational or geographic gaps. These problems were particularly prevalent in Medieval Europe where mass was always conducted in Latin and in the American backwoods where the regular presence of an ordained minister was a rare luxury. Despite these issues, however, cemetery law in the United States bears the indelible imprint of 17th and 18th century Protestant belief.

Since the time of the apostles, resurrection has been an essential Christian doctrine. The Apostle Paul argued Christianity was in vain and Christians were without hope if the dead were not raised. Without resurrection, Christ had not conquered sin and Christians were saved for now but doomed the death in the afterlife. The Church Fathers, early Church creeds, and Ecumenical Councils expounded upon this belief. The Apostles' Creed and Nicene Creed both affirm belief in the resurrection of the dead. The Councils clarified the physical, bodily nature of Christ's life, death, and resurrection, thus affirming the bodily resurrection of Christians.

The doctrine of resurrection created a respect for the dead. Christian burial practices, therefore, disfavored cremation, dissection, and mutilation of the dead body. Catholic and High church Protestants (e.g. Anglicans, some Methodists, and some Presbyterians) afforded the body much respect, practiced ornate funerals, and some venerated the remains of saints and martyrs. Low church Protestants (e.g. Presbyterians, Puritans, and Baptists) regarded such practices as superstitious Catholic beliefs harmful to the living and not beneficial for the dead. All Christians, however, agreed body and soul were united at resurrection. A corpse was not merely a useless, shell of a person; rather, it was a seed sown in hope of resurrection. The body would be raised eternal but how and when were divine mysteries.

The nature of this divine mystery gave rise to much debate and speculation. Neither Scripture nor Church teaching specify exactly how the dead are raised. St. Augustine believed the bodies of the dead would be made anew at resurrection. Thomas Aquinas believed the corpse would be remade into a new body at resurrection. Many medieval Christians, perhaps through the influence of pagan culture, came to believe the treatment of the corpse affected its resurrection. Although orthodox Christianity never taught cremation or desecration of the dead affected resurrection, the prevalence of this belief directed the course of medieval burial practices and English ecclesiastical law.

The early Church followed the example of Abraham, Jacob and Joseph by burying in the ground or in tombs, among family members. Jesus Christ himself was buried in this manner. As Christianity gained influence in Rome, cemeteries and burials moved into the city. The Church developed doctrines encouraging burial in a churchyard or near saints or martyrs. St. Augustine argued church burial benefited the souls of the dead by encouraging the living to pray for the dead. Being buried near a saint or a martyr was a further benefit because of their intercession for the deceased. Thus, Christians buried in or near churches within the city.

When Rome legalized, then established, Christianity burial replaced cremation as the prevailing social norm. According to Minucius Felix, Christians did not fear cremation but "[adopted] the ancient and better custom of burying in the earth." Cremation reflected a pagan disdain for the dead which Christian and Jewish teaching rejected. Much of the Church opposed the 19th century reemergence of cremation because it was often done in protest of the Church and affirmation of specifically non-Christian beliefs. Since then, relying upon earlier teachings, most Christians have relaxed their opposition to cremation.

❖   ❖   ❖

Salem Cemetery, Winston-Salem, North Carolina
Photo by Tanya D. Marsh

CHAPTER 3.2

HISTORY OF SEPULTURE

Stephen Wickes, SEPULTURE (1884)

> Bury me with my fathers. ... There they buried Abraham and Sarah, his wife; there they buried Isaac and Rebecca, his wife; and there I buried Leah.
>
> —GEN. xlix, 29-31.

Inhumation was practised from the earliest times. The dead were buried in the wilderness, and in places inhabited. Abraham, who was a "mighty prince," upon the death of Sarah, "stood up before his dead and spake unto the sons of Heth ... give me a possession of a burying place with you that I may bury my dead out of my sight." He thereupon purchased the cave of Machpelah for money.

Jacob's remains were transported from Egypt by his son Joseph with great pomp, and laid in Canaan, according to his desire made known before his death. Moses was buried in the valley of Moab, Miriam, his sister; in the desert of Zin, Aaron in Mount Hor, Eleazer, his son, and Joshua, on the mountains of Ephraim. The bones of Joseph, which the children of Israel brought up out of Egypt, were buried in Shechem in a parcel of ground which Jacob had bought, three hundred years before, of the sons of Hamor, and where he erected an altar to Jehovah.

After the Israelites came into the quiet possession of the promised land and were brought under the requirements of their ceremonial laws, their habits in regard to the dead and their methods of sepulture were somewhat changed. According to the precepts of their law, the touch of a corpse rendered them unclean. ...

The Hebrews were very careful in the burial of their dead. It was considered to be a great calamity to be deprived of it, and denied it to none—not even their enemies. This concern for burial proceeded from a persuasion of the soul's immortality. Jeremiah (viii, 2) threatens the kings, priests and false prophets, who were idolators, that their bones should be cast out of their graves and be thrown like dung upon the earth. The same prophet foretold that Jehoiakim, King of Judah, who was guilty of all manner of vice, among other severe punishments, should be buried with "the burial of an ass." Jason (2 Macc. v: 10), who had denied burial to many Jews, was himself treated in the same manner. He died in a foreign land, and was thrown like carrion upon the earth. Good men made it a part of their religious devotion to inter the dead ...

After the Jews were settled in Canaan, they buried their dead in various places. Their law made no provision for the mode or place of interment. Sepulchres were in the towns and country, by the highways, in gardens and on mountains. ...

Ancient Customs and Methods of Burial

The Egyptians embalmed their dead. Joseph commanded that his father's body should be embalmed. Joseph's body was also embalmed in Egypt.

The Hebrew people were buried in sepulchres, or in graves in the open fields. ... Our Saviour compares the Pharisees to "graves that appear not, so that the men that walk over them are not aware of them." In the case of those who died of leprosy, the tumuli of the graves, or other evidences of the dead beneath, were avoided, lest uncleanness should be contracted.

A few passages of scripture refer to burning of the dead. The cases are exceptional. ... The ceremony of burning of the body is spoken of as a rite in honor of kings. If the practice did exist it was of short duration and limited to a few.

Excepting the cases of Jacob and Joseph, whose bodies were embalmed as a mark of distinguished honor, at the expense of the state, we have no distinct account of embalmment among the earlier Hebrews. In later times the Jews adopted it in the case of persons of rank and fortune. ...

Interment Among the Early Christians

The new testament furnishes many passages to show that the Jews buried without their cities. The sepulchre in which the body of our Saviour was laid was in the place where He was crucified. ...

The interment of the first Christians was undistinguished, and was like that of the common people. After they became a distinct class, they had their own peculiar funeral ceremonies, which partook of usages both Jewish and Gentile, but uniformly by burial. It was not long before the persecutors of the Christians under the Roman Empire and the carnage under Nero, greatly increased the number of martyrs. The tenderest emotions of nature and the impulses of their religion led them to provide a resting place for the slain, to protect their bodies from the rage of the people. They were taken charge of, and with secrecy and great caution transported under cover of the night to the public cemeteries. The catacombs soon became the repository of their remains, but anticipating the evils which must necessarily result from the accumulation of so many bodies in the place where they were accustomed to assemble for religious worship, they were abandoned.

Large tracts of land in the suburbs of Rome, given by the Patricians and some pious, wealthy women, were appropriated to purposes of burial. These were the origin of cemeteries (place of repose). More than forty such burial places are reckoned to have been opened in the suburbs of Rome. ... Here were erected altars and chapels, constructed for funeral ceremonies. The latter were also used for religious worship. The cemeteries were cared for with the greatest attention, and all became the sites of consecrated temples. ...

In the law of the twelve tables, enacted by the Decemviri (A. D. about 200), burial or burning of the dead within the city was forbidden. The statute was in force for a long period. The admission of the remains of even holy personages was positively forbidden.

The Christian church in three centuries rested in comparative quiet, and finally perfect peace, by the conversion of Constantine, and by his memorable edict of toleration, in A. D. 313. The Pagan temples of idols ceased to be resorted to and were transferred to the worship of God. The altars at which the Christians worshipped in the catacombs and cemeteries in the suburbs, were transferred to the cities, and the relics of the martyrs took the places of the Pagan deities. Now it was, that a general desire was manifest for providing tombs within their cities. A wish to be buried near the temples of their worship is a natural one. They thought, too, that proximity to the places where the prayers of the holy were offered, would benefit the souls of the departed dead, and that the emanations from the bodies of the saints would warm the hearts of the faithful and encourage them in pious works.

Burials within or near a church had their origin in the request of the Emperor Constantine to be buried in the vestibule of the Basilica of the Holy Apostles, which he himself had built. His wish was granted as a mark of the highest honor. The successors of Constantine obtained a like distinction. Benefactors to the church received the same. The priesthood, by their sanctity and rank, were deemed worthy of the high privilege. The revolution thus begun was neither general nor rapid.

The bishops who granted the privileges adopted each his own regulations, which were stringent or otherwise, according to his views. In half a century interments within the city of Constantinople and other Roman cities became general, for in A. D. 381, Theodosius renewed the edicts of his predecessors and prohibited interments in cities. He ordained that the bodies, urns, and sarcophagi within the walls of Rome should be removed to a distance. His design was to prevent infection of the air. ... "The Christian Emperors always censured the burial of the dead in cities; they feared contagion."

The edict was observed for a considerable time, but it came to be disregarded long before Gregory the Great, by whom it was restored in Italy. "Whatever difference there might have been in the opinion between the Pagans and Christians as to the fate which awaits us after our mortal career, whatever variety the principles laid down in the Christian church, we always see the most enlightened princes maintaining, by their laws in relation to interments, those rules which were most in conformity with the real good of the community. The ancient ecclesiastical constitutions, the letters of the Pontiffs, that sacred tradition which they are bound to preserve, all concurred in delivering cities from the infection of dead bodies... At length tyrannical custom overcame the law. The prerogative which was reserved for Emperors was at last the inheritance of the lowest class of citizens, and that which was at first a particular privilege became at length the common right of all."

❖ ❖ ❖

Zentralfriedhof [Central Cemetery], Vienna, Austria
Photo by Tanya D. Marsh

CHAPTER 3.3
THE OLD TESTAMENT
(King James Version)

Genesis 23

And Sarah was an hundred and seven and twenty years old: these were the years of the life of Sarah.

2 And Sarah died in Kirjatharba; the same is Hebron in the land of Canaan: and Abraham came to mourn for Sarah, and to weep for her.

3 And Abraham stood up from before his dead, and spake unto the sons of Heth, saying,

4 I am a stranger and a sojourner with you: give me a possession of a buryingplace with you, that I may bury my dead out of my sight.

5 And the children of Heth answered Abraham, saying unto him,

6 Hear us, my lord: thou art a mighty prince among us: in the choice of our sepulchres bury thy dead; none of us shall withhold from thee his sepulchre, but that thou mayest bury thy dead.

7 And Abraham stood up, and bowed himself to the people of the land, even to the children of Heth.

8 And he communed with them, saying, If it be your mind that I should bury my dead out of my sight; hear me, and intreat for me to Ephron the son of Zohar,

9 That he may give me the cave of Machpelah, which he hath, which is in the end of his field; for as much money as it is worth he shall give it me for a possession of a buryingplace amongst you.

10 And Ephron dwelt among the children of Heth: and Ephron the Hittite answered Abraham in the audience of the children of Heth, even of all that went in at the gate of his city, saying,

11 Nay, my lord, hear me: the field give I thee, and the cave that is therein, I give it thee; in the presence of the sons of my people give I it thee: bury thy dead.

12 And Abraham bowed down himself before the people of the land.

13 And he spake unto Ephron in the audience of the people of the land, saying, But if thou wilt give it, I pray thee, hear me: I will give thee money for the field; take it of me, and I will bury my dead there.

14 And Ephron answered Abraham, saying unto him,

15 My lord, hearken unto me: the land is worth four hundred shekels of silver; what is that betwixt me and thee? bury therefore thy dead.

16 And Abraham hearkened unto Ephron; and Abraham weighed to Ephron the silver, which he had named in the audience of the sons of Heth, four hundred shekels of silver, current money with the merchant.

17 And the field of Ephron which was in Machpelah, which was before Mamre, the field, and the cave which was therein, and all the trees that were in the field, that were in all the borders round about, were made sure.

18 Unto Abraham for a possession in the presence of the children of Heth, before all that went in at the gate of his city.

19 And after this, Abraham buried Sarah his wife in the cave of the field of Machpelah before Mamre: the same is Hebron in the land of Canaan.

20 And the field, and the cave that is therein, were made sure unto Abraham for a possession of a buryingplace by the sons of Heth.

Genesis 47

28 And Jacob lived in the land of Egypt seventeen years: so the whole age of Jacob was an hundred forty and seven years.

29 And the time drew nigh that Israel must die: and he called his son Joseph, and said unto him, If now I have found grace in thy sight, put, I pray thee, thy hand under my thigh, and deal kindly and truly with me; bury me not, I pray thee, in Egypt:

30 But I will lie with my fathers, and thou shalt carry me out of Egypt, and bury me in their buryingplace. And he said, I will do as thou hast said.

31 And he said, Swear unto me. And he sware unto him. And Israel bowed himself upon the bed's head.

Genesis 49

And Jacob called unto his sons, and said, Gather yourselves together, that I may tell you that which shall befall you in the last days. …

29 And he charged them, and said unto them, I am to be gathered unto my people: bury me with my fathers in the cave that is in the field of Ephron the Hittite,

30 In the cave that is in the field of Machpelah, which is before Mamre, in the land of Canaan, which Abraham bought with the field of Ephron the Hittite for a possession of a buryingplace.

31 There they buried Abraham and Sarah his wife; there they buried Isaac and Rebekah his wife; and there I buried Leah.

32 The purchase of the field and of the cave that is therein was from the children of Heth.

33 And when Jacob had made an end of commanding his sons, he gathered up his feet into the bed, and yielded up the ghost, and was gathered unto his people.

Genesis 50

And Joseph fell upon his father's face, and wept upon him, and kissed him. …

24 And Joseph said unto his brethren, I die: and God will surely visit you, and bring you out of this land unto the land which he sware to Abraham, to Isaac, and to Jacob.

25 And Joseph took an oath of the children of Israel, saying, God will surely visit you, and ye shall carry up my bones from hence.

26 So Joseph died, being an hundred and ten years old: and they embalmed him, and he was put in a coffin in Egypt.

❖ ❖ ❖

Zentralfriedhof [Central Cemetery], Vienna, Austria
Photo by Tanya D. Marsh

CHAPTER 3.4
THE NEW TESTAMENT
(King James Version)

Matthew 27

57 When the even was come, there came a rich man of Arimathaea, named Joseph, who also himself was Jesus' disciple:

58 He went to Pilate, and begged the body of Jesus. Then Pilate commanded the body to be delivered.

59 And when Joseph had taken the body, he wrapped it in a clean linen cloth,

60 And laid it in his own new tomb, which he had hewn out in the rock: and he rolled a great stone to the door of the sepulchre, and departed.

John 19

38 And after this Joseph of Arimathaea, being a disciple of Jesus, but secretly for fear of the Jews, besought Pilate that he might take away the body of Jesus: and Pilate gave him leave. He came therefore, and took the body of Jesus.

39 And there came also Nicodemus, which at the first came to Jesus by night, and brought a mixture of myrrh and aloes, about an hundred pound weight.

40 Then took they the body of Jesus, and wound it in linen clothes with the spices, as the manner of the Jews is to bury.

41 Now in the place where he was crucified there was a garden; and in the garden a new sepulchre, wherein was never man yet laid.

42 There laid they Jesus therefore because of the Jews' preparation day; for the sepulchre was nigh at hand.

1 Corinthians 15

35 But some man will say, How are the dead raised up? and with what body do they come?

36 Thou fool, that which thou sowest is not quickened, except it die:

37 And that which thou sowest, thou sowest not that body that shall be, but bare grain, it may chance of wheat, or of some other grain:

38 But God giveth it a body as it hath pleased him, and to every seed his own body.

39 All flesh is not the same flesh: but there is one kind of flesh of men, another flesh of beasts, another of fishes, and another of birds.

40 There are also celestial bodies, and bodies terrestrial: but the glory of the celestial is one, and the glory of the terrestrial is another.

41 There is one glory of the sun, and another glory of the moon, and another glory of the stars: for one star differeth from another star in glory.

42 So also is the resurrection of the dead. It is sown in corruption; it is raised in incorruption:

43 It is sown in dishonour; it is raised in glory: it is sown in weakness; it is raised in power:

44 It is sown a natural body; it is raised a spiritual body. There is a natural body, and there is a spiritual body.

45 And so it is written, The first man Adam was made a living soul; the last Adam was made a quickening spirit.

46 Howbeit that was not first which is spiritual, but that which is natural; and afterward that which is spiritual.

47 The first man is of the earth, earthy; the second man is the Lord from heaven.

48 As is the earthy, such are they also that are earthy: and as is the heavenly, such are they also that are heavenly.

49 And as we have borne the image of the earthy, we shall also bear the image of the heavenly.

50 Now this I say, brethren, that flesh and blood cannot inherit the kingdom of God; neither doth corruption inherit incorruption.

51 Behold, I shew you a mystery; We shall not all sleep, but we shall all be changed,

52 In a moment, in the twinkling of an eye, at the last trump: for the trumpet shall sound, and the dead shall be raised incorruptible, and we shall be changed.

53 For this corruptible must put on incorruption, and this mortal must put on immortality.

54 So when this corruptible shall have put on incorruption, and this mortal shall have put on immortality, then shall be brought to pass the saying that is written, Death is swallowed up in victory.

55 O death, where is thy sting? O grave, where is thy victory?

56 The sting of death is sin; and the strength of sin is the law.

57 But thanks be to God, which giveth us the victory through our Lord Jesus Christ.

❖　❖　❖

Hollywood Cemetery, Richmond, Virginia
Photo by Tanya D. Marsh

CHAPTER 3.5

AUGUSTINE ON DEATH

Phillip Schaff, NICENE AND POST-NICENE FATHERS (1886-1900)

[Augustine of Hippo (354 – 430 AD) was an early Christian theologian. He was the Bishop of Hippo (modern day Annaba, Algeria) and one of the most important Church Fathers and is recognized by modern Catholics and Protestants for his theological contributions. In particular, his work *De Civitate Dei* (The City of God) was highly influential on the development of orthodox Christian thought. He was beatified and is the patron of the Augustinian monks.]

THE CITY OF GOD

Book 13: Chapter 20

Thus the souls of departed saints are not affected by the death which dismisses them from their bodies, because their flesh rests in hope, no matter what indignities it receives after sensation is gone. For they do not desire that their bodies be forgotten, as Plato thinks fit, but rather, because they remember what has been promised by Him who deceives no man, and who gave them security for the safe keeping even of the hairs of their head, they with a longing patience wait in hope of the resurrection of their bodies, in which they have suffered many hardships, and are now to suffer never again. For if they did not "hate their own flesh," when it, with its native infirmity, opposed their will, and had to be constrained by the spiritual law, how much more shall they love it, when it shall even itself have become spiritual! For as, when the spirit serves the flesh, it is fitly called carnal, so, when the flesh serves the spirit, it will justly be called spiritual. Not that it is converted into spirit, as some fancy from the words, "It is sown in corruption, it is raised in incorruption," but because it is subject to the spirit with a perfect and marvellous readiness of obedience, and responds in all things to the will that has entered on immortality,—all reluctance, all corruption, and all slowness being removed. For the body will not only be better than it was here in its best estate of health, but it will surpass the bodies of our first parents ere they sinned.

Book 22: Chapters 19-21

What am I to say now about the hair and nails? Once it is understood that no part of the body shall so perish as to produce deformity in the body, it is at the same time understood that such things as would have produced a deformity by their excessive proportions shall be added to the total bulk of the body, not to parts in which the beauty of the proportion would thus be marred. Just as if, after making a vessel of clay, one wished to make it over again of the same clay, it would not be necessary that the same portion of the clay which had formed the handle should again form the new handle, or that what had formed the bottom should again do so, but only that the whole clay should go to make up the whole new vessel, and that no part of it should be left unused. Wherefore, if the hair that has been cropped and the nails that have been cut would cause a deformity were they to be restored to their places, they shall not be restored; and yet no one will lose these parts at the resurrection, for they shall be changed into the same flesh, their substance being so altered as to preserve the proportion of the various parts of the body. ...

But the love we bear to the blessed martyrs causes us, I know not how, to desire to see in the heavenly kingdom the marks of the wounds which they received for the name of Christ, and possibly we shall see them. For this will not be a deformity, but a mark of honor, and will add lustre to their appearance, and a spiritual, if not a bodily beauty. And yet we need not believe that they to whom it has been said, "Not a hair of your head shall perish," shall, in the resurrection, want such of their members as they have been deprived of in their martyrdom. But if it will be seemly in that new kingdom to have some marks of these wounds still visible in that immortal flesh, the places where they have been wounded or mutilated shall retain the scars without any of the members being lost. While, therefore, it is quite true that no blemishes which the body has sustained shall appear in the resurrection, yet we are not to reckon or name these marks of virtue blemishes. ...

Far be it from us to fear that the omnipotence of the Creator cannot, for the resuscitation and reanimation of our bodies, recall all the portions which have been consumed by beasts or fire, or have been dissolved into dust or ashes, or have decomposed into water, or evaporated into the air. Far from us be the thought, that anything which escapes our observation in any most hidden recess of nature either evades the knowledge or transcends the power of the Creator of all things. ...

Whatever, therefore, has been taken from the body, either during life or after death shall be restored to it, and, in conjunction with what has remained in the grave, shall rise again, transformed from the oldness of the animal body into the newness of the spiritual body, and clothed in incorruption and immortality. But even though the body has been all quite ground to powder by some severe accident, or by the ruthlessness of enemies, and though it has been so diligently scattered to the winds, or into the water, that there is no trace of it left, yet it shall not be beyond the omnipotence of the Creator,—no, not a hair of its head shall perish.

THE CARE TO BE HAD FOR THE DEAD (DE CURA PRO MORTUIS)

Long time, my venerable fellow-bishop Paulinus, have I been thy Holiness's debtor for an answer; even since thou wrotest to me by them of the household of our most religious daughter Flora, asking of me whether it profit any man after death that his body is buried at the memorial of some Saint...

There is a certain kind of life by which is acquired, while one lives in this body, that it should be possible for these things to be of some help to the departed; and, consequently, it is "according to the things done by the body," that they are aided by the things which shall, after they have left the body, be religiously done on their behalf. For there are whom these things aid nothing at all, namely, when they are done either for persons whose merits are so evil, that neither by such things are they worthy to be aided; or for persons whose merits are so good, that of such things they have no need as aids. Of the kind of life, therefore, which each hath led by the body, doth it come, that these things profit or profit not, whatever are piously done on his behalf when he has left the body. For touching merit whereby these things profit, if none have been gotten in this life, it is in vain sought after this life. So it comes to pass as well that not unmeaningly doth the Church, or care of friends, bestow upon the departed whatever of religion it shall be able; as also that, nevertheless, each receiveth "according to the things which he hath done by the body, whether it be good or bad," the Lord rendering unto each according to his works. For, that this which is bestowed should be capable of profiting him after the body, this was acquired in that life which he hath led in the body...

"But" (say I) "in such a slaughter-heap of dead bodies, could they not even be buried? not this, either, doth pious faith too greatly dread, holding that which is foretold that not even consuming beasts will be an hindrance to the rising again of bodies of which not a hair of the head shall perish. Nor in any wise would Truth say, "Fear not them which kill the body, but cannot kill the soul;" if it could at all hinder the life to come whatever enemies might choose to do with the bodies of the slain. Unless haply any is so absurd as to contend that they ought not to be feared before death, lest they kill the body, but ought to be feared after death, lest, having killed the body, they suffer it not to be buried. Is that then false which Christ says, "Who kill the body, and afterwards have no more that they can do," if they have so great things that they can do on dead bodies? Far be the thought, that that should be false which Truth hath said...

So, then, all these things, care of funeral, bestowal in sepulture, pomp of obsequies, are more for comfort of the living, than for help to the dead. If it at all profit the ungodly to have costly sepulture, it shall harm the godly to have vile sepulture or none. Right handsome obsequies in sight of men did that rich man who was clad in purple receive of the crowd of his housefolk; but far more handsome did that poor man who was full of sores obtain of the ministry of Angels; who bore him not out into a marble tomb, but into Abraham's bosom bore him on high. All this they laugh at, against whom we have undertaken to defend the City of God: but for all that their own philosophers, even, held care of sepulture in contempt; and often whole armies, while dying for their earthly country, cared not where they should after lie, or to what beasts they should become meat...

Yet it follows not that the bodies of the departed are to be despised and flung aside, and above all of just and faithful men, which bodies as organs and vessels to all good works their spirit hath holily used. For if a father's garment and ring, and whatever such like, is the more dear to those whom they leave behind, the greater their affection is towards their parents, in no wise are the bodies themselves to be spurned, which truly we wear in more familiar and close conjunction than any of our putting on. For these pertain not to ornament or aid which is applied from without, but to the very nature of man...

If this be true, doubtless also the providing for the interment of bodies a place at the Memorials of Saints, is a mark of a good human affection towards the remains of one's friends: since if there be religion in the burying, there cannot but be religion in taking thought where the burying shall be. But while it is desirable there should be such like solaces of survivors, for the showing forth of their pious mind towards their beloved, I do not see what helps they be to the dead save in this way: that upon recollection of the place in which are deposited the bodies of those whom they love, they should by prayer commend them to those same Saints, who have as patrons taken them into their charge to aid them before the Lord...

But then the only reason why the name Memorials or Monuments is given to those sepulchres of the dead which become specially distinguished, is that they recall to memory, and by putting in mind cause us to think of, them who by death are withdrawn from the eyes of the living, that they may not by forgetfulness be also withdrawn from men's hearts. For both the term Memorial most plainly shews this, and Monument is so named from monishing, that is, putting in mind. For which reason the Greeks also call that μνημεῖον which we call a Memorial or Monument: because in their tongue the memory itself, by which we remember, is called μνήμη. When therefore the mind recollects where the body of a very dear friend lies buried, and thereupon there occurs to the thoughts a place rendered venerable by the name of a Martyr, to that same Martyr doth it commend the soul in affection of heartfelt recollection and prayer. And when this affection is exhibited to the departed by faithful men who were most dear to them, there is no doubt that it profits them who while living in the body merited that such things should profit them after this life...

When therefore the faithful mother of a faithful son departed desired to have his body deposited in the basilica of a Martyr, forasmuch as she believed that his soul would be aided by the merits of the Martyr, the very believing of this was a sort of supplication, and this profited, if aught profited. And in that she recurs in her thoughts to this same sepulchre, and in her prayers more and more commends her son, the spirit of the departed is aided, not by the place of its dead body, but by that which springs from memory of the place, the living affection of the mother...

For wheresoever the flesh of the departed may lie or not lie, the spirit requires rest and must get it: for the spirit in its departing from thence took with it the consciousness without which it could make no odds how one exists, whether in a good estate or a bad: and it does not look for aiding of its life from that flesh to which it did itself afford the life which it withdrew in its departing, and is to render back in its returning; since not flesh to spirit, but spirit unto flesh procureth merit even of very resurrection, whether it be unto punishment or unto glory that it is to come to life again...

We read in the Ecclesiastical History which Eusebius wrote in Greek, and Ruffinus turned into the Latin tongue, of Martyr's bodies in Gaul exposed to dogs, and how the leavings of those dogs and bones of the dead were, even to uttermost consumption, by fire burned up; and the ashes of the same scattered on the river Rhone, lest any thing should be left for any sort whatever of memorial. Which thing must be believed to have been to no other end divinely permitted, but that Christians should learn in confessing Christ, while they despise this life, much more to despise sepulture. For this thing, which with savage rage was done to the bodies of Martyrs, if it could any whit hurt them, to impair the blessed resting of their most victorious spirits, would assuredly not have been suffered to be done. In very deed therefore it was declared, that the Lord in saying, "Fear not them which kill the body, and afterward have no more that they can do," did not mean that He would not permit them to do any thing to the bodies of His followers when dead; but that whatever they might be permitted to do, nothing should be done that could lessen the Christian felicity of the departed, nothing thereof reach to their consciousness while yet living after death; nothing avail to the detriment, no, not even of the bodies themselves, to diminish aught of their integrity when they should rise again...

And yet, by reason of that affection of the human heart, whereby "no man ever hateth his own flesh," if men have reason to know that after their death their bodies will lack any thing which in each man's nation or country the wonted order of sepulture demandeth, it makes them sorrowful as men; and that which after death reacheth not unto them, they do before death fear for their bodies...By reason then of this, the natural love which every man hath for his own flesh, it was both to the one a punishment to learn that he should not be in the sepulchre of his fathers, and to the other a care to take order beforehand that his own bones should be spared, if he should lie beside him whose sepulchre no man should violate...

Why then are those who buried Saul and his son said to have done mercy, and for this are blessed by that godly king, but because it is a good affection with which the hearts of the pitiful are touched, when they grieve for that in the dead bodies of other men, which, by that affection through which no man ever hateth his own flesh, they would not have done after their own death to their own bodies; and what they would have done by them when they shall have no more feeling, that they take care to do by others now having no feeling while themselves have yet feeling?...

Howbeit it is a question which surpasses the strength of my understanding, after what manner the Martyrs aid them who by them, it is certain, are helped; whether themselves by themselves be present at the same time in so different places, and by so great distance lying apart one from another, either where their Memorials are, or beside their Memorials, wheresoever they are felt to be present: or whether, while they themselves, in a place congruous with their merits, are removed from all converse with mortals, and yet do in a general sort pray for the needs of their suppliants…

Which things being so, let us not think that to the dead for whom we have a care, any thing reaches save what by sacrifices either of the altar, or of prayers, or of alms, we solemnly supplicate: although not to all for whom they are done be they profitable, but to them only by whom while they live it is obtained that they should be profitable. But forasmuch as we discern not who these be, it is meet to do them for all regenerate persons, that none of them may be passed by to whom these benefits may and ought to reach. For better it is that these things shall be superfluously done to them whom they neither hinder nor help, than lacking to them whom they help. More diligently however doth each man these things for his own near and dear friends, in order that they may be likewise done unto him by his. But as for the burying of the body, whatever is bestowed on that, is no aid of salvation, but an office of humanity, according to that affection by which "no man ever hateth his own flesh." Whence it is fitting that he take what care he is able for the flesh of his neighbor, when he is gone that bare it. And if they do these things who believe not the resurrection of the flesh, how much more are they beholden to do the same who do believe; that so, an office of this kind bestowed upon a body, dead but yet to rise again and to remain to eternity, may also be in some sort a testimony of the same faith? But, that a person is buried at the memorials of the Martyrs, this, I think, so far profits the departed, that while commending him also to the Martyrs' patronage, the affection of supplication on his behalf is increased.

❖   ❖   ❖

Glasnevin Cemetery, Dublin, Ireland
Photo by Tanya D. Marsh

CHAPTER 3.6

PRIMARY SOURCES ON CHRISTIAN BELIEFS ABOUT BURIAL

Phillip Schaff, NICENE AND POST-NICENE FATHERS (1886-1900)

TERTULLIAN, ON THE RESURRECTION OF THE FLESH

Chapter LVII

What is the good of believing in the resurrection, unless your faith embraces the whole of it? If the flesh is to be repaired after its dissolution, much more will it be restored after some violent injury. Greater cases prescribe rules for lesser ones. Is not the amputation or the crushing of a limb the death of that limb? Now, if the death of the whole person is rescinded by its resurrection, what must we say of the death of a part of him? If we are changed for glory, how much more for integrity! Any loss sustained by our bodies is an accident to them, but their entirety is their natural property. ...

If God raises not men entire, He raises not the dead. For what dead man is entire, although he dies entire? Who is without hurt, that is without life? What body is uninjured, when it is dead, when it is cold, when it is ghastly, when it is stiff, when it is a corpse? When is a man more infirm, than when he is entirely infirm? When more palsied, than when quite motionless? Thus, for a dead man to be raised again, amounts to nothing short of his being restored to his entire condition,—lest he, forsooth, be still dead in that part in which he has not risen again.

God is quite able to re-make what He once made.

TERTULLIAN, TREATISE ON THE SOUL

Chapter LI

Yet even this partial survival of the soul finds a place in the opinions of some men; and on this account they will not have the body consumed at its funeral by fire, because they would spare the small residue of the soul. There is, however, another way of accounting for this pious treatment, not as if it meant to favour the relics of the soul, but as if it would avert a cruel custom in the interest even of the body; since, being human, it is itself undeserving of an end which is also inflicted upon murderers. The truth is, the soul is indivisible, because it is immortal; (and this fact) compels us to believe that death itself is an indivisible process, accruing indivisibly to the soul, not indeed because it is immortal, but because it is indivisible.

MINUCIUS FELIX, OCTAVIUS

Chapter XXXIV

But who is so foolish or so brutish as to dare to deny that man, as he could first of all be formed by God, so can again be re-formed; that he is nothing after death, and that he was nothing before he began to exist; and as from nothing it was possible for him to be born, so from nothing it may be possible for him to be restored? Moreover, it is more difficult to begin that which is not, than to repeat that which has been. Do you think that, if anything is withdrawn from our feeble eyes, it perishes to God? Every body, whether it is dried up into dust, or is dissolved into moisture, or is compressed into ashes, or is attenuated into smoke, is withdrawn from us, but it is reserved for God in the custody of the elements.

Nor, as you believe, do we fear any loss from sepulture, but we adopt the ancient and better custom of burying in the earth. See, therefore, how for our consolation all nature suggests a future resurrection. The sun sinks down and arises, the stars pass away and return, the flowers die and revive again, after their win-try decay the shrubs resume their leaves, seeds do not flourish again. unless they are rotted: thus the body in the sepulchre is like the trees which in winter hide their verdure with a deceptive dryness.

❖　❖　❖

CHAPTER 4

DEATH AND BURIAL
IN CATHOLIC EUROPE

Kaisergruft [Imperial Crypt], Capuchin Church, Vienna, Austria
Photo by Tanya D. Marsh

CHAPTER 4.1
DEATH AND BURIAL IN CATHOLIC EUROPE
Tanya D. Marsh

In a significant departure from Roman Custom, the early Christians forbid cremation and insisted upon interment in consecrated ground. This meant, despite the legal prohibition on interments within the city walls, that Christians were interred or entombed within the church building itself or in the surrounding yard—the churchyard. With a few exceptions, Christians did not banish the dead beyond city walls until the 19th and 20th centuries. Because Christian doctrine limited the available placement of human remains, space-saving techniques like grave recycling and ossuaries were implemented. The close proximity between the living and the dead in Christian houses of worship was quite different from Roman custom.

In Chapter 4.2, Edward Gibbon argues that the pagan practices of the pre-Christian Romans heavily influenced the development of certain Christian funerary practices. Writing in 1826, Gibbon articulated a key critique of the Reformation—that the "religious adoration" of "Christians for the martyrs of the faith" and the integration of relics into consecrated buildings were pagan, not Christian, practices. For example, Christ Church Cathedral in Dublin, Ireland, once held relics that (allegedly) included a fragment of a cloth that wrapped the baby Jesus, a thorn from the crown of thorns, and the Staff of Jesus. In 1538, these relics were publicly burned. A reliquary containing the heart of Laurence O'Toole, the archbishop of Dublin from 1162 to 1180, survived that destruction but was stolen from the Cathedral in 2012 by unknown persons.

Material on relics is included in this Chapter 4 for several reasons. First, the heavy use of relics and reliquaries in 17th and 18th century Europe is foreign to most modern Americans, even those who faithfully attend Catholic Church. Second, the doctrine regarding relics, and the desire of the people to be interred in close proximity to relics, influenced funerary practices and methods of disposition in Catholic Europe. Those customs and practices were imported to the United States by millions of immigrants, particularly from Ireland, Germany, and Italy. European Catholics and Protestants in the 17th and 18th centuries shared a similar hierarchy of disposition options that hinged on family wealth and status. Interment or entombment within the church was preferred, followed by entombment in a family tomb or crypt located in the churchyard, and finally undifferentiated burial in the churchyard. That hierarchy of preferences came to the United States and is clearly reflected in the churches and churchyards of the colonial period and the early 19th century, particularly in urban areas. Many of the photographs in this book from St. Paul's Chapel in New York City, a colonial era church and churchyard, King's Chapel Cemetery in Boston, and St. Louis #1 in New Orleans are indistinguishable from contemporary European cemeteries and churchyards. A series of photographs after Chapter 4.6 highlights the similarities.

❖   ❖   ❖

Kaisergruft [Imperial Crypt], Capuchin Church, Vienna, Austria
Photo by Tanya D. Marsh

CHAPTER 4.2
INTRODUCTION OF THE WORSHIP OF SAINTS, AND RELICS, AMONG THE CHRISTIANS

Edward Gibbon,
THE HISTORY OF THE DECLINE AND FALL OF THE ROMAN EMPIRE (1826).

The destruction of the pagan religion, A.D. 378-395

The ruin of paganism, in the age of Theodosius, is perhaps the only example of the total extirpation of any ancient and popular superstition; and may therefore deserve to be considered as a singular event in the history of the human mind. …

The pagan religion is prohibited, A.D. 390

The temples of the Roman empire were deserted, or destroyed; but the ingenious superstition of the pagans still attempted to elude the laws of Theodosius, by which all sacrifices had been severely prohibited. The inhabitants of the country, whose conduct was less exposed to the eye of malicious curiosity, disguised their religious, under the appearance of convivial, meetings. On the days of solemn festivals, they assembled in great numbers under the spreading shade of some consecrated trees; sheep and oxen were slaughtered and roasted; and this rural entertainment was sanctified by the use of incense, and by the hymns, which were sung in honour of the gods. But it was alleged, that, as no part of the animal was made a burnt offering, as no altar was provided to receive the blood, and as the previous oblation of salt cakes, and the concluding ceremony of libations, were carefully omitted, these festal meetings did not involve the guests in the guilt, or penalty, of an illegal sacrifice. Whatever might be the truth of the facts, or the merit of the distinction, these vain pretenses were swept away by the last edict of Theodosius; which inflicted a deadly wound on the superstition of the pagans. This prohibitory law is expressed in the most absolute and comprehensive terms. "It is our will and pleasure," says the emperor, "that none of our subjects, whether magistrates or private citizens, however exalted or however humble may be their rank and condition, shall presume, in any city, or in any place, to worship an inanimate idol, by the sacrifice of a guiltless victim." …

The violent and repeated strokes of the orthodox princes, were broken by the soft and yielding substance against which they were directed; and the ready obedience of the pagans protected them from the pains and penalties of the Theodosian Code. Instead of asserting, that the authority of the gods was superior to that the emperor, they desisted, with a plaintive murmur, from the use of those sacred rites which their sovereign had condemned. If they were sometimes tempted, by a sally of passion, or by the hopes of concealment, to indulge their favourite superstition; their humble repentance disarmed the severity of the Christian magistrate, and they seldom refused to atone for their rashness, by submitting with some secret reluctance, to the yoke of the Gospel. The churches were filled with the increasing multitude of these unworthy proselytes, who had conformed, from temporal motives, to the reigning religion; and whilst they devoutly imitated the postures, and recited the prayers, of the faithful, they satisfied their conscience by the silent and sincere invocation of the gods of antiquity. …

The worship of the Christian martyrs

… The grateful respect of the Christians for the martyrs of the faith, was exalted, by time and victory, into religious adoration; and the most illustrious of the saints and prophets were deservedly associated to the honours of the martyrs. One hundred and fifty years after the glorious deaths of St. Peter and St. Paul, the Vatican and the Ostian road were distinguished by the tombs, or rather by the trophies, of those spiritual heroes. In the age which followed the conversion of Constantine, the emperors, the consuls, and the generals of armies, devoutly visited the sepulchers of a tentmaker and a fisherman; and their venerable bones were deposited under the altars of Christ, on which the bishops of the royal city continually offered the unbloody sacrifice. The new capital of the eastern world, unable to produce any ancient and domestic trophies, was enriched by the spoils of dependent provinces. The bodies of St. Andrew, St. Luke, and St. Timothy, had reposed, near three hundred years, in the obscure graves, from whence they were transported, in solemn pomp, to the church of the Apostles, which the magnificence of Constantine had founded on the banks of the Thracian Bosphorus. About fifth years afterward, the same banks were honoured by the presence of Samuel, the judge and prophet of the people of Israel. His ashes, deposited in a golden vase, and covered with a silken veil, were delivered by the bishops into each other's hands. The relics of Samuel were received by the people, with the same joy and reverence which they would have shown to the living prophet; the highways, from Palestine to the gates of Constantinople, were filled with an uninterrupted procession; and the emperor Arcadius himself, at the head of the most illustrious members of the clergy and senate, advanced to meet his extraordinary guest, who had always deserved and claimed the homage of kings. The example of Rome and Constantinople confirmed the faith and discipline of the Catholic world. The honours of the saints and martyrs, after a feeble and ineffectual murmur of profane reason, were universally established; and in the age of Ambrose and Jerom, something was still deemed wanting to the sanctity of a Christian church, till it had been consecrated by some portion of holy relics, which fixed and inflamed the devotion of the faithful.

General reflections

In the long period of twelve hundred years, which elapsed between the reign of Constantine and the reformation of Luther, the worship of saints and relics corrupted the pure and perfect simplicity of the Christian model; and some symptoms of degeneracy may be observed even in the first generations which adopted and cherished this pernicious innovation.

Fabulous martyrs and relics

The satisfactory experience, that the relics of saints were more valuable than gold or precious stones, stimulated the clergy to multiple the treasures of the church. Without much regard for truth or probability, they invented names for skeletons, and actions for names. The fame of the apostles, and of the holy men who had imitated their virtues, was darkened by religious fiction. To the invincible land of genuine and primitive martyrs, they added myriads of imaginary heroes, who had never existed, except in the fancy of crafty or credulous legendaries; and there is reason to suspect, that Tours might not be the only diocese in which the bones of a malefactor were adored, instead of a saint. A superstitious practice, which tended to increase the temptations of fraud and credulity, insensibly extinguished the light of history, and of reason, in the Christian world. ...

Miracles

... [T]he relics of the first martyr [St. Stephen] were transported, in solemn procession, to a church constructed in their honour on Mount Sion; and the minute particles of those relics, a drop of blood, or the scrapings of a bone, were acknowledged, in almost every province of the Roman world, to possess a divine and miraculous virtue. The grave and learned Augustine, whose understanding scarcely admits the excuse of credulity, has attested the innumerable prodigies which were performed in Africa by the relics of St. Stephen; and this marvelous narrative is inserted in the elaborate work of the City of God, which the bishop of Hippo designed as a solid and immortal proof of the truth of Christianity. Augustin solemnly declares, that he has selected those miracles only which were publicly certified by the persons who were either the objects, or the spectators of the power of the martyr. ... And yet the bishop enumerates above seventy miracles, of which three were resurrections from the dead, in the space of two years, and within the limits of his own diocese. If we enlarge our view to all the dioceses, and all the saints, of the Christian world, it will not be easy to calculate the fables, and the errors, which issued from this inexhaustible source. ...

Introduction of pagan ceremonies

As the objects of religion were gradually reduced to the standard of the imagination, the rites and ceremonies were introduced that seemed most powerfully to affect the senses of the vulgar. If in the beginning of the fifth century, Tertulian, or Lactantius, had been suddenly raised from the dead, to assist at the festival of some popular saint, or martyr, they would have gazed with astonishment and indignation, on the profane spectacle, which had succeeded to the pure and spiritual worship of a Christian congregation. As soon as the doors of the church were thrown open, they must have been offended by the smoke of incense, the perfume of flowers, and the glare of lamps and tapers, which diffused at noonday, a gaudy, superfluous, and, in their opinion, a sacrilegious light. If they approached the balustrade of the altar, they made their way through the prostrate crowd, consisting, for the most part, of strangers and pilgrims, who restored to the city on the vigil of the feast; and who already felt the strong intoxication of fanaticism, and, perhaps, of wine. Their devout kisses were imprinted on the walls and pavement of the sacred edifice; and their fervent prayers were directed, whatever might be the language of their church, to the bones, the blood, or the ashes of the saints, which were usually concealed, by a linen or silken veil, from the eyes of the vulgar. The Christian frequented the tombs of the martyrs in the hope of obtaining, from their powerful intercession, every sort of spiritual, but more especially of temporal blessings. They implored the preservation of their health or the cure of their infirmities; the fruitfulness of their barren wives, or the safety and happiness of their children. Whenever they undertook any distant or dangerous journey, they requested that the holy martyrs would be their guides and protectors on the road; and, if they returned, without having experienced any misfortune, they again hastened to the tombs of the martyrs, to celebrate, with grateful thanksgivings, their obligations to the memory and relics of those heavenly patrons. The walls were hung round with symbols of the favours, which they had received; eyes, and hands and feet of gold and silver; and edifying pictures, which could not long escape the abuse of indiscreet or idolatrous devotion, represented the image, the attributes, and the miracles of the tutelary saint. The same uniform original spirit of superstition might suggest, in the most distant ages and countries, the same methods of deceiving the credulity, and of affecting the senses, of mankind; but it must ingeniously be confessed, that the ministers of the Catholic church imitated the profane model, which they were impatient to destroy. The most respectable bishops had persuaded themselves, that the ignorant rustics would more cheerfully renounce the superstitions of paganism, if they found some resemblance, some compensation, in the bosom of Christianity. The religion of Constantine achieved in less than a century, the final conquest of the Roman empire; but the victors themselves were insensibly subdued by the arts of their vanquished rivals.

❖   ❖   ❖

St. Martin's Cathedral, Bratislava, Slovakia
Photo by Tanya D. Marsh

CHAPTER 4.3
ON THE SAINTS AND THEIR RELICS

Francois Veron, THE RULE OF CATHOLIC FAITH: OR, THE PRINCIPLES AND DOCTRINES
OF THE CATHOLIC CHURCH (1833)
[translated by Rev. J. Waterworth]

On the Invocation of the Saints

"I firmly hold that the saints reigning together with Christ, are to be venerated, and invoked, and that they offer prayers to God for us." These are the words of our Profession of Faith. The Council of Trent, in the 25th session, explains this doctrine more fully, and explicitly: "The Holy Synod admonishes all those, to whom the office of teaching has been entrusted, diligently to instruct the faithful, relatively to the invocation, and intercession of the Saints; teaching them that the Saints, who reign together with Christ, offer up their prayers to God for man; that it is good, and profitable, suppliantly to invoke them, and to fly to their prayers, help, and aid, in order to obtain favours from God, through his Son Jesus Christ, who is alone our Saviour, and our Redeemer; that it is an impious opinion which denies that the Saints who enjoy eternal happiness are to be invoked; or which asserts that they do not pray for man; or that to invoke their intercession is our favour as individuals, is idolatrous, or opposed to the word of God, and the honour of the only Mediator between God, and man, Christ Jesus; or that it is foolish to pray either mentally or vocally, to those who are reigning in Heaven." ...

On the Relics of the Saints

On this point, our Profession of Faith says,—"I firmly hold that the relics of the saints are to be venerated." The Council of Trent "enjoins, that the bishops, and others, instruct the faithful, on the honor to be paid to the relics of the saints; teaching them that the bodies of the holy martyrs, and others, now living with Christ, which once were the living members of Christ, and the temples of the Holy Ghost,—and which shall be raised by him to eternal life, and shall be glorified, are to be venerated by the faithful. Through them the Almighty bestows many benefits on man; so that they who affirm, no veneration, or honor to be due to the relics of the saints; or, that to honor these, and other sacred monuments, is useless,—are absolutely to be condemned; as the church has condemned, and does not condemn them." This, and only this, is decreed by the Council; and this, consequently, is an article of our Faith, being proposed to our belief, by a General Council.

❖ ❖ ❖

Stift Melk (Melk Abbey), Melk, Austria
Photo by Tanya D. Marsh

CHAPTER 4.4
RELICS
Charles George Herbermann, et al., THE CATHOLIC ENCYCLOPEDIA (1911)

The word *relics* comes from the Latin *reliquiae* ... which already before the propagation of Christianity was used in its modern sense, viz., of some object, notably part of the body or clothes, remaining as a memorial of a departed saint. The veneration of relics, in fact, is to some extent a primitive instinct, and it is associated with many other religious systems besides that of Christianity. ...

Doctrine regarding relics
The teaching of the Catholic Church with regard to the veneration of relics is summed up in a decree of the Council of Trent (Sess. XXV), which enjoins the bishops and other pastors to instruct their flocks that "the holy bodies of holy martyrs and of others now living with Christ—which bodies were the living members of Christ and 'the temple of the Holy Ghost' (I. Cor., vi, 19) and which are by Him to be raised to eternal life and to be glorified are to be venerated by the faithful for through these [bodies[many benefits are bestowed by God on men, so that they who affirm that veneration and honour are not due to the relics of the saints, or that these and other sacred monuments are uselessly honoured by the faithful, and that the places dedicated to the memories of the saints are in vain visited with the view of obtaining their aid, are wholly to be condemned, as the Church has already long since condemned, and also now condemns them.

Further, the council insists that "in the invocation of the saints the veneration of relics and the sacred use of images, every superstition shall be removed and all filthy lucre abolished." Again, "the visitation of relics must not be by any perverted into revellings and drunkenness." To secure a proper check upon abuses of this kind, "no new miracles are to be acknowledged or new relics recognized unless the bishop of the diocese has taken cognizance and approved thereof." ...

The justification of Catholic practice, which is indirectly suggested here by the reference to the bodies of the saints as formerly temples of the Holy Ghost and as destined hereafter to be eternally glorified, is further developed in the authoritative "Roman Catechism" drawn up at the instance of the same council. Recalling the marvels witnessed at the tombs of the martyrs, where "the blind and cripples are restored to health, the dead recalled to life, and demons expelled from the bodies of men," the Catechism points out that these are facts which "St. Ambrose and St. Augustine, most unexceptionable witnesses, declare in their writings that they have not merely heard and read about, as many did, but have seen with their own eyes." ... And from thence, turning to Scriptural analogies, the compilers further argue: "If the clothes, the kerchiefs, if the shadow of the saints before they departed from this life, banished diseases and restored strength, who will have the hardihood to deny that God wonderfully works the same by the sacred ashes, the bones, and other relics of the saints? This is the lesson we have to learn from that dead body which, having been accidentally let down into the sepulcher of Eliseus, "when it had touched the bones of the Prophet, instantly came to life" (4 Kings, xiii, 21). We may add that this miracle as well as the veneration shown to the bones of Moses only gains additional force from their apparent contradiction to the ceremonial laws against defilement, of which we read in Num., xix, 11-22. The influence of this Jewish shrinking from contact with the dead so far lingered on that it was found necessary in the "Apostolical Constitutions," to issue a strong warning against it and to argue in favour of the Christian cult of relics.

According to the common opinion of theologians, relics are to be honoured—St. Thomas ... does not seem to consider even the word *adorare* inappropriate ... [W]hile we love and venerate the saints who were so dear to God, we also venerate all that belonged to them, and particularly their bodies, which were once the temple of the Holy Spirit and which are some day to be conformed to the glorious body of Jesus Christ. ...

There is nothing, therefore, in Catholic teaching to justify the statement that the Church encourages belief in a magical virtue, or physical curative efficacy residing in the relic itself. ...

Early History

Few points of faith can be more satisfactorily traced back to the earliest ages of Christianity than the veneration of relics. The classical instance is to be found in the letter written by the inhabitants of Smyrna, about 156, describing the death of St. Polycarp. After he had been burnt at the stake, we are told that his faithful disciples wished to carry off his remains, but the Jews urged the Roman officer to refuse his consent for fear that the Christians "would only abandon the Crucified One and begin to worship this man." Eventually, however, as the Smyrneans say, "we took up his bones, which are more valuable than precious stones and finer than refined gold, and laid them in a suitable place, where the Lord will permit us to gather ourselves together, as we are able, in gladness and joy, and to celebrate the birthday of his martyrdom." ...

[The worship of relics] flourished to its greatest extent as early as the fourth century and no Church doctor of repute restricted it. ... The numerous miracles which were wrought by bones and relics seemed to confirm their worship. ...

St. Gregory of Nyssa, in his sermons on the forty martyrs, after describing how their bodies were burned by command of the persecutors, explains that "their ashes and all that the fire had spared have been so distributed throughout the world that almost every province has had its share of the blessing. I also myself have a portion of this holy gift and I have laid the bodies of my parents beside the relics of these warriors that in the hour of the resurrection they may be awakened together with these highly privileged comrades." We have here also a hint of the explanation of the widespread practice of seeking burial near the tombs of the martyrs. It seems to have been felt that when the souls of the blessed martyrs on the day of general resurrection were once more united to their bodies, they would be accompanied in their passage to heaven by those who lay around them and that these last might on their account find more ready acceptance with God. ...

During the Merovingian and Carlovingian period the cultus of relics increased rather than diminished. Gregory of Tours abounds in stories of the marvels wrought by them, as well as of the practices used in their honour ... Very significant ... is the prologue to the text of the Salic Laws, probably written by a contemporary of Gregory of Tours in the sixth century. "That nation," it says, "which has undoubtedly in battle shaken off the hard yoke of the Romans, now that it has been illuminated through Baptism, has adored the bodies of the holy martyrs with gold and precious stone, those same bodies which the Romans burnt with fire, and pierced with the sword, or threw to wild beasts to be torn to pieces." In England we find from the first a strong tradition in the same sense derived from St. Gregory himself. Bede records how the pope "forwarded to Augustine all the things needful for the worship and service of the church, namely sacred vessels, altar linen, church ornaments, priestly and clerical vestments, relics of the holy Apostles and martyrs and also many books." ...

After the Second Council of Nicaea, in 787, had insisted with special urgency that relics were to be used in the consecration of churches, and that the omission was to be supplied if any church had been consecrated without them, the English Council of Celehyth (probably Chelsea) commanded that relics were to be used, and in default of them the Blessed Eucharist. ...

Reliquaries

It would follow of necessity from the data given in the article *Relics* that reliquaries—by which we understand in the wider sense any box, casket, or shrine destined for the reception of relics— must have existed in some shape or form almost from the beginning of Christianity.

❖　❖　❖

Officers' Burial Ground, Kilmainham, Dublin, Ireland
Photo by Tanya D. Marsh

CHAPTER 4.5

BURIAL

Edward Pace, et al., THE CATHOLIC ENCYCLOPEDIA (1922)

Ecclesiastical burial consists in bringing the corpse to the church, and after the funeral service has been held there, interring the body in a place blessed and lawfully appointed as a resting-place for the dead. Nobody may be buried in churches, even basement or lower churches, except popes, royal personages or cardinals, or residential bishops, or abbots or prelates nullius, who may be interred in their own churches. The Catholic Church has a right to have its own cemeteries. If this right is violated and the majority of those who are being interred in a cemetery are Catholics, local ordinaries should see that the public cemeteries are blessed, or at least that a part is reserved for Catholics and blessed. Where this cannot be done each grave must be blessed as often as there is a burial. The canonical regulations concerning the interdiction, violation, and reconciliation of churches apply also to cemeteries.

Every parish should have its own cemetery unless the ordinary allows one in common for two or more parishes. He may allow moral personalities and private families to have their own places of interment away from the general cemetery. The faithful may erect private burial-places of vaults for themselves and their families in parochial cemeteries, with the written consent of the ordinary or his delegate, or in the private cemetery of an association, with the written leave of its superior. These private burial-places may be alienated with the consent of the ordinary or superior. The graves of priests and clerics should, if possible, be separate from those of the laity and should be located in a more respectable place; furthermore, if it can be conveniently done, the graves of priests should be apart from those of the inferior clergy. The cemetery, should be enclosed and carefully guarded, and the proper authorities should see that no epitaphs, inscriptions or decorations unworthy of our religion are allowed therein. If possible there should be, in addition to the cemetery that has been blessed, an enclosed protected place for the interment of those who have not been allowed Christian burial. No burial is to be permitted, especially in case of sudden death, until after a lapse of time sufficient to remove all doubt as to the reality of the party's death, and no remains that have received definitive Christian burial may be exhumed without the ordinary's consent, which must never be granted if the body cannot undoubtedly be distinguished from the other corpses. ...

Any person is free to select his funeral church or cemetery, if the canons do not expressly deprive him of this right; a wife or child who has reached the age of puberty may make this choice even contrary to a husband's or a father's desire; but professed religious who are not bishops and children below the age of puberty have not this power of selection. In order, however, for the selection to be made validly, one must choose the parish church, or a church of a regular order ... or, in the case of a patron, the church of which he enjoys the patronage, or any other church authorized to hold funeral services. ... If anyone desires to be buried in a cemetery other than that of his parish, his wish should be carried out if the administrator of the cemetery in question raises no objection; should one desire to be buried in the cemetery of a religious order, this may be done if the religious superior consents. A deceased person who has a family burial-ground should be buried in it if possible if he has not selected any place; a widow in a similar case is to be buried with her husband, or if she has had more than one, with the last; if there are several family burial-places, the decedent's family or heirs are to decide in which of them the interment is to take place. ...

❖ ❖ ❖

Glasnevin Cemetery, Dublin, Ireland
Photo by Tanya D. Marsh

CHAPTER 4.6

TOMBS

B. Kleinschmidt, THE CATHOLIC ENCYCLOPEDIA (1912)

A memorial for the dead at the place of burial, customary, especially for distinguished persons, among nearly all peoples. It is of much importance in the history of art because the development of plastic art can be traced almost in its entirety by means of tombs, for the tombs, having, as a rule, been erected in churches, are better preserved. Apart from the sepulchral slabs in the Catacombs, sarcophagi ornamented with portraits, and scattered examples of mausolea, tombs may be divided into four special classes.

The first class consists of tombs with recumbent tombstones; among such are the stone or metal plates inserted in the flooring of churches. These are the oldest Christian monuments. Originally, at least in Germany, they were ornamented with a cross having a long shaft; from the eleventh century they also bore the figure of the deceased. The monumental metal plate of the tomb of King Rudolph of Swabia (d. 1081), in the cathedral of Merseburg, is of this era. During the Gothic period an engraved brass plate was the favourite sepulchral monument, while the Renaissance returned to the plate cast in relief, such as the plates by Peter Vischer of Nuremberg.

The second class consists of detached altar-tombs, that is, a raised tomb containing the body of the deceased. One variety rises like a table above the place of burial. Romanesque art generally left the side walls of the altar-tomb without ornament, while Gothic art adorned them with numerous small figures, as those of relatives, mourners, praying figures, and allegorical forms. On the lid the deceased was represented at full length. Numerous examples are to be found in all the medieval cathedrals and monastic churches. Even England, where there are but scanty plastic remains, has a rich treasure of such monuments. Probably no altar-tomb is more celebrated than that of Emperor Maximilian at Innsbruck. Another worthy of mention is Charles the Bold's tomb at Dijon by Claus Sluter. More elaborate

St. Michael's Church, Vienna, Austria

monuments have frequently an additional structure above and around them, as a baldachin, e.g. the tomb of the Della Scala at Verona; chiefly that of Cansignorio (d. 1375). During the Renaissance the baldachin assumed an entirely monumental form, almost that of a triumphal arch; fine examples are the monuments of Galleazzo Visconti in the Certosa at Pavia and of Francis I at Saint-Denis.

The third class may be called mural tombs, that is, altar-tombs set originally in a niche against a wall, and later raised upon pillars, caryatides, or a solid under-structure. They were decorated on all sides with rich plastic ornamentation. They were customary as early as the Gothic period and attained their highest development in Italy, where the inordinate craving for fame and the longing to be remembered by posterity led to the production of those magnificent sepulchral monuments for physicians, lawyers, professors, statesmen, and, by no means last, prelates, which fill the churches from Venice to Naples. During the period of the early Renaissance it was a favourite custom to place a recumbent statue of the deceased upon a state

Tomb of Strongbow, Christ Church Cathedral, Dublin, Ireland

bed or a sarcophagus and to set this at a moderate height; this structure is surrounded by standing or kneeling angels who draw back a curtain of the niche in which the Madonna is often visible. A fine example is the tomb of Leonardo Bruni (d. 1444) in Santa Croce at Florence. During the late Renaissance undue consideration was paid to architecture, as in the sepulchral monument of Giovanni Pesaro in the Frari church at Venice. In the seventeenth and eighteenth centuries the art of sculpture obtained again a greater opportunity in the treatment of tombs, but unfortunately only in the monotonous Baroque style. Hardly more than the figure of the deceased was brought into prominence. It was placed within an altar of similar style or upon a broad podium and was surrounded by all kinds of symbolical figures in the most daring positions. In a material sense these tombs are often very fine but they frequently lack the desired spiritual earnestness and repose.

The fourth class consists of hanging sepulchral monuments (memorial tablets). These occur as early as Gothic art in the form of funeral escutcheons and coats of arms made of wood or leather; and are especially prominent in the period of the Rococo and Baroque styles. Besides the altar-shaped table often constructed in several stories, the cartouche containing a portrait of the deceased was very popular in sepulchral monuments of this class.

Since the modern era put an end nearly everywhere to the burial of the dead within the church building, a new form of sepulchral art has gradually developed; it has produced works of the greatest beauty in all countries, but has also shown great perversions of the artistic sense, especially in Italy where the tendency is more to an excess of technic than to the conception of the eternal. The finest sepulchral monument of modern times is perhaps the one designed by A. Bartholome and erected at Pere Lachaise.

Minoritenkirche (Minorities Church), Vienna, Austria

❖　❖　❖

Memorial Tablet, New York City, New York

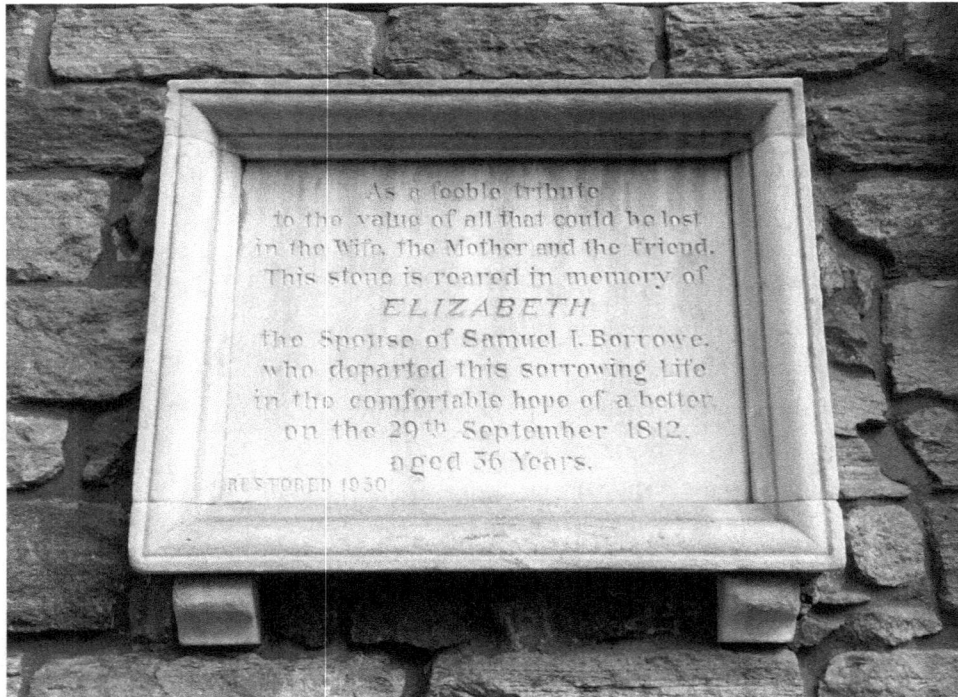

St. Paul's Chapel, New York City, New York
Photo by Tanya D. Marsh

Memorial Tablets, Vienna, Austria

St. Stephen's Cathedral, Vienna, Austria
Photo by Tanya D. Marsh

19th Century Memorial Tablet, New York City, New York

THIS TABLET
recalls to the recollection of their
FAMILY and FRIENDS
THOMAS BARROW,
who died 15th. Sept. 1825,
Aged 89 Years and 11 Months.
AND HIS WIFE
SARAH BARROW,
who died 22nd. Jan. 1786,
Aged 40 Years and 7 Months.
PIETY JUSTICE and BENEVOLENCE
ADORN'D their LIVES.
Their surviving Son, with Filial Piety
and Veneration erected this little
MONUMENT to their MEMORY.

St. Paul's Chapel, New York City, New York
Photo by Tanya D. Marsh

21st Century Memorial Tablet, Dublin, Ireland

Shane MacThomáis
1967 – 2014

"So, unquiet wanderer
and gather the glasnevin coverlet
about your head"

Glasnevin Cemetery, Dublin, Ireland
Photo by Tanya D. Marsh

19th Century Family Tomb, Rural Ohio

Winchester Cemetery, Winchester, Ohio
Photo by Tanya D. Marsh

19th Century Family Tombs, Dublin, Ireland

Glasnevin Cemetery, Dublin, Ireland
Photo by Tanya D. Marsh

Wall Vaults, Bratislava, Slovakia

St. Martin's Cathedral, Bratislava, Slovakia
Photo by Tanya D. Marsh

Wall Vaults, New Orleans, Louisiana

Lafayette Cemetery #1, New Orleans, Louisiana
Photo by Tanya D. Marsh

Passage Tomb circa 3200 BC, County Meath, Ireland

Newgrange, County Meath, Ireland
Photo by Tanya D. Marsh

Tombs, Vienna, Austria

Zentralfriedhof [Central Cemetery], Vienna, Austria
Photo by Tanya D. Marsh

CHAPTER 5

ENGLISH LAW AND CUSTOMS

Glasnevin Cemetery, Dublin, Ireland
Photo by Tanya D. Marsh

CHAPTER 5.1
ENGLISH LAW AND CUSTOMS
Tanya D. Marsh

The first contacts between Rome and Britain were the expeditions of Julius Caesar in 55 and 54 BC. These brief invasions resulted in the establishment of diplomatic relations and trade between some of the Celtic tribes and Rome, but no permanent Roman presence on the island. The Roman invasion of Britain finally took place in 43 AD.

Following the invasion, temples to Roman gods were installed in Britain, but the Celtic Britons continued to worship their own gods as well. In 61 AD, Rome attempted to strengthen its hold on the island by outlawing the Druid priests and destroying their sacred groves. The introduction of Christianity to Britain has not been conclusively established, although it was certainly transmitted to the island through the Romans. The earliest evidence is a statement by Tertullian, around 200 AD, where he described "all the limits of the Spains, and the diverse nations of the Gauls, and the haunts of the Britons, inaccessible to the Romans, but subjugated to Christ." Christianity was legalized in the Roman Empire by Constantine I in 313 AD, and Theodosius I made Christianity the official religion of the empire in 391 AD. Not long thereafter, Rome abandoned Britain to the Saxons. The Germanic Saxons were pagan, and for a century and a half, Christianity retreated in Britain. Although official Roman influence in Britain ended in the fourth century, the history of English ecclesiastical law, as described in Chapter 5.2, demonstrates that the customs and laws of the Roman Empire left a lasting imprint on Britain.

The Church of England was established after the end of Roman Britain. History records that the Church of England began with the mission of Saint Augustine of Canterbury in AD 597. From the beginning, it appears that the Church of England asserted jurisdiction over places of burial. It is generally reported that burial in churchyards began in Britain in 750 AD, but it should be noted that when Augustine died in 604 AD, he was buried in the portico of what is now known as St. Augustine's in Canterbury. As explained in the *Ruggles Report* (Chapter 7.3):

> The exclusive power of the ecclesiastics denominated, in legal phrase, "ecclesiastical cognizance," became not only executive, but judicial. It was executive, in taking the body into their actual, corporeal possession, and practically guarding its repose in their consecrated grounds; and it was judicial, as well in deciding all controversies involving the possession or the use of holy places, or the pecuniary emoluments which they yielded, as in a broader field, in adjudicating who should be allowed to lie in consecrated earth, and, in fact, who should be allowed to be interred at all.

The Acts of Supremacy

The Church of England was subject to the authority of the Roman Catholic Church until the 1534 Act of Supremacy, an act of Parliament that declared King Henry VIII the "Supreme Head of the Church of England." This doctrine, known as "royal supremacy," subverted the Church of England to the civil authority of the English sovereign.

King Henry VIII was succeeded by his young son Edward in 1547. During the short reign of King Edward VI, the realm was governed by a Regency Council that supported the Act of Supremacy. Edward VI died in 1553 and was succeeded by his older sister Mary, the daughter of Henry VIII and the Catholic Catherine of Aragon. Queen Mary I, raised in her mother's faith, caused Parliament to repeal the Act of Supremacy in 1554. Parliament passed the Second Act of Supremacy in 1559, a year after the death of Mary. Her successor, Queen Elizabeth I, was declared the "Supreme Governor of the Church of England." The official Anglican Church of England was established by Queen Elizabeth I's Second Act of Supremacy. The ruling monarch of England remains the Supreme Governor of the Church of England, and the Archbishop of Canterbury is the Primate of all England. Although the Church of England is Protestant, the religious settlements during the reign of Queen Elizabeth I caused it to retain significant continuity with the pre-Reformation Church, particularly in its structure, buildings, and liturgy. It is said that the Church of England is both "catholic and reformed."

The conservatism of the Church of England clashed with more radical Protestant dissenters, including the Puritans, during the 17th century. The Church was allied with the Royalists during the English Civil War, so during the Commonwealth (1649 – 1660), its bishops were abolished and the Book of Common Prayer was banned. With the restoration of the monarchy in 1660, these decisions were reversed. The Book of Common Prayer was revised in 1662 and adopted by Parliament. That version (excerpted in Chapter 5.3) was carried to the American colonies. Protestant dissenters were persecuted freely until 1689, when the Toleration Act gave legal existence to Protestants outside the Church of England that accepted the doctrine of the Trinity.

The settlement of 1689 established the structure of the modern Church of England and its relationship with the state. The Church of England was, and remains, the established Church with particular legal privileges and obligations, but significant liberalization has occurred in the past 300 years with respect to those of other faiths (or no faith at all).

Organization of the Church of England

As established by the Second Act of Supremacy, the monarch of Britain is the Supreme Governor of the Church of England. In this role, she appoints archbishops, bishops, and deans of cathedrals with the advice of the Prime Minister. The two archbishops and 24 senior bishops sit in the House of Lords.

The Church of England is organized into two provinces, each led by an archbishop. The Archbishop of Canterbury is responsible for the southern province and the Archbishop of York is responsible for the northern province. Each province is subdivided into dioceses. There are 12 dioceses in the north and 29 in the south. Each diocese has a cathedral and a bishop.

The most fundamental unit in the Church of England is the parish. A parish typically consists of a single church building and a churchyard. The parish is run by a parish priest. Historically, there were several types of parish priests, including vicars, rectors, and perpetual curates. They were distinguished by the method and amount of their compensation. Today, there is no distinction between rectors and vicars and the terms are used interchangeably. All rectors and vicars are appointed by patrons, who may be private individuals, corporate entities such as cathedrals, colleges, or trusts, by the bishop, or directly by the Crown.

The Incumbent

The vicar or rector may also be known as the "incumbent." In English ecclesiastical law, an "incumbent" is the holder of a Church of England parochial charge or benefice (a grant of land for life in return for certain services). The Church linked some spiritual duties with some forms of assets (the "temporalities") in order to generate revenue to support the incumbent. Under English ecclesiastical law, an incumbent is a "corporation sole," meaning "a legal entity vested in an individual and his successors by reason of his office."

The incumbent is significant to the study of cemetery law because in the Church of England, legal ownership of a churchyard is vested in the incumbent. Historically, the incumbent was responsible for maintaining the churchyard and fences in good condition, although individual tombstones were the responsibility of those who erected them and, after their death, the heirs-at-law of the decedent.

The materials in Chapter 5.4 and Chapter 5.5 often refer to the "incumbent." In Chapter 6.3, Justice Joseph Story mentions the importance of the incumbent in his discussion of the development of cemetery law in the United States.

❖ ❖ ❖

Highgate Cemetery, London, England
Photo by Harold Lloyd

CHAPTER 5.2

THE ECCLESIASTICAL LAW OF ENGLAND

Richard Burn, THE ECCLESIASTICAL LAW, VOLUME I (9th ed., 1842)

The Ecclesiastical Law of England is compounded of these four main ingredients: the Civil law, the Canon law, the Common law, and the Statute law. And from these, digested in their proper rank and subordination, to draw out one uniform law of the Church, is the purport of this book.

Where these laws do interfere and cross each other, the order of preference is this: The Civil law submitteth to the Canon law; both of these to the Common law; and all the three to the Statute law.

So that from any one or more of these without all of them together, or from all of these together without attending to their comparative obligation, it is not possible to exhibit any distinct prospect of the English ecclesiastical constitution.

I. By the CIVIL law is meant, the law of the ancient Romans, which had its foundation in the Grecian republics, and received continual improvements in the Roman state during the space of upwards of a thousand years, and did not expire at last even with the empire itself.

For the distinct knowledge whereof, it is to be remembered, that after the abolishing of the regal government at Rome, and the establishment of the republic, they sent three men into Greece, to collect the laws of the Athenian and other Grecian states; and from these were compiled and digested by ten commissioners, well known by the name of the *Decemviri*, the laws of the Twelve Tables (so called from their being engraved on twelve tables of brass), which were the first and principal foundation of the Roman law.

To the twelve tables were added the *Responsa Prudentum*, or interpretation of the lawyers; who accommodated the same to the use and practice of their courts. And this was denominated, in contradistinction to the laws of the twelve tables, the *jus non scriptum*, or unwritten law: and having no other name, begun then to be called the civil law; and is that which is styled by Justinian the *jurisprudentia media*, because it came in between the laws of the twelve tables and the Imperial constitutions.

Next to these were the *Leges* or laws emphatically so called, because they were enacted by the whole body of the people, reckoning both the nobility and commonalty together: and this was particularly, when a new case happened that was not provided for by the former laws; the consuls on this occasion caused the people to be assembled together, and informed them what the case was, and asking their opinions, that is, putting it to the vote, they decided the same according to the rules of equity as the matter appeared to them; and this decision being made, was ever afterwards in the like cases observed as a law. For after the abolition of the regal government, the magistracy was lodged with the people; one principal branch whereof is the power of making laws.

Afterwards, the common people mutinying, upon some differences with the nobility, retired and separated themselves from the nobility for some time; and during this secession they enacted laws of their own, which were called *Plebiscita*: and upon a reconciliation with the nobility afterwards, it was agreed and consented to that these also should have the force of law, and be obligatory upon the whole Roman people, the nobility as well as others.

But on the daily increase of the Roman state, it appearing almost impossible to assemble the whole body of the people, at least without some tumult and commotion, It was thought expedient, whenever any new case arose, to trust the senate with this power. And when any new law was made by them, it was styled *Senatus consultum*, or a decree of the senate; and it was, in like manner as the *plebiscita*, incorporated into the Roman civil law. ...

II. The CANON law sprung up out of the ruins of the Roman empire, and from the power of the Roman pontiffs. When the seat of the empire was removed to Constantinople, many of the European princes and states fell off from the dominion of the emperors: and Italy amongst the rest. And the bishops of Rome, having been generally had in esteem 88 presiding in the capital city of the empire, began to set up for themselves, and by degrees acquired a temporal dominion in Italy, and a spiritual dominion throughout Italy and almost all the rest of Europe.

And thereupon the several princes and states did willingly receive into the body of their own laws, the canons of councils, the writings of the holy fathers, and the decrees and constitutions of popes.

Concerning the Canons of Councils, it was established by Justinian himself, that the canons of the Councils of Nice and of Constantinople, of the First Council of Ephesus, and of the Council of Chalcedon, should be observed for laws; and that their decrees, as to matters of faith and doctrine, should be esteemed even as the Holy Scriptures.

After Justinian, the authority of canons made in general or provincial councils, and of the writings of the fathers, still prevailed; and the decision of ecclesiastical controversies, which could not be drawn from the councils and the fathers, was sought for from the Roman pontiffs, who writ answers to those that consulted them, in like manner as the Roman emperors; and their determinations were called rescripts and decretal epistles, and obtained the force of laws.

More particularly, of the canon law there are two principal parts, the *Decreu* and the *Decretals.*

The Decrees are ecclesiastical constitutions made by the pope and cardinals, at no man's suit. These were first collected by Ivo, in the year 1114. And afterwards polished and perfected by Gratian, a monk of Bononia, in the year 1149(1).

The Decretals are canonical epistles written by the popes...

Ill. The COMMON LAW is so called, because it is the common municipal law or rule or justice throughout the kingdom. For although there are divers particular laws, some by custom applied to particular places, and some to particular causes: yet that law, which is common to the generality of all persons, things, and causes, and hath a superintendency over those particular laws that are admitted in relation to particular places or matters, is the common law of England.

This is usually called *lex non scripta*; not as if all those laws of which it consisteth were only oral. or communicated from the former ages to the latter merely by word; for all those laws have their several monuments in writing, whereby they are transferred from one age to another, and without which they would soon lose all kind of certainty for as the civil and canon laws have their canons, decrees, and decretal determinations in writing, so those laws of England which are not comprised under the title of acts of parliament, are for the most part extant in records of pleas, proceedings and judgments, in books of reports and judicial decisions, in tractates of learned men's arguments and opinions, preserved from ancient times, and still extant in writing. But they are styled unwritten laws, because their authoritative and original institutions are not set down in writing in that manner, or with that verbal explicitness, that acts of parliament are; but they are grown into use, and have acquired their binding power and the force of laws, by a long and immemorial usage, and by the strength of custom and reception in this kingdom; the matter indeed, and the substance of those laws, are in writing, but the formal and obliging force or power of them grows by long use and custom. For custom generally received in this kingdom obtains the force of law, and is that which gives power sometimes to the canon law and sometimes to the civil law, in the respective courts wherein they are in use; and again, controls both, when they cross other customs that are generally received in the kingdom.

As to the rise and original of this common law, it is to be understood, that after the decay of the Roman empire, this nation was invaded by several different people; each of whom, more or less, introduced their own Iaws in the place where they settled. When the kingdom became united under one monarch, the several laws were collected and formed into one general law of the realm. ...

IV. The STATUTE LAW is made by the king, the lords spiritual and temporal, and commons in parliament assembled; that is, by the united suffrages of the whole kingdom, either in person or by representative. And this is that which gives unto acts of parliament their strength and superiority above all other laws in this kingdom whatsoever; by virtue whereof they control, alter, mitigate, repeal, revive, explain, amend, both the common, canon, and civil laws, and actually have done so in abundance of instances. These statutes or acts of parliament bear date (as was observed before) from the reign of King Henry the Third; and new statutes have been enacted in every king and queen's reign since that time, except only during the short reign of King Edward the Fifth. By which means, in the space of upwards of 500 years, they have necessarily become very numerous, and not a little confused, so that there is need of another Justinian to revise and digest them.

Under this head, we are also to reckon the Thirty-Nine Articles of Religion, agreed upon in Convocation, in the year 1562; and, in like manner, the Rubric of the Book of Common Prayer: which, being both of them established by act of parliament, are to be esteemed as part of the statute law.

These are the constituent parts of the English ecclesiastical law, as practised and exercised in the ecclesiastical courts and in the courts of common law. But besides these, there are other courts which in many instances have concurrent jurisdiction; and in which indeed most ecclesiastical matters of considerable consequence are now usually determined, namely, the courts of equity in the exchequer and in the chancery. In these are cognizable matters of tithes and moduses for the same, causes matrimonial and testamentary and other things relative thereunto, as appointing of guardians, ordering executors and administrators, taking care of the interests of infants, payment of debts and legacies, and many other such like. And in these courts the determinations are made according to the rules of equity and good conscience; and more especially they take cognizance in cases where no provision, or not sufficient provision, is made by the ordinary course of law; and sometimes they will mitigate the rigour of the common law, where by circumstances there happens to be a peculiar hardship or inconvenience in the particular case in question; but, ordinarily, they will not determine against the known and established maxims of the common law, much less relieve against an act of parliament, for that cannot be altered but by the same authority which established it.

❖ ❖ ❖

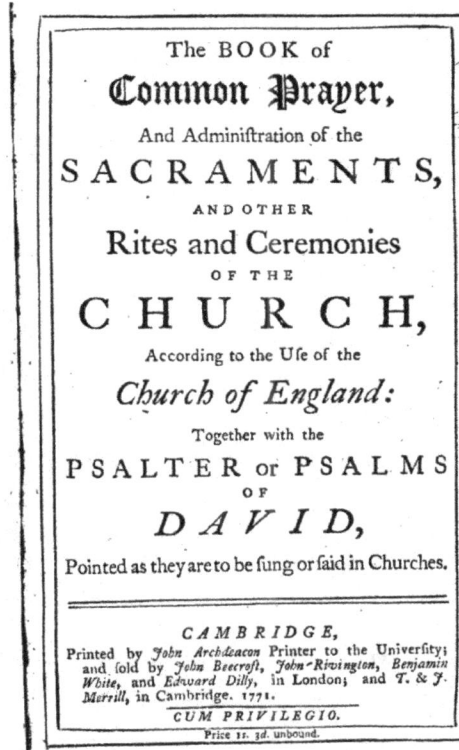

CHAPTER 5.3

THE ORDER OF THE BURIAL OF THE DEAD

THE BOOK OF COMMON PRAYER (1662)

Here is to be noted, that the Office ensuing is not to be used for any that die unbaptized, or excommunicate, or have laid violent hands upon themselves.

The Priest and Clerks meeting the Corpse at the entrance of the Church-yard, and going before it, either into the Church, or towards the Grave, shall say, or sing,

I am the resurrection and the life, saith the Lord: he that believeth in me, though he were dead, yet shall he live: and whosoever liveth and believeth in me shall never die. St. John xi. 25, 26.

I know that my Redeemer liveth, and that he shalt stand at the latter day upon the earth. And though after my skin worms destroy this body, yet in my flesh shall I see God: whom I shall see for myself, and mine eyes shall behold, and not another. Job xix. 25, 26, 27.

We brought nothing into this world, and it is certain we can carry nothing out. The Lord gave, and the Lord hath taken away; blessed be the Name of the Lord. 1 Tim. vi. 7. Job I. 21.

After they are come into the Church, shall be read one or both of these Psalms following.
Dixi, custodiam. Psalm 39.

I said, I will take heed to my ways: that I offend not in my tongue.

I will keep my mouth as it were with a bridle: while the ungodly is in my sight.

I held my tongue, and spake nothing: I kept silence, yea, even from good words; but it was pain and grief to me.

My heart was hot within me, and while I was thus musing the fire kindled: and at the last I spake with my tongue;

Lord, let me know mine end, and the number of my days: that I may be certified how long I have to live.

Behold, thou hast made my days as it were a span long: and mine age is even as nothing in respect of thee; and verily every man living is altogether vanity.

For man walketh in a vain shadow, and disquieteth himself in vain: he heapeth up riches, and cannot tell who shall gather them.

And now, Lord, what is my hope: truly my hope is even in thee.

Deliver me from all mine offences: and make me not a rebuke unto the foolish.

I became dumb, and opened not my mouth: for it was thy doing.

Take thy plague away from me: I am even consumed by means of thy heavy hand.

When thou with rebukes dost chasten man for sin, thou makest his beauty to consume away, like as it were a moth fretting a garment: every man therefore is but vanity.

Hear my prayer, O Lord, and with thine ears consider my calling: hold not thy peace at my tears.

For I am a stranger with thee: and a sojourner, as all my fathers were.

O spare me a little, that I may recover my strength: before I go hence, and be no more seen.

Glory be to the Father, and to the Son: and to the Holy Ghost;

As it was in the beginning, is now, and ever shall be: world without end. Amen.

Domine, refugium. Psalm 90.

Lord, thou hast been our refuge: from one generation to another.

Before the mountains were brought forth, or ever the earth and the world were made: thou art God from everlasting, and world without end.

Thou turnest man to destruction: again thou sayest, Come again, ye children of men.

For a thousand years in thy sight are but as yesterday: seeing that is past as a watch in the night.

As soon as thou scatterest them, they are even as a sleep: and fade away suddenly like the grass.

In the morning it is green, and groweth up: but in the evening it is cut down, dried up, and withered.

For we consume away in thy displeasure: and are afraid at thy wrathful indignation.

Thou hast set our misdeeds before thee: and our secret sins in the light of thy countenance.

For when thou art angry all our days are gone: we bring our years to an end, as it were a tale that is told.

The days of our age are three-score years and ten; and though men be so strong, that they come to fourscore years: yet is their strength then but labour and sorrow; so soon passeth it away, and we are gone.

But who regardeth the power of thy wrath: for even thereafter as a man feareth, so is thy displeasure.

So teach us to number our days: that we may apply our hearts unto wisdom.

Turn thee again, O Lord, at the last: and be gracious unto thy servants.

O satisfy us with thy mercy, and that soon: so shall we rejoice and be glad all the days of our life.

Comfort us again now after the time that thou hast plagued us: and for the years wherein we have suffered adversity.

Shew thy servants thy work: and their children thy glory.

And the glorious Majesty of the Lord our God be upon us: prosper thou the work of our hands upon us, O prosper thou our handy-work.

Glory be to the Father, and to the Son: and to the Holy Ghost;

As it was in the beginning, is now, and ever shall be: world without end. Amen.

Then shall follow the Lesson taken out of the fifteenth Chapter of the former Epistle of Saint Paul to the Corinthians.

1 Cor. 15. 20.

Now is Christ risen from the dead, and become the first-fruits of them that slept. For since by man came death, by man came also the resurrection of the dead. For as in Adam all die, even so in Christ shall all be made alive. But every man in his own order: Christ the firstfruits; afterward they that are Christ's, at his coming. Then cometh the end, when he shall have delivered up the kingdom to God, even the Father; when he shall have put down all rule, and all authority, and power. For he must reign, till he hath put all enemies under his feet. The last enemy that shall be destroyed is death. For he hath put all things under his feet. But when he saith, all things are put under him, it is manifest that he is excepted, which did put all things under him. And when all things shall be subdued unto him, then shall the Son also himself be subject unto him that put all things under him, that God may be all in all. Else what shall they do which are baptized for the dead, if the dead rise not at all? Why are they then baptized for the dead? and why stand we in jeopardy every hour? I protest by your rejoicing, which I have in Christ Jesus our Lord, I die daily. If after the manner of men I have fought with beasts at Ephesus, what advantageth it me, if the dead rise not? Let us eat and drink, for to-morrow we die. Be not deceived: evil communications corrupt good manners. Awake to righteousness, and sin not: for some have not the knowledge of God. I speak this to your shame. But some man will say, How are the dead raised up? and with what body do they come? Thou fool, that which thou sowest is not quickened, except it die. And that which thou sowest, thou sowest not that body that shall be, but bare grain, it may chance of wheat, or of some other grain: But God giveth it a body, as it hath pleased him, and to every seed his own body. All flesh is not the same flesh; but there is one kind of flesh of men, another flesh of beasts, another of fishes, and another of birds. There are also celestial bodies, and bodies terrestrial; but the glory of the celestial is one, and the glory of the terrestrial is another. There is one glory of the sun, and another glory of the moon, and another glory of the stars; for one star differeth from another star in glory. So also is the resurrection of the dead: It is sown in corruption; it is raised in incorruption: It is sown in dishonour; it is raised in glory: It is sown in weakness; it is raised in power: It is sown a natural body; it is raised a spiritual body. There is a natural body, and there is a spiritual body. And so it is written, The first man Adam was made a living soul; the last Adam was made a quickening spirit. Howbeit, that was not first which is spiritual, but that which is natural; and afterward that which is spiritual. The first man is of the earth, earthy: the second man is the Lord from heaven. As is the earthy, such are they that are earthy: and as is the heavenly, such are they also that are heavenly. And as we have borne the image of the earthy, we shall also bear the image of the heavenly. Now this I say, brethren, that flesh and blood cannot inherit the kingdom of God; neither doth corruption inherit incorruption. Behold, I shew you a mystery: We shall not all sleep, but we shall all be changed, in a moment, in the twinkling of an eye, at the last trump, (for the trumpet shall sound,) and the dead shall be raised incorruptible, and we shall be changed. For this corruptible must put on incorruption, and this mortal must put on immortality. So when this corruptible shall have put on incorruption, and this mortal shall have put on immortality; then shall be brought to pass the saying that is written, Death is swallowed up in victory. O death, where is thy sting? O grave, where is thy victory? The sting of death is sin, and the strength of sin is the law. But thanks be to God, which giveth us the victory through our Lord Jesus Christ. Therefore, my beloved brethren, be ye stedfast, unmoveable, always abounding in the work of the Lord, forasmuch as ye know that your labour is not in vain in the Lord.

When they come to the Grave, while the Corpse is made ready to be laid into the earth, the Priest shall say, or the Priest and Clerks shall sing:

Man that is born of a woman hath but a short time to live, and is full of misery. He cometh up, and is cut down, like a flower; he fleeth as it were a shadow, and never continueth in one stay.

In the midst of life we are in death: of whom may we seek for succour, but of thee, O Lord, who for our sins art justly displeased?

Yet, O Lord God most holy, O Lord most mighty, O holy and most merciful Saviour, deliver us not into the bitter pains of eternal death.

Thou knowest, Lord, the secrets of our hearts; shut not thy merciful ears to our prayer; but spare us, Lord most holy, O God most mighty, O holy and merciful Saviour, thou most worthy judge eternal, suffer us not, at our last hour, for any pains of death, to fall from thee.

Then, while the earth shall be cast upon the Body by some standing by, the Priest shall say,

Forasmuch as it hath pleased Almighty God of his great mercy to take unto himself the soul of our dear *brother* here departed, we therefore commit his body to the ground; earth to earth, ashes to ashes, dust to dust; in sure and certain hope of the Resurrection to eternal life, through our Lord Jesus Christ; who shall change our vile body, that it may be like unto his glorious body, according to the mighty working, whereby he is able to subdue all things to himself.

Then shall be said or sung,

I heard a voice from heaven, saying unto me, Write, From henceforth blessed are the dead which die in the Lord: even so saith the Spirit: for they rest from their labours.

Then the Priest shall say,

Lord, have mercy upon us.

Christ, have mercy upon us.

Lord, have mercy upon us.

Our Father, which art in heaven, Hallowed be thy Name. Thy kingdom come. Thy will be done in earth, as it is in heaven. Give us this day our daily bread. And forgive us our trespasses, As we forgive them that trespass against us. And lead us not into temptation; But deliver us from evil. Amen.

Priest.

Almighty God, with whom do live the spirits of them that depart hence in the Lord, and with whom the souls of the faithful, after they are delivered from the burden of the flesh, are in joy and felicity: We give thee hearty thanks, for that it hath pleased thee to deliver this our brother out of the miseries of this sinful world; beseeching thee, that it may please thee, of thy gracious goodness, shortly to accomplish the number of thine elect, and to hasten thy kingdom; that we, with all those that are departed in the true faith of thy holy Name, may have our perfect consummation and bliss, both in body and soul, in thy eternal and everlasting glory; through Jesus Christ our Lord. Amen.

The Collect

O merciful God, the Father of our Lord Jesus Christ, who is the resurrection and the life; in whom whosoever believeth shall live, though he die; and whosoever liveth, and believeth in him, shall not die eternally; who also hath taught us, by his holy Apostle Saint Paul, not to be sorry, as men without hope, for them that sleep in him: We meekly beseech thee, O Father, to raise us from the death of sin unto the life of righteousness; that, when we shall depart this life, we may rest in him, as our hope is this our brother doth; and that, at the general Resurrection in the last day, we may be found acceptable in thy sight; and receive that blessing, which thy well-beloved Son shall then pronounce to all that love and fear thee, saying, Come, ye blessed children of my Father, receive the kingdom prepared for you from the beginning of the world: Grant this, we beseech thee, O merciful Father, through Jesus Christ, our Mediator and Redeemer. Amen.

The grace of our Lord Jesus Christ, and the love of God and the fellowship of the Holy Ghost, be with us all evermore. Amen.

❖ ❖ ❖

Metairie Cemetery, Metairie, Louisiana
Photo by Tanya D. Marsh

CHAPTER 5.4

BURIAL OF THE DEAD

Richard Grey, A SYSTEM OF ENGLISH ECCLESIASTICAL LAW (2nd ed., 1732)

For the use of Young Students in the Universities, who are designed for Holy Orders.

Q. May the Minister refuse or delay to bury any Corpse, that is brought to the Church or Church-yard, convenient Warning being given him thereof before?

> A. No; (except the Party deceased who were denounced Excommunicate Majori Excommunicatione, for some grevious and notorious Crime, and no Man able to testify of his Repentance, or were unbaptized, or had laid violent Hands upon himself,) upon Pain of Suspension for three Months. Can. 68.

Q. Are there any other Cases in which Christian Burial was antiently denied?

> A. Yes. Particularly, 1. To Hereticks. 2. Persons not receiving the Holy Sacrament, at least at Easter. And, 3. Persons kill'd in Duels, Tilts, or Tournaments.

Q. Is there any Fee due for Burial?

> A. *A Fee for Burial may be due by Custom; and where it is so, belongs to the Minister of the Parish where the Deceased heard Divine Service, and received Sacraments, wheresoever the Corpse be buried.

Q. Upon what does the Proportion of the Burial Fees depend?

A. The Proportion of Fees due for the Burial of Persons, whether to Incumbent or Churchwardens, whether for burying in or out of the Parish, depends upon the particular Usage and Custom of each Parish respectively.

Q. May a person be buried in the Church, or any Part of it, without Consent of the Incumbent?

A. *No; unless a Burying-Place within the Church is prescrib'd for, as belonging to a Manor-House.

Q. Upon what Account does this Right of giving Leave belong to the Incumbent?

A. It belongs to him, not as having the Freehold, at least not in that respect alone, but in his general Capacity of Incumbent, and as the Person whom the Ecclesiastical Laws have appointed the Judge of the Fitness or Unfitness of this or that Person, to have the Favour of being buried in the Church.

Q. May Monuments, Coat-Armour, and other Ensigns of Honour set up in Memory of the Deceased, be removed at the Pleasure of the Ordinary or Incumbent?

A. *No: On the Contrary, if either they, or any other Person, shall take away, or deface them, when set up with the Consent of the Ordinary, the Person who set them up shall have an Action against them during his Life; and after his Death the Heir of the Deceased shall have the same.

Q. Can a Corpse once buried be taken up or removed?

A. *Not without License from the Ordinary.

Q. What is the Import of the *Acts for burying in Woolen?

A. 'Tis enacted, That no Person (except dying of the Plague) shall be buried in Sheet, Shirt, Shift, or Shroud, or any thing whatever, made or mingled with Flax, Hemp, Silk, Hair, Gold, or Silver, or in any Stuff, or Thing, other than what is made of Sheeps-Wool only, or be put into any Coffin lined, or faced with any sort of Cloth or Stuff, or any other Thing whatever, that is made of any other Material but Sheeps-Wool only, upon Pain of forfeiting five Pounds. 18 Car. II. c.4.

❖   ❖   ❖

Highgate Cemetery, London, England
Photo by Harold Lloyd

CHAPTER 5.5
THE ECCLESIASTICAL LAW OF BURIAL IN ENGLAND
Richard Burn, THE ECCLESIASTICAL LAW, VOLUME I (9th ed., 1842)

Original of Burying Places

As to the original of burying places, many writers have observed, that at the first erection of churches, no part of the adjacent ground was allotted for interment of the dead, but some place for this purpose was appointed at a farther distance; especially in cities and populous towns, where agreeably to the old Roman law of the Twelve Tables, the place of inhumation was without the wall, first indefinitely by the way side, then in some peculiar inclosure assigned to that use. Therefore the Roman pontifical, ... appoint[ed] twenty-five churches in Rome to bury martyrs in; when at that time laws and customs did forbid all burial within the city. Hence the Augustine monastery was built without the walls of Canterbury (as Ethelbert and Augustine in both their charters intimate), that it might be a dormitory to them and their successors, the kings and archbishops for ever. This practice of remoter burials continued to the age of Gregory the Great, when the monks and priests beginning to offer for souls departed, procured leave, for their greater ease and profit, that a liberty of sepulture might be in churches or in places adjoining to them. This mercenary reason seems to be acknowledged by Pope Gregory himself, whilst he allows that when the parties deceasing are not burthened with heavy sins, it may then be a benefit to them to be buried in churches, because their friends and relations, as often as they come to these sacred places, seeing their graves, may remember them and pray to God for them.

After this, Cuthbert Archbishop) of Canterbury, brought over from Rome this practice into England about the year 750, from which time they date the original of churchyards in this island. … The practices of burying within the churches, did indeed (though more rarely) obtain before the use of churchyards, but was by authority restrained when churchyards were frequent and appropriated to that use. [A]t the first it was the nave or body of the church that was permitted to be a repository of the dead, and chiefly under arches by the side of the walls. Lanfranc, Archbishop of Canterbury, seems to have been the first who brought up the practice of vaults in chancels, and under the very altars, when he had rebuilt the church of Canterbury, about the year 1075. …

Burying in the Church

No person may be buried in the church, or in any part of it, without the consent of the incumbent. In some of the foreign canons it is said, "without consent of bishop and incumbent;" in others, "without consent of bishop or incumbent." But our common law hath given this privilege to the parson only, exclusive of the bishop, in a resolution in the case of *Frances and Ley*, H. 12 Jac., that neither the ordinary himself nor the churchwardens can grant licence of burying to any within the church, but the parson only; because the soil and freehold of the church is only in the parson, and in none other. Which right of giving leave will appear to belong to the parson, not as having the freehold (at least not in that respect alone), but in his general capacity of incumbent, and as the person whom the ecclesiastical laws appointed the judge of the fitness or unfitness of this or that person to have the favour of being buried in the church. For anciently (as was said) the burying not only in temples and churches, but even in cities, was expressly prohibited. And afterwards, when the burying in churches came to be allowed and practised, the canon law directeth that none but persons of extraordinary merit shall be buried there; of which merit (and by consequence of the reasonableness of granting or denying that indulgence) the incumbent was in reason the most proper judge, and was accordingly so constituted by the laws of the church, without any regard to the common law notion of the freehold's being in him, which if it proves any thing in the present case, proves too much, that neither without the like leave may they bury in the churchyard, because the freehold of that is also declared to be in him.

Upon the like foundation of freehold, the common law hath one exception to this necessity of the leave of the parson, namely, where a burying place within the church is prescribed for as belonging to a manor house, the freehold of which they say is in the owner of that house, and that by consequence he hath a good action at law if he is hindered to bury there. Yet nevertheless the churchwardens also by custom may have a fee for every burial within the church, by reason the parish is at the charge of repairing the floor.

But there is good reason that any parishioner, at his discretion, shall not have the liberty of burying there; especially upon account of the health of the inhabitants to be assembled there for religious worship. …

Burying in the Church-yard

The reason given by Gregory the Great, why it was more profitable to be buried within the precincts of the church, than at a distance, was, because their neighbours, as often as they come to those sacred places, remembering those whose sepulchers they behold, do put forth prayers for them unto God.

Which reason was afterwards transferred into the body of the canon law. And this superstition of praying for the dead, seems to have been the true original of churchyards, as incompassing or adjoining to the church: which being laid out and inclosed for the common burial places of the respective parishioners, every parishioner hath and always had a right to be buried in them.

["About the year 750, spaces of ground adjoining the churches were carefully inclosed, and solemnly consecrated and appropriated to the burial of those who had been entitled to attend divine service in those churches, and who now become entitled to render back into those places their remains to earth, the common mother of mankind, without payment for the ground which they were to occupy, or for the pious offices which solemnised the act of interment." The Court will not grant a mandamus to compel a rector to bury the corpse of a parishioner in any particular part of a churchyard.—Ed.]

For by the custom of England, any person may be buried in the churchyard of the parish where he dies, without paying any thing for breaking the soil. But a fee may be due by prescription or immemorial custom.

In the case of *The King v. Taylor*, it was held that information was grantable against a parson for opposing the burial of a parishioner in the churchyard; but as to refusing to read the service over the deceased, because he was never baptised, the court would not interpose; that being a matter cognizable in the ecclesiastical court. [But a custom in a parish for the inhabitants to bury as near as possible to their ancestors, is bad.—Ed.]

Whether Strangers may be buried therein

But ordinarily it seemeth that a person may not be buried in the churchyard of another parish than that wherein he died, at least without the consent of the parishioners or churchwardens, whose parochial right of burial is invaded thereby, and perhaps also of the incumbent whose soil is broken; as in the case of *The Churchwardens of Harrow on the Hill*, it is said, that upon a process against them some years ago, for suffering strangers to be buried in their churchyard, and their appearing and confessing the charge, they were admonished by the ecclesiastical judge, not to suffer the same for the future. ...

But where a parishioner dieth in his journey, or otherwise, out of the parish, perhaps it may be otherwise: as it seemeth to be, where there is a family vault or burying place in the church, or chancel, or aisle thereof. ...

Whether Burial may be hindered for Debt

By the civil law, dead bodies ought not to be hindered from burial for debt, as vulgarly supposed; which seemed to be allowed by the law of the Twelve Tables. No law of the Twelve Tables handed down to us allows a dead body to be arrested for debt, although a famous law of the third table gave to creditors, according to most interpreters, a singular power of cutting into pieces the body of a living debtor, who after a certain process refused to pay. On the contrary, the tenth table prescribes imperatively the various solemnities which were to be observed in the burial of the dead; and a law of the digest protects from citation even persons who are employed in performing the funeral rites. ... But Huber, although he is clear that a dead body cannot be kept from burial, thinks that creditors may, by an arrest, prevent the relations of the deceased from carrying the corpse to a distant family monument. ... And Lindwood says, heretofore the law was, that the burial of a dead person might be delayed for debt; but this was afterwards abolished; for death dissolved all things; and albeit a man in his life-time may in some cases be imprisoned for debt, yet his dead body shall not be disturbed. ...

Burial of Murderers and Rebels

It is certain, that after execution, the bodies being at the king's disposal, are, for the public example, and for the greater terror unto others, never admitted to Christian burial; and this seemeth to have been the law of the Church of England from two ancient canons, by the former of which it is ordained as follows: "Concerning those who by any fault inflict death upon themselves, let there be no commemoration of them in the oblation, as likewise for them who are punished for their crimes; nor shall their corpses be carried unto the grave with psalms." By the latter—"If any shall voluntarily kill himself by arms, or by any instigation of the devil, it is not permitted that for such a person any masses be sung, nor shall his body be put into the ground with any singing of a psalm, nor shall he be buried in pure sepulchre. The same shall be done to him, who for his guilt endeth his life by torments, as a thief, murderer, and betrayer of his lord."

Mode of Burial is of Ecclesiastical Cognizance

Burial in the parish church yard is a common law right inherent in the parishioners, but the mode of burial is of ecclesiastical cognizance, and therefore the Court refused a mandamus to inter the body of a parishioner in an iron coffin.

This was the celebrated case which afterwards formed the subject of one of Lord Stowell's most elaborate judgments ... the case of *Gilbert v. Buzzard.* Lord Stowell permitted the interment of bodies in patent iron coffins, subject to an increased rate of payment to the parish. Some involucra or coverings (he said) have been deemed necessary in all civilized and Christian countries, but chests or trunks containing the bodies descending along with them to the grave and remaining there till their own decay, cannot plead either the same necessity or same general use. In our own countries, the use of coffins is extremely ancient, though most probably by no means general; they are not nominatim, or directly required by any authority whatever; and it is to be observed, that in the funeral service of the Church of England there is no mention, indeed, there is rather an apparently studious avoidance of any mention of coffins. It is throughout the whole service the corpse or the body. Funerals were anciently coffined and uncoffined, and were charged for accordingly. From which I might venture to draw this conclusion, that even at that time (1627), it was recognized as not unjust, that where the deceased by the use of his coffin took a larger occupancy of the ground, he should compensate the parish by an increased payment."

Burying in Woollen

By the 30 Car. 2, st. I, c. 3, s. 3, "For the encouragement of the woolen manufactures, and prevention of the exportation of money for the importing of linen, it is enacted, that no corpse of any person shall be buried in any shirt, shift, sheet, or shroud or any thing whatsoever, made or mingled with flax, hemp, silk, hair, gold or silver, or in any stuff or thing other than what is made of sheep's wool only, on pain of 5l." ...

Minister not to refuse Burial, except in certain cases

Can. 68, "No minister" shall refuse or delay to bury any corpse that is brought to the church or churchyard (convenient warning being given him thereof before), in such manner and form as is prescribed in the Book. of Common Prayer. And if he shall refuse so to do, except the party deceased were denounced excommunicated *majori excommunicatione*, for some grievous and notorious crime, and no man able to testify of his repentance, he shall be suspended by the bishop of the diocese from his ministry, by the space of three months."

Were denounced excommunicated. But by the rubric before the office for burial of the dead, the said office likewise shall not be used for any that die unbaptized, or that have laid violent hands upon themselves. ...

There were anciently other causes of refusal of burial, particularly of heretics, against whom there was an especial provision in the canon law, that if they continued in their heresy, they should not have a Christian burial: of which we have a remarkable instance a little before the Reformation, in the case of one Tracy, who was publicly accused in convocation of having expressed heretical tenets in his will; and being found guilty, a commission was issued to dig up his body, which was accordingly done.

Also persons *not receiving the holy sacrament*, at least at Easter, were excluded from Christian burial by a decree of the fourth Lateran council, which became afterwards a law of the English Church.

In like manner, persons killed in *duels, tilts or tournaments*.

But at this day it seemeth that these prohibitions are restrained to the three instances before mentioned; of persons excommunicated, unbaptized, and that have laid violent hands upon themselves.

And of this last sort are to be understood, not all who have procured death unto themselves, but who have done it voluntarily, and consequently have died in the commission of a mortal sin; and not idiots, lunatics, or persons otherwise of insane mind. ...

Office of Burial

By the rubric: "The priests and clerks meeting the corpse at the entrance of the churchyard, and going before it either into the church or towards the grave, shall say as is there appointed."

By which it seemeth to be discretionary in the minister whether the corpse shall be carried into the church or not. And there may be good reason for this, especially in cases of infection.

Ringing at Funerals

Can. 67. "After the party's death, there shall be rung no more but one short peal, and one before the burial, and one other after the burial."

Fee for Burial

"We do firmly enjoin that burial shall not be denied to anyone, upon the account of any sum of money; because if any thing hath been accustomed to be given by the pious devotion of the faithful, we will that justice be done thereupon to the churches by the ordinary of the place afterwards." ...

Right of Interment distinct from Right of Erecting any Memorial

The distinction between the right of mere interment and of erecting any memorial over the interred, is clearly stated *Bardin, &c. v. Calcott.* The churchyard as well as the church (says the same great authority) is the freehold of the minister, subject to the rights of the parishioners for interment. Ancient custom often annexes fees for erecting a stone or anything else by which the grave may be protected, and the memory of the person interred, preserved. It is no general common law right; but custom will interpose, and where it is shown to be customary, such practice will be supported.

Funeral Charges

Funeral expenses, according to the degree and quality of the deceased, are to be allowed of the goods of the deceased, before any debt or duty whatsoever. ...

Stealing Shrouds

The carcase that is buried belongeth to no one, but is subject to ecclesiastical cognizance, if abused or removed. Though, as Lord Coke says, a corpse is *nullius in bonis*; yet taking up a dead body, though for the purpose of dissection, is an indictable offence at law, as an act highly indecent and *contra bonos mores*. The 1 Jac. 1, c. 12, made it felony to steal dead bodies for the purposes of witchcraft, but is repealed by 9 Geo. 2, c. 5.

And a corpse once buried cannot be taken up or removed without licence from the ordinary.

That is, to be buried in another place, or the like; but in the case of a violent death the coroner may take up the body for his inspection if it is interred before he comes to view it. ...

Monuments

Lord Coke says, concerning the building or erecting of tombs, sepulchres, or monuments for the deceased, in church, chancel, common chapel, or churchyard, in convenient manner, it is lawful; for it is the last work of charity that can be done for the deceased, who whilst he lived was a lively temple of the Holy Ghost, with a reverend regard and Christian hope of a joyful resurrection. And the defacing of them is punishable by the common law ... But the building or erecting of the sepulchre, tomb, or other monument, ought not to be to the hindrance of the celebration of divine service. And again, he says, if a nobleman, knight, esquire, or other, be buried in a church, and have his coat armour and pennions with his arms, and such other ensigns of honour as belong to his degree or order, set up in the church, or if a grave-stone or tomb be laid or made for a monument of him, in this case, although the freehold of the church be in the parson, and that these be annexed to the freehold, yet cannot the parson or any other take them or deface them, but he is subject to an action to the heir and his heirs in the honour and memory of whose ancestor they were set up. …

Action of Trespass for removing a Tombstone

The courts of common law will in some cases punish, as well as the Ecclesiastical Courts, the removal of a tombstone. In *Horner v. Brewster*, trespass was maintained for taking away a tombstone from a churchyard, and obliterating an inscription made upon it, at the suit of the party by whom it was erected, although the freehold of the churchyard is in the parson; as the right to a tombstone vests in the person who erects it, or in the heirs of the deceased in whose memory it is set up. …

❖   ❖   ❖

Highgate Cemetery, London, England
Photo by Harold Lloyd

CHAPTER 5.6

INTERNMENT IN ENGLAND

Stephen Wickes, SEPULTURE (1884)

Prior to and during the sixth century interments in cities were greatly increased. … The Council of Bracar contained a celebrated canon which forbade interment in churches, and proved also that cities have the right to prohibit any person from burying within its walls. [At the end of the eighth century, one of Charlemagne's bishops] complained that the churches in France had become almost burial places. The capitularies of Charlemagne forbade interments of the laity within the churches, and subsequently that of all persons, without discrimination. He ordered the tombs to be destroyed, and wished for the future that they should never be raised above the level of the ground. Notwithstanding the measures enforced by Charlemagne, they were modified by subsequent councils, though the church desired that the prohibition should be obeyed. It fell into such a degree of neglect that the Emperor Leo, in the close of the ninth century, in codifying and publishing the canons of the church, erased in one of his statutes the old prohibition of burying in churches. The terms of his decree show that the old law had fallen into complete discredit, and had become a dead letter. He gives two reasons for its falling into disuse. The first was the distress of the people to see the bodies of their relatives carried so far from them; and the second was the expense of transportation or great vexation of the poor.

Excerpts from Edwin Chadwick's 1843 Report on the Sanitary Condition of the Laboring Population of Great Britain—Supplementary Report on the Results of a Special

Inquiry into the Practice of Interments in Towns:

"There are 39 burial-grounds within the borough of Liverpool. The interments take place in graves, vaults or pits. In 23 burial-grounds, graves only are used; in 7, graves and vaults only; in 4, graves and pits; in 2, graves, vaults and pits, and in 1, pits only. The aggregate annual number of interments within the borough is, in ordinary years, from 10,000 to 11,000. Of this number, as nearly as can be estimated, about two-thirds take place in pits and one-third in graves. The interments in vaults probably do not exceed 20 annually.

"The pits vary in depth from eighteen to twenty feet, being from seven to twelve feet long and three and a half to nine feet wide. The number of bodies deposited in each pit varies from 30 to 120. In St. James' Cemetery, about six inches of earth are placed over the coffins after each day's interments. In the others the coffins are covered with two and a half feet of soil, which is removed previous to the next interments but, with this exception, the pits remain open or only covered with a frame work of boards until filled with coffins—a period varying from ten days in the case of the smaller, to ten weeks in the case of the larger pits.

"It has been estimated that an acre of ground is capable of affording decent interment to not more than 130 bodies yearly; but in the thirty-seven burial-grounds of Liverpool, taking one with another, the number of burials to an acre is fully double of that just stated. Were the calculations confined to those most in use, the proportion would be greatly augmented. In some of these places it is almost impossible to dig a new grave without disturbing bodies previously buried, and in some the soil when opened up appears to consist chiefly of human remains in a state of decomposition. ...

The length of time necessary to effect complete decomposition varies according to the soil. It is shorter in one porous and open than in one either dense or clayey. The regulations of the Home Office (British) prescribe that no unwalled grave shall be reopened within fourteen years after the burial of a person above twelve years of age, or within eight years after a burial of a child under twelve years of age, unless to bury another member of the same family, in which case a layer of earth not less than one foot thick shall be left undisturbed above the previously-buried coffin. If, on reopening any grave, the soil be found to be offensive, such soil shall not be disturbed, and in no case shall human remains be removed from the grave. ...

The size of grave spaces, as adopted by the British Home Office, and so prescribed, is nine feet long by four feet broad, four square yards for an adult, and for a child under twelve, two square yards, either four and a half by four feet, or six by three feet. This size, which may be recommended by sanitary authorities for general adoption, allows the retention of a strip of undisturbed ground about two feet in width between two adjacent graves. In any case it is important that each grave should be at least a foot distant from the nearest graves on every side...

The modes of interments in the British cemeteries are in graves, vaults and tombs. The former are in general use. Their depth varies from five to six feet, the same being prescribed by the cemetery companies, or by the authorities of the towns or cities where they are situated. Graves are the safest place for burial, and furnish conditions for the most rapid progress of decomposition.

Coffins

... In the time of Edward II and III, even persons of distinction preferred to have their bodies committed to the bare earth. It was a common custom in the time of Queen Elizabeth to bury only in winding sheets. ...

It was a custom observed in various parts of Christendom before and since the seventeenth century, to bury the clergy with their feet towards the east, that they may meet their flocks on the morning of the great day and conduct them to the tribunal. Tradition has fostered the expectation that our Lord will appear in the east. Therefore, all the faithful dead are buried with their feet to the east, to meet him. Hence, in Wales, the east wind is called the wind of the dead men's feet. ...

It would seem, from the apparently studious avoidance of any mention of coffins in the burial service of the Church of England, that at the period of the compilation of that service (1546-7), uncoffined interments were common; corpse, or body, alone is spoken of. Sir Henry Spelman says in his works: "Interments without coffins were common amongst the humbler classes even so late as the year 1650.

Linen was the customary fabric for swathing the dead by those who were able to purchase. As it was imported from "beyond the seas," an act was passed by Parliament in 18th of Charles II, "for burying in woolen only," intended to lessen the importation of linen, and for the encouragement · of the woolen manufacturers of the kingdom. It provided that no corpse should be buried but in woolen only; penalty, £5. A register to be kept in every parish of persons buried there, affidavit to be made within eight days after each burial that the person was buried in woolen; penalty, £5.

The very poor were sewed up in sheets and carried to the grave in a "parish shell," which was a coarser kind of coffin with a movable lid, and used as a bier for the purpose of conveying the body to the place of sepulture. Interment in the bare earth was the common method among the Jews and other nations as well. ... The body of our Saviour was wrapped in linen. The stone at the door of the sepulchre was, to the minds of the holy women, the only apprehended hindrance to their approach to his body.

Through all English history the distinguished alone, as we have seen, were laid in coffins. It is reasonable to infer that the dead bodies of the pilgrims at Plymouth, so many of whom died during the first winter, were laid in the bare earth. ...

Burial in coffins, as a universal custom, commenced with the last century. ...

A reverent respect for the dead and the purest sentiments of affection are in harmony with the method of depositing, in proper swathing, in mother earth, the bodies of those who "return to their dust." ...

The most of the governments in Europe have prohibited intra-mural interments absolutely. In our own country the disposal of the dead has not been a subject of legislation by State legislatures, to whom it belongs. The regulation of burials has been left to municipal authority, liable to be governed in its action by local influences.

The question how and where the dead shall be disposed of is one eminently sanitary. It is a civil affair. The religion of all peoples modifies and renders traditionally sacred their methods of burial; but among Christian nations "such is the harmony always existing between religion and sound policy, that what is acknowledged as decorous and useful by one is also commanded and prescribed by the other." The dead should be so buried that *the living may not suffer*.

❖   ❖   ❖

Highgate Cemetery, London, England
Photo by Harold Lloyd

CHAPTER 5.7

SELECTED BURIAL FEES IN 1840 LONDON

John Cauch, THE FUNERAL GUIDE; OR, A CORRECT LIST OF THE BURIAL FEES OF THE VARIOUS PARISH AND PRIVATE GROUNDS, IN THE METROPOLIS (1840)

St. Paul, Shadwell

Vault under Church	£. 4	19	0
Ditto under School	3	3	0
First Ground	1	18	0
Second ditto	1	4	6
Third ditto	0	9	0
Lead or Iron Coffin in Ground	6	0	0
Church Service	0	13	0
Bells, 5s. and	0	12	0
Head and Foot Stone	3	7	6

Half the above Dues, and 6d. for Ground and Vaults for Children under 10 years. Double Dues for Non-Parishoners, except for Church Service. Bury at 3 o'Clock on Week-days—1/4 past 4 on Sundays. Early Dues, Fittings.

Mr. Thurley, Sexton, High Street, Shadwell.

All Saints, Poplar

First Ground, Common Grave	£. 0	5	0
Second ditto, ditto	0	11	0
Third ditto, ditto	1	1	0
Vault under Church	5	15	0
Purchase of the Site for a Vault or Brick Grave in Ground, at per Ft. in Width	1	3	6
Opening the same, or Vault under Church	1	10	0
Burial in the same, or Vault under ditto	0	15	0
Going into Church	0	10	0
Head and Foot Stone	2	0	0
Flat Stone	3	5	0
Tomb, not railed in	5	0	0
Ditto, railed in	7	0	0
Bells, 2s., 5s. 6d., and	0	13	0
Palls, if carried into Church, 5s.—If not	0	2	0
Second Pall, or for Child	0	1	0
Removing Corpse	0	2	0
Extra Digging, at per Foot	0	1	6

Non-Parishoners in all the above (except for extra Digging and removing Corpse) to pay Double Fees. Bury on Week-days at 3 o'clock, and Sundays in Summer, ¼ before 5 and in Winter after the Afternoon Service.

Mr. Simpson, Sexton, near the Church

St. Peter's, Cornhill

Middle Aisle of Church and Great Bell	£. 3	14	0
[Side Isle or under Organ, 10s. less]			
Vault	4	4	0
Six-ft. Grave, in Ground	1	14	6
If in Lead, (extra)	5	0	0
Desk Service, (extra)	0	10	0
Great Bell	0	10	0
Laying down Grave Stone in any part of Church	15	15	0

Non-Parishoners Double. Bury at any time on Week-days—1/4 past 1 o'Clock on Sundays.

Mrs. Cox, Sextoness, Lamb Passage, Leadenhall Market.

Trinity Church, Marylebone

Vault	£. 9 9 0
Catacomb	12 0 0
Children under 8 years	5 0 0
Ditto under 14 years	6 6 0
Family Vault for 2 Coffins	24 0 0
" 3 ditto	36 0 0
" 4 ditto	48 0 0
" 5 ditto	60 0 0
" 6 ditto	72 0 0
" 12 ditto	105 0 0
" 16 ditto	120 0 0
Rector and Clerk in addition	1 11 0

Including Bell and Desk Service.

Mr. Cheshire, Clerk, 6, Norton Street

❖   ❖   ❖

Glasnevin Cemetery, Dublin, Ireland
Photo by Tanya D. Marsh

CHAPTER 5.8
THE ENGLISH ECCLESIASTICAL LAW OF BURIAL
Percival Jackson, THE LAW OF CADAVERS (1950)

The ecclesiastical regulation of interment went unchallenged throughout the Middle Ages, and the law of the clergy controlled burial and cemeteries in England without serious lay interference until the adoption of the English Burial Acts in 1855. ...

Ecclesiastical cases had been decided, like civil cases, in shire or hundred court, jointly presided over by the bishop and either an ealdorman or sheriff. By an ordinance of William the Conqueror, the temporal and spiritual jurisdictions were severed and control of churchyards and burials was absorbed by the ecclesiastical authorities. ...

Relationship to civil, common, and statutory law
The ecclesiastical law of England is not, however, to be thought exclusive of the common law. On the contrary, it is a composite of civil law, canon law, common law, and statute law. And conflict between these components yielded, in the order just stated, the statutory law, as at present, prevailing over all others. The canon law, the growth of which we have traced, was based on the civil law of Rome. The influence of civil and canon law upon the proceedings of courts of equity presided over by chancellors, who during the period of church supremacy from the time of the Roman conquest to the Reformation were ecclesiastics, must be manifest. But even in the ecclesiastical courts, the canon law did not bind the laity *proprio vigore*, and except as it

was incorporated into the common law by act of Parliament or by local custom, its enforcement would be restrained by the common law courts.

Authority over sepulture

The English ecclesiastical courts exercised over the burial of the dead "a legal secular authority which they had gradually abstracted from the ancient civil courts to which it originally belonged." The historical development through early periods that committed the care of the dead to spiritual control found counterpart in England by reason of the practice of burial in churchyards. Every person except the felon, the heretic, and the suicide was entitled to be buried in the consecrated ground of the parish churchyard.

This right was akin to that of the pew holder. It was a right of use for the specific purpose of burial, the fee and control being vested in the church authorities. Indeed, by ancient practices under canon law, the taking of any fee for a burial was prohibited, the right to burial being one's religious privilege and the necessity of according it a corresponding duty. This is evidenced by the statement in Lyndwood's Provinciale, "Let the right of burial and the sacraments of the Church be denied to none for lack of money, neither be anything demanded for Christening, let him that demandeth it be anathema."

These rights were confirmed by the common law courts upon the theory that no exaction for burial would be permitted unless, by invariable custom, such practice was confirmed and this, impliedly at least, affirmed the common law's jurisdiction to enforce the right of burial of a parishioner, without fee, in his parish graveyard. These rights were later confirmed and modified by acts of Parliament.

The ecclesiastical jurisdiction of burial in churchyards continues, to a modified extent, by reason of the right of regulation by the religious society of church matters and their appurtenances, which jurisdiction, of course, is now subject to general governmental control. With the passage of the first of the burial acts in England (1852), the control of interment was authorized in private burial societies and municipalities and thus generally passed under lay domination.

❖ ❖ ❖

CHAPTER 6

JUSTICE JOSEPH STORY AND U.S. CEMETERY LAW

FIRST CHURCH BUILDING.
Erected 1769.
(*Drawn from Description.*)

German Lutheran Church, Georgetown, District of Columbia
History of the Evangelical Lutheran Church of Georgetown, D.C. 1769 – 1909 *(1909)*

CHAPTER 6.1
JUSTICE JOSEPH STORY AND U.S. CEMETERY LAW
Tanya D. Marsh

Joseph Story was born in Marblehead, Massachusetts in 1779. He graduated from Harvard University in 1798, then read law in Marblehead and Salem. Story was admitted to the bar at Salem, Massachusetts in 1801. In 1811, at the age of 32, Story became the youngest Associate Justice of the Supreme Court of the United States. A vigorous opponent of slavery, Story wrote the majority opinion in the famous case *United States v. Amistad*, 40 U.S. 518 (1841). In 1829, Story was appointed as a Professor Law at Harvard University while retaining his position on the Court.

Justice Story made two significant contributions to the development of U.S. cemetery law that are the subject of this Chapter 6. First, he wrote the majority opinion in *Beatty v. Kurtz*, 27 U.S. 566 (1829), one of the few cases where the Supreme Court of the United States addressed any aspect of cemetery law.

In 1829, the United States Supreme Court was called upon to adjudicate competing claims of title to a parcel of land in Georgetown. Charles Beatty and George Frazier Hawkins laid out "Beatty and Hawkins' addition to Georgetown" in 1769. A parcel was designated for the German Lutheran church to be used for religious purposes and the use of the congregation. The Lutherans erected a church and a burying-ground. Approximately forty years later, the church building "fell down" as a "consequence of inevitable decay," although the parcel remained in use as a cemetery. The heirs of Beatty and Hawkins asserted that the Lutherans had conditional title to the parcel, which terminated when the church fell down and was not replaced. They entered the cemetery and "threw down the fence and tombstones." The Lutherans filed a complaint to quiet title and for an injunction. Justice Joseph Story, writing on behalf of the Court, affirmed a perpetual injunction against the defendants. "This is not the case of a mere private trespass; but a public nuisance, going to the irreparable injury of the Georgetown congregation of Lutherans. The property consecrated to their use by a perpetual servitude or easement, is to be taken from them; the sepulchres of the dead are to be violated; the feelings of religion, and the sentiment of natural affection of the kindred and friends of the deceased are to be wounded; and the memorials erected by piety or love, to the memory of the good, are to be removed so as to leave no trace of the last home of their ancestry to those who may visit the spot in future generations. It cannot be that such acts are to be redressed by the ordinary process of law. The remedy must be sought, if at all, in the protecting power of a court of chancery; operating by its injunction to preserve the repose of the ashes of the dead, and the religious sensibilities of the living. [emphasis added]" This brief pronouncement—that the remedy must be sought in the protecting power of a court of chancery—established a foundational principle in the U.S. law of human remains: courts of equity have jurisdiction over the dead and serve as their protectors.

The second contribution made by Justice Story to cemetery law was his 1831 address at the dedication of Mount Auburn Cemetery in Cambridge, Massachusetts. In a speech that often referred to the Bible, Story articulated the increasingly popular argument, at least in urban communities, that the English practice of burial in city churchyards should be replaced by burial in a new kind of cemetery—the rural cemetery. The address is set forth in Chapter 6.3. Professor Al Brophy describes the significance of that address in Chapter 6.4.

Joseph Story died in 1845 and was buried in Mount Auburn Cemetery. His son, William Wetmore Story, created the monument at his gravesite as well as the bust that is on display at the Supreme Court of the United States.

In his *Commentaries on the Constitution of the United States* (1833), Story explained his views on the separation of church and state, a central issue in cemetery law:

> ... Article VI, paragraph 3 of the U.S. Constitution declares, that "no religious test shall ever be required as a qualification to any office or public trust under the United States." This clause is not introduced merely for the purpose of satisfying the scruples of many persons, who feel an invincible repugnance to any religious test, or affirmation. It had a higher objective: to cut off for ever every pretence of any alliance between church and state in the national government.

> The real object of the First Amendment was, not to countenance, much less to advance Mahometanism, or Judaism, or infidelity, by prostrating Christianity; but to exclude all rivalry among Christian sects, and to prevent any national ecclesiastical establishment, which should give to an hierarchy the exclusive patronage of the national government. It thus cut off the means of religious persecution, (the vice and pest of former ages,) and of the subversion of the rights of conscience in matters of religion, which had been trampled

upon almost from the days of the Apostles to the present age. The history of the parent country had afforded the most solemn warnings and melancholy instructions on this head; and even New England, the land of the persecuted puritans, as well as other colonies, where the Church of England had maintained its superiority, would furnish out a chapter, as full of the darkest bigotry and intolerance, as any, which should be found to disgrace the pages of foreign annals. Apostacy, heresy, and nonconformity had been standard crimes for public appeals, to kindle the flames of persecution, and apologize for the most atrocious triumphs over innocence and virtue.

Thus, the whole power over the subject of religion is left exclusively to the state government, to be acted upon according to their own sense of justice, and the state constitutions; and the Catholic and the Protestant, the Calvinist and the Arminian, the Jew and the Infidel, may sit down at the common table of the national councils, without any inquisition into their faith, or mode of worship.

❖ ❖ ❖

Central United Methodist Church, Arlington, Virginia
Photo by Tanya D. Marsh

CHAPTER 6.2

BEATTY AND RITCHIE V. KURTZ AND OTHERS, TRUSTEES OF THE GERMAN LUTHERAN CHURCH OF GEORGETOWN

Supreme Court of the United States, 27 U.S. 566 (1829)

Mr Justice STORY delivered the opinion of the Court.

This is an appeal in a suit in equity from a decree of the circuit court of the district of Columbia, sitting for the country of Washington. ...

In the year 1769, Charles Beatty and George F. Hawkins laid out a town, known by the name of Beatty and Hawkins's addition to Georgetown; and which is now included within its corporate limits. ... Upon the original plan so recorded, one lot was marked out and inscribed with these words, "for the Lutheran church;" and this lot was in fact part of the land of which Charles Beatty was seised.

The bill was brought up by the original plaintiffs, alleging themselves to be trustees and agents for the German Lutheran church composed of the members of the German Lutheran church of Georgetown, duly organized as such, in behalf of themselves and the members of the said church. It charges the laying out of the lot in question for the sole use and benefit of the Lutheran church, to be held by them for religious purposes and the use of the congregation, as abovementioned. That soon afterwards the lot was taken possession of by the said German Lutherans in Georgetown; who organized themselves into a church or congregation, and erected a church or house of worship thereon; and the lot was enclosed by them and a church erected thereon; and hath been kept and held by them during a period of fifty years; and hath been used as a burying ground for the members of the church, with the avowed intention of building thereon another church or place of worship, the first building erected thereon being decayed, whenever their funds would enable them so to do. That during all this period their possession has never been questioned, and the lot has been exempted from taxation as property set apart for a religious purpose. ... It further charges that Charles Beatty died about sixteen years ago, without having made any conveyance of the said lot, and that Charles A. Beatty, the defendant, is his heir, and has the title by descent; and prays that he may be compelled to convey it to them. It further charges that Ritchie, the other defendant, has unwarrantably disputed their title; and has entered upon the lot and removed some of the tomb stones erected thereon, and means to dispossess the plaintiffs and to remove the tomb stones and graves. The bill therefore prays that they may be quieted in their possession, and that a writ of injunction may issue, and for further relief.

The defendants ... admitted that the lot was so marked in the plot as the bill states, and that it was Charles Beatty's intention to appropriate the same to the use of the Lutheran congregation, provided they would build thereon, within a reasonable time, a house of public worship. They deny that the German Lutherans were ever organized, as stated in the bill; or that any such church has been built; or that there has been any such possession or enclosure as the bill asserts; or that Charles Beatty ever made any conveyance of the property to transfer his title. They admit that the lot has been used as a grave yard, but not exclusively appropriated to the use of the Lutheran congregation. They admit that a building was erected thereon, but that it was used as a school house. They admit that the defendant, Beatty, is heir at law, and as such, that he claims the lot in question, and has authorized the defendant, Ritchie, to take possession thereof. They deny all the equity in the bill, as well as the authority of the plaintiffs to sue; declaring them to be mere volunteers, and demanding proof of their authority, & c.

The general replication was filed, and the cause came on for a hearing upon the bill, answer, exhibits and depositions; and the court decreed a perpetual injunction against the defendants, with costs. The appeal is brought from that decree. ...

This is not the case of a mere private trespass; but a public nuisance, going to the irreparable injury of the Georgetown congregation of Lutherans. The property consecrated to their use by a perpetual servitude or easement, is to be taken from them; the sepulchres of the dead are to be violated; the feelings of religion, and the sentiment of natural affection of the kindred and friends of the deceased are to be wounded; and the memorials erected by piety or love, to the memory of the good, are to be removed so as to leave no trace of the last home of their ancestry to those who may visit the spot in future generations. It cannot be that such acts are to be redressed by the ordinary process of law. The remedy must be sought, if at all, in the protecting power of a court of chancery; operating by its injunction to preserve the repose of the ashes of the dead, and the religious sensibilities of the living. ...

❖ ❖ ❖

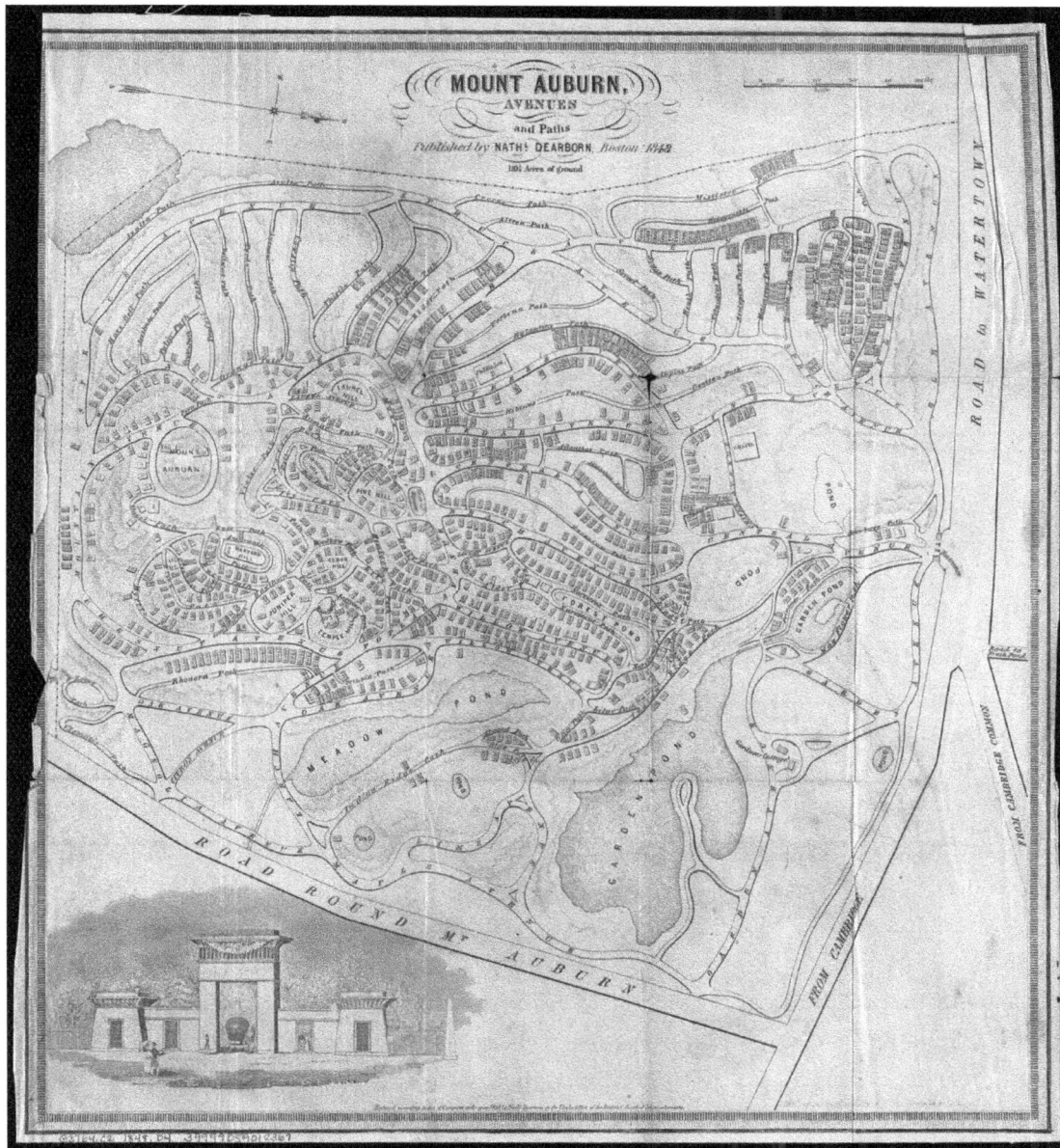

Mount Auburn Cemetery, Cambridge, Massachusetts
Nathaniel Dearborn, Mount Auburn Avenues and Paths *(1848)*

CHAPTER 6.3
ADDRESS AT THE CONSECRATION OF MOUNT AUBURN
Justice Joseph Story

September 24, 1831

My Friends,

The occasion, which brings us together, has much in it calculated to awaken our sensibilities, and cast a solemnity over our thoughts. We are met to consecrate these grounds exclusively to the service and repose of the dead.

The duty is not new; for it has been performed for countless millions. The scenery is not new; for the hill and the valley, the still, silent dell, and the deep forest, have often been devoted to the same pious purpose. But that, which must always give it a peculiar interest, is, that it can rarely occur except at distant intervals; and, whenever it does, it must address itself to feelings intelligible to all nations, and common to all hearts.

The patriarchal language of four thousand years ago is precisely that, to which we would now give utterance. We are "strangers and sojourners" here. We have need of "a possession of a burying-place, that we may bury our dead out of our sight." Let us have "the field, and the cave which is therein; and all the trees, that are in the field, and that are in the borders round about;" and let them "be made sure for a possession of a burying-place." [*Note: Justice Story refers to Genesis 23, which is excerpted in Chapter 3.3.*]

It is the duty of the living thus to provide for the dead. It is not a mere office of pious regard for others; but it comes home to our own bosoms, as those who are soon to enter upon the common inheritance.

If there are any feelings of our nature, not bounded by earth, and yet stopping short of the skies, which are more strong and more universal than all others, they will be found in our solicitude as to the time and place and manner of our death; in the desire to die in the arms of our friends; to have the last sad offices to our remains performed by their affection; to repose in the land of our nativity; to be gathered to the sepulchres of our fathers. It is almost impossible for us to feel, nay, even to feign, indifference on such a subject. ...

It is in vain, that Philosophy has informed us, that the whole earth is but a point in the eyes of its Creator,—nay, of his own creation; that, wherever we are,—abroad or at home,—on the restless ocean, or the solid land,—we are still under the protection of his providence, and safe, as it were, in the hollow of his hand. It is in vain, that Religion has instructed us, that we are but dust, and to dust we shall return,—that whether our remains are scattered to the corners of the earth, or gathered in sacred urns, there is a sure and certain hope of a resurrection of the body and a life everlasting. These truths, sublime and glorious as they are, leave untouched the feelings, of which I have spoken, or, rather, they impart to them a more enduring reality. Dust as we are, the frail tenements, which enclose our spirits but for a season, are dear, are inexpressibly dear to us. We derive solace, nay, pleasure, from the reflection, that when the hour of separation comes, these earthly remains will still retain the tender regard of those, whom we leave behind;— that the spot, where they shall lie, will be remembered with a fond and soothing reverence;—that our children will visit it in the midst of their sorrows; and our kindred in remote generations feel that a local inspiration hovers round it.

Let him speak, who has been on a pilgrimage of health to a foreign land. Let him speak, who has watched at the couch of a dying friend, far from his chosen home. Let him speak, who has committed to the bosom of the deep, with a sudden, startling plunge, the narrow shroud of some relative or companion. Let such speak, and they will tell you, that there is nothing, which wrings the heart of the dying,—aye, and of the surviving,—with sharper agony, than the thought, that they are to sleep their last sleep in the land of strangers, or in the unseen depths of the ocean.

"Bury me not, I pray thee," said the patriarch Jacob, "bury me not in Egypt: but I will lie with my fathers. And thou shalt carry me out of Egypt; and bury me in their burying-place." — "There they buried Abraham and Sarah his wife; there they buried Isaac and Rebecca his wife; and there I buried Leah." [*Note: Justice Story refers to Genesis 49, which is excerpted in Chapter 3.3.*]

Such are the natural expressions of human feeling, as they fall from the lips of the dying. Such are the reminiscences, that forever crowd on the confines of the passes to the grave. We seek again to have our home there with our friends, and to be blest by a communion with them. It is a matter of instinct, not of reasoning. It is a spiritual impulse, which supersedes belief, and disdains question.

But it is not chiefly in regard to the feelings belonging to our own mortality, however sacred and natural, that we should contemplate the establishment of repositories of this sort. There are higher moral purposes, and more affecting considerations, which belong to the subject. We should accustom ourselves to view them rather as means, than as ends; rather as influences to govern human conduct, and to moderate human suffering, than as cares incident to a selfish foresight.

It is to the living mourner—to the parent, weeping over his dear dead child—to the husband, dwelling in his own solitary desolation—to the widow, whose heart is broken by untimely sorrow—to the friend, who misses at every turn the presence of some kindred spirit— It is to these, that the repositories of the dead bring home thoughts full of admonition, of instruction, and slowly but surely, of consolation also. They admonish us, by their very silence, of our own frail and transitory being. They instruct us in the true value of life, and in its noble purposes, its duties, and its destination. They spread around us, in the reminiscences of the past, sources of pleasing, though melancholy reflection.

We dwell with pious fondness on the characters and virtues of the departed; and, as time interposes its growing distances between us and them, we gather up, with more solicitude, the broken fragments of memory, and weave, as it were, into our very hearts, the threads of their history. As we sit down by their graves, we seem to hear the tones of their affection, whispering in our ears. We listen to the voice of their wisdom, speaking in the depths of our souls. We shed our tears; but they are no longer the burning tears of agony. They relieve our drooping spirits, and come no longer over us with a deathly faintness. We return to the world, and we feel ourselves purer, and better, and wiser, from this communion with the dead.

I have spoken but of feelings and associations common to all ages, and all generations of men—to the rude and the polished—to the barbarian and the civilized—to the bond and the free—to the inhabitant of the dreary forests of the north, and the sultry regions of the south—to the worshipper of the sun, and the worshipper of idols—to the Heathen, dwelling in the darkness of his cold mythology, and to the Christian, rejoicing in the light of the true God. Every where we trace them in the characteristic remains of the most distant ages and nations, and as far back as human history carries its traditionary outlines. They are found in the barrows, and cairns, and mounds of olden times, reared by the uninstructed affection of savage tribes; and, every where, the spots seem to have been selected with the same tender regard to the living and the dead; that the magnificence of nature might administer comfort to human sorrow, and incite human sympathy.

The aboriginal Germans buried their dead in groves consecrated by their priests. The Egyptians gratified their pride and soothed their grief, by interring them in their Elysian fields, or embalming them in their vast catacombs, or enclosing them in their stupendous pyramids, the wonder of all succeeding ages. The Hebrews watched with religious care over their places of burial. They selected, for this purpose, ornamented gardens, and deep forests, and fertile valleys, and lofty mountains; and they still designate them with a sad emphasis, as the "House of the Living." The ancient Asiatics lined the approaches to their cities with sculptured sarcophagi, and mausoleums, and other ornaments, embowered in shrubbery, traces of which may be seen among their magnificent ruins. The Greeks exhausted the resources of their exquisite art in adorning the habitations of the dead. They discouraged interments within the limits of their cities; and consigned their reliques to shady groves, in the neighborhood of murmuring streams and mossy fountains, close by the favorite resorts of those, who were engaged in the study of philosophy and nature, and called them, with the elegant expressiveness of their own beautiful language, CEMETERIES, or "Places of Repose." The Romans, faithful to the example of Greece, erected the monuments to the dead in the suburbs of the eternal city, (as they proudly denominated it,) on the sides of their spacious roads, in the midst of trees and ornamental walks, and ever-varying flowers. The Appian way was crowded with columns, and obelisks, and cenotaphs to the memory of her heroes and sages; and, at every turn, the short but touching inscription met the eye,—Siste Viator,—Pause Traveller,—inviting at once to sympathy and thoughtfulness. Even the humblest Roman could read on the humblest gravestone the kind offering—"May the earth lie lightly on these remains!" And the Moslem Successors of the emperors, indifferent as they may be to the ordinary exhibitions of the fine arts, place their burying-grounds in rural retreats, and embellish them with studious taste as a religious duty. The cypress is planted at the head and foot of every grave, and waves with a mournful solemnity over it. These devoted grounds possess an inviolable sanctity. The ravages of war never reach them; and victory and defeat equally respect the limits of their domain. So that it has been remarked, with equal truth and beauty, that while the cities of the living are subject to all the desolations and vicissitudes incident to human affairs, the cities of the dead enjoy an undisturbed repose, without even the shadow of change.

But I will not dwell upon facts of this nature. They demonstrate, however, the truth, of which I have spoken. They do more; they furnish reflections suitable for our own thoughts on the present occasion.

If this tender regard for the dead be so absolutely universal, and so deeply founded in human affection, why is it not made to exert a more profound influence on our lives? Why do we not enlist it with more persuasive energy in the cause of human improvement? Why do we not enlarge it as a source of religious consolation? Why do we not make it a more efficient instrument to elevate Ambition, to stimulate Genius, and to dignify Learning? Why do we not connect it indissolubly with associations, which charm us in Nature and engross us in Art? Why do we not dispel from it that unlovely gloom, from which our hearts turn as from a darkness, that ensnares, and a horror, that appalls our thoughts?

To many, nay, to most of the heathen, the burying-place was the end of all things. They indulged no hope, at least, no solid hope, of any future intercourse or re-union with their friends. The farewell at the grave was a long, and an everlasting farewell.

At the moment, when they breathed it, it brought to their hearts a startling sense of their own wretchedness. Yet, when the first tumults of anguish were passed, they visited the spot, and strewed flowers, and garlands, and crowns around it, to assuage their grief, and nourish their piety. They delighted to make it the abode of the varying beauties of Nature; to give it attractions, which should invite the busy and the thoughtful; and yet, at the same time, afford ample scope for the secret indulgence of sorrow.

Why should not Christians imitate such examples? They have far nobler motives to cultivate moral sentiments and sensibilities; to make cheerful the pathways to the grave; to combine with deep meditations on human mortality the sublime consolations of religion. We know, indeed, as they did of old, that "man goeth to his long home, and the mourners go about the streets." But that home is not an everlasting home; and the mourners may not weep as those, who are without hope. What is the grave to Us, but a thin barrier dividing Time from Eternity, and Earth from Heaven? …

Why then should we darken with systematic caution all the avenues to these repositories? Why should we deposit the remains of our friends in loathsome vaults, or beneath the gloomy crypts and cells of our churches, where the human foot is never heard, save when the sickly taper lights some new guest to his appointed apartment, and "lets fall a supernumerary horror" on the passing procession? Why should we measure out a narrow portion of earth for our graveyards in the midst of our cities, and heap the dead upon each other with a cold, calculating parsimony, disturbing their ashes, and wounding the sensibilities of the living? Why should we expose our burying-grounds to the broad glare of day, to the unfeeling gaze of the idler, to the noisy press of business, to the discordant shouts of merriment, or to the baleful visitations of the dissolute? Why should we bar up their approaches against real mourners, whose delicacy would shrink from observation, but whose tenderness would be soothed by secret visits to the grave, and holding converse there with their departed joys? Why all this unnatural restraint upon our sympathies and sorrows, which confines the visit to the grave to the only time, in which it must be utterly useless—when the heart is bleeding with fresh anguish, and is too weak to feel, and too desolate to desire consolation?

It is painful to reflect, that the Cemeteries in our cities, crowded on all sides by the overhanging habitations of the living, are walled in only to preserve them from violation. And that in our country towns they are left in a sad, neglected state, exposed to every sort of intrusion, with scarcely a tree to shelter their barrenness, or a shrub to spread a grateful shade over the new-made hillock.

These things were not always so among christians. They are not worthy of us. They are not worthy of christianity in our day. There is much in these things, that casts a just reproach upon us in the past. There is much, that demands for the future a more spiritual discharge of our duties.

Our Cemeteries rightly selected, and properly arranged, may be made subservient to some of the highest purposes of religion and human duty. They may preach lessons, to which none may refuse to listen, and which all, that live, must hear. Truths may be there felt and taught in the silence of our own meditations, more persuasive, and more enduring, than ever flowed from human lips. The grave hath a voice of eloquence, nay, of superhuman eloquence, which speaks at once to the thoughtlessness of the rash, and the devotion of the good; which addresses all times, and all ages, and all sexes; which tells of wisdom to the wise, and of comfort to the afflicted; which warns us of our follies and our dangers; which whispers to us in accents of peace, and alarms us in tones of terror; which steals with a healing balm into the stricken heart, and lifts up and supports the broken spirit; which awakens a new enthusiasm for virtue, and disciplines us for its severer trials and duties; which calls up the images of the illustrious dead, with an animating presence for our example and glory; and which demands of us, as men, as patriots, as christians, as immortals, that the powers given by God should be devoted to his service, and the minds created by his love, should return to him with larger capacities for virtuous enjoyment, and with more spiritual and intellectual brightness.

It should not be for the poor purpose of gratifying our vanity or pride, that we should erect columns, and obelisks, and monuments to the dead; but that we may read thereon much of our own destiny and duty. We know, that man is the creature of associations and excitements. Experience may instruct, but habit, and appetite, and passion, and imagination, will exercise a strong dominion over him. These are the Fates, which weave the thread of his character, and unravel the mysteries of his conduct. The truth, which strikes home, must not only have the approbation of his reason, but it must be embodied in a visible, tangible, practical form. It must be felt, as well as seen. It must warm, as well as convince.

It was a saying of Themistocles, that the trophies of Miltiades would not suffer him to sleep. The feeling, thus expressed, has a deep foundation in the human mind; and, as it is well or ill directed, it will cover us with shame, or exalt us to glory. The deeds of the great attract but a cold and listless admiration, when they pass in historical order before us like moving shadows. It is the trophy and the monument, which invest them with a substance of local reality. Who, that has stood by the tomb of Washington on the quiet Potomac, has not felt his heart more pure, his wishes more aspiring, his gratitude more warm, and his love of country touched by a holier flame? Who, that should see erected in shades, like these, even a cenotaph to the memory of a man, like Buckminster, that prodigy of early genius, would not feel, that there is an excellence over which death hath no power, but which lives on through all time, still freshening with the lapse of ages.

But passing from those, who by their talents and virtues have shed lustre on the annals of mankind, to cases of mere private bereavement, who, that should deposit in shades, like these, the remains of a beloved friend, would not feel a secret pleasure in the thought, that the simple inscription to his worth would receive the passing tribute of a sigh from thousands of kindred hearts? That the stranger and the traveller would linger on the spot with a feeling of reverence? That they, the very mourners themselves, when they should revisit it, would find there the verdant sod, and the fragrant flower, and the breezy shade? That they might there, unseen, except of God, offer up their prayers, or indulge the luxury of grief? That they might there realize, in its full force, the affecting beatitude of the scriptures; "Blessed are they that mourn, for they shall be comforted?"

Surely, surely, we have not done all our duty, if there yet remains a single incentive to human virtue, without its due play in the action of life, or a single stream of happiness, which has not been made to flow in upon the waters of affliction.

Considerations, like those, which have been suggested, have for a long time turned the thoughts of many distinguished citizens to the importance of some more appropriate places of sepulture. There is a growing sense in the community of the inconveniences, and painful associations, not to speak of the unhealthiness of interments, beneath our churches. The tide, which is flowing with such a steady and widening current into the narrow peninsula of our Metropolis, not only forbids the enlargement of the common limits, but admonishes us of the increasing dangers to the ashes of the dead from its disturbing movements. Already in other cities, the church-yards are closing against the admission of new incumbents, and begin to exhibit the sad spectacle of promiscuous ruins and intermingled graves.

We are, therefore, but anticipating at the present moment, the desires, nay the necessities of the next generation. We are but exercising a decent anxiety to secure an inviolable home for ourselves and our posterity. We are but inviting our children and their descendants, to what the Moravian Brothers have, with such exquisite propriety, designated as "the Field of Peace." [*Note: The Moravian Church calls its cemeteries "God's Acre," from the German* Gottesacker, *literally meaning "Field of God."*]

A rural Cemetery seems to combine in itself all the advantages, which can be proposed to gratify human feelings, or tranquillize human fears; to secure the best religious influences, and to cherish all those associations, which cast a cheerful light over the darkness of the grave.

And what spot can be more appropriate than this, for such a purpose? Nature seems to point it out with significant energy, as the favorite retirement for the dead. There are around us all the varied features of her beauty and grandeur—the forest-crowned height; the abrupt acclivity; the sheltered valley; the deep glen; the grassy glade; and the silent grove. Here are the lofty oak, the beech, that "wreathes its old fantastic roots so high," the rustling pine, and the drooping willow;—the tree, that sheds its pale leaves with every autumn, a fit emblem of our own transitory bloom; and the evergreen, with its perennial shoots, instructing us, that "the wintry blast of death kills not the buds of virtue." Here is the thick shrubbery to protect and conceal the new-made grave; and there is the wild-flower creeping along the narrow path, and planting its seeds in the upturned earth. All around us there breathes a solemn calm, as if we were in the bosom of a wilderness, broken only by the breeze as it murmurs through the tops of the forest, or by the notes of the warbler pouring forth his matin or his evening song.

Ascend but a few steps, and what a change of scenery to surprise and delight us. We seem, as it were in an instant, to pass from the confines of death, to the bright and balmy regions of life. Below us flows the winding Charles with its rippling current, like the stream of time hastening to the ocean of eternity. In the distance, the City,—at once the object of our admiration and our love,—rears its proud eminences, its glittering spires, its lofty towers, its graceful mansions, its curling smoke, its crowded haunts of business and pleasure, which speak to the eye, and yet leave a noiseless loneliness on the ear. Again we turn, and the walls of our venerable University rise before us, with many a recollection of happy days passed there in the interchange of study and friendship, and many a grateful thought of the affluence of its learning, which has adorned and nourished the literature of our country. Again we turn, and the cultivated farm, the neat cottage, the Village church, the sparkling lake, the rich valley, and the distant hills, are before us through opening vistas; and we breathe amidst the fresh and varied labors of man.

There is, therefore, within our reach, every variety of natural and artificial scenery, which is fitted to awaken emotions of the highest and most affecting character. We stand, as it were, upon the borders of two worlds; and as the mood of our minds may be, we may gather lessons of profound wisdom by contrasting the one with the other, or indulge in the dreams of hope and ambition, or solace our hearts by melancholy meditations. ...

And we are met here to consecrate this spot, by these solemn ceremonies, to such a purpose. The Legislature of this Commonwealth, with a parental foresight has clothed the Horticultural Society with authority (if I may use its own language) to make a perpetual dedication of it, as a Rural Cemetery or Burying-Ground, and to plant and embellish it with shrubbery, and flowers, and trees, and walks, and other rural ornaments. And I stand here by the order and in behalf of this Society, to declare that, by these services, it is to be deemed henceforth and forever so dedicated. Mount Auburn, in the noblest sense, belongs no longer to the living, but to the dead. It is a sacred, it is an eternal trust. It is consecrated ground. May it remain forever inviolate!

What a multitude of thoughts crowd upon the mind in the contemplation of such a scene. How much of the future, even in its far distant reaches, rises before us with all its persuasive realities. Take but one little narrow space of time, and how affecting are its associations! Within the flight of one half century, how many of the great, the good, and the wise, will be gathered here! How many in the loveliness of infancy, the beauty of youth, the vigor of manhood, and the maturity of age, will lie down here, and dwell in the bosom of their mother earth! The rich and the poor, the gay and the wretched, the favorites of thousands, and the forsaken of the world, the stranger in his solitary grave, and the patriarch surrounded by the kindred of a long lineage! How many will here bury their brightest hopes, or blasted expectations! How many bitter tears will here be shed! How many agonizing sighs will here be heaved! How many trembling feet will cross the path-ways, and returning, leave behind them the dearest objects of their reverence or their love!

And if this were all, sad indeed, and funereal would be our thoughts; gloomy, indeed, would be these shades, and desolate these prospects.

But—thanks be to God—the evils, which he permits, have their attendant mercies, and are blessings in disguise. The bruised reed will not be laid utterly prostrate. The wounded heart will not always bleed. The voice of consolation will spring up in the midst of the silence of these regions of death. The mourner will revisit these shades with a secret, though melancholy pleasure. The hand of friendship will delight to cherish the flowers, and the shrubs, that fringe the lowly grave, or the sculptured monument. The earliest beams of the morning will play upon these summits with a refreshing cheerfulness; and the lingering tints of evening hover on them with a tranquilizing glow. Spring will invite thither the footsteps of the young by its opening foliage; and Autumn detain the contemplative by its latest bloom. The votary of learning and science will here learn to elevate his genius by the holiest studies. The devout will here offer up the silent tribute of pity, or the prayer of gratitude. The rivalries of the world will here drop from the heart; the spirit of forgiveness will gather new impulses; the selfishness of avarice will be checked; the restlessness of ambition will be rebuked; vanity will let fall its plumes; and pride, as it sees "what shadows we are, and what shadows we pursue," will acknowledge the value of virtue as far, immeasurably far, beyond that of fame.

But that, which will be ever present, pervading these shades, like the noon-day sun, and shedding cheerfulness around, is the consciousness, the irrepressible consciousness, amidst all these lessons of human mortality, of the higher truth, that we are beings, not of time but of eternity—"That this corruptible must put on incorruption, and this mortal must put on immortality." [*Note: Justice Story refers to I Corinthians 15, which is excerpted in Chapter 3.4.*] That this is but the threshold and starting point of an existence, compared with whose duration the ocean is but as a drop, nay the whole creation an evanescent quantity.

Let us banish, then, the thought, that this is to be the abode of a gloom, which will haunt the imagination by its terrors, or chill the heart by its solitude. Let us cultivate feelings and sentiments more worthy of ourselves, and more worthy of christianity. Here let us erect the memorials of our love, and our gratitude, and our glory. Here let the brave repose, who have died in the cause of their country. Here let the statesman rest, who has achieved the victories of peace, not less renowned than war. Here let genius find a home, that has sung immortal strains, or has instructed with still diviner eloquence. Here let learning and science, the votaries of inventive art, and the teacher of the philosophy of nature come. Here let youth and beauty, blighted by premature decay, drop, like tender blossoms, into the virgin earth; and here let age retire, ripened for the harvest. Above all, here let the benefactors of mankind, the good, the merciful, the meek, the pure in heart, be congregated; for to them belongs an undying praise. And let us take comfort, nay, let us rejoice, that in future ages, long after we are gathered to the generations of other days, thousands of kindling hearts will here repeat the sublime declaration, "Blessed are the dead, that die in the Lord, for they rest from their labors; and their works do follow them."

❖ ❖ ❖

Tombstone of Joseph Story, Mount Auburn Cemetery, Cambridge, Massachusetts
Nathaniel S. Dearborn, Dearborn's Guide Through Mount Auburn *(8th ed. 1854)*

CHAPTER 6.4

JUSTICE JOSEPH STORY AND THE MOUNT AUBURN CEMETERY

Alfred L. Brophy, *"these great and beautiful republics of the dead": Constitutionalism and the Antebellum Cemetery*, Florida State University Law Review (2016)

Supreme Court Justice Joseph Story, in the beginning of his fifty-second year, spoke in front of thousands of Boston's citizens at the dedication of the Mount Auburn Cemetery on September 24, 1831. Mount Auburn, the United States' first "rural cemetery," had been in the making for several years, a joint venture of the Massachusetts Horticultural Society and a group of Bostonians who sought a more appropriate place for burials than the overcrowded downtown Boston cemeteries. It used a private charitable corporation to organize for public missions—the dignified burial of the dead, the preservation of their memory, and the elevation of those who visited cemeteries. Story began his address with a statement about natural law—the universal human respect for the dead and the desire to have a place of repose as well as veneration. This was a principle common to humans throughout history, from the time of Egypt to Rome and Greece, down to the present. Such universal sentiments could serve noble purposes. "We should accustom ourselves to view" cemeteries "as influences to govern human conduct, and to moderate suffering." After visiting a cemetery, "we feel ourselves purer, and better, and wiser, from this communion with the dead." For Story thought—as did other people of his time, like Washington Irving—that cemeteries might be turned from places of gloom to places of moral uplift. "Why," he asked, "do we not enlist it with more persuasive energy in the cause of human improvement? ... Why do we not make it a more efficient instrument to elevate Ambition, to stimulate Genius, and to dignify Learning?"

The cemetery was part of a Christian mission to teach people about the eternal life of the soul; that lesson separated civilized Christians from barbarians. By visiting the graves of ancestors individuals engaged in a sentimental project of learning from the past and interacting with it. "[W]e gather up, with more solicitude, the broken fragments of memory, and weave, as it were, into our very hearts, the threads of their history." By removing graveyards from cities, where there was no opportunity to reflect on their lessons, where they were disturbed by commerce, and where they had to be gated to prevent further violation, and putting them in rural settings where people might visit them in quiet moments, Story planned to enlist cemeteries in "the highest purposes of religion and human duty."

Story sought to enlist sentiment to accomplish moral uplift. Here he drew upon common sense philosophy, which emphasized the role that sentiment could play in motivating and shaping character. Often Americans tried to speak to considerations of sentiment and reason both—or what many referred to at the time as the "heart" and "head." Such religious purposes overlapped with secular purposes in antebellum America, for religion worked in conjunction with the Constitution, the government, and individual sentiment to create a godly, civilized nation.

All these pieces operated together in Justice Story. From his 1826 Harvard Phi Beta Kappa address that linked the common law to Christianity and those two together to moral and economic progress, to his *Commentaries on the Constitution*, through to his opinions on the Supreme Court, Story's world was one of moral duties that restrained vice, preserved the republic through patriotism and Christianity, and preserved property rights.

Americans learned about those constitutional values in many places. They heard about constitutional values in church pulpits, at debates and addresses of college literary societies, at gatherings of civic organizations, at militia and military meetings. Another prominent place for discussions of constitutional values—the places where those sentiments of Union, economy, and law were put into action—were legislative halls. Story saw a unique ability of cemeteries to contribute to the mission of those related institutions. Cemeteries taught moral truths differently (and in some ways better) than anywhere else, for they spoke with a voice that everyone could hear. "They may preach lessons, to which none may refuse to listen, and which all, that live, must hear. Truths may be there felt and taught in the silence of our own meditations, more persuasive, and more enduring, than ever flowed from human lips." Indeed, there was an eloquence—a phrase of particular importance to antebellum Americans who often communicated orally—in cemeteries that spoke to everyone:

> The grave hath a voice of eloquence, nay, of superhuman eloquence, which
> speaks at once to the thoughtlessness of the rash, and the devotion of the good;
> which addresses all times, and all ages, and all sexes; which tells of wisdom to
> the wise, and of comfort to the afflicted; which warns us of our follies and our
> dangers; which whispers to us in accents of peace, and alarms us in tones of
> terror; which steals with a healing balm into the stricken heart, and lifts up and
> supports the broken spirit; which awakens a new enthusiasm for virtue, and
> disciplines us for its severer trials and duties; which calls up the images of the
> illustrious dead, with an animating presence for our example and glory; and

which demands of us, as men, as patriots, as christians, as immortals, that the powers given by God should be devoted to his service, and the minds created by his love, should return to him with larger capacities for virtuous enjoyment, and with more spiritual and intellectual brightness.

Cemeteries, thus, had a unique call on the mind, which fit with Story's desire to "use every possible incentive to human virtue." Cemeteries exercised a sentimental pull because of the people buried there. They also caused people to reflect on life. The rural setting amplified their appeal to visitors' emotions. Mount Auburn was within sight of Boston and Harvard and farms. Thus, "within our reach, every variety of natural and artificial scenery, which is fitted to awaken emotions of the highest and most affecting character." The cemetery furnished a useful school for instruction. As the *North American Review* commented in 1841, "The appropriate burial of the dead ... is fraught with moral and religious uses, which the thoughtful will readily interpret."

Story concluded with a call to "cultivate feelings and sentiments more worthy of ourselves, and more worthy of Christianity." Story's address operated at a high level of generality as it tapped a well of cultural ideas. It also set the model for many addresses down to the Civil War, just as Mount Auburn set the standard for subsequent rural cemeteries. Several books detailed the monument art and layout of Mount Auburn and travel memoirs recorded the thoughts of important tourists. Within a few years rural cemeteries were opening through the United States. ...

At a high level of generality, then, cemeteries functioned to promote republican values. They taught lessons about the early Republic, about change over centuries. Their monuments' inscriptions as well as the historical importance of their setting and the beauty of their landscaped gardens inspired citizens to more moral thinking. But in other ways the cemetery was part of the mission of creating a republican government. Richmond's periodical *Southern Literary Messenger* wrote in 1853, shortly after the dedication of the Hollywood Cemetery, of the need for permanent rural cemeteries. When children moved away from their ancestral homes, family cemeteries fell into disrepair; perhaps they were even forgotten entirely and often the cemeteries fell to development and farming. "Change is the order of the day," was the explanation. Where in England families would stay and thus were able to provide care for family plots, in the United States things were entirely different. Because of the constant migration, "the father plants and stranger to his blood and family waters." There could not —indeed should not—be laws prohibiting development. "The character of our institutions forbid a change in our laws and nature demands, as well an the good of society, that they shall not be altered." This led the *Messenger* to ask whether the problem of the desecration of family cemeteries could "be remedied without an abrogation of a policy so essentially necessary to the freedom and prosperity of our country?" It could, if there were a place where the dead would be cared for in perpetuity. "These great and beautiful republics of the dead" served that purpose.

It was not just that cemeteries inspired patriotic sentiments; they actually were examples of democracies and republics. Rural cemeteries brought everyone together regardless of religious affiliation. There was a democracy in cemeteries, where rich and poor mingled. The lawyer John Thompson, who was elected to the United States House of Representatives in 1856 as a Republican, spoke of such democracy of cemeteries in his 1854 dedication address at

Poughkeepsie's cemetery:

> Here the rich and the poor—the lofty and the lowly, friends and foes, meet and mingle in a fellowship that knows no rivalries; admits of no distinctions. Whatever the affection or opulence of survivors may erect, "of storied urn, or animated bust," to mark the merit of the lost—the dwellers in this quiet city of the dead, will experience no difference—rank and precedence are unknown, and peace sits enthroned in every chamber of these silent realms.

❖   ❖   ❖

CHAPTER 7

THE RUGGLES
REPORT

CHAPTER 7.1
THE RUGGLES REPORT

Tanya D. Marsh

In 1766, the City of New York sold the Presbyterian Congregation a parcel of ground at the northeast corner of Beekman and Nassau Streets, "expressly for the purpose of erecting thereon a church edifice and using the ground for a cemetry [sic] or church yard." The Brick Presbyterian Church opened on that site in 1768.

By the 1830s, the leaders of the congregation had concluded that the site was no longer feasible for continued use and desired to sell the church and surrounding land. Part of the reason they desired to relocate may have been the 1822 New York City ordinance that prohibited burials south of Grand Street. Unlike parish churches in England, which were required to provide burial spaces for free, the sale of graves and vaults was an important source of revenue for colonial American churches. The prohibition on new interments surely put financial pressure on the church.

A number of pew holders and vault owners objected to the proposed sale, and the church asked the Chancery Court of New York for leave to sell in 1837. Citing the dissension in the congregation to the proposed sale, and the importance of maintaining the graves and vaults on the property, the court dismissed the petition: "Many of those revered and good men, whose names are on its earliest records, are entombed within its precincts. Their ashes have mingled with the earth, and have helped to consecrate the spot. Let it stand as a valued monument, sacred to religion and to the memory of its founders, until, indeed, it can be no longer useful." In the court's discussion of the rights of the vault owners, it drew upon the lessons of the Old Testament, highlighting the enduring significance of that legacy: "A vault, in reference to interment, is but a place to entomb; and when so used, becomes a tomb; a receptacle for the dead—a last resting place. A grant of such a place gives an exclusive right; and why may it not be perpetual? Abraham's purchase of the cave in the field of Machpelah, 'for a possession of a burying-place,' was of that character. There, according to sacred history, the patriarch buried his wife Sarah,

The Brick Presbyterian Church, New York City, New York

and was himself buried; there, were Isaac and Rebecca also laid; in that cave Jacob buried Leah, and while sojourning in Egypt and about to die, he made his son Joseph swear to him to remove his body and bury it with his fathers."

During the 1850s, the City of New York widened and straightened many downtown streets, including Beekman Street. The fifteen-foot widening disturbed thirteen vaults in the churchyard that contained the remains of approximately one hundred people. The "Minister's Vault" was owned by the church; the other twelve vaults were owned or leased (for 99 year terms) by congregants. The sum of $28,000 was determined as just compensation for the loss and damage to the churchyard, and the Surrogate's Court of New York was tasked with dividing that sum between the Brick Presbyterian Church and the vault owners. Finding no applicable precedent in U.S. law, the Surrogate's Court appointed a referee, attorney Samuel B. Ruggles, to provide a summary of the relevant legal principles. The resulting report, included as Chapter 7.3, is a foundational authority in the U.S. law of human remains.

Ruggles explained the inapplicability of English legal precedent and argued that it was appropriate to "banish [the] maxims, doctrines, and practices [of English ecclesiastical law] from our jurisprudence, and to prevent [it] from guiding, in any way, our judicial action."

> The English emigration to America—the most momentous event in political history—commenced in the very age when Chief-Justice Coke was proclaiming, as a legal dogma, the exclusive authority of the Church over the dead. The liberty-loving, God-fearing Englishmen, who founded these American States, had seen enough and felt enough of "ecclesiastical cognizance," and they crossed a broad and stormy ocean to a new and untrodden continent, to escape from it for ever.

But Ruggles warned that a void would therefore be created in the common law:

> The necessity for the exercise of such authority, not only over the burial, but over the corpse itself, by some competent legal tribunal, will appear at once, if we consider the consequences of its abandonment. ... The dead deprived of the legal guardianship, however partial, which the church so long had thrown around them, and left unprotected by the civil courts, will become, in law, nothing but public nuisances; and their custody will belong only to the guardians of the public health, to remove and destroy the offending matter, with all practicable economy and dispatch.

"In the new, transplanted England of the Western continent," Ruggles argued, "the dead will find protection, if at all, in the secular tribunals, succeeding, by fair inheritance, to the primeval authority of the ancient, uncorrected common law." This "ancient, uncorrected common law" described by Ruggles bears a striking similarity to Roman civil law and Anglican canon law. He argued it was illegitimate for U.S. courts to follow English ecclesiastical law, but Ruggles was more critical of the "exclusive authority of the Church over the dead" than the underlying principles of Church doctrine. The rules that Ruggles proposed to settle the dispute between the Brick Presbyterian Church and the vault holders essentially mimic the rules found in seventeenth century ecclesiastical law and place them in a secular context.

The *Ruggles Report* proposed five foundational principles:

1.   That neither a corpse, nor its burial, is legally subject, in any way, to ecclesiastical cognizance, nor to sacerdotal power of any contract.

2.   That the right to bury a corpse and to preserve its remains, is a legal right, which the courts of law will recognize and protect.

3.   That such right, in the absence of any testamentary disposition, belongs exclusively to the next of kin.

4.   That the right to protect the remains includes the right to preserve them by separate burial, to select the place of sepulture, and to change it at pleasure.

5.   That if the place of burial be taken for public use, the next of kin may claim to be indemnified for the expense of removing and suitably reentering their remains.

❖   ❖   ❖

St. Paul's Chapel, New York City, New York
Photo by Tanya D. Marsh

CHAPTER 7.2

IN THE MATTER OF THE PETITION OF THE CORPORATION OF THE BRICK PRESBYTERIAN CHURCH IN THE CITY OF NEW YORK

Chancery Court of New York, 3 Edw.Ch. 155 (1837)

[The Brick Presbyterian Church petitioned the City to sell the church building and its cemetery to the City and use the purchase money to buy and build another church building. The congregation and trustees had settled upon at least $150,000 as the purchase price. Upon selling the land and the building, the bodies interred in the cemetery would have to be moved. Because some of the congregation opposed the sale, the court ordered a master investigate and report to the court.

The church had sold several vaults upon the terms granted by the "Dutch consistory." The Dutch consistory terms were fee simple subject to burial charges. John DeWitt and John Quackenboss purchased two such deeds. The church also sold deeds under similar terms with 999 year leases. Thomas Ash and William Ash purchased two such deeds.]

The matter before the court, as it now appears upon the master's report and the mass of testimony connected with it, presents questions which go first to the right of the corporation to sell; and secondly, to the expediency of a sale and consequent removal of the church? ...

The case, then, resolves itself into the question, whether the trustees have a right and can lawfully sell, without the consent of all the pew holders, but especially of the vault owners;

and if the trustees have such right, then, as to the expediency of the measure? The first of these questions, that is, as to the right, affects the interest of some who are not, at present, members of the congregation, and have no connection with the church as a spiritual body; and the other, as to the expediency of a sale, affects those exclusively who are in the latter point of view connected with the church as stated hearers, communicants and worshippers, whether they be pew-holders or not. ...

The objection, on the ground of the legal rights of pew-holders, I consider not insuperable to the granting of the present application.

Then, as to the vault owners: what are their rights?

In order to determine the point embraced by this question, it will be necessary to look into the grants under which the property is held and through which ground for vaults has been disposed of. ...

One of the heirs of a lessee produces this lease and claims to hold under it.

The great question, with respect to these instruments, is: what rights do they confer? Do they confer a mere right of interment, an exclusive right to inter in those particular spots, or is it a right to the land—an estate or interest in the land itself to endure for ever in the one case, and, until the expiration of the term, in the other?

This is a question not entirely free from difficulty. It is argued that, with the exception of the deed and lease, conferring an exclusive right to bury within the walls of the vaults, it is a right of no greater extent and of no longer duration than is conferred when the privilege of burying in a grave or a public vault is granted or sold, and that such a grant confers no right of property in the soil, but only a temporary use. And the case of *Gilbert v. Buzzard and Boyer*, 3 Phillimore, 335, is cited, as containing a full explanation of the law on the subject of interments. That case certainly has an important bearing upon the one now before the court. The plaintiff, there, claimed the right to bury his deceased wife in the church-yard in an iron coffin, on paying the usual fees. The churchwardens refused to put the iron coffin in the ground upon any terms, on account of its durability. This, necessarily, led to the consideration of what right was acquired by interment in a grave—whether it was an exclusive right to the spot for ever, or one which terminated with the decay of the body. If the former, then it was immaterial in what manner the body was deposited, whether enclosed in wood, iron or lead; but if the latter, then it was important that the ground should not be occupied with durable coffins of metal. And here it will be necessary for me to quote somewhat at large from the very eloquent opinion of Sir William Scott. After an historical sketch of the ancient and modern modes of interment, and observing upon the comparative durability of materials, the learned judge thus proceeds:

"It being assumed that the court is justified in holding this opinion upon the fact of comparative duration, the pretension of these coffins to be admitted on equal terms must resort to the other proposition, which declares that the difference of duration ought to make no difference in the terms of admission. Accordingly it has been argued, that the ground once given to the interment of a body is appropriated for ever to that body; that it is not only the *domus ultima*, but the *domus æterna* of that tenant, who is never to be disturbed, be the condition of that tenant himself what it may. It is his for ever; and the insertion of any other body into that space, at any other time, however distant, is an unwarrantable intrusion. If these positions be true, the question of comparative duration sinks into utter insignificance."

"In support of them it seems to be assumed, that the tenant himself is imperishable; for, surely, there cannot be an inextinguishable title, a perpetuity of possession, belonging to a perishable thing: but obstructed in a portion of it, by public authority, the fact is, that "man" and "for ever" are terms quite incompatible in any state of his existence, dead or alive, in this world. The time must come when his posthumous remains must mingle with and compose a part of the soil in which they have been deposited. Precious embalmments and splendid monuments may preserve for centuries the remains of those who have filled the more commanding stations of human life: but the common lot of mankind furnishes them with no such means of conservation. With reference to men, the *domus æterna* is a mere flourish of rhetoric. The process of nature will resolve them into an intimate mixture with their kindred earth, and will furnish a place of repose for other occupants of the grave in succession. It is objected that no precise time can be fixed at which the mortal remains, and even the chest which contains them, shall undergo the complete process of dissolution; and it certainly cannot, being dependent upon circumstances that differ, upon difference of soils and exposure, of climate and seasons: but observation can ascertain it sufficiently for practical use. The experience of not many years is required to furnish a certainty sufficient for such purposes. Founded on these facts and considerations, the legal doctrine certainly is, and remains unaffected, that the common cemetery is not *res unius ætatis*, the exclusive property of one generation now departed; but is likewise the common property of the living, and of generations yet unborn, and subject only to temporary appropriation. There exists a right of succession in the whole, a right which can only be lawfully obstructed in a portion of it, by public authority, that of the ecclesiastical magistrate, who gives occasionally an exclusive title in a part of the public cemetery to the succession of a single family, or to an individual who has a claim to such a distinction: but he does not do that without just consideration of its expediency, and a due attention to the objections of those who oppose such an alienation from the common use. Even a brick grave without such authority is an aggression upon the common freehold interest, and carries the pretensions of the dead to an extent that violates the just rights of the living."

"If this view of the matter be just, all contrivances that, whether intentionally or not, prolong the time of dissolution beyond the period at which common local usage has fixed it, are acts of injustice, unless compensated for in one way or other. In country parishes, where the population is small and the cemetries are large, it is a matter less worthy of consideration. More can be spared, and less is wanting. But in populous parishes, in large and crowded cities, the exclusive possession is unavoidably limited; for, unless limited, evils of formidable magnitude would take place. Church-yards cannot be made commensurate to a large and increasing population; the period of decay and dissolution does not arrive fast enough in the accustomed mode of depositing bodies in the earth, to evacuate the ground for the use of succeeding claimants. New cemeteries are to be purchased at an enormous expense to the parish, and to be used at an increased expense to the families, and at the inconvenience of their being compelled to resort to very incommodious distances for attendance upon the offices of interment. Three additional burial grounds in this very parish have been so bought. This is the known progress of things in their ordinary course; and if to this is to be added the general introduction of a new mode of interment, which is to insure to the bodies a much longer possession, the evil will be intolerable. A comparatively small portion of the dead will shoulder out the living and their posterity. The whole environs of this metropolis must be surrounded by a circumvallation of church-yards, perpetually enlarging, by becoming themselves surcharged with bodies; if indeed landowners can be found willing to divert their ground from the beneficial uses of the living to the barren preservation of the dead, contrary to the humane maxim quoted by Tully from Plato's Republic, *'Quæ terra fruges ferre, et, ut mater, cibos suppeditare, possit, eam nequis nobis minuat neve vivus neve mortuus.'"*

"If, therefore, these iron coffins are to bring additional charges upon parishes, they ought to bring with them a proportionate compensation; upon all common principles of estimated value, one must pay for the longer lease which you actually take of the ground. And what is the exception to be pleaded for iron? If you wish to protect your deceased relative from the spoliators of the dead, by additional securities, which will press upon the convenience of the parish, we do not blame the purpose, nor reject the measure; but it is you, and not the parish, who must pay for that purpose. I am aware (as I have already hinted,) that very ancient canons forbid the taking of money for interment, upon the notion that consecrated grounds were among the res sacra; and that money payments for them were, therefore, acts of a demoniacal complexion. But this has not been the way of considering that matter since the Reformation, (for the practice certainly goes back at least as far;) it appears founded upon reasonable considerations, and is subjected to the proper control of an authority of inspection. To inland and populous parishes, where funerals are very frequent, the expense of keeping church-yards in an orderly and seemly condition is not small; and that of purchasing new church-yards, when the old ones are likely to become surcharged, is extremely oppressive. To answer such charges, both certain and contingent, it is surely not unreasonable that the actual use should contribute when it is called for."

From this it will be perceived that, while the common cemetry is subject only to a temporary appropriation, yet there may be a grant of an exclusive title to a part of the public cemetry from the ecclesiastical authority. A faculty or grant from the bishop will authorize the erection of tombs and monuments. The person who sets them up has a right of action for injuring or defacing them during his life; and the heir of the deceased has a like right of action. The heir has a right of property in the monuments and escutcheons of his ancestors; and may bring an action against those who take or deface them. But the heir has no right of property in the bodies or ashes of his ancestor and can bring no civil action against those who may indecently violate and disturb their remains when buried. And yet the property in the shroud and winding-sheet are in the executor or other person who was at the charge of the funeral; and a stealing of it will be felony.

Since, then, there may be a right of property acquired in monuments or tombs erected by a faculty or grant, why may not such a right be acquired by purchase from the corporation of a religious society?

A vault, in reference to interment, is but a place to entomb; and when so used, becomes a tomb; a receptacle for the dead—a last resting place. A grant of such a place gives an exclusive right; and why may it not be perpetual? Abraham's purchase of the cave in the field of

Machpelah, "for a possession of a burying-place," was of that character. There, according to sacred history, the patriarch buried his wife Sarah, and was himself buried; there, were Isaac and Rebecca also laid; in that cave Jacob buried Leah, and while sojourning in Egypt and about to die, he made his son Joseph swear to him to remove his body and bury it with his fathers. Here we have an instance of a purchase, which enured to the purchaser and his heirs even to the fourth generation.

It is certainly competent for a man, at this day, to buy the fee simple of an estate in land for the purposes of sepulture; and when converted to that use, the title may descend or be again the subject of sale.

The conveyance from the city corporation to the church, in the year one thousand seven hundred and sixty-six, was a conveyance of the fee of the land, a base or determinable fee, being subject to a quit rent and to a condition that the land should be appropriated to a particular purpose—that of a church and cemetry. This renders it a conveyance to a pious and charitable use; but it was still a conveyance of the land and conferred on the grantees an estate and interest in land for the purposes intended. In appropriating this land to such intended purposes, it was competent for the trustees to dispose of it as they might think proper not inconsistent with the grant and the use for which they expressly held it, namely, on a part of the ground to erect a church edifice; in another part to construct vaults for public use, reserving a space for graves to be opened, on such terms as they might think proper to prescribe; and the residue to lay out for private vaults and to sell the sites or ground for that purpose. And such sales might be of the fee of the land;—true, Sonly a base fee, such as had been conveyed to them. The trustees proceeded to dispose of lots or parcels of the land within the conditions on which they had received the property, as we have seen by their resolutions passed in the years 1769, 1786 and 1788. The intention obviously was, to sell and dispose of the land; and not to grant a mere temporary use or privilege to construct vaults in the land with a reserve of the title to the church. It was a grant of the land itself, such as passed the title to the purchasers or lessees. And hence the form of the conveyances, describing each lot or parcel by metes and bounds, with all the apt words generally used to pass the title to the land; still, the use and enjoyment is limited to that which is below the surface—there is to be no building above ground. A good reason, of course, exists for this. And yet, such a limited use is not inconsistent with a grant of the soil. A man who has a title to lands in fee simple, may build his house beneath as well as above the surface. I cannot but conclude that the deed and the lease in question confer title to the land and not a mere easement or privilege to inter the dead.

If I am correct in this, it can make no difference that any further interments are now prohibited within these vaults, and certainly no argument drawn from this circumstance can give the petitioners any right to resume the control of the vaults, to break them up or desecrate the ground. The corporation ordinance, which restricts burials in our city, may have been intended as a prohibition, but the practical effect, as we know, has not been such. The fine imposed, of two hundred and fifty dollars, has rather operated as a tax upon this privilege than as a prevention. Many vault holders have continued to use their family resting places by paying this penalty; and the very objectors on the present occasion may desire to do so. This view of the case renders it unnecessary to examine into the expediency or propriety of the proposed sale and removal of the church. If the petitioners have not the right without obtaining the consent of the vault-holders, then it cannot be done, however much it may be desired by a large portion of the congregation.

Even if I should be mistaken as to the right of the vault-holders and it could appear that the petitioners can lawfully sell and raze the foundations of the church and destroy these resting places of the dead, still the necessity and expediency of the step, when coupled with the interest and welfare of the church and its congregation, are not so apparent. Great difference of opinion exists among the members and congregation on the subject. The elders, deacons and trustees are divided; and although a majority of them are in favor of a sale and removal, yet a majority of the congregation at large appears to be against it. There is great danger that a removal may be attended by a dispersion and scattering of the flock; but, leave the old hallowed church in its conspicuous and commanding situation and it will always be attractive. Something is due to its venerated walls. Many of those revered and good men, whose names are on its earliest records, are entombed within its precincts. Their ashes have mingled with the earth, and have helped to consecrate the spot. Let it stand as a valued monument, sacred to religion and to the memory of its founders, until, indeed, it can be no longer useful.

I must dismiss this petition.

❖　❖　❖

Central Burying Ground, Boston, Massachusetts
Photo by Tanya D. Marsh

CHAPTER 7.3

AN EXAMINATION OF THE LAW OF BURIAL IN A REPORT TO THE SUPREME COURT OF NEW-YORK BY SAMUEL B. RUGGLES, REFEREE, IN THE MATTER OF TAKING A PORTION OF THE CEMETERY OF THE BRICK PRESBYTERIAN CHURCH, IN WIDENING BEEKMAN-STREET IN THE CITY OF NEW-YORK (1856)

[As New York City expanded in nineteenth century, the City began various street widening projects. One such project was the widening of Beekman Street in lower Manhattan. The widening of Beekman Street, however, encroached upon the Brick Presbyterian Church's cemetery. The land taken for the road included twelve vaults that the church had sold to parishioners in fee simple or leased for terms of 999 years. A thirteenth vault, belonging to the church, was also taken.

The City Commissioners of Estimate and Assessment created a $28,000 fund for the damages to the owners of the vaults. A dispute arose between the parishioners and the Brick Presbyterian Church regarding who was entitled to the damages, and what division was appropriate.

The human remains were removed from their vaults and placed temporarily under the church. Moses Sherwood was among the disturbed dead. Maria Smith, his daughter, was able to identify his body by a ribbon he was buried with. Ms. Smith sought to have Moses and four others re-interred at the church's expense.

The court asked New York attorney Samuel B. Ruggles to report on both issues.] Upon these facts, the opinion of Mr. Ruggles, the Referee, which was reported to the Court, pursuant to its order, was as follows:

1. What are the respective rights of the Brick Presbyterian Church, and of the vault-owners, in the said fund?

It is claimed in behalf of the vault-owners, that the grants from the church were intended to convey, and did legally convey, the fee of the land occupied by the vaults and their steps: that the church retained no legal estate or interest in the land so conveyed, and can not rightfully claim any portion of the sum awarded as its value: but that said vault-owners are entitled each to their rateable proportion of the sum awarded, to wit, in the ratio borne by the area of the land occupied by said vaults and steps, to the area of the whole of the land taken, being, as shown by the proofs, $2,052.80 for each vault.

This claim is contested by the church, on the ground that the grants of the vaults were not intended to convey, and did not convey, any portion of the legal fee, but only a privilege or easement in the land to bury the dead; that the whole legal estate in the laud remained in the church, subject only to such privilege or easement; and that the possession of such of the vault-owners who produce no grant or paper title proves only that, as occupants, they were enjoying a similar privilege or easement.

The Referee does not feel at liberty to inquire how far this legal view of the grants was correct, for the reason that the question has been distinctly and authoritatively settled by his Honor Vice-Chancellor McCoun. in the case reported in 3 Edwards' Chancery Reports, p. 155, involving the legal construction of these very grants. The judgment in that case was, that the grants conferred a title to the land, and not a mere "easement or privilege to inter the dead." The Vice-Chancellor, however, expressed his opinion that the grants conveyed a "base fee," and not a fee simple absolute; and it is therefore necessary to determine practically the pecuniary value of the interest defined to be a base-fee, by ascertaining how far it falls short of a fee simple absolute. The one is necessarily less than the other. The unqualified estate in fee simple absolute is shown, as above, to be $2,052.80. How much is abstracted from that value, by the qualification of its mode of enjoyment? What is the extent of that qualification? How much, and how far does it "debase" the fee?

The qualification does not debase or impair the fee, by any limitation of time. The habendum of the grant of the vault No. 11 is to the grantees, their heirs and assigns for ever. The lease of the vault No. 7 is for 999 years, which for all practical purposes is equivalent to a grant in perpetuity. The usufruct being thus perpetual, it is practically unimportant whether the grant which secures it operates technically to convey a "fee," or only an "easement." The proprietor of a perpetual easement to bury the dead virtually possesses a right, in all pecuniary respects as valuable, as a technical fee in the land restricted to that single use. The mode of enjoyment, the power of enjoyment, and the perpetuity of enjoyment, are precisely alike in both. But a perpetuity of enjoyment of land does not necessarily comprise its whole pecuniary value. A "fee" in land means nothing but an estate of inheritance therein, and not necessarily its whole usufruct.

It may embrace, as in the present case it does embrace, only a portion of the usufruct. The word measures only the duration of the estate. It defines its quantity, but not its quality. A fee is rendered "base," by debasing not the quantity, but the quality of the estate-by limiting not the duration, but the mode of enjoyment. It is "qualified," and thereby debased, by narrowing, by abridging, by defining, the otherwise unlimited power of enjoyment by singling out the "quails" modo, the specific mode of usufruct, and thereby excluding all other modes.

The only pecuniary value of land is in its usufruct; and the whole pecuniary value of a fee in land can therefore only be found in the absolutely unrestricted right to every possible mode of usufruct. If any mode whatever be subtracted or withheld, the pecuniary value is reduced precisely to that extent. In the case above cited, his Honor the Vice-Chancellor, in stating that the vault-owners took "a base fee, such as had been conveyed to the church," evidently intended to assert only, that the two estates were of the same legal species, not that they were equal or equivalent in a pecuniary sense. They were both "base" fees, but they differed most essentially in the extent of the qualification of their modes of enjoyment, and consequently in their comparative degrees of debasement. The restrictions on the usufructuary right of the church, debarred it only from uses which should be both private and secular, leaving open, without stint or limit, the whole field of public usufruct, whether religious or secular; while the vault-owners were absolutely cut off from every possible or imaginable mode of use, except the one, single, solitary office of interring the dead.

Nor must we unduly enlarge the legal comprehensiveness of the word "land," as used in these grants, or of "ground," if taken to be synonymous with it. The remarkably comprehensive definitions of "land" by legal writers, cannot be taken in the present case without due restriction. Blackstone declares that it includes "not only the face of the earth, but everything under it or over it:" that "by the name of land, which is *nomen generalissimum*, every thing terrestrial will pass!" (2 Comm. 19.) Sir Edward Coke, in the *First Institute*, 4 a, in an animated eulogy of "land," as the "habitation and resting-place of man," and "the best of the four elements," expatiates glowingly on its various uses. "Out of it," says he, "cometh man's food, and bread that strengthens man's heart, and wine that gladdeth the heart of man, and oyle that maketh him a cheerful countenance; ... it is replenished with hidden treasures, metals, and precious stones, and many other things, for profit, ornament and pleasure;" and in a still higher strain, concludes, that "the earth hath in law a great extent upwards, not only of water, as hath been said, but of ayre and all other things even up to heaven: for *cujus est solum, ejus est usque ad coelom*"—to which legal definition, some of the older writers, either penetrating more deeply into the subject, or regarding it from a different point of view, have subjoined, "*usque ad inferos!*"

If these, then, are the proper boundaries, and attributes, and properties of "land," when conveyed in fee simple absolute, which of them can legally be assigned to the "land" or ground now under consideration? Does it, in truth, embrace "everything terrestrial?" Does it, in fact, include "not only the face of the earth, but everything under it and over it?" If it include the whole of the "solum," does it indeed extend upwards, "usque ad coelom?" Does it extend a single hairbreadth above the surface of the earth? The grant expressly describes and defines it as a "piece of ground under the earth." No monument, or memorial, or structure of any kind, could be erected upon the land, or over the land, for the stone which was to cover it was to be "even with the surface of the ground." That stone was, in fact, a landmark and a boundary. It defined the upper limit of the land conveyed. It distinctly established the dividing line, the horizontal plane, bisecting the fee simple of the "land," and separating the underlying "solum" from all above it. The superincumbent portion was appropriately retained by the church, *usque ad calum*, subject only to a right of passage through it, attached as an easement to the subterranean portion conveyed.

The reservation of the portion of the "land" above the surface, resulting from the boundary line confining below the surface the portion of the land granted, necessarily left in the church a present estate in fee in the part reserved; and the fact is important, because it distinguishes their right in the land, as a present existing estate in possession, from that mere, naked, contingent possibility of a forfeiture, reserved by the City Corporation in the land conveyed by them to the church. A separate estate of inheritance in real property above the surface, physically surmounting an underlying estate at and below the surface, is familiar to the law, and was recognized as recently as the case of Miss Coutts' box in Drury Lane Theatre, reported in 2 Gale & D., 426. Through their own upper stratum, or division of the "land," extending from the surface "*usque ad calum*," the church indisputably had the right of way into their edifice, and the right of view from its front windows out to the street. Nay, more; they might have erected over these very vaults any addition to the edifice, so that they left the proprietors a sufficient and proper access; and that addition, by inclosing the vaults within the walls of the sanctuary, so far from injuring, would have enhanced their proper value.

The usufructuary interest, then, of the vault-owners was wholly subterranean—not on the earth, but wholly under the earth. The usufruct, restricted by the very force of the term "interment," was wholly within the earth. It lay in utter darkness, cut off from every imaginable purpose of "business, profit, or ornament." It derived no advantage from contact with the living world, but in its own single, peculiar, and narrow office, was impaired rather than benefited by the human activity, which enhanced the usufructuary value of all above it.

In estimating, then, the pecuniary value of "land," thus deprived of all its ordinary attributes and capacities, we cannot properly measure it by land in the vicinity, unrestrictedly devoted to traffic, or any other active mode of usufruct. In truth, it should not be estimated or regarded at all as lying within a commercial city, but only as forming part of a "cemetery;" by its very appellation, a "sleeping-place," a dormitory of the dead, and in that true sense, deriving its primary and principal, if not its only value, from its repose and security from disturbance.

The proper pecuniary value of a cemetery may, however, be enhanced by its religious accessories, and particularly by its position in a church-yard, whether the ground be consecrated in form by ecclesiastical solemnities, or in feeling by proper religious associations. Anything, whether real or imaginary, which renders land more desirable as a place of interment, necessarily adds to its pecuniary value. In this sense, the vaults of the Brick Presbyterian Church might derive, and doubtless did derive, a superadded money value, from their proximity to the venerable edifice, casting its shadow over the successive generations, going out from its honored walls to their last repose. But even this element was subject to contingency. The continuance of the church edifice was by no means certain. Considerations of duty might well carry the edifice to portions of the city, opening a broader field of usefulness. Indeed, it appears in evidence that a sale of the church, even for private, secular purposes, had been actively agitated by its trustees, which, if effected, would wholly extinguish everything like value in the vaults, derived from religious association, and virtually compel the owners to remove their dead to some more suitable locality. The conversion of the Middle Dutch Church into a Post Office, as shown by the proofs, strikingly shows the pecuniary effect upon the vaults of a church, produced by secularizing the edifice to which they were attached. A vault in a city church-yard may also possess a peculiar element of value in its greater security from violation counterbalanced, however, by the hazard; that it may be invaded, as in the present case, under the form of legal proceedings, by the overpowering demands of commerce. The vaults in question were surrounded by a substantial iron fence, including them and the church in one common inclosure. Equal security appears, however, to be furnished by the inclosures of the vaults in the other city church-yards, and in the Marble Cemetery in the Second Avenue, and which may now be purchased for $100 or $150. It appears, also, that the dead are practically secure in Greenwood Cemetery, the inclosure of which has fully protected from disturbance the remains of the 45,349 individuals that have been buried there in the twelve years from 1842 to 1854.

A vault in a city church-yard may also possess an element of value in its cheap and easy accessibility, saving, as it appears, about $15 in carriage-hire for each interment. But it does not exceed, in this respect, the vaults above referred to in the other city church-yards, worth only $150.

It further appears, that the proprietors of the vaults in question paid several penalties of $250 each for several interments during the period between the years 1823 and 1839, when city vaults were subjected to that burthen. The fact does not, however, prove that the same penalties would now be paid. The general change of sentiment in the last few years, produced by the establishment and embellishment of rural cemeteries at Greenwood, and elsewhere in the vicinity of the city, would undoubtedly lead the proprietors of city vaults to select those cemeteries as places of interment, rather than pay such penalties. The proofs also show the extent to which interments in city vaults has fallen into disuse, being, in the last year, only 25 in Trinity church-yard, 20 in St. Thomas's, and 25 in St. Mark's; and in the two Dutch church-yards, only two.

It appears, then, from this analysis of the usufructuary value of the vaults in question, that its elements consist all but exclusively of security, accessibility, and repose. If this be true, their pecuniary value might be justly measured by assuming the price of vaults in other city church-yards, possessing the same elements in the same degree; and this would not exceed $150. It seems quite apparent that a vault in Greenwood Cemetery, notwithstanding the additional expense of carriage hire, would afford, in its superior attractions in many other respects, an ample equivalent; and the Referee therefore adopted it, to make sure of doing no injustice to the proprietors of a property, the taking of which against their consent, had naturally excited peculiar sensibilities. If public opinion may be taken as a guide, a vault in Greenwood, surrounded by a proper iron railing, is very far preferable to any of the vaults in question. In fact, the action of the vault-owners themselves has manifested quite distinctly their preference for places of interment out of the city. The remains removed from the twelve vaults have been deposited in only two instances in any other city church-yard or city cemetery. In several cases, they were removed to Greenwood; in one, to New Jersey; in another, to a church-yard in Westchester: while Mr.

Washington Irving has selected a permanent resting-place for his ancestors and himself amid "the tranquil solitudes of Sleepy Hollow"—a locality consecrated by those ever-living elements of genius, taste, and feeling, which will preserve it from profanation through every mutation of human creeds or human laws. In truth, it is more the office of the moralist and the poet than of the lawyer or the conveyancer to weigh these delicate equivalents in the sleep of the grave. It is Gray and Goldsmith, and not Coke or Blackstone, who can best decide whether the calm repose of the rural cemetery, the "solemn stillness" of the country church-yard, be not preferable, in every element of proper value, to any "easement," or place of deposit, however perpetual, amid the din, and dust, and turmoil of a crowded, trading city.

The cost of a vault in Greenwood Cemetery, 9 feet by 15, including the land and the iron railing, and the expense of removing and re-interring the bodies, is proved to be $590. The remains were removed from the vaults in question in the year 1853, and, generally, as early as the 1st of May. The Referee therefore reports that, in his opinion, the sum of $590 should be allowed to the owners of each of said twelve vaults, with interest from the 1st of May, 1853, to the 15th of January, 1856, being $113.57—in all, $703.57—and amounting, for the twelve, to $8,482.84. There should, however, be deducted from said twelve sums of $703.57 respectively, such amounts as are shown by the proofs to have been expended by the church in removing the remains. These expenditures are, in the aggregate, $209.25, and reduce to $8,233.59, the total amount payable for the vaults, by the fund in court.

2. Is the claimant, Maria Smith, entitled to payment out of the said fund, for the expense of re-interring the remains of her father, Moses Sherwood, whose grave was taken away in widening the street, or to damages for disturbing the grave?

The proper disposal of this question by this court will be important, not so much in the pecuniary amount involved in the present instance, as in furnishing a rule for other cases where cemeteries may be disturbed, either by their proprietors or by public authority. It broadly presents the general question, which does not appear to be distinctly settled in this State: Who is legally and primarily entitled to the custody of a dead body? and as a necessary result, Who is legally bound to bury it? and further, if a body be ejected from its place of burial, Who then is legally and primarily entitled to its custody, and who is bound to re-bury it?

The widening of Beekman-street by the Corporation of New-York removed every building and other impediment which stood in its way. Among them was the grave, the "*domus ultima*" of Moses Sherwood, over which a marble tombstone, inscribed with his name, had been standing more than fifty years. His skull and bones, and portions of his grave-clothing, were found lying in his grave. Had anyone any legal interest in that grave, or any right to preserve the repose of its occupant? or any legal interest in the monument, or right to preserve its repose? Do these rights come within the legal denomination of "private property," which the Constitution forbids to be taken for public use without just compensation?

Property has been concisely defined to be, "the highest right a man can have to a thing." Blackstone spreads out the definition into the "sole and exclusive dominion which one man claims and exercises over the external things of the world, in total exclusion of the right of any other individual in the universe:" (2 Black. Comm., 2.)

The things which may thus be exclusively appropriated, and thereby made "private property," are not confined to tangible or visible objects; for light and air are "property," and belong exclusively to the occupant, so long as he has possession. The right to the mere repose of a grave, although intangible or invisible, may none the less be property. The dividing line between "property" as a thing objectively appropriated by a person, and a "personal right" as subjectively belonging to a person, is not always entirely distinct. The proprietary right to a grave-stone, and the personal right to its undisturbed repose, may measurably partake of both. In a certain sense, even a purely personal right may be said to be appropriated. Nor is the distinction very essential; for if there be a right in a grave, or its contents or appendages, which the law will recognize, it matters little whether the right is appropriated by, or belongs to its possessor. Is there, then, a right of which a court of justice will take cognizance?

In resorting to England for light on this subject, we encounter a body of law grown up under circumstances differing widely from our own. The jurisprudence of that country is peculiarly compounded, embracing largely the ecclesiastical element, from which ours is exempt; and it has given birth to anomalies which we are hardly required to adopt. This is strikingly manifest in the matter of the dead, in which the partition of judicial authority between the Church and the State, forming one composite system, has materially narrowed the powers and the action of the courts of common law. It is believed that an attentive examination of the history of this division of judicial power will show that it is wholly peculiar to England, and that the decisions and dicta of their courts and legal writers on this subject, ought not to exert any controlling influence over our legal tribunals. In surveying the various changes in the organization and powers of the British courts of justice, produced successively by the Roman, Saxon, and Norman conquests, it is difficult to fix with precision the period when the judicial authority began to be divided between the State and the Church. Christianity had made some progress in Britain while yet remaining under the Roman power, but does not appear to have mingled itself materially with the governmental administration. The Saxon conquerors, who succeeded the Roman in the fifth century, brought in Paganism for about one hundred and fifty years; but it was extirpated about the close of the sixth century, by the vigor of St. Augustin, under the pontificate of Gregory the Great. ... Occasional interments in places of worship, or their immediate vicinity, had indeed been made by the early Christians as far back as the reign of Constantine; but it was not until after the pontificate of Gregory, and the rapid increase, under his successors, of the temporal power of the Church, that burial grounds were generally attached to places of worship, and subjected by formal consecration to ecclesiastical authority.

The juridical history of the Church in England, from the sixth century to the thirteenth, exhibits its steady, and all but uninterrupted progress, in obtaining the exclusive temporal, judicial cognizance of all matters touching the ecclesiastical edifices and their appendages, and especially their places of burial. During that period, the office of sepulture, originally only a secular duty, came to be regarded as a spiritual function-so much so, that the secular courts, in cases as early as the 20th and 21st Edward L, cited in 2 Inst. 363, in determining whether or not a building was a church, inquired only whether it had sacraments and sepulture.

It is generally stated, that burial in churchyards was introduced into England by Cuthbert, Archbishop of Canterbury, in the year 750. The form of their consecration is even yet preserved, in some of its essential features, by the Established Church. The invocation, as given by Burns in his *Ecclesiastical Law*, 1 vol. p. 334, after declaring that the duty has been taught by God, "through his holy servants, in all ages, to assign places where the bodies of the saints may rest in peace and be preserved from all indignities," asks the Divine acceptance "of the charitable work, in separating the portion of ground to that good purpose." ...

During the early portion of the Anglo-Saxon period, the power of the clergy over the dead was kept in check, by uniting the lay with the clerical order in the ecclesiastical tribunals; but their jurisdictions were separated soon after the Norman conquest; and the effect upon the dead is plainly discernible. The exclusive power of the ecclesiastics denominated, in legal phrase, "ecclesiastical cognizance," became not only executive, but judicial. It was executive, in taking the body into their actual, corporeal possession, and practically guarding its repose in their consecrated grounds; and it was judicial, as well in deciding all controversies involving the possession or the use of holy places, or the pecuniary emoluments which they yielded, as in a broader field, in adjudicating who should be allowed to lie in consecrated earth-and, in fact, who should be allowed to be interred at all. ...

An attentive examination of the progress and the proceedings of the Ecclesiastical tribunals, will show that the ancient civil courts of England gradually lost their original, legitimate authority, over places of interment, as private property, and their proper and necessary control over the repose of the dead. The clergy, monopolizing the judicial power over the subject, burial was committed solely to ecclesiastical cognizance; while the secular courts, stripped of all authority over the dead, were left to confine themselves to the protection of the monument and other external emblems of grief erected by the living. But these they guarded with singular solicitude. The tomb-stone, the armorial escutcheons—even the coat and pennons, and ensigns of honor, whether attached to the church edifice or elsewhere were raised, as "heir-looms," to the dignity of inheritable estates, and descended from heir to heir, who could hold even the parson liable for taking them down or defacing them.

The reverent regard of the common law for these memorials is curiously manifested by Coke in the *Third Institute*, p. 203, where he expatiates upon a monumental stone, in his time more than four hundred years old, inscribed with the name of a Jewish rabbi, and inlaid in the ancient wall of London; as if to intimate, that the law would protect from injury that venerable piece of antiquity.

But at this point the courts of the common law stopped; and held, in deference to the ecclesiastical tribunals, that the heir could maintain no civil action for indecently, or even impiously, disturbing the remains of his buried ancestor, declaring the only remedy to belong to the parson, who, having the freehold of the soil, could maintain trespass against such as should dig or disturb it. The line of legal demarkation, established in this subject between the ecclesiastical and the common law courts, is thus defined by Coke: "If a nobleman, knight, esquire, etc., be buried in a church, and have his coat-armour and pennons, with his armes, and such other insigns of honour as belong to his degree or order, set up in the church; or if a grave-stone be laid or made for memory of him, albeit the freehold of the church be in the parson, and that these be annexed to the freehold, yet cannot the parson, or any, take or deface them, but he is subject to an action to the heire and his heirs, in the honour and memory of whose ancestor they were set up." (1st Inst.. 4,18b.) In the *Third Institute*, page 203, he asserts the authority of the church, as follows: "It is to be observed;" says he, "that in every sepulchre that hath a monument, two things are to be considered: viz., the monument, and the sepulchre, or buriall of the dead. The burial of the cadaver, that is, *caro data cermibus* (flesh given to worms), is *nullius in bonis*, and belongs to ecclesiastical cognizance; but as to the monument, action is given, as hath been said, at the common law for the defacing thereof."

With all proper respect for the legal learning of this celebrated Judge, we may possibly question both the wisdom and the etymology of this verbal conceit, this fantastic and imaginary gift, or outstanding grant to the worms. In the English jurisprudence, a corpse was not given or granted to the worms, but it was taken and appropriated by the Church. In Latin, it was a "*cadaver*," only because it was something fallen (a *cadendo*), even as the remains of fallen cities, in the letter of Sulpicius to Cicero (Lit. Faro. 7), are denominated "*cadavera oppidorum.*"

The learned lexicographers and philologists, Martinius and the elder Vossius, both of them contemporaries of Coke, wholly dissent from his whimsical derivation. Martinius dervives "*cadaver*" from "*cadendo, quia stare non potest*," *Lexicon Philologicum Martinii*, 1720; while Vossius unequivocally reproves the derivation in question, as an act of pleasant, but inflated trifiing. "*Suavite nugantur*," says he, "*qui cadaver conflatum aiunt, ex tribus vocibus, caro data vermibus.*" *Etymologicon Linguce Latinae*, Amsterdam, 1662. And yet this inflated Latin trifle, the offspring only of Coke's characteristic and inordinate love of epigram, has come down through the last three hundred years, copied and recopied, and repeated again and again by judges and legal writers, until it has imparted its tincture to the law of the dead, throughout every portion of the earth which listens to the English tongue.

But even the dictum itself, if closely examined, will not be found to assert, that no individual can have any legal interest in a corpse. It does not at all assert that the corpse, but only that the "buriall," is "*nullius in bonis*" and this assertion was legally true in England, where it was made, for the peculiar reason above stated—that the temporal office of burial had been brought within the exclusive legal cognizance of the Church, who could and would enforce all necessary rules for the proper sepulture and custody of the body, thus rendering any individual action in that respect unnecessary. The power thus exercised by the ecclesiastical tribunals was not spiritual in its nature, but merely temporal and juridical. It was a legal, secular authority, which they had gradually abstracted from the ancient civil courts, to which it had originally belonged; and that authority, from the very necessity of the case, in the State of New-York, must now be vested in its secular courts of justice.

The necessity for the exercise of such authority, not only over the burial, but over the corpse itself, by some competent legal tribunal, will appear at once, if we consider the consequences of its abandonment. If no one had any legal interest in a corpse, no one can legally determine the place of its interment, nor exclusively retain its custody. A son will have no legal right to retain the remains of his father, nor a husband of his wife, one moment after death. A father cannot legally protect his daughter's remains from exposure or insult, however indecent or outrageous, nor demand their reburial, if dragged from the grave. The dead, deprived of the legal guardianship, however partial, which the Church so long had thrown around them, and left unprotected by the civil courts, will become, in law, nothing but public nuisances; and their custody will belong only to the guardians of the public health, to remove and destroy the offending matter, with all practicable economy and dispatch. The criminal courts may punish the body-snatcher who invades the grave, but will be powerless to restore its contents. The honored remains of Alexander Hamilton, reposing in our oldest church-yard, wrapped in the very bosom of the community, built up to greatness by his consummate genius, will become *"nullius in bonis,"* and belong to that community no longer. The sacred relics of Mount Vernon may be torn from their "mansion of rest," and exhibited for hire in our very midst, and no civil authority can remand them to the tomb.

Applied to the case now under examination, the doctrine will deny to a daughter, whose filial love had followed her father to the grave, and reared a monument to his memory, all right to ask that his remains, uprooted by the City authorities, and cast into the street, shall again be decently interred. In England, with judicial functions divided between the State and the Church, the secular tribunals would protect the monument, the winding-sheet, the grave-clothes, even down to the ribbon (now extant) which tied the queue; but the Church would guard the skull and bones. Which of these relics best deserves the legal protection of the Supreme Court of law and equity of the State of New-York? Does not every dictate of common sense and common decency demand a common protection for the grave and all its contents and appendages? Is a tribunal like this under any legal necessity for measuring its judicial and remedial action by the narrow rule and fettered movement of the common law of England, crippled by ecclesiastical interference? But may it not put forth its larger powers and nobler attributes as a court of enlightened equity and reason?

The due protection of the dead engaged the earnest attention of the great lawgivers of the polished nations of antiquity. The laws of the Greeks carefully guarded the private rights of individuals in their places of interment; and a similar spirit shines forth in the clear intelligence and high refinement of the Roman jurisprudence. In the *Digest of the Civil Law*, pl. 46, tit. 12, we find the beneficent and salutary provision which gave a civil remedy, by the *"Sepulchri violati actio,"* to everyone interested, for any wanton disturbance of a sepulchre; and where *"Ulpian, praetor, ait--Cujus dolo malo sepulchrum violatum esse dicetur in eum in factum judicium dabo ut ei ad quem pertineat, quanti ob eam rem aequum videbitur, condamnetur. Si nemo erit ad quem pertineat, sive agere nolet; quicunque agere volet, ei centum aureorum actionem dabo;"*— a sepulchre being comprehensively defined by another clause to be, any place in which the body or bones of a man were deposited—*"Sepulchrum est, ubi corpus ossave hominis, condita sunt."*—(Dig. pl. 7, § 2.) Nor does the dictum of Coke, now under consideration, assert—for, historically, it would not be true—that no individual right to protect the repose of the dead had ever existed under the common law of England. So far from that, we see in the provision above extracted from the Digest, that the individual right did exist during the greater part of the four hundred years when England, then called Britain, formed part of the Roman empire. In the six centuries of Saxon rule which succeeded, as is forcibly observed by Chancellor Kent, "the Roman civilization, laws, usages, arts, and manners, must have left a deep impression, and have become intermixed and incorporated with Saxon laws and usages, and constituted the body of the ancient English common law." (1 Kent Comm. 547.)

The provision in question had been introduced into the Roman jurisprudence long before its systematic codification by Justinian. It bears on its face the name of Ulpian, the great

Roman jurist, who not only lived as early as the second century of the Christian era, but actually assisted (as Selden states in his Appendix to Fleta), in the judicial administration of Britain. He was the contemporary, and doubtless the personal and professional friend, of the celebrated praetorian-prefect, Papinian—himself the most distinguished lawyer of his age, and chief administrator, in the year 210, of the Roman government at York. Selden glowingly depicts the judicial illumination of that early British age, as flourishing alike under the "*Jus Caesareum,*" the imperial law, and its able administration by those two most accomplished and illustrious Romans, "*viri peritissimi, illustrissimique e Romanis.*" (Selden App. to Fleta, 478.)

Nor is there any reason to believe that the Romanized British, when released, in the fifth century, from their political allegiance to the Empire, abandoned the civilization, or abrogated the laws or usages which they had so long enjoyed; still less that they would seek or desire, in any way, to withdraw from their sepulchres and graves the protection which those laws had so fully secured. There is not a shadow of historical evidence that, under the Saxon invaders, who succeeded the Roman governors, any less respect was shown for the buried dead. On the contrary, it is distinctly shown by the Scandinavian historians, that these partially civilized Saxons had been specially taught to reverence their places of burial by their great leader, Odin, the father of Scandinavian historians, distinguished for his eloquence and persuasive power, and especially commemorated as being the first to introduce the custom of erecting grave-stones in honor of the dead.

In the dim and flickering light by which we trace the laws of these long-buried ages, the fact is significant and instructive, that of the several founders of the seven little Saxon kingdoms constituting the Heptarchy, nearly all deduced their descent, more or less remotely, from Odin himself. Hengist, who led the Saxon forces into Britain, and became first King of Kent, claimed, with peculiar pride, to be his great-grandson-rendering it quite improbable that during the rule of himself or his race, or that of his kindred sovereigns, which lasted from three to four hundred years, Saxonized Britain learned to abandon its buried ancestors, or hold them, in law, "*nullius in bonis.*"

Nor do we find in the occasional inroads of the Danes, temporarily disturbing the Saxon governments of England, any evidence that they obliterated, in the slightest degree, the reverential usages in the matter of the dead, coming down from Odin. The early laws of that rude people, carefully collected in the twelfth century by the learned antiquary Saxo Grammaticus, speak with abhorrence of those who insult the ashes of the dead, not only denouncing death upon the "*alieni corruptor cineris,*" but condemning the body of the offender to lie forever unburied and unhonored. (Law of Frotho, Saxo Grammaticus, Lib. 5.).

The law of the Franks, near neighbors of the Saxons, cited by Montesquieu (Spirit of Laws, Lib. 30, ch. 19), not only banished from society him who dug up a dead body for plunder, but prohibited anyone from relieving his wants, until the relatives of the deceased consented to his readmission thus legally and distinctly recognizing the peculiar and personal interest of the relatives in the remains.

We are, indeed, so surrounded by proof of the universal reverence of the Gothic nations for their buried ancestors, that we are justified in assuming it to be historically certain, that the barbarous idea of leaving the dead without legal protection never originated with them; that the enlightened provision of the Roman jurisprudence, which protected in Britain the individual right to their undisturbed repose, not only remained unaffected by the Saxon invasion, but was implanted by that event still more deeply in the ancient common law of England; and that it must have been vigorously enforced, as well by the earliest secular courts of the Anglo-Saxons, as in that transition period of their judicial history, when the sheriff and the bishop, sitting side by side on the bench, united the lay and the ecclesiastical authority in a single tribunal.

Nor was the right to protect the dead eradicated by the Norman conquest. It is true that the ecclesiastics who poured into England with the Conqueror exerted themselves actively and indefatigably to monopolize for the Church the temporal authority over the dead; but that by no means proves that they were left unprotected. On the contrary, it was a concentration in the ecclesiastical body, of every light which any individual had previously possessed to secure their repose. The individual right was not extinguished; it was only absorbed by the Church.

The ecclesiastical element was not eradicated from the framework of the English government, either by the Reformation, or the Act of Parliament establishing the Protestant Succession; but in the portion of the world which we inhabit, the work has been more thoroughly accomplished. The English emigration to America—the most momentous event in political history—commenced in the very age when Chief Justice Coke was proclaiming, as a legal dogma, the exclusive authority of the Church over the dead. The liberty-loving, God-fearing Englishmen, who founded these American States, had seen enough and felt enough of "ecclesiastical cognizance," and they crossed a broad and stormy ocean to a new and untrodden continent, to escape from it for ever. ...

It certainly is not for us to interfere with the ecclesiastical law of England, nor needlessly to criticize its claims to the respect of the people whom it binds. We only ask to banish its maxims, doctrines, and practices from our jurisprudence, and to prevent them from guiding, in any way, our judicial action. The fungous excrescence which required centuries for its growth, may need an efflux of ages to remove. Burial, in the British Islands, may possibly remain, for many generations, subject exclusively to "ecclesiastical cognizance;" but in the new, transplanted England of the Western continent, the dead will find protection, if at all, in the secular tribunals, succeeding, by fair inheritance, to the primeval authority of the ancient, uncorrupted common law.

It is gratifying, however, to perceive that, even in the English courts, traces are becoming discernible of a disposition to recognize the ancient right of burial at common law. In the year 1820, a legal claim was made by one Gilbert, to bury, in a London church-yard, the body of his wife in an iron coffin; but it was resisted by the Churchwardens, Buzzard and Boyer, on the ground that it would injuriously prolong the period when the natural decay of the body, and of a wooden inclosure, would make room in the grave for another occupant. An application had been previously made in the same matter, to the King's Bench, for a mandamus, (reported in 2 Bam. &: Ald., 806) on which occasion the distinguished counsel, Mr. Scarlett and Mr. Chitty, claimed that the right of interment existed at common law. In refusing the application, Chief Justice Abbott said: "It may be admitted, for the purpose of the present question, that the right of sepulture is a common law right, but I am of opinion, that the mode of burial is a subject of ecclesiastical cognizance." Mr. Justice Holroyd, after duly reproducing Coke's *"caro data vermibus,"* declared, that "burial is as much a matter of ecclesiastical cognizance, as the prayers that are to be used, or the ceremonies that are to be performed at the funeral."

London, was thereupon carried into the Ecclesiastical Court, then adorned by the learning and talents of Sir William Scott (since Lord Stowell). In the very elaborate and eloquent opinion delivered by the accomplished judge on that occasion (reported in 3 Phillmore, p. 335), he reviews the whole history of burial, from the remotest antiquity, philosophically tracing the progress of interment through the heathen and the Christian ages. Drawing a distinction between the coffined and uncoffined funerals of early times, he admits that many authoritative writers assert the right of a parishioner to be buried in his own parish church-yard; but he denies that it necessarily includes the right to bury a "trunk or chest," with the body. "The right," says he, "strictly taken, is, to be returned to the parent earth for dissolution, and to be carried there in a decent and inoffensive manner." The honest sense and feeling of the judge were evidently struggling with the ecclesiastical law and usage, but he came to the conclusion, that no mode of burial could be permitted which would prolong the natural decay of the body, or needlessly preserve its identity—that the lapse of a single generation is practically sufficient for mingling human remains with the earth, and destroying their identity—that the dead having no legal right to crowd the living, each buried generation must give way to its successor-and that, therefore, an iron coffin, which would unduly and. unlawfully prolong the period for identifying the remains, was ecclesiastically inadmissible—unless an extra fee were paid to the church.

It will be perceived, by the proofs in the case now under examination, that the remains of the exhumed body are identified beyond doubt or question. The skeleton of the "posthumous man" is now legally "standing in court," distinctly individualized, with his daughter, next and nearest of kin; at his side, to ask, that the tribunal whose order for widening the street ejected him from the grave, will also direct his decent re-interment.

It was the pride of Diogenes, and his disciples of the ancient school of Cynics, to regard burial with contempt, and to hold it utterly unimportant whether their bodies should be burned by fire, or devoured by beasts, birds, or worms; and a French philosopher of modern days, in a kindred spirit, descants upon the "glorious nothingness" of the grave, and that "nameless thing," a dead body. The secular jurisprudence of France holds it in higher and better regard. In the interesting case reported in *Merlin's Répertoire*, Tit. *Sépulture*, where a large tract of land near Marseilles had necessarily been taken for the burial of several thousand bodies, after the great plague of 1720, it was adjudicated by the secular court, that the land should not be profaned by culture even of its surface, until the buried dead had mouldered into dust. The eloquent *plaidoyer* [advocacy] of the *acovat-général* upon that occasion dwells with emphasis on the veneration which all nations, in all ages, have shown for the grave-adding, however, with some little tinge of national irreverence, "C'est une *vénération toujours révocable!* et toujours subordonne au bien public." [This is a revocable veneration! and always subject to the public good.]

In portions of Europe, during the semi-barbarous state of society in the middle ages, the law permitted a creditor to seize the dead body of his debtor; and in ancient Egypt, a son could borrow money by hypothecating his father's corpse; but no evidence appears to exist, in modern jurisprudence, of a legal right to convert a dead body to any purpose of pecuniary profit.

It will be seen that much of the apparent difficulty of this subject arises from a false and needless assumption, in holding that nothing is property that has not a pecuniary value. The real question is not of the disposable, marketable value of a corpse, or its remains, as an article of traffic, but it is of the sacred and inherent right to its custody, in order decently to bury it, and secure its undisturbed repose. The dogma of the English ecclesiastical law, that a child has no such claim, no such exclusive power, no peculiar interest in the dead body of its parent, is so utterly inconsistent with every enlightened perception of personal right, so inexpressibly repulsive to every proper moral sense, that its adoption would be an eternal disgrace to American jurisprudence. The establishment of a right so sacred and precious, ought not to need any judicial precedent. Our courts of justice should place it, at once, where it should fundamentally rest for ever, on the deepest and most unerring instincts of human nature; and hold it to be a self-evident right of humanity, entitled to legal protection, by every consideration of feeling, decency, and Christian duty. The world does not contain a tribunal that would punish a son who should resist, even unto death, any attempt to mutilate his father's corpse, or tear it from the grave for sale or dissection; but where would he find the legal right to resist, except in his peculiar and exclusive interest in the body?

The right to the repose of the grave necessarily implies the right to its exclusive possession. The doctrine of the legal right to open a grave in a cemetery; after a certain lapse of time, to receive another tenant, however it may be sanctioned by custom in the English churchyards, or by Continental usage at Pere-La-Chaise, and elsewhere, will hardly become acceptable to the American mind; still less the Italian practice of hastening the decomposition of the dead by corrosive elements. The right to the individuality of a grave, if it exist at all, evidently must continue so long as the remains of the occupant can be identified-and the means of identifying can only be secured and preserved by separate burial. The due and decent preservation of human remains by separate burial, is pre-eminently due to Christian civilization, which, bringing in the coffin and the sarcophagus, superseded the custom of burning, and "gave," in Lord Stowell's vivid phrase, "final extinction to the sepulchral bonfires."

The monument erected over a grave is expressly intended to individualize its occupant; but it would be a most singular mockery to protect the monument, and leave the grave itself to be filled with other tenants. The church, in the present case, as keeper of the cemetery, by permitting the erection of the monument, virtually consented that it should stand, to perform its appropriate, individualizing office. Such a monument could not be disturbed in England, even by the Established Church: for the daughter, as the lawful heir, could at once arrest the sacrilege, or obtain an ample indemnity. By every principle of enlightened reason, she is equally entitled, as next of kin, to protect her father's remains. No one will deny, that the moral, if not the legal duty of re-burying them, first devolves on her, and it is because their ejection from the grave thus burthens her with the duty, that she is plainly entitled to claim, that the expense shall be defrayed by the fund awarded to indemnify the parties damaged. The father, identified by the monument, had lain separate for more than fifty years. The church could not have lawfully mingled any other remains with his, nor can the daughter now be required, either in justice or decency, to destroy their individuality, still less to permit them to be cast into any common receptacle of undistinguishable rubbish.

To throw a dead body into a river was held, by the Supreme Court of Maine, to be an indictable offence (1 Greenl. 226), and it would not be less indecent and criminal to empty into the streets of the city, or into the waters which wash its shores, the bones and ashes of an ancient cemetery. The criminality of the act, as of any other violation of the grave, is not, as is erroneously asserted, in invading the imaginary rights of the dead, but in outraging the Christian sensibilities of the living. The "*conditio sepulturae*," [the condition of burial] in the expressive language of St. Augustine is, "*magis vivorum solatia quam subsidia mortuorum*." [comforts of the living rather than the dead.] It was the special punishment, not of the buried dead, but of the living sinners of unhappy Jerusalem, that spread the bones of her inhabitants "before the sun, and the moon, and all the host of heaven." It is not the buried Moses Sherwood, but his living daughter, Maria. Smith, who now claims the right to his quiet repose, in the grave where she laid him. That repose has been disturbed, under the forms of law, against her will. As the only reparation the case admits, she asks for the re-interment of the remains in a separate grave, to be individualized by the monument which, as her lawful "heir-loom," the law preserves, from generation to generation, for that very purpose. The cemetery which contained them was expressly taken by the church, to perform this very office of sepulture. As a cemetery, its use was a charitable as well as a religious use—a trust which this court, in the exercise of its undisputed equity powers, and wholly irrespective of any assumption or resumption of authority ever possessed by any ecclesiastical body, may now duly control and regulate.

The claimant, after fifty years' occupancy by her father of the grave, may rightfully be held to be one of the beneficiaries, for whom the charitable use was created, and for whose benefit and protection it should be carried into full effect. The fund representing a part of the very land thus devoted to the charitable use, is now in possession of the court, its legitimate guardian, and subject to its equitable discretion.

The Referee is therefore of opinion, that it is proper to retain from the fund a sum sufficient to cover the expense of re-interring the remains of Moses Sherwood in a separate grave, in such reasonable locality as the said Maria Smith might select.

The proofs taken on the reference shows, that eighty graves, in all, were disturbed by the widening of the street,—but no claim for damages, or for re-interment, has been presented, except in the case above stated. The remains of the bodies in the other graves have been temporarily deposited under the church in Beekman street, to be properly re-interred elsewhere, in case of its sale.

The Referee respectfully submits the following conclusions as justly deducible, from the fact, that no ecclesiastical element exists in the jurisprudence of this State, or in the frame-work of its government:

1. That neither a corpse, nor its burial, is legally subject, in any way, to ecclesiastical cognizance, nor to sacerdotal power of any kind.

2. That the right to bury a corpse and to preserve its remains, is a legal right, which the courts of law will recognize and protect.

3. That such right, in the absence of any testamentary disposition, belongs exclusively to the next of kin.

4. That the right to protect the remains includes the right to preserve them by separate burial, to select the place of sepulture, and to change it at pleasure.

5. That if the place of burial be taken for public use, the next of kin may claim to be indemnified for the expense of removing and suitably re-interring their remains.

[The case was brought to hearing on this Report, before the Special Term of the Supreme Court in April, 1856. After hearing counsel, the Court confirmed the Report in all respects, directing payment for the vaults, as valued by the Referee, awarding $100 to Maria Smith, as next of kin of Moses Sherwood, directing her with that sum to re-inter his remains, and erect at his grave the monument taken in widening the street, and declaring her entitled to the possession of the remains, and of the monument for that purpose. The order further directed the church to re-inter separately the remains found in any other of the graves whenever identified by the next of kin.]

NOTES

Following the widening of Beekman Street, the Trustees of the Brick Presbyterian Church were granted the authority to sell. The last sermon was preached there on May 25, 1856, and the new building in Murray Hill was dedicated on October 31, 1858. The congregation moved to 91st and Park Avenue in 1938, where it remains today.

Although the *Ruggles Report* is merely a referee's report to a trial court and has no formal precedential power, it remains a respected and highly cited authority in modern times. The most enduring legacy of the *Ruggles Report* is that it provided a strong justification for the assertion by the United States Supreme Court in *Beatty et al v. Kurtz et al.* that U.S. courts of equity have authority over human remains. The Indiana Supreme Court's reliance on the Ruggles Report in *Renihan v. Wright*, 25 N.E. 822, 824 (Ind. 1890) is typical:

> The [*Ruggles Report*] contains a statement of the learned referee's investigation of the law of burial, and it is believed to be the most accurate and elaborate collection and statement of the law, upon that subject, yet published. ... As we have no division of power between the church and the state in this country, it follows that much of the power exercised by ecclesiastical tribunals in England is vested, of necessity, in the secular courts here charged with the general administration of the law. The necessity for the existence and exercise of such power must be apparent to all.

❖ ❖ ❖

CHAPTER 8

OVERVIEW OF
U.S. CEMETERY LAW

I think when it comes to the sort of essentials for a good death, a good funeral, essentials are a corpse, mourners, somebody to broker the changed relationship between the living and the dead, the peace between them, something to say a version of "behold, I show you a mystery." And then transport; some movement from here to there, we get them home again, we get them to the further shore, we get them to their grave, their tomb, their fire. Up into the tree we get them, if we live elsewhere, into the side of the mountain where the birds come and pick the bones clean and we describe the birds as holy. Its what we do. Humans, we've been doing it for 40,000 or 50,000 years. And the routine, the fashions change a little bit, the fundamental business is the same: a corpse, mourners, sacred text, transport. We move them.

Thomas Lynch, Poet and Undertaker
DEATH AND THE CIVIL WAR, directed by Ric Burns (2012)

Tomb of James Whitcomb Riley, Crown Hill Cemetery, Indianapolis, Indiana
Photo by Cass Pyatt

CHAPTER 8.1
OVERVIEW OF U.S. CEMETERY LAW
Tanya D. Marsh

English colonization of North America began with the establishment of Jamestown, Virginia in 1606 and quickly spread along the East Coast. Although there were important religious, social, and legal differences between the colonies, it is not surprising that the practices of the colonists were heavily rooted in the customs of seventeenth century English villages and English ecclesiastical law. However, there were several problems adapting English practices and laws to colonial America.

First, early colonists and pioneers died before churchyards could be established. This disrupted one of the fundamental assumptions of English practices—burial in the consecrated ground of a churchyard. The widespread burial of the dead outside of churchyards, originally by necessity and later by social evolution, highlighted the dearth of common law relating to human remains. English burials were presumptively in consecrated ground and therefore subject to ecclesiastical cognizance. That division of authority was ill-suited for the American experience.

Although many of the colonies had rules consistent with English ecclesiastical law, the states expressly refused to adopt it. The repudiation of ecclesiastical law, coupled with the widespread departure from burial in churchyards, left an enormous gap in early American law. Courts struggled to address disputes for which they had no common law precedent, and

169

mourned the loss of ecclesiastical precedent. As a New York chancery court judge complained in 1820: "Are the principles of natural law, and of Christian duty, to be left unheeded, and inoperative, because we have no ecclesiastical Courts recognized by law?"

State legislatures did not immediately fill this void with a statutory law of human remains. Instead, courts were forced to attempt to sift through the doctrines, principles, and values of English ecclesiastical and common law and determine which could be adapted for use in a country with greater cultural and religious diversity than England and, significantly, with no established church. The authority of state courts to create the U.S. common law of human remains was affirmed by the United States Supreme Court in 1829 in the landmark case *Beatty v. Kurtz*. That opinion also established the authority of U.S. courts of equity over human remains, particularly after interment.

An eminent domain action by the City of New York in 1856 provided an opportunity to better develop the law of cemeteries in the United States. Unsure of how to divide the award of damages between the Brick Presbyterian Church and the families that owned vaults disturbed by the widening of Beekman Street, the Surrogate's Court appointed New York attorney Samuel B. Ruggles to prepare a report on the common law of human remains. The resulting *Ruggles Report* articulates the fundamental principles of U.S. cemetery law and has been cited by countless courts in the past 160 years.

❖ ❖ ❖

America on the eve of the Civil War was a profoundly religious place. A place of deeply rooted and almost universally held assumptions and beliefs about the meaning of death and dying, about the nature of God and the afterlife, and about what constituted a good death and the right way to die.

One of the most striking differences between us in the twenty-first century and the inhabitants of the nineteenth century is our attitudes about death. Death was then very much a part of life and seen as something that needed to be thought about constantly in order to live well and ultimately to die well. This was very much a Christian approach to dying and the United States was overwhelming Christian at this time. Approximately four times as many people attended church every week as voted in the election of 1860. You could tell by watching how someone died what that life before had meant and what the eternal life beyond was likely to be like. An individual who was dying would die at home, this was very much a part of Victorian culture and defined a good death. Would be surrounded by loved ones, would indicate a readiness to die, a welcoming and embrace of salvation and Christian principles and then often last words for the loved ones surrounding the dying person. That was the idealized good death.

Drew Gilpin Faust
DEATH AND THE CIVIL WAR, directed by Ric Burns (2012)

Crown Hill Cemetery, Indianapolis, Indiana
Photo by Cass Pyatt

CHAPTER 8.2
CHANGING PERSPECTIVES ON THE DEAD
Daniel Gibson

A small knot of men stood above the grave. Downward they dug, like grave-robbers. By order of the Bishop of Lincoln they searched for the remains of John Wycliffe.

Wycliffe's remains rested in peace for forty-one years beside the River Avon. On May 4, 1451, however, the Church declared him a heretic. His translation of the Bible to English and distribution to the masses made him an enemy of the Church. His posthumous punishment? To be "ungraved" and burned—provided his body could be "discerned from the bodies of other faithful people."

So they dug him up, burned him up, and threw his ashes into the Avon. The Bishop of Lincoln, the Pope, and the other members of the Council of Constance never doubted they had doled out an appropriate punishment to the heretic John Wycliffe.

The burning of Wycliffe's body illustrates the traditional Christian European perspective on the dead—they exist in stasis between life and resurrection. In that mindset, the desecration of Wycliffe's remains was meant to punish Wycliffe himself, not his friends, family, and disciples. Such a punishment would make little sense to many of us today. Instead, we would presume that Wycliffe's loved ones could seek a remedy in tort law because of the infliction of emotional distress. The emphasis has shifted in our collective minds from protecting the corpse to protecting the survivors. This shift in thought is reflected in our changed law, policy, and funerary practices.

Traditional Christian European burial practices were rooted in doctrine that emphasized the importance of the condition and placement of remains in anticipation of the resurrection of the dead. As discussed in Chapter 5.6, bodies were often buried with their feet towards the east so they would face Jerusalem at the resurrection, where tradition says Jesus Christ will appear. The Church mandated burial in consecrated ground, and burials were almost always within the churchyard so the priest could lead his congregation at the resurrection. Particularly before the Reformation, burial in close proximity to the relics of a martyr or saint (inside the church building) was preferred because of the belief that the saints and martyrs interceded on behalf of the dead. Burial was a preparation for the coming life.

Particularly before the Reformation, Christians strongly believed that the physical condition of their remains was tied to the promise of eternal life. With that in mind, the last funeral rites and the method and location of burial was focused more on the interests of the dead than the living. One benefit to the living was the comfort of the social contract that all members of community would care for and respect the dead. The promise of a proper burial—our "tender regard for the dead"—was comfort to dying. A guarded grave brought peace while a desecrated grave brought sorrow in part because it represented a violation of the social contract.

English ecclesiastical law and U.S. common law reflect this belief, perhaps more literally than pre-Reformation Christians, who were comfortable with common graves and ossuaries. Justice Joseph Story's *Address at the Consecration of Mount Auburn* eloquently summarized:

> If there are any feelings of our nature, not bounded by earth, and yet stopping short of the skies, which are more strong and more universal than all others, they will be found in our solicitude as to the time and place and manner of our death; in the desire to die in the arms of our friends; to have the last sad offices to our remains performed by their affection; to repose in the land of our nativity; to be gathered to the sepulchres of our fathers. It is almost impossible for us to feel, nay, even to feign, indifference on such a subject.

Justice Story's opinion in *Beatty v. Kurtz* brought this belief into secular U.S. law. The Supreme Court undertook to protect "the sepulchres of the dead," "the feeling of religion," and "the sentiment of natural affection of the kindred and friends of the deceased" from violation. The Court defended the "repose of the ashes of the dead and the religious sensibilities of the living." Justice Story and the Court did so in a time where most Christians, and most Americans, still believed that the physical condition of human remains was related to resurrection. The orthodoxy of those beliefs had weakened since the Reformation, but they were still theologically and culturally relevant.

The Ruggles Report also reflected these tenets. The right of the next of kin to protect a grave was "self-evident" from "every consideration of feeling, decency, and Christian duty." Ruggles asserts that the common law rejected the "barbarous idea" of refusing to protect the dead. Instead, the English had long enjoyed the common law right to "undisturbed repose." Ruggles wrote that "[e]very dictate of common sense and decency" demanded such protection. Justice Story and Samuel Ruggles both illustrate the prevailing belief in the early-to-mid 19th century that the desecration of a grave or a corpse did not merely offend the living; it also injured the dead.

Therefore, the law's protection of the grave and the corpse was not primarily motivated by sanitary, economic, or psychological concerns but rather by moral and religious duty. As Story and Ruggles both recognized, the lack of an established church in the United States meant that the guardian of the dead must be found elsewhere—the courts of equity and the next of kin. But the shift in the identity of the protector of the dead did not change the emphasis from the interests of the dead to the concerns of the living.

Between the mid-19th century and the 21st century, that emphasis has changed in the United States—dramatically. Although the majority of Americans still self-identify as "Christians," a multitude of creeds have replaced religious homogeneity. The once ubiquitous belief that the physical condition of the remains was related to the promise of resurrection is no longer dominant. That does not, however, mean modern Americans no longer care about the physical condition of human remains. Indeed, arguably, modern Americans care more than any of our ancestors. The reason that we care, however, has changed, and that shift in religious belief and cultural practice and influenced the law.

Wilson v. Read signaled this cultural-legal shift. According to the *Wilson* court, burial of the dead "is a civil affair." Christian teaching and sound policy harmonize to command one thing: "the dead should be so buried that *the living may not suffer.*" Although it has always been true that Christians have sought to balance the protection of the dead and the interests of the living, modern Americans place far greater emphasis on the needs of the living, from the planning of the funeral through final disposition. U.S. cemetery law reflects these priorities.

Poet and funeral director Thomas Lynch sums up modern views in four words: "the dead don't care."

> Being a dead saint is no more worthwhile that being a dead philodendron or a dead angelfish. Living is the rub, and always has been… . Once dead, they let their relics do the legwork, because, as I was trying to tell the priest, the dead don't care.
>
> Only the living care.
>
> And I am sorry to be repeating myself, but this is the central fact of my business—that there is nothing, once you are dead, that can be done *to you* or *for you* or *with you* or *about you* that will do you any good or harm; that any damage or decency we do accurse to the living, to whom your death happens, if it really happens to anyone. The living have to live with it. You don't.

English common law assumes an established church. American common law assumes the opposite. For most of our nation's history, the prevailing culture has been dominated by English Protestant beliefs and practices, long after they constituted a majority of the population. Those beliefs and practices were reflected in the common law and the deliberations of legislatures. The prevailing culture of modern America is increasingly secular and diverse. Our statutory law is beginning to reflect this diversity, but the common law remains strongly rooted in a 17th century English Protestant worldview.

Most modern Americans would agree with Thomas Lynch—the dead don't care. This makes the "ungraving" of John Wycliffe seem primitive, foolish, or pointless. These changing perspectives on the dead have resulted in a disconnect between law and culture, which has created cognitive dissonance and frustrates attempts to understand or change the law.

❖   ❖   ❖

St. Paul's Chapel, New York City, New York
Photo by Tanya D. Marsh

CHAPTER 8.3
INTRA-MURAL BURIAL IN THE UNITED STATES
Stephen Wickes, SEPULTURE (1884)

["Intra-mural burial" refers to burial within the city limits.]

… The first settlers of America came with the traditions of the land of their fathers. They buried their dead in their midst, and their descendants do so still. …

[The cemetery of Trinity Church, in lower Manhattan, was described by Dr. Ackerly in 1822]:

"Trinity churchyard is on high ground, west of Broadway, and contains about two and a half acres. … The church was first built in 1698, and its graveyard has been receiving the dead from that time to the present—a period of 124 years. More persons are probably interred within its precincts than in any burying-ground in the city, and it is supposed to contain the remains of human beings almost equal in number to the present population of New York. A burial can scarcely take place without disturbing a previous one…" …

There were other graveyards and vaults in proximity to that of Trinity. The South Reformed Church having a space of 25,000 square feet in Garden street, which was narrow and confined; and Wall Street Church, covering with the building 20,000 square feet, nearly the whole of which was excavated for vaults, and an additional range constructed under the sidewalk.

Between Pine and Cedar streets were the burying grounds of the Associate Reformed and French Protestant Churches.

The Middle Dutch Church Cemetery was a considerable place of interment and appropriated to vaults; as also St. Paul's Church and the North Dutch Church, in Fulton street. St. Paul's was contiguous to Broadway. The monument now standing in it bear testimony to its being the resting place of large numbers of the dead. Nearly opposite to it was the cemetery of Brick Church which, in 1823 was entirely filled. Pascalis, in commenting upon these, and other burial places of which he makes "of less account," says "there is, as all know, in the slightest computation, ten acres or 500,000 square feet of ground in the city exclusively appropriated to interments in graves or vaults." ...

❖   ❖   ❖

Arlington National Cemetery, Arlington, Virginia
Photo by Tanya D. Marsh

CHAPTER 8.4

THE LAW OF BURIAL IN THE UNITED STATES

Percival Jackson, THE LAW OF CADAVERS (1950)

English ecclesiastical law not adopted here

In adopting the common law of England, our states fixed various dates as the genesis of the substantive common law in their jurisdictions. Some states which formed part of the original colonies took the years of their own settlement. Adopting the common law as it existed in 1607, the date of the founding of Jamestown, Virginia later could find no precedents therein concerning burial, since the English jurisdiction, as we have seen, was then exercised by the ecclesiastical courts. And since our institutions have been predicated upon objection to spiritual control of temporal affairs, it was natural that we should say that while adopting the common law of England in organizing our state governments, by the weight of authority we have never considered ourselves bound by the ecclesiastical decisions, many of which were inapplicable to our form of government.

> Ecclesiastical Law is not a part of the law of this State, nor are equitable rights to be determined by it; on the contrary, when a court of equity exercises its powers, it does so only upon equitable principles, irrespective of ecclesiastical or any other law. As was said in *Matter of Donn*: "When an ecclesiastical body assumes jurisdiction and control over a corpse, its acts are of a temporal and

juridical character and not in any sense spiritual; and, under our laws and institutions, when it attempts so to do it is acting outside of its proper jurisdiction and domain."

Temporal jurisdiction over sepulture
"The repudiation of the ecclesiastical law and of ecclesiastical courts by the American colonies left the temporal courts the sole protector of the dead and of the living in their dead."

Influence of English ecclesiastical law
But many flagrant civil injuries would be without remedy if only matters which were cognizable in the old courts of common law were subject to adjudication in our courts, for in England many matters purely civil in their nature were within the exclusive jurisdiction of the ecclesiastical courts. For example, cases arising out of the contract of marriage were originally deemed purely religious in character. Although in English practice the administration of certain branches of the law was committed to the chancery, the admiralty and spiritual courts and had fallen into settled courses, resulting in customary rules of conduct, it might well be said that these rules had become part of the common law and might be accepted as guides, to the extent applicable to our local situation and circumstances and not repugnant to our constitutions and to our laws.

While ecclesiastical law and canonical corporations here have been unknown in the sense in which they existed in medieval Europe, many of our early settlements were created about the parish church, with its accompanying graveyard. In New England, particularly, the English parish system found its way into the foundations of American government, and consequently some traces of canon law still are found in parts of New England. Early American burial was in the churchyard, and though always yielding to temporal sovereignty, through the colonial adherence to the equitable principles of the English common law, the commands of the church found their way into our law of burial.

Law of sepulture largely statutory
Before the enactment of general statutes authorizing and regulating cemetery corporations throughout the United States, the control of the churchyards was vested in the trustees of the respective religious societies controlling them, under the general or special acts under which they were organized. In rural communities church cemeteries were and are common, but right of burial therein in the United States is largely derivative of membership in the religious society rather than being a privilege of geographic location. We also have public burial grounds in this country, controlled by the municipality or other public authorities; and, as in England under the burial acts, the various states of the United States have authorized the organization of non-religious societies, profit and nonprofit making, for the acquisition and maintenance of private and public burial grounds, wholly separate and apart from those maintained by the churches and other religious societies. These societies are by statute authorized to regulate burial in their respective cemeteries with or without regard to religious practice or creed. The control of burial in the United States is now wholly secular, affected by ecclesiastical dictates only to the extent that a religious corporation owns the burial ground. The control of burial is affected similarly by

lay ownership of a public or private cemetery.

The consideration of the law of burial must now depend almost wholly upon the provision of statutes which supplement and, in a great measure, supersede both the common law and the equitable principles derived from practices and customs that are based upon the ecclesiastical tenets and regulations once exclusively controlling burial.

❖   ❖   ❖

CHAPTER 9

THE LEGAL STATUS
OF HUMAN REMAINS

Lafayette Cemetery #1, New Orleans, Louisiana
Photo by Tanya D. Marsh

CHAPTER 9.1
THE LEGAL STATUS OF HUMAN REMAINS
Tanya D. Marsh

In 1859, the Indiana Supreme Court declared: "we lay down the proposition, that the bodies of the dead belong to the surviving relations, in the order of inheritance, as property, and that they have the right to dispose of them as such, within restrictions analogous to those by which the disposition of other property may be regulated."

In 1868, the Supreme Judicial Court of Massachusetts held that "A dead body is not the subject of property, and after burial it becomes a part of the ground to which it has been committed, 'earth to earth, ashes to ashes, dust to dust.' The only action that can be brought for disinterring it is *trespass quare clausum*."

The Massachusetts court, in relying upon William Blackstone's statement in Commentaries on the Laws of England that "though the heir has a property in the monuments and escutcheons of his ancestors, yet he has none in their bodies or ashes..." held in accordance with the common law rule that human bodies are not property, before or after burial. In *Guthrie v. Weaver*, 1 Mo. App. 136, 141 (1876), the Missouri Court of Appeals explained the rule: "When a human body has been interred with the knowledge and consent of those who, up to that moment, may have owned the coffin and shroud, these articles are irrevocably consigned to earth, and all property in the purchasers of them is at an end. They become mere adjuncts to the more worthy object, the human body which they serve to inclose whilst it is resolved into the dust from whence it springs; with the coffined clay that they surround, 'they have said to corruption, thou art my father, and to the worm, thou art my sister and my mother.' They are no longer property, and their relations with the living are at an end. There can be no property in a corpse, and there is none in the shroud which surrounds it, when that corpse has been once committed to the tomb. Of the truth of these propositions we entertain no doubt."

Samuel B. Ruggles criticizes the reasoning of Lord Coke and William Blackstone in his report, arguing that Lord Coke mischaracterized the Latin translations of Roman legal principles upon which he relied. However, Roman law is generally consistent with the idea that human remains are not property. Ulpian wrote that under Roman law, the creator of life, God, owns the human body and man is simply the *administrator et custos*.

❖ ❖ ❖

Glasnevin Cemetery, Dublin, Ireland
Photo by Tanya D. Marsh

CHAPTER 9.2

REPLEVIN & LARCENY

Sidney Perley, MORTUARY LAW (1898)

Replevin

There is no property nor right of property in a coffin or shroud after burial sufficient to support an action of replevin. So that proceeding cannot be used to recover a coffin and its contents, especially when such contents are a corpse. Articles after burial are a portion of the earth itself, in the eye of the law, whether they have begun to decay or not, provided they are deposited in the ground with the consent of those who had any pecuniary interest in them, and for the purpose of interment. They are no longer articles of merchandise, nor the property of those who furnished them. If replevin would lie in such cases, how many petty disputes would arise compelling the tomb to be unearthed, and all the sacredness surrounding our friends' remains and their last resting place to be at the mercilessness of anyone who would swear that he was entitled to the possession of a shroud, or of some petty article buried with the body. The question of ownership could not be tried and determined until the desecration was complete. Such things must not be. The case of *Guthrie v. Weaver*, 1 Mo. App. 136 (1876), was one where a sheriff, being possessed of a replevin writ authorizing him to take a certain coffin, opened the grave, and took the coffin with the remains therein, to hold the same until the question of the title to the coffin—and body too, for that matter—should be determined in the courts of law.

The court used exceedingly strong language against such a practice, saying that "no civilized community would endure such a rule of law as this."

Larceny

A corpse cannot be stolen at common law, as it is not property; but articles buried with it, which were merchandise before the interment, are also subjects of larceny after burial. These articles are the coffin, grave clothes, etc. In an indictment therefor they should be alleged to be the property of the person who furnished them and buried the deceased.

It is larceny to take articles of dress from the body of a drowned man with the intention of stealing them; and in such a case the articles may be alleged in the indictment to be the property of the administrator of the estate of the deceased, though no administrator has been appointed. It is also a misdemeanor at common law to attempt to commit such larceny.

❖　❖　❖

Crown Hill Cemetery, Indianapolis, Indiana
Photo by Tanya D. Marsh

CHAPTER 9.3
BOGERT V. THE CITY OF INDIANAPOLIS
Supreme Court of Indiana
13 Ind. 134 (1859)

Suit by the city of Indianapolis against Charles Bogert, charging him with a violation of the cemetery ordinance. The only complaint filed in the case, before the mayor, was the affidavit of one Garrison W. Allred, that said Bogert did violate the ordinance in question, by entering a certain cemetery in said city, and interring therein a dead body.

A motion to dismiss for want of a sufficient cause of action, was denied.

There was judgment before the mayor against Bogert.

In the Common Pleas, motions to dismiss, &c., were again overruled, and the judgment of the mayor was affirmed.

Without passing upon the sufficiency of the causes of action, we proceed at once to the main questions in the suit, viz., the validity of the ordinance under which it is claimed that the suit is instituted, and can be maintained.

The city charter provides that the city council shall have power "to establish cemeteries or burial places, within or without said city, and to provide for the sanctity of the dead."

The question in the case is, what power does this provision of the charter confer upon the city council.

The second clause of the provision, to-wit, "to provide for the sanctity of the dead," may be laid out of the case. It has no reference to the subject-matter of this suit. It does not involve the questions, who shall bury the dead? and in which cemetery shall they be laid? The council may pass ordinances to punish the unauthorized disturbance of their repose, and the desecration of their resting places, no matter by whom or where, within the city limits, they were buried.

The question is, then, what power is conferred by these words, viz., "to establish cemeteries or burial places within or without such city."

It will be observed that the power conferred is alike to act under the grant within or without the city. What can be done in the premises within the city, can be done without the city.

Now, two different meanings are put upon the words above quoted from the city charter. Bogert contends that the words "to establish cemeteries," means to purchase, or receive by way of donation, grounds for public city cemeteries, and to devote them to that use, as the public necessity or convenience may demand.

The city council contend that the meaning is, that the council may seize upon existing private burying grounds, make them public, and exclude the proprietors from their management. In other words, that to establish means to assume the control of that which is established.

If this be the true interpretation, then, as the city may act without or within the city, it seems to have been intended that the city council should assume the control of all the cemeteries in the county, and place them in charge of the city sexton. This, surely, the city could not do; but the city could purchase, or receive by way of donation, a tract of land without the city, and devote it to the use of the dead, and put it in the care of an agent or officer, and time will render it necessary that this be done.

Again; such a construction places the charter in conflict with the general laws of the state, while a more limited construction leaves it in harmony with them. Those laws authorize any individuals to unite themselves together for the purpose of receiving donations of lands, or purchasing the same, for cemeteries …

Now, it is not uncommon for religious and charitable societies to procure cemetery grounds for their special use. We know, historically, that close beside, or more remote from the church, or the synagogue, has usually been the consecrated churchyard, in which rested the deceased members and their children. The power claimed by the city council would entitle them to invade the privacy of these sacred inclosures, and subject burials in them to the control of the city sexton; for by the ordinance enacted, no person can enter to bury, but by his permission, to be obtained only by paying him the price of digging a grave; and then the body must, by $7, be deposited in the place designated by him, thus enabling him to scatter, in different parts of the ground, the members of the same family.

The incorrectness of the meaning claimed by the city council, for the provision of the charter in question may be further illustrated by a reference to other provisions. For example, the charter authorizes the council to establish gas works. Would it be pretended that, therefore, the council was authorized to seize the gas works already erected by a private company?

We conclude, then, that the city charter does not empower the city council to subject to the control of the city sexton, cemeteries other than those belonging to the city.

And if it did, a grave question would arise as to the validity, itself of so much of the charter. This is a point not necessary here to be decided, and we are not, therefore, in what we say upon it, speaking for the Court. But we lay down the proposition, that the bodies of the dead belong to the surviving relations, in the order of inheritance, as property, and that they have the right to dispose of them as such, within restrictions analogous to those by which the disposition of other property may be regulated. They cannot be permitted to create a nuisance by them. Hence, a by-law might be reasonable, where population was dense, requiring those buried to be sunk to a certain depth, or to be buried outside of where population was, or was likely to become dense, and within a reasonable time after death, &c.; but we doubt if the burial of the dead can, as a general proposition, be taken out of the hands of the relatives thereof, they being able and willing to bury the same.

Having ascertained by the law governing the case, we give its facts, as presented by the record, on which the law is to be applied.

It is agreed by the parties that the following are the facts in the case:

Union Cemetery in the city of Indianapolis, was laid off into lots, about twenty years ago, by a company of private individuals, who were, at the time, the owners of the ground.

The lots have been sold, and deeded in fee simple, to private individuals, by the original owners.

Henry Hobner was the owner of one of said lots, and, in May, 1859, employed Weaver and Williams, undertakers, to bury a deceased child of his therein.

Pursuant to said employment, Weaver and Williams directed Charles Bogert to dig the grave in said lot, for the burial of said child, and he proceeded to execute the work by virtue, alone, of such direction.

For that act, he was sued by the city, and judgment given against him, under the ordinance which has been previously noted.

The proprietors have never surrendered the Union Cemetery to the city.

Henry Hobner had a right to bury his own child in his own lot, being in limits where burial was allowed, without purchasing the consent of anybody.

Since the foregoing opinion was written, an additional brief has been filed by the city, raising the question of jurisdiction, but, under the circumstances, we shall not examine it.

The judgment is reversed with costs. Cause remanded.

❖ ❖ ❖

King's Chapel Burying Ground, Boston, Massachusetts
Photo by Tanya D. Marsh

CHAPTER 9.4

THOMAS F. MEAGHER V. JAMES DRISCOLL

Supreme Judicial Court of Massachusetts, 99 Mass. 281 (1868)

A grantee who has buried the remains of his child in a lot in a cemetery, of which he holds possession under a deed from the proprietor which sets forth that such grantee is entitled to the lot, habendum to him and his heirs and assigns, to his and their use as a place of burial for the dead, may maintain an action of tort in the nature of trespass *quare clausum fregit* against the superintendent of the cemetery for disinterring and removing the remains therefrom, although the cemetery has never been licensed under the Gen. Sts. c. 28, § 5, for purposes of burial, and although the plaintiff's deed is on condition that the lot shall not be transferred without consent of the proprietor, and shall be subject to his regulations in the care and management of the cemetery; and in measuring damages the jury may take into consideration the injury of the plaintiff's feelings, if it appears that the defendant acted in wilful disregard or careless ignorance of the plaintiff's rights.

TORT in the nature of trespass *quare clausum fregit* for the removal of the remains of the plaintiff's deceased child from Lot No. 4 in Holyhood Cemetery in Brookline, on September 23, 1865. Answer, that the plaintiff had forfeited any right of burial which he ever had in that lot, and that the defendant removed the remains and buried them elsewhere in the discharge of his duty as superintendent of the cemetery.

At the trial in the superior court, before Ames, C. J., there was evidence that in December 1863 the plaintiff selected the lot on account of its neighborhood to a place where the remains of his father were buried; paid to the defendant (who was in charge of the cemetery as superintendent) five dollars towards the purchase of it, which was all that he was required to pay at that time; and soon afterwards buried there the remains of the child. The evidence was conflicting as to the length of credit given for the balance of twenty-five dollars due on the price of the lot; the plaintiff testifying that he was told to pay as soon as he could do so conveniently, and the defendant testifying that the sale was on condition that the balance of the purchase money should be paid in thirty days.

There was also evidence that in February 1865, by the direction of the plaintiff, who was then living in Woburn, his wife went to the defendant's house and paid the balance to the defendant's son, who was then acting as superintendent of the cemetery in the absence of his father by reason of sickness, and who delivered to her the following deed, and entered the transaction on the defendant's official records; and that in the following September the remains of the plaintiff's child were disinterred, and removed by the defendant to a lot known as a "charity lot," and there buried in a grave containing two other bodies.

"Holyhood Catholic Cemetery. Brookline, Mass., Dec. 6th, 1863. Mr. T. F. Meagher, having paid thirty dollars, the receipt whereof is hereby acknowledged, is entitled to one Lot, No. 4, in Holyhood Cemetery, to have and to hold the same to said Meagher, his heirs and assigns, to his and their use as a place of burial for the dead; yet upon the following conditions, to wit: That said lot shall not be transferred without the consent of the proprietor; shall be subject to the regulations made or to be made in the care and management of said cemetery by the proprietor, who shall also have the right to prevent the erection of any offensive or improper monument or inscription thereon; that no remains shall be deposited therein for hire; and that persons dying in drunkenness, duel, or by self destruction, unbaptized, non-Catholics, or otherwise opposed to the Catholic Church, shall not be there interred. In case of a violation of any of the foregoing conditions, said premises shall revert to me, the said proprietor, my legal heirs and assigns. Three dollars will be charged for every opening of graves after the first. Jos. M. Finotti. Witness, James Driscoll. Lot No. 4, Walk A, Left. By instrument recorded February 1st, 1858, lib. 262, fol. 267, in the Dedham Registry of Deeds, the cemetery is bonded to the Rt. Rev. J. B. Fitzpatrick, Bishop of the Diocese of Boston." …

The defendant then contended "that, as the action was an action for trespass on real estate, the plaintiff could at all events only recover for the actual damage done to such real estate; and that, the alleged trespass on the lot and removal of the body not being wilful or with wrongful intent, but wholly from accident and mistake, the plaintiff for that reason also would be restricted to nominal damages only;" and further, that he could not recover at all, because the execution of the deed quoted, and the payment therefor to the defendant's son, did not invest him with a title which would support the action. But the judge ruled "that, as the plaintiff was in possession of the lot, having selected and taken the instrument usually given to purchasers of lots, and was holding and using the lot for the purposes and in the manner intended by the terms of the instrument, he was entitled to maintain the action; that, if it appeared that the defendant had acted in the removal of the body of the child either with a wilful disregard of the plaintiff's rights, or under a mistake arising from gross carelessness and want of ordinary attention or diligence in making proper inquiry, and with the opportunity, by means of his records or by inquiry, to know that the plaintiff had paid for the lot, the jury in assessing damages would have a right to consider the injury to the plaintiff's feelings, and would not be restricted to the mere pecuniary loss or damage to his property."

The jury returned a verdict for the plaintiff, assessing damages in the sum of $837.50; and the defendant alleged exceptions.

FOSTER, J.

By the common law, "though the heir has a property in the monuments and escutcheons of his ancestors, yet he has none in their bodies or ashes; nor can he bring any civil action against such as indecently at least, if not impiously, violate and disturb their remains when dead and buried. The person, indeed, who has the freehold of the soil may bring an action of trespass against such as dig and disturb it; and if any one, in taking up a dead body, steals the shroud or other apparel, it will be felony, for the property thereof remains in the executor or whoever was at the charge of the funeral." A dead body is not the subject of property, and after burial it becomes a part of the ground to which it has been committed, "earth to earth, ashes to ashes, dust to dust." The only action that can be brought for disinterring it is *trespass quare clausum*. But any person in the actual possession of land may maintain this action against a wrongdoer. The title of the plaintiff was more than a burial right in soil the freehold and possession of which remained in another. The written instrument from Father Finotti, the owner of the fee, conferred a right to the exclusive occupation of a particular lot. ...

The measure of damages was correctly stated. The gist of the action is the breaking and entering of the plaintiff's close. But the circumstances which accompany and give character to a trespass may always be shown either in aggravation or mitigation. He who is guilty of a wilful trespass, or one characterized by gross carelessness and want of ordinary attention to the rights of another, is bound to make full compensation. Under such circumstances, the natural injury to the feelings of the plaintiff may be taken into consideration in trespasses to real estate as well as in other actions of tort. Acts of gross carelessness, as well as those of wilful mischief, often inflict a serious wound upon the feelings, when the injury done to property is comparatively trifling. We know of no rule of law which requires the mental suffering of the plaintiff, or the misconduct of the defendant, to be disregarded. The damages in such cases are enhanced, not because vindictive or exemplary damages are allowable, but because the actual injury is made greater by its wantonness.

❖ ❖ ❖

Salem Cemetery, Winston-Salem, North Carolina
Photo by Liam Sherman

CHAPTER 9.5

RETHINKING LAWS PERMITTING THE SALE OF HUMAN REMAINS

Tanya D. Marsh, THE HUFFINGTON POST (October 13, 2012)

Etsy, the online marketplace for handcrafted items, updated its "prohibited items" policy last week to ban the listing of human remains or body parts, including skulls, bones, articulated skeletons, bodily fluids, preserved tissues and organs. (Hair and teeth are still allowed to be sold on Etsy.) A few online news outlets picked up the story, and the resulting chatter focused on several questions. "You can buy human remains on the Internet?" And even more fundamentally: "You can buy human remains?"

Perhaps surprisingly, the answer to both questions is "yes." The only federal law which restricts the sale of human remains is the 1990 Native American Graves Protection and Repatriation Act, which generally attempts to protect the burial sites of Native Americans by prohibiting the possession and trade of Native American funerary objects and human remains. No federal law prohibits the disturbance of the burial sites of non-Native Americans, or the possession and trade of funerary objects and human remains. Instead, the laws regarding the disposition, possession, and trade of human remains and the disturbance of graves is handled by the states. Only three states currently restrict the trade in human remains: Georgia, New York, and Tennessee.

A few Google searches reveal a surprising trade in human remains online. Ebay's "Human Remains and Body Parts Policy" prohibits the sale of Native American grave-related items and "humans, the human body, or any human body parts" but expressly permits "clean, articulated (jointed), non-Native American skulls and skeletons used for medical research." To comply with the policy, the seller must list that the remains are to be used for medical research, but there is no requirement that the buyer actually demonstrate that they will be used for that purpose. Interested buyers can currently pick up a set of human ribs for $14.50, an articulated hand for $135, a complete spine with pelvis bone for $300, a skull for $1300, or an entire human skeleton (including a display case) for the "Buy It Now" price of $1900.

A website called "The Bone Room," which describes itself as a natural history store, sells a wide range of items including fossils, mounted butterflies, animal bones, and human bones. The website explains that prices for human bones have risen in recent years because the major sources were India (which banned their export in 1987) and China (which banned their export shortly before the 2008 Beijing Olympics). The Bone Room sells standard articulated human skeletons for around $5,000 and standard adult skulls from $800 to $1700.

The sale of human remains is not limited to the Internet. On the April 27, 2011 episode of "Storage Wars," entitled "Skullduggery," Dave Hester purchased a storage locker that included a human skull and collection of bones. He sold it at a local store and made a profit on the locker. Many antique stores and flea markets sell human remains and funerary objects.

Few laws restrict the possession and trade in non-Native American human remains in the United States, but the commercialization of human remains is dramatically inconsistent with the respect that by law and custom we generally provide to deceased human beings. American courts have long assumed a universal human concern with the disposition of our mortal remains. Seventeen states have laws that forbid "abuse of a corpse," which generally means that it is a criminal offense to "treat a corpse in a way that [a person] knows would outrage ordinary family sensibilities." Americans of varied backgrounds treat the disposition of their deceased loved ones with reverence. More tellingly, we treat the disposition of strangers with respect. Cars pull over the side of the road to allow a funeral procession to pass. When anonymous bodies are found, particularly when those bodies are of children, strangers often donate to provide for a funeral and decent burial. When stories are published concerning the mistreatment of corpses, or the mishandling of cremated remains, the predominant response is disgust and anger.

How do we explain the difference between these commonly accepted social and legal norms regarding the decent treatment of remains, and legal permissiveness toward the seemingly cavalier commercial treatment of certain remains? I think that the failure of the law to prevent the commercialization of human remains is consistent with the neglect of the American law of the dead by legal scholars, policy makers, and the public. This disregard is symptomatic of a broader disconnect between the living and the dead in American society. Thinking about how we feel about death and about how we want to treat human remains is an uncomfortable topic that we'd rather avoid.

But that neglect has consequences. In 2011, a Craiglist seller in Phoenix advertised the skull of a 12 to 14-year old child that he had purchased at a garage sale. Both of those sales were perfectly legal. It is valid to argue that we should make human remains available for medical or anthropological research. It is much harder to justify that we should be allowed to display the skull of a dead child as an object of curiosity, or to profit from the sale of that child's body. But if we remain unwilling to have a public discussion about the trade of human remains, the lines will continue to be drawn by private entities like Etsy and Ebay, and the choices they make may not reflect society's values.

❖   ❖   ❖

CHAPTER 10

CEMETERIES
AS A LAND USE

Arborville Cemetery, Arborville, Nebraska
Photo by Tanya D. Marsh

CHAPTER 10.1

CEMETERIES AS A LAND USE

Tanya D. Marsh

American colonists generally followed seventeenth century English customs regarding the disposition of human remains. But English burial practices were not as easily adapted. Colonists and pioneers began dying before churchyards could be established. The earliest colonial and frontier burials were typically isolated, located wherever death occurred, and usually unmarked. These practical challenges, combined with the lack of a single established church in the United States, resulted in a variety of burial options that were uniquely American.

Burial in cemeteries owned by a religious organization remains an option—in some communities it is the primary option. In colonial America, many followed English custom and buried their dead in churchyards. In more densely populated cities like New York City, burial sites were also available inside the church and in subterranean vaults. Today, the Catholic Church is one of the largest owners of cemeteries in the United States. Particularly in smaller cities and rural areas, it is common to see a cemetery adjacent to a Protestant church. For reasons discussed below, few churchyards remain in large cities.

From the beginning, many colonists rejected English custom and established domestic burial grounds. These clusters of graves were located on farms, usually near the home on a hill. There was very little precedent in seventeenth century Europe for domestic burial grounds. The few wealthy Europeans who established private graveyards on their property usually sanctified the ground and established a private church alongside. In contrast, family burying grounds in the colonial era were the modest product of necessity. On the edge of settled civilization, pioneers were separated from formal places of worship by bad roads and other difficulties. Private cemeteries were more popular in the southern colonies than in New England. Thomas Jefferson drew up plans for a private cemetery at Monticello in 1771. Family graveyards—private burying grounds on private land—were a uniquely American invention. In sheer numbers, they still represent the lion's share of cemeteries in the United States. Their current legal status is consistent with the patchwork nature of their creation. In many cases, no documentation separates them from the surrounding parcel of land, and buyers purchase a home or farm subject to the rights of its former inhabitants. Family graveyards may consist of a handful of graves, while others have dozens. In some states, if a family graveyard lacks a self-appointed caretaker, title and/or maintenance obligations revert to the government, usually at the county or township level. Historical and genealogical organizations have also adopted family graveyards and assumed responsibility for their continuing care.

As towns developed; haphazard family and neighborhood cemeteries gave way to organized cemeteries. In colonial cities in particular, the location of cemeteries followed the pattern of English village life and were located in the center of town. Not all of these early cemeteries were owned by religious organizations. Many communities in the colonies, and later in the United States, established municipally-owned cemeteries for the benefit of their residents. Often, the cemeteries that were owned by the public and open to the public reserved a corner for the potter's field, the final resting place for those unable to afford a burial spot.

Although cemeteries in the center of a small town caused few problems, the rapid urban growth in the nineteenth century led to significant changes in burial practices in the United States and Europe. Boston's population tripled in the years between the Revolution and the 1820s. Epidemics of cholera, yellow fever, typhoid, and smallpox caused widespread death and triggered progressive (for the time) public health policies. Before the causes of infectious disease were understood, there was a belief that disease was caused by miasma, an invisible vapor created by decomposing organic matter. Overcrowded cemeteries in town, struggling to keep pace with the burgeoning population, were seen as a threat to public health. Compounding problems, many cemeteries were neglected and perceived as a nuisance to neighbors. In addition, property values were rising and land dedicated for cemetery purposes was desirable for other uses.

In 1822, the Boston City Council called "for the immediate termination of inner–city burials, as well as the exhumation of all crammed or shallow–buried corpses." That measure was defeated, but similar measures were adopted in other cities. In 1823, ground burials were forbidden south of Canal, Sullivan, and Grant Streets in Manhattan. In 1851, ground burials were forbidden south of 86th Street and no new cemeteries were permitted in Manhattan.18 A significant number of Manhattan burials were moved to Queens in the nineteenth century. Chicago's sanitary superintendent pushed for the abandonment of that city's cemetery in 1858. By 1866, all burials in Chicago were disinterred and relocated to cemeteries on the edge of town. In 1900, the Board of Supervisors voted to prohibit any future interments in San Francisco. After the great fire of 1906, most burials were removed to Colma. These decisions were not without controversy, and many state courts considered the balance between the needs of the living and the sanctity of the grave. The California Supreme Court's 1907 decision in Laurel Hill Cemetery v. City & County of San Francisco is typical.

European cities faced similar overcrowding and public health issues in the nineteenth century. In response, the rural cemetery was created. Père Lachaise, established by the French government outside Paris in 1804, applied Romantic ideals to offer moral instruction and comfort. In 1831, the principles showcased at Père Lachaise were applied to the first rural cemetery in the United States—Mount Auburn Cemetery in Cambridge, Massachusetts. The success of Mount Auburn inspired the construction of rural cemeteries in cities across the United States. These new cemeteries were, as their names imply, located in the "rural" outskirts of the city rather than in the city center.

They are also significantly larger than the traditional burying grounds they replaced. Mount Auburn occupies 72 acres outside Boston. Laurel Hill, established in Philadelphia in 1836, occupies 74 acres. Green-Wood Cemetery, established in Brooklyn in 1838, occupies 478 acres. The rural cemeteries, like Père Lachaise, were more linked to nature than religion. The same landscape architects employed to design the significant parks in the nineteenth century were also engaged to design rural cemeteries. Frederick Law Olmsted, the architect of Central Park in New York City and the Biltmore Estate grounds at the Vanderbilt summer home in Asheville, North Carolina, designed a number of rural cemeteries including Elmwood Cemetery in Detroit and Mountain View Cemetery in Oakland, California. The design of Mount Auburn was coordinated by the Massachusetts Horticultural Society.

The rural cemeteries were often established by non-profit organizations created for the purpose, although some were initially envisioned as profit-making enterprises. The cemeteries were typically open to all who could afford to pay. Many of the rural cemeteries sold plots to families, who could improve them in accordance with the cemetery's aesthetic requirements. Family lots in Mount Auburn were 300 square feet, more than sufficient for several generations. Single lots were also sold to those who could not afford a family lot.

At the 1831 dedication of Mount Auburn, Justice Joseph Story argued that the goal of Mount Auburn should be to "make cheerful the pathways to the grave; to combine with deep meditations on human mortality the sublime consolations of religion." He expressed outrage at the condition of cemeteries in the United States and the moral duty of Christians to improve them.

❖ ❖ ❖

Crown Hill Cemetery, Indianapolis, Indiana
Photo by Cass Pyatt

CHAPTER 10.2

CEMETERIES IN THE CITY PLAN

AMERICAN SOCIETY OF PLANNING OFFICIALS

INFORMATION REPORT NO. 16 (July 1950)

Men have devised an almost endless number of uses for land, but the one that seems most nearly permanent is its use for interment of the dead. This permanence is reinforced by the phrases used to sell cemetery lots—"perpetual care" and "perpetual charter."

If we are realistic, we may question how long "perpetual" will be. We do know, however, that courts have held that the legal rule against perpetuities does not apply to cemetery funds. Such funds are in the nature of charitable trusts.

Extent of Cemeteries

If the idea of "perpetual care" were pursued far enough, we should eventually use all our land for the interment of the dead and have no land left for the living. While we can be sure this state of affairs will not come about, we have already reached the point at which the distribution of land between the living and the dead is a serious problem.

As far back as 1821, Sir William Scott said in deciding the case of *Gilbert v. Buzzard and Boyer* (161 English Reports 1342):

> A comparatively small portion of the dead will shoulder out the living and their
> posterity. The whole environs of this metropolis must be surrounded by a

circumvallation of churchyards, perpetually enlarging by becoming themselves surcharged with bodies; if indeed land owners can be found willing to divert their ground from the beneficial uses of the living to the barren preservation of the dead.

In 1935, the U. S. Department of Commerce published an estimate of 15,000 cemeteries in the United States. There are no official estimates of the acreage contained in these cemeteries. If we assume the conservative figure of one acre per thousand population cemetery land in the United States would be approximately 140,000 acres. Quite probably the greater part lies within city limits.

Little, if any, cemetery land in the United States is used for reburial. Each year, therefore. more land is used for cemetery purposes. There were 1,445,370 deaths in this country in 1947. Of these, it is estimated that 96% of the bodies were disposed of by burial and 4% by cremation. If we assume the current figure of 620 burials per acre, we required 2,238 acres of cemetery land in 1947.

The actual amount of land, 3-1/2 square miles annually in a nation of 3 million square miles, is of minor importance. The serious aspect is that the cemetery land is for the most part situated in or near our cities, where land is _not_ in over supply. ...

In the sample shown in the table" there is an obvious difference between United States and British cities. Cemetery acreage per thousand population is greater on this side of the Atlantic. There are several reasons for this:

    a)   Greater supply of land in the U. S. allows a more liberal use.

    b)   Burials in churches and churchyards takes care of a negligible portion of U.S. burials.

    c)   Intensity of use of cemeteries (through "family" and "common" graves) is higher in Great Britain, in some cases running as much as 6,000 burials per acre.

    d)   Cremation, which uses little cemetery land, i$ more extensively used in Great Britain than in this country.

The Cemetery Problem

The first thing that strikes the city planner when he tackles a problem involving a cemetery is that he is faced with pressures, ideas and laws which are not paralleled in any other city planning question, The disposal of the dead is enmeshed in religious doctrine, custom, fear, superstition, complicated statutory law, and crusading burial reform, Probably the most important single technique in handling the removal of cemeteries is the delicate public relations job.

Cemetery problems divide generally into two groups: those involving existing cemeteries, and those involving proposed cemeteries.

Existing cemeteries become problems when they fall into dis-use, when their care is neglected, when the land is needed for another use, when they lie in the path of some needed public improvement. The old cemetery may become a health hazard. Even when it is carefully maintained, many persons feel that a cemetery in a neighborhood will depress property values. Municipal administrators dislike cemeteries because they are a part of the ever-increasing list of tax-exempt properties.

Planning for the new cemetery requires determining in the first place whether a cemetery is needed at all. If it is needed, what size should it be? Where can it best be located where it will not be an obstacle to municipal growth, where it will not be a public health hazard? How can it be designed so that it may be used for additional purposes such as recreation? Do cemeteries depress property values, and if so, how can real estate depreciation be minimized? How can the cemetery (and the community!) be protected against future neglect? How can land designated for cemetery use be reclaimed for other uses should the developmental pattern of the community change? How can the planner be sure, when asked to project his estimates for a cemetery fifty to a hundred years or more into the future?

Cemetery Removal

An old and neglected cemetery may be rehabilitated. If it is not susceptible to being cleaned up, it may have to be removed. Those cemeteries occupying space desired by the community for other uses may have to be moved, in whole or in part. The most convincing case for moving the cemetery (i.e. the bodies) to another location is when its continued existence and use is a nuisance. The cemetery, however, must be proved to be a nuisance in fact. The universal weight of authority has held that a cemetery is not a nuisance per se. When the cemetery is in fact a nuisance, it may be enjoined. The most frequent proof of nuisance has been connected with the existing or possible pollution of a water supply or of the atmosphere. If it can be proved that a cemetery is a public health hazard, the city will have little difficulty in getting the right to remove it. It is difficult to prove that a cemetery is a health hazard. However, all the early court cases considered the effect of the cemetery on public physical health, while a recent Connecticut decision (on funeral homes) indicated that public mental health should also be considered. The neglect and dis-use of a cemetery for a long time has been grounds for declaring it a nuisance and requiring its removal. Legislative bodies, moved to prohibit all cemeteries within the city limits, have been buttressed in their actions by court rulings that this prohibition may be extended to include compulsory discontinuance of the use of existing cemeteries, together with disinterment and re-burial of the bodies.

Eminent Domain

If the cemetery is a nuisance, the municipality uses its police power to abate the nuisance. It is a rule of law that damages suffered because of the operation of the police power are not compensable. For this reason, courts will probably stop short of requiring disinterment of an entire cemetery as the method of abating the nuisance. Rather, they would be inclined to order clean-up and less drastic measures. Besides. it is more than likely lesser measures will end a true nuisance.

If civic advance, however, requires removal of all or a part of a cemetery, the method will usually be condemnation. Cities are creatures of the state, having only those powers specifically delegated to them by the state. One of these delegated powers is the right of eminent domain for the purpose of carrying out municipal improvements, such as streets. But unless it is specifically authorized, the city does not generally have the right to condemn cemetery property. In some cases cemeteries are granted general immunity from appropriation by condemnation. In most states, this statutory immunity applies to specific and designated purposes. The majority of states allow taking if consent of the owner is obtained. ...

In some instances. it may be necessary to condemn. even though consent is, or can be, obtained. When the City of San Francisco cleared out all cemeteries within the city limits, no permission was sought from relatives of those interred. The city counsel felt that if, in asking permission, the city had received a single refusal, the policy of the California statute would have been negated. The California law (1923 statutes 1 Chapter 312, page 46) permits the abandonment of cemeteries and removal of bodies in all cities of more than 100,000 population.

The Tennessee Valley Authority moved thousands of graves in assembling land for its many reservoirs. In most cases the Authority arranged with next of kin for the removal of the bodies to a suitable site. However, when a fee title was involved. the Authority brought a friendly condemnation suit to assure a clear title. Such procedure was also necessary where owners were unknown.

In most cases, cemetery lot "owners" do not actually "own" the land, i.e., have a title in fee simple. Instead, they own burial rights and the fee remains with the cemetery corporation. The value of the fee in such cases is nominal; the damage, when the cemetery is taken, is suffered by the owner of the burial rights. If the land now used for burial might have greater value when subdivided into building lots—and such use were possible under the conditions of ownership— the cemetery corporation might claim such value. Where the land can not be freed of its burial trust, then its value will be that for burial purposes. When the burial trust is removed, (Matter of Albany Street Opening (New York) 11 Wend. 148) the unencumbered title has been held to be worth the value of the fee, less the cost of removal and re-interment of the bodies, plus the cost of new momunents to mark the new graves. (Matter of Board of Transportation of City of New York, 251 N. Y.S. 409) ...

Use of Discontinued Cemeteries

If a cemetery is discontinued and the bodies removed, the land is, of course. available for any appropriate use. In many cases, the reason for removal is the need of the land for another use. Its use as an airport in Baltimore has been noted. St. Louis recently moved its "Potter's Field" to make way for a housing project. For the most part, public sentiment and the courts have stopped the conversion of cemetery land to commercial purposes. The Missouri Supreme Court has ruled definitely on this point in *Campbell v. Kansas City* 161 S.W. 261.

The small cemetery in the built-up section of a city may be the only open space left. On this point C.M. Robinson wrote in MODERN CIVIC ART, (Putnam, New York, 1918. P. 292, 349):

"In many cities—most strikingly in London—where land values have become so high as almost to discourage municipal purchases for the creation of open spaces, and where the crowding is so severe that there is excuse for fear that an arbitrary reduction of the habitable area in a given section may increase rather than diminish suffering and the pushing of the urban boundaries into a distance that the poor cannot traverse make pitiful appeal for public open areas, there has been a utilization of ancient graveyards. They are transformed, with excellent sanitary effect, to serve as breathing places, garden spots, and playgrounds. But their location as regards the street plan is obviously without system.

"…Finally, the community use of the cemetery as a park is simply a pathetic confession of the public need of park reservations. Speaking artistically, the cemeteries have lately shown vast improvement. From a type originally comparable to stoneyards they tend to become more and more park-like. … But the great significance of a community's park-use of a cemetery is the proof of the need of park. It is a use to be encouraged and approved, until the park is provided, for all the reasons for which parks are approved."

Forecasting Cemetery Requirements

… There is danger in projecting burial habits and custom far into the future. For example, burial expenses are rising. One of the arguments used in Great Britain to promote cremation is that it is less expensive. This could certainly influence persons toward its use. In the United States, the difference in cost is not so great. In this country, the difference can be calculated by setting off the cost of cremation and disposal of the ashes against the cost of the cemetery lot. Funeral costs, including coffin and embalming, are the same up to the point of final disposal. If the "single-grave" burial lot is used the difference is not great. …

It is also questionable as to how long religious and social customs will hold. The experience in Basel [Switzerland—where 48.1% of bodies were disposed of by cremation in 1941, even though 33.2% of the population were members of religious faiths that did not permit cremation] would indicate that as much as 77% of the population not affected by strict religious sanctions, would turn to cremation as the method of disposal of the dead.

The disposal of the ashes of cremation, sometimes called "cremains," does require some cemetery land. In some cases regular cemetery lots are used. Most of the disposal is in a special building called a "columbarium," in which the ashes are placed in urns, to be kept in individual niches. In some cemeteries the ashes are spread over a "garden of repose," especially set aside and dedicated for the purpose. …

The proportion of cemetery area available for burials will vary widely. Hare and Hare (THE CEMETERY HANDBOOK (2nd Ed.) p. 200) have listed cemeteries ranging from thirteen saleable lots (20 feet by 20 feet) per gross acre, to 72.5 lots per gross acre. They offer from their experience the average figure of 62 lots per gross acre on an 80 acre cemetery. Ordinarily, smaller cemeteries devote a greater portion of the area to non-burial purposes—drives, service buildings, chapel, landscaping, etc. Rugged terrain and low land may decrease the usable area on large sites. On the other hand, churchyards used for cemeteries, and certain small sectarian cemeteries will have a more intensive use. …

Hare and Hare estimate the number of burials on a 20-foot square lot as ten —or from their figures, 620 burials per gross acre in an 30-acre cemetery. The lower cost "single-grave" sections in the cemetery will provide more burials than this.. The average single-grave occupies 20 to 25 square feet (2-1/2 - 3 feet by 8 feet). The burials per acre devoted to single-graves will probably be around 1,000.

In laying out cemeteries as well as in estimating cemetery land requirements, the single-grave section requires careful study. The single-grave is the cheapest in the cemetery. Usually the sections are in the least desirable part of the cemetery. This is normally the lowest usable part, in view of the premium on hills and high spots. Most single-graves are purchased after the death of the individual, few are bought "pre-need."

Because they are cheaper, single-graves will be more in demand from families in the lower income groups. Thus, cemetery land requirements are definitely tied in with the average income in a city.

To offset the intensive use of the single-grave areas, many family lots are never more than half filled, the unused portion being landscaped, or occupied by a monument. The very large lots of the wealthy are even less intensively used. ...

Any survey of cemeteries must consider sectarian cemeteries. Some large cemeteries, both municipal and private, have sectarian areas; but in large cities, certain religious faiths have their own cemeteries. The same is true of different races. The planner must be familiar with the religious and racial distribution within his city. Unused capacity in a sectarian cemetery will not he available to non-members of the sect. Nor will unused capacity in a non-sectarian cemetery satisfy the requirements of all races and religions. ...

Considerations in Location

The problems associated with a cemetery are many. Because of this, there may be a temptation for municipal officials to relegate the cemetery to an area outside the city limits. Cities do have the right to prohibit burial within the city limits. However, the courts do not look with favor on the prohibition of cemeteries where the area is sparsely settled, and where, therefore, little danger to human life or health could result.

The use of negative control of location, however, is limited in value. "Outside the city limits" is no answer if the planning is for a county, for a metropolitan area, or for a region. It is a shortsighted solution for even those who are only concerned with the area within city corporate boundary lines. Many cities may be expected to grow and annex additional land. In the future, these cities may be faced with annexing a previously banned cemetery, or the logical direction of city growth may be thwarted by the presence of the cemetery.

A cemetery should be considered as a necessary part of a community, and its location should be carefully planned. At the beginning of this report, it was pointed out that in urban land use statistical summaries, cemeteries are rarely listed separately. They are normally included under "semi-public open spaces." The significance of this grouping is that the cemetery does serve as an open space, and it should be considered as benefiting the city because of this. In some communities, cemeteries may be combined with certain park and recreation uses. In others, where cemeteries are located on the perphery of communities, the cemetery can be an asset in civic design, if there is any advantage to the greenbelt concept. In fact, the cemetery (not combined with recreational uses) has a certain advantage over the public park in that it is nota focus for as much traffic as a popular city park would be.

In passing judgment on the location of a new cemetery, the city planner must ask two basic questions. First, is the proposed location one which does not interfere with and better still, is it one which even aids, a good and logical development of the city? Second, is the proposed location one which will give reasonable assurance that the cemetery will be a successful venture?

It is necessary, before the first question can be answered, that there be the most complete knowledge possible as to what is a good and logical pattern for the future growth of the city. In other words, there should be a master plan. The relative immobility of a cemetery, once established, makes it important for the planner to extend this plan, in some phases, far into the future. It is especially desirable for him to project the major thoroughfare and land-use plans as far as possible. ...

Perpetual Care

For obvious reasons, neglected cemeteries create problems and become nuisances. Cemeteries become neglected because they have been poorly financed. There can be no doubt that leaving the care of graves to the lot owners, that is, to the owners of the burial rights, always results in neglect. Proper care must be a responsibility of the cemetery association or authority and it must be soundly financed. The care should not be financed out of profits on the sale of burial rights, nor has it proved successful to pay for it from taxes.

The only successful method for assuring continuing maintenance is the "perpetual care" fund. This is a trust fund and only the earnings may be used to pay for maintenance.

Perpetual care costs are generally calculated by one of two methods. The charge may be a percentage of the lot cost, or it may be a flat rate per square foot of land sold for burial purposes. Since the cost of maintaining a cemetery lot does not depend upon the price paid for it, the flat rate per square foot is the more equitable way to charge. The average cost throughout the country is about 50 cents per square foot, although small cemeteries with fewer buildings or without lawn sprinkling may be able to operate on half this amount. Where the percentage of lot price is used, it may vary from ten to twenty-five percent, In Minnesota, a state law requires that 20% of the income from the sale of lots be set aside for perpetual care.

One weakness has begun to show up in the perpetual care plan. Earnings on perpetual care funds have dropped and maintenance costs, particularly for labor, have risen. If this trend continues, the ability of the funds to provide perpetual care is speculative.

❖ ❖ ❖

Verdon Cemetery, Richardson County, Nebraska
Photo by Tanya D. Marsh

CHAPTER 10.3

THE CEMETERY: ITS NATURE AND REGULATION

DEFINITIONS

Percival Jackson, THE LAW OF CADAVERS (1950)

The word "cemetery" is derived from a Greek term which means "to sleep" and denoting "sleeping places," the term used for their extra-mural burial grounds by the early Christians. Cemeteries are of ancient origin, segregated burial in numbers, having been practiced early. A burial field was maintained for the Kings of Judah, and there Isaiah was buried. The purchase of the field of Ephron for a private cemetery is the first recorded mercantile transaction; there, in the cave of Machpelah, Abraham was buried with Sarah, his wife, and their children. Subsequently the practice of burial in churchyards grew up. To quote from Pardovan, an eminent church lawyer: "Churchyards are dormitories for human bodies, and ordinarily that spot of ground within which the church stands." With the advent of private burial grounds the term "cemetery" has generically designated a place where dead bodies, commonly those of human beings, are buried. The term "cemetery" is used interchangeably with "graveyard," "burial ground," "place of burial" and includes not only the ground in which interments are made, but also the roads, paths, and appurtenant grounds used and ornamented in connection therewith. The definition of a cemetery does not preclude maintenance of a mortuary and includes the use of lands for erection of a crematory and columbarium. A cemetery may be public or private.

Actual interment not necessary.

A cemetery may be created, without actual interment by setting the necessary ground apart for burial. "What creates the cemetery is the act of setting the ground apart for the burial of the dead, marking it, and distinguishing it from the adjoining ground as a place of burial."

Distinguished from place of casual burial.

To create a cemetery there must be something more than a casual or single burial. By [California] statute, "six or more human beings being buried at one place constitutes the place a cemetery." [Jackson cites additional statutory definitions in a footnote. In Texas, "a cemetery is a place dedicated to and used and intended to be used for permanent interment of human dead. In Vermont, "a cemetery is any plot of ground used or intended to be used for permanent disposition and burial of human dead."]

Difference in protection.

A single burial will entitle the interred cadaver to protection, and land containing a human being will be maintained inviolate. But a cemetery is entitled to broader protection, since it includes, in addition to the ground actually used for burial purposes, such avenues, walks, grounds, buildings, and improvements as may be necessary for or appurtenant to its use or embellishment.

Distinguished from abandoned burial grounds.

Where burials have been discontinued, it has been said that the land is no longer called a place of burial, but a former place of burial. However, a cemetery remains such and is to be so considered until its abandonment and until all bodies are removed therefrom.

❖　❖　❖

Zentralfriedhof [Central Cemetery], Vienna, Austria
Photo by Tanya D. Marsh

CHAPTER 10.4
GRAVE RECYCLING
Dana Horlick

Traditional practices concerning the burial and disposition of remains vary from country to country. Many countries, especially Western European countries, have long utilized grave recycling to cope with crowded cemeteries. Grave recycling involves burying a corpse in a manner that encourages decomposition, and after a set period of time (usually 20-50 years, although it does vary by country), whatever remains are left are unearthed and deposited in a communal ossuary. The grave is then available for the next occupant. This is in direct contrast to the uniquely American idea of a grave being committed to a single person in perpetuity. The unique approach towards death is reflected by the typical United States funeral, consisting of embalming, an open-casket viewing, a service held in a funeral home, and ground burial in a casket and vault.

In keeping with the idea that a single individual should be the sole occupant of a gravesite for eternity, Americans have employed a number of strategies to slow decomposition and preserve the body. These strategies include embalming, placing remains in a metal or hardwood casket with a steel and/or concrete vault or grave liner, and ground burial in a single grave dedicated to an individual for perpetuity. All of these practices hinder the use of grave recycling since they are intended to discourage the decomposition of the remains, a critical process in order to re-use the grave. Countries that practice grave recycling seek to hasten decomposition by forbidding or discouraging embalming, metal caskets, and vaults.

Grave recycling first developed primarily due to practical concerns with limited space available for burial. By the early Middle Ages, burial in the churchyard had become the Christian norm. However, churchyards were not large spaces and thus quickly reached capacity. As a solution to the overcrowding and lack of available space, it became customary to remove decomposed remains from vaults and graves to create new space for the newly deceased. The disinterred bones could not simply be discarded; they needed to be preserved to ensure eventual resurrection, and it was important that they remain somewhere on the church grounds, near the saints under whose protection they had been placed. The solution was to establish within the church or cemetery a bone house, or carnarium (also know as a charnel house or an ossuary).

Many charnel houses handled the remains of these individuals using a similar process. Bones, with special attention given to the skull, were disinterred, washed with wine, and placed in a room annexed to the chapel where rites for the deceased were performed. Once the bones were removed, that gravesite became available for re-use since there was no longer an occupant present within the grave. Increasing the special attention given to the skull, many of the Athonite monasteries adopted the practice of painting or inscribing the name of the deceased upon the skull. This allowed the skull, the most human part of the skeleton, to be more easily identified as belonging to a particular individual. Marking the skulls in this manner was more than a form of commemoration; it also allowed the remains to be identified later, in case members of the monastery were raised to sainthood.

In contrast to the Eastern monastic ossuaries, the early charnels in the West were intended only as storage spaces for human remains, not meant to be viewed. This reflects the practical motivation behind the use of grave recycling - the lack of available space. By the late fourteenth century, however, it was becoming increasingly common to use the bones to create displays. The bones used to decorate these ossuaries generally came from local cemeteries. Elaborate designs were introduced by the beginning of the seventeenth century, when fantastic bone-encrusted chapels were constructed, some of which even incorporated preserved corpses. The elaborate arrangements and displays of bones became enough of a concern that in some areas mandates were issued regarding them. For example, in France there were periodic inspections to ensure that the bone stacks were decent and not badly arranged or covered with debris.

Despite the increasingly elaborate arrangements of the remains, traditionally the charnels were models of equality, "imposing anonymity on the remains to remind visitors that all of humanity is equally subject to death's grasp, worldly honors and vanities notwithstanding." However, during the nineteenth century, it became a popular practice to enshrine or decorate privileged bones, and to label them with the name and status of the person to whom they had once belonged.

This new trend created a hierarchy within the charnel that replicated that of society at large, and conferred the aura of a sacred relic upon certain remains. Previously, ossuaries had placed every individual on the same level—containing numerous bones, unassociated with any particular person or status. The later trend, however, allowed some individuals to elevate their status over others, even in death. Even though the ossuaries became a reflection of the societal hierarchy, they were first and foremost primarily religious sites.

Despite the morbidity that a typical American would perhaps associate with a charnel house or ossuary, these bones houses were sacred sites, many of which incorporated chapels for worship, making them places "not of fear, but of eschatological hope." The charnels were built on consecrated ground and the bones themselves were considered blessed, as it was believed that they would be resurrected and clothed in divine glory at the Second Coming of Christ.

In addition, many of these ossuaries encouraged interaction between the living and the dead. The Fontanelle Cemetery, a large ossuary created in a cave system in Naples during the seventeenth century, was one such ossuary. For over 200 years, the living would come to solicit aid from the remains of the deceased, asking for advice on various domestic and personal problems, and expressing their gratitude by providing the dead with shrines, prayers, and various forms of offerings. The elaborately decorated and fantastically arranged ossuaries created between the sixteenth and nineteenth centuries bear witness to the dialogue with the dead that was once an important part of the spiritual life of many Christians.

In present day America, we have instead chosen to separate ourselves from the dead, entrusting the funeral industry to provide adequate burial services. Once the deceased is buried, it becomes an issue of "out of sight, out of mind," wherein many graves become abandoned or neglected. Historically, ossuaries provided an opportunity where family members and friends of the deceased can continue to interact with their loved one. Being able to visit the ossuary and see your loved one's bones makes for a much more engaging process as opposed to visiting a gravestone.

In Christian theology, ossuaries performed an additional function, containing memento mori, or reminders of death. This imagery conveys the message that "regardless of earthly honors and social status, death reduces us all equally to base matter; one should therefore put aside worldly vanities and repent from sin." In addition, many ossuaries contained the inscription "As you are now so once was I; as I am now so you shall be," although it may vary somewhat. This forces the visitor to confront his or her own mortality. "No people who turn their back on death can be alive ... The presence of the dead among the living will be a daily fact in any society that encourages its people to live." In essence, it is only when you are confronted with death and mortality that you can truly live. Thus, ossuaries can serve purposes other than conserving space.

Although many individuals living today would probably find it odd to visit an ossuary and ask for advice or aid from the remains of the deceased, those who lived during those times would likely find it odd that we do not interact with the dead today. Instead, we have become a death-denying culture. We have undergone an evolution in which little by little, the dead cease to exist. "As the dialogue with the dead fell silent, our relation to the charnel houses, where death was made visible, was radically altered." We shift responsibility to the funeral industry to handle the remains of our loved ones. We bury our family members in cemeteries, visit for a few years, and forget or simply move on. The current model that we utilize in America, preserving our dead as much as physically possible and placing them in a single grave for perpetuity, does not acknowledge that reality.

We may feel that we need a permanent place where we can visit our deceased loved one or feel that it is disrespectful to disturb their eternal rest, but allowing a single individual to rest in a single grave for eternity does not acknowledge the reality that many gravesites are unattended and have been for decades. If no one visits a grave in 75 years, does it really make sense to keep that gravesite dedicated to that single individual? This places spatial constraints on burials in that available gravesites are limited due to preexisting burials. Although many parts of America still have grave space available, in some areas, especially urban areas with high populations, space is limited.

An additional concern presented by the current model utilized here in America is a financial one. Cemeteries make money by selling gravesites and this money goes towards, among other things, maintaining the cemetery and the graves. When a cemetery is full and no longer has any gravesites available for sale, it no longer has a source of revenue and cannot continue to maintain the cemetery or graves without revenue. This means that many older cemeteries, with either no space remaining or very few gravesites available, will eventually fall into disrepair and a state of neglect. Even if you wanted to visit the grave of someone who was buried 100 years ago, the conditions of the cemetery itself may make it unsafe for you to do so.

Even though there are both spatial and financial issues with our current model that could be ameliorated by utilizing a model similar to many other developed countries, many Americans would find the idea of an ossuary to be distasteful or morbid. One reason why, focuses on how we define ourselves - one scholar has stated that "the epidermis has come to define our modern concept of individual boundary and its dissolution implies the loss of individuality. To modern eyes, then, the display of bones in a charnel is not only a violation of the bodily canon, it undermines our fundamental concept of individuality." This conceptualization of identity and individuality would make it difficult to accept a grave-recycling model.

When learning of these types of practices - grave recycling and the use of ossuaries - many Americans would probably assume that this is something that occurred far into the past and does not occur in modern society. Thus, they would likely be surprised to learn that many developed countries utilize these practices. Europeans have practiced grave recycling since at least the Middle Ages. In Greece, for example, remains are buried and then disinterred after they decompose for a period of time ranging from 20 to 50 years. The remnants are then placed in a communal ossuary located at the cemetery. The grave is typically marked to identify the temporary occupant, and then the gravestone is removed when the remains are transferred to the ossuary.

In Greece, once the rental period is up, a relative must appear at the gravesite to witness a cemetery worker dig up the grave, exhume the body, pry it from the coffin, and then collapse the bones into a container roughly the size of a shoebox for storage in a communal ossuary. If no one shows up on the appointed date, or if you stop payment on the fee for the ossuary, the cemetery destroys the bones.

In Switzerland, graves are rented for 25 years, after which the graves are dug up and the site re-used. Families often buy the space, or rent it on a very long-term basis. In fact, if you visit a Swiss cemetery it is likely that the only old headstones you'll see are the ones on family graves.

These graves tend to hold generations of relatives. For everyone else, however, after 25 years the grave is dug up and the headstone is either returned to the family or recycled by being broken up into gravel chips.

In Germany, graves are usually leased for 20 to 25 years. At the end of the lease period, most cemeteries place a yellow-tag notice on the grave to let any relatives or friends know that the time is up. Usually, this one notice on the grave is the only notice provided to friends and family of the imminent termination of the lease. This serves the purpose of ensuring that people who regularly visit their loved ones are given the opportunity to renew the lease or to prepare themselves for the removal of their loved ones. Those who object after the fact have less standing given that had they been regular visitors, they would have seen the notice. Therefore, this practice protects the relatives of the deceased who have not abandoned or neglected the grave, by giving them a voice in the process.

If the cemetery director does not hear from the family and a new lease period is not contracted, the headstone will be pulled up and, when the need arises, the site will be leased to a new occupant, the plot dug up, and a new tenant buried there. When individuals are buried in Germany their body is placed in a simple wooden coffin. This is to ensure that the body and the coffin decompose relatively quickly. If a lease is not renewed for a gravesite, the bones are left in the ground. If a new grave is dug, those bones will be dug up too and placed back with the dirt when the new inhabitant is settled into the ground.

Similarly to Norway, Germany is also currently experiencing issues with its grave recycling practice. For a body to decompose quickly and fully, it needs oxygen to be present, and a little moisture (but not too much). The problem in Germany is that when many communities created their newest cemeteries, they purchased cheap soil with high clay content from local farmers. This clay-heavy soil drains very poorly, keeps the bodies cool, and prevents oxygen from reaching them. Instead of decomposing, the bodies turn into a gray-white, paste-like soft mass. This creates numerous difficulties when trying to reuse the grave: since an essential element of grave recycling is that the body has decomposed, at least partially, before the grave is reused.

Cemetery reforms in Australia would offer families of the deceased a choice between renewable interment rights of 25 years or a permanent 99-year lease. In the case of renewable tenure on future graves and wall niches containing ashes, rights would be granted for 25 years, with a right to renew every 25 years, up to a maximum of 99 years. This right of renewal would allow families that are struggling with the loss of their loved one and who cannot yet cope with the idea of someone else being buried on top of the deceased, more time to come to grips with the idea. By the time 99 years has passed, those closest to the deceased will likely be deceased themselves, making the re-use of the grave much less emotionally charged.

Urban areas of Australia currently practice a method known as lift and deepen. This allows old graves to be opened up to provide stacking space for as many as three extra coffins. This process involves exhuming the deceased, digging the grave to a greater depth - around 10 feet - and reinterring the previous remains. This allows multiple other individuals to be buried in the same grave, conserving the limited space available.

Under the 1934 Local Government Act for burials, South Australia listed a maximum 99-year lease for gravesites. After the lease expires, if a living relative can be found, the cemetery may offer an extension on the lease. If living relatives cannot be located or leases are not renewed, the cemetery may then decide to recycle the grave. Advertisements are often placed in local print media prior to such works taking place in an attempt to locate difficult to find living relatives. This is in contrast to the method in Germany whereby the notice is placed on the grave itself to notify family members of the impending reuse of the gravesite. Both strategies indicate a concern for the reaction of the living relatives of the deceased.

Durban, a port city in South Africa, has had to deal with issues concerning the capacity of their cemeteries. Only 2 of the 53 cemeteries in Durban, which have to cover a population of 3.5 million, have space for fresh graves. To cope with this shortage of burial sites, Durban has turned to grave recycling. Legally, the city is permitted to re-use gravesites after 10 years. The law allows this grave recycling as long as both the family of the previous occupant and the family of the newly deceased agree. Bones from the old grave are supposed to be put in a bag and buried deeper in the ground, so that the site appears fresh.

Only graves that are the results of conflicts or of national importance or over 60 years and outside of local municipal cemeteries are considered protected, requiring approval by the South African Heritage Resources Agency before re-use. In the absence of a lease or objection, the only other exclusion to reuse is a negative environmental impact. This allows the government quite a bit of leeway in determining whether to reuse a grave or not.

However, Durban has had an issue with the inability to recycle graves more than a limited amount of times. One cemetery was closed after each gravesite had been recycled five times. After that, the corpses no longer decomposed because the microorganisms that normally putrefy the bodies were saturated. This issue is likely due to the short turn around in Durban. Allowing re-use of the grave only 10 years after the deceased was buried does not leave enough time for the first corpse to decay. Extending the time allotted to a single occupant in the grave space may help to ease this problem.

In Norway, the government provides use of a cemetery plot without charge for 20 years. After that, rent must be paid or the grave is re-used and the decomposing remains and casket are left in the ground under the new coffin. However, Norway is currently having issues with its grave recycling practice. Shortly after World War II, Norwegians began a practice of wrapping their dead in plastic before laying them to rest in wooden caskets, believing the practice was more sanitary.

Three decades and hundreds of thousands of burials later, gravediggers realized the airtight conditions kept the corpses from decomposing. This limits the ability of the government to recycle the graves. The law states that if you open a grave from the period when they used plastic, you are not allowed to reuse the grave. This poses challenges for a country that practices grave recycling in an effort to conserve space. The issues that Norway is currently facing demonstrates the importance of both the methods of burial and the materials utilized.

In Vienna, Austria, the *Zentralfriedhof* ("Central Cemetery") contains 3 million interments in just 300,000 graves, demonstrating the prevalence of grave recycling. In addition, the numbers also demonstrate the effectiveness and practicality of grave recycling. Interring 3 million deceased while using up only 300,000 graves saves a lot of land and makes that land available for other persons, likely to serve the living instead of the dead.

In Great Britain, where burial grounds are most often small, ancient churchyards, the government has permitted the reuse of graves that have been untended for more than 75 years. This reclamation of graves has been going on since 1976, when councils were granted the power to add bodies to existing graves that had room, as long as the bodies already there were not disturbed. In addition, under the London Local Authorities Act 2007, councils have powers to disturb graves older than 75 years, with the consent of any relatives. This means that remains can be buried deeper down in the same grave, creating new space for bodies to be buried on top. The method utilized in London is somewhat different than that used in many other countries in that it may not involve an ossuary. In addition, the remains may not even be removed from the grave, and occupants can be buried one on top of the other.

In London, before the cemetery reuses any of its graves, it has to announce that it is doing so, with public notices in the cemetery and advertisements in papers. It tries to contact the families of those buried there, who have the right to veto any reuse for a generation. However, this often does not pose much of a practical constraint. Recently, the City of London Cemetery claimed 200 graves for reuse; only one family wrote back saying they did not want the grave disturbed. This demonstrates that, at least after quite some time passes, the majority of people do not maintain a connection with the cemetery plot their loved one is buried in, demonstrating that grave recycling may not be as emotionally sensitive of a topic as some may think.

Although reuse of graves in London is legal, this is not the case in most of Britain. Prior to the 1850s, it was a common practice to stack graves, reusing plots after 100 years. However, the grave recycling process itself is currently banned in most of Britain by a Victorian law that also allowed interment outside churchyards, where reuse of graves was common. The 1865 Burial Act, which makes it illegal to disturb existing bodies, was introduced partly because churchyards were so overcrowded that bodies were regularly being dug up after only a few months to make way for more. This law also made graves in cemeteries permanent, partly to deter grave robbing.

Due to limited available space, the prohibition on grave recycling in most of Britain has had consequences for the friends and family members of the deceased. More people are having to travel longer distances to visit graves, they are paying more to bury their loved ones (local authorities often charge non-residents higher fees for the grave), and cemeteries are being spoiled as pathways and trees are dug up to create more space. These problems could be ameliorated if the rest of Great Britain adopts a model similar to the one used in London and begins practicing grave recycling.

London's 75-year limit on grave use is significantly longer than the 20 years allowed in Norway, provided that the relatives do not purchase the use of the grave for a longer period of time. The extended time frame is likely intended to reduce concerns about the negative impact on family and friends of the deceased. After this amount of time, the emotions relating to the death of the deceased would likely have died down to a certain extent and the situation will not be as difficult. The variation between London and Norway demonstrates that the length of time a grave is dedicated to a single occupant varies significantly among countries that utilize grave recycling.

For instance, Singapore only allows interment for 15 years, followed by mandatory exhumation and cremation. Hong Kong and Taiwan both have similar programs. In Hong Kong, however, the bones are cleaned and placed in an urn, which is reburied, allowing a time of remembrance for the friends and family of the deceased. The relatively shorter time frame allotted to a single occupant in Singapore is likely due to the nation-state's small size and population size (four million) making the availability of land a more pressing concern. In Singapore, government newspaper advertisements announce exhumation programs so people can identify late relatives. Any remains that are not identified are kept for three years, then scattered at sea. Therefore, grave recycling is not just a historical practice, but it is also one that continues today, especially in countries with limited space for graves and those with low cremation rates.

There are also countries that practice grave recycling to a limited extent. In British Columbia, for example, the regulations permit graves to be reused, but only by family members. In British Columbia, reuse involves removing—with family permission—whatever remains are left in a grave. The grave is dug a little deeper, the older remains returned to the grave, and the fresh remains are placed on top. This is similar to the method used in London, although London does not restrict the availability of this method to family members. In fact, prior to adopting its current approach to grave recycling, London also chose to reuse only the graves of family members. Prior to the regulations allowing the current method of grave recycling, the City of London Cemetery had some family graves containing the remains of as many as 20 people.

Therefore, starting out restricting the practice to solely family members may be the first step towards allowing the practice on a more widespread level. In addition, the choice to only allow grave recycling when the deceased are family members may make the process more palatable for a public unaccustomed to such approach. This means that decades after you pass away and are buried, you will not be sharing your grave space with a complete stranger but rather a family member. The approach taken by British Columbia may be one way to introduce grave recycling to the United States in a way so as it is not rejected outright.

In fact, the United States has utilized grave recycling to a limited extent. For example, wall vaults line the perimeters of the older New Orleans cemeteries. The Church generally rented these wall vaults for a year and a day and after that time period ended, the remains were removed, bagged, and placed in a communal ossuary. Additionally, even the family vaults and in-ground graves in New Orleans cemeteries contain multiple remains. Therefore, although the concept of grave recycling may seem completely foreign and abnormal to the typical American, the United States has used it before.

It would be possible to implement grave recycling in the United States, but it would likely be a slow process. Many of the countries that utilize grave recycling require the practice, due to overcrowding and lack of available land for additional gravesites. However, some places limit the practice to family members. Thus, it may be beneficial to take a two-prong approach. First, grave recycling should be made available for family members. If there are people who are related that wish to share a gravesite, they should be allowed to do so.

The second prong would force people to accept, or at least tolerate, the practice of grave recycling. In areas that have limited gravesites available, especially urban areas dealing with overcrowding on a large scale, grave recycling would be beneficial. Therefore, in areas that do not have the space to continue burying its residents, grave recycling should be made mandatory. Mandatory grave recycling is more easily justified under these circumstances than in more rural areas with more available land.

Attempting to introduce grave recycling on a large scale in the United States would force Americans to change the way we conceptualize burial. Not only would we have to reconsider the gravesite being dedicated to a single individual in perpetuity, but we also would need to alter the way we deal with the dead. There are certain aspects of the typical American funeral that do not comport with grave recycling. For example, we would need to move away from embalming since this slows the decomposition process of the remains, meaning that the gravesite is not available for re-use until a longer period of time has passed.

Americans would also need to reconsider what their loved ones are buried in. Expensive caskets made of wood or steel, as well as steel or concrete vault liners, also slow decomposition. Use of these items would therefore need to be discontinued in order to make grave recycling a viable option. Burying loved ones, without embalming them, in something as simple as a shroud would be more practical for grave recycling. This would allow nature to decompose the remains at a pace quick enough for the gravesite to be available for re-use within a few decades.

Since Americans are not used to grave recycling and are accustomed to a certain type of funeral and disposal of remains, there is likely to be pushback from the public over introducing such a method. In addition, the funeral industry may be critical of such a process as well. In the long run, the funeral industry could benefit from grave recycling since it allows cemeteries to re-use their gravesites, and therefore re-sell the same gravesites after a certain period of time has passed. This means more income without having to buy more land to create more gravesites.

However, the funeral industry is currently committed to the typical American funeral, involving embalming and selling fancy caskets and grave liners to their customers. Prohibiting the use of these methods and items means immediate decreased revenue for the funeral industry. Thus, although the funeral industry can sell the same gravesite over and over again, it will make less money on each and every burial that it conducts given the restrictions that would be in place. The funeral industry is a very powerful lobby and may succeed in preventing grave recycling from being implemented on a national level.

If, however, the legislature does succeed in passing legislation requiring grave recycling, the variety among countries that do practice grave recycling indicates that there are numerous ways to implement the practice. The most viable method seems to involve limiting the amount of time dedicated to a single individual in a single gravesite to a period of 75 years. By this time, the remains will have decomposed to the point that there is not going to be much left to reinter. In addition, this allows the family and friends of the deceased time to process their grief over their loss. By the time 75 years has passed, many of the people personally affected by the individual's death will be deceased themselves. This means that there are unlikely to be numerous people deeply affected by re-using the gravesite.

Once the remains are unearthed from the gravesite, the issue becomes what to do with them. Although using an ossuary may be an option, it is likely that the public will strenuously object to this. Putting the dead on display or piling everyone from the cemetery in one room would likely be a difficult practice for Americans to accept. The more viable solution would be to bag the remains removed from the gravesite and return the bag to the grave. Then the newly deceased individual would be buried on top of the previous occupant's bagged remains. Although there likely will be objections to burying one person on top of another, this seems to be the best solution for what to do with the unearthed remains.

One of the major issues with implementing grave recycling in the United States, other than the reactions of the public and the funeral industry, deals with previous burials. As mentioned previously, the typical American funeral involves embalming, use of a casket, and possibly the use of a steel or concrete grave liner. These aspects serve to slow decomposition, which poses problems when it comes to re-using fairly recent gravesites. Gravesites cannot be re-used unless the individual currently buried in the grave has decomposed to the point where the remains are small enough to be bagged and placed in the bottom of the grave.

This echoes the issues faced in Norway, dealing with the plastic liners previously used during burials. The government in Norway has prohibited re-using gravesites where a plastic liner was used, limiting the availability of gravesites that can be used for grave recycling. It is possible that it may take hundreds of years before gravesites that are currently in use are available for grave recycling, given the way in which the individual was buried. If grave recycling is implemented on a large scale in the United States, for the first 75 years or so, there will be a limited supply of gravesites. However, once 75 years has passed and those that have been buried within that time frame comply with the restrictions concerning burial (i.e., no embalming and no grave liner), there will be a multitude of gravesites available to be re-used, allowing grave recycling to be practiced on a large scale.

If the legislature manages to pass a law requiring grave recycling and includes restrictions as far as the available burial practices, then grave recycling could be a viable solution to overcrowding in the United States. However, there is likely to be opposition from both the public, who are not used to confronting the realities of death, and the funeral industry, whose profits are based on the current typical funeral practices here in the United Stations. If these obstacles can be overcome, the United States can join numerous countries around the world that practice grave recycling.

❖ ❖ ❖

Crown Hill Cemetery, Indianapolis, Indiana
Photo by Tanya D. Marsh

CHAPTER 10.5

GRAVE NEW WORLD

Tyler Gardner

The "traditional" American burial is both a hazard and a waste of land resources. The current system must change in the coming generations.

The average plot size for traditional American graves are approximately 4 feet by 12 feet, and occupied by a single person, in perpetuity. This consumes a significant amount of land. In response to the economic and environmental consequences of the traditional American burial system, there has been a movement towards cremation and green burial. This article hopes to identify the current problems with traditional burials in regards to efficient land usage and offers regulatory laws and policies that could address these concerns.

A traditional burial typically refers to embalming a body, and then displaying the body for visitation and typically a funeral service at a funeral home. Traditional burials have been the primary process by which the majority of Americans will have their body disposed. The historical consensus is that embalming began en mass during the American Civil War and gained even more publicity when Abraham Lincoln was himself embalmed in order to transport his body between Illinois and Washington D.C. Embalming began in response to problems of body transportation in the American Civil War, but today the funeral industry argues that embalming the body is important, because it allows the body to be viewed and gives mental and emotional solace to the loved ones left behind. The term that was in vogue for a time was 'grief therapy,' however, recently the term seems to have been abandoned. Instead the typical line is more about gaining closure. Even before cremation, embalming and viewing are seen as important to gain closure and not have regrets of not seeing the body before disposition.

The funeral industry is unique in regards to other industries that sell products or services as costly as the average traditional funeral. The reason for this uniqueness is that considering the high costs of a traditional burial those having to make decisions regarding purchasing funeral services have little information, experience, have limited time, and are emotionally stressed. Lack of public awareness and law makers willingly assenting to funeral industry interests have resulted in widespread traditional burials that have created multiple problems. Two problems will be addressed in this paper, the first being environmental concerns created by popular embalming techniques and the second being inefficient land use in the creation and planning of cemeteries. These problems can be addressed effectively by the creation of tax incentives for non-traditional burials and uniformed federal regulations for cemeteries.

How We Got Here

A full understanding of the problems of America's current body disposition practices can be ascertained by a clear explanation of how the practice of embalming and burial became the standard in America. Initially Americans disposition of the dead was typically performed by the deceased's family and the body was taken care of and buried by the family. The bodies were predominantly buried in church cemeteries, family land, or in city cemeteries. The American Civil War changed this dramatically because huge numbers of men were dying far away from home. Transporting these bodies back to their homes was not possible due to the speed in which decomposition of the body occurred. However, embalming changed this, by embalming the bodies they could then be transported back to their homes and funerals could be given to these men with the body present. Thus a 'professional' class of embalmers was born, and with events such as Abraham Lincoln's body being embalmed, the embalmers continued to survive as an industry after the civil war.

Overtime the industry and culture of America changed, funeral homes became predominantly responsible for handling the deceased, coffins were replaced with more stylish expensive caskets, and embalming was routinely used. As time went on, the idea of cemeteries changed and cemeteries began to take on a 'park' like quality, a place to be at peace spiritually. All of these combined to create cultural norms and solidify an industry that could provide such services to satisfy the norm. The key fact of this history is that these changes created an economic industry around burial, bigger equipment was needed and funeral homes became the entities that handled funerals. Thus the ritual of burial had shifted away from home burials to a commercial entity designed to perform all the culturally significant duties of burial. Superficially this shift does not seem bad, however, it has created serious problems in land-use efficiency and the laws and subsequent regulations have stifled out alternatives to traditional burial. The continuation of embalming and traditional burial practices is primarily driven by the funeral industry and cultural norms in America. However, traditional burials have ignored two important considerations. The first is that traditional burial results in inefficient land usage and second, traditional burial results in environmental degradation and potential health hazards. In order to mitigate these problems a push to increase cremation, green burial, and to change laws and tax incentives are needed. The most important issue to be addressed by these changes are the environmental concerns because there is potential for environmental degradation and human health concerns.

Environmental Concerns

Formaldehyde is overwhelming used in almost all embalmings performed in America. Embalming preserves and sanitizes the body, which allows for the body to be preserved long enough for a viewing and funeral service. The funeral industry has an obvious economic interest in maintaining the status quo for using embalming, because the embalming is a service that can be charged and it preserves the body temporarily from decomposition which allows for a traditional burial to occur. Embalming's preservation quality allows the body to be viewed, this is important because noticeable decomposition begins as soon as the heart stops pumping blood, once this happens the body begins to quickly decompose and discolor. This is a core component of the funeral industry's economy, a fundamental part because a large source of revenue is the traditional funeral service and burial, preserving the body is a necessary condition in order to have visitation and a traditional funeral service in memory of the deceased. Formaldehyde is the primary ingredient in embalming fluid for all embalmings in America. To understand how large of an economic industry would be affected by a change from using formaldehyde consider that the National Funeral Directors Association estimates approximately two million Americans are embalmed in a year. Each embalming uses approximately 3.5 gallons of fluid containing primarily formaldehyde, resulting in roughly seven million gallons of formaldehyde being placed into the ground every year.

As long ago as 2004 the International Agency for Research on Cancer declared formaldehyde a known human carcinogen. Further, the U.S. Department of Health and Human Services' National Toxicology Program declared formaldehyde a carcinogen. The U.S. Department of Health and Human Services designation garnered a response from Mellissa Johnson Williams, executive director of the American Society of Embalmers, saying 'Today everything is a carcinogen' and openly questioned the validity of the study. A more artful answer may have been to express concern first, state there was a need to have more studies done, and finally explore alternatives to formaldehyde. Analogous to this approach would be the Bisphenol-A (BPA) studies that indicated BPA caused potential health problems. Many plastic makers initially expressed skeptic concern and then responded by taking out BPA from their products. Interestingly though there is an argument that BPA's replacement is just as problematic and are also often unknown. This is likely to occur in the funeral industry in regards to replacing formaldehyde, there are little options for them to take currently and the ones that are available appear to present the same problem formaldehyde does. Which is why a movement away from traditional burial is all the better.

There are other problems and need for change. Older cemeteries contain bodies that were embalmed in the late 19th and early 20th century using embalming fluid containing. The practice of using arsenic-based embalming lasted into the early 20th century until it was eventually banned. Further the caskets in used in this time contained high levels of copper, zinc and lead which if ingested in large enough amounts can become health hazards. Studies of cemeteries in Iowa and New York suspected of using arsenic based embalming fluids and caskets containing high levels copper, zinc, and lead showed elevated levels of all these elements in groundwater 'downstream' of these cemeteries.

While at the time these burials occurred it was difficult to predict that groundwater would be affected it is difficult to correct the problem. Not even considering the regulatory hurdles involved in buying a cemetery, converting the land is a financial burden, involving the digging up and relocating of bodies. Further this kind of tasks is usually only taken up by the government, which means the government must have an interest in the land and investing the resources to convert the land. Further cemeteries are unlikely to come up for sale or lose their usefulness for body disposition. This is because there is an economic incentive for the funeral industry to keep the custom and tradition of funeral services. The average cremation costs around $3,725 compare this to the $8,565 cost of a traditional burial. Traditional burial generates by far the most revenue for funeral homes which make it highly unlikely that the industry, as currently constructed, would make any moves to change embalming practices as they stand today.

Inefficient Land Use

For the purposes of this paper efficient land use will be a reference to land that has potential for multiple usable purposes and is readily convertible to meet market demand. In contrast inefficient land use references land containing cemeteries, which as discussed are not easily converted. The inefficient land use problem is caused by a lack of systematic and uniform regulation on cemeteries and burial plots, as well as the financial challenge of converting cemeteries to useful parcels of land. Determining just how much land is already in use by cemeteries is quite difficult. It is far easier to attempt to give an approximate projection of how much land will be needed for cemeteries in the future. There is no overarching federal system keeping track of the amount and size of cemeteries in this country. Even from my own research there are mismatches between multiple sources of cemetery documentation. Hard copies on record can overlap or be unclear, as some rely on very old land markers that are no longer present, resources such as findagrave.com do have a substantial amount of cemeteries documented but because of overall poor documentation there are mismatches in between historical records, zoning documentation, and findagrave.com purported cemeteries. Often there can be issues of duplication, of multiple cemeteries having the same name, private and farm cemeteries not documented, and abandoned cemeteries.

These challenges illustrate two serious problems created by America's cemetery system, or lack thereof. The first problem is that the documentation issues make it difficult to easily identify how much land is already being used by cemeteries. It is very difficult to re-convert cemeteries into efficient parcels of land which means it is unlikely a significant of cemeteries are being or going to be converted. The second problem is the unsystematic and spread out nature of cemeteries in general. This is best illustrated particularly in rural areas of the country, because many cemeteries are spread out by virtue of city cemeteries, church cemeteries, and farm cemeteries miles apart from each other. Their potential impact on surrounding land can be greater than if the cemeteries were in more concentrated areas. For example formaldehyde can leak into the ground, because cemeteries are more spread out in rural areas there is higher likelihood of formaldehyde entering into water streams and surrounding areas. Whereas if cemeteries were concentrated and better planned their impact on potential water sources could be minimized by placing concentrated cemeteries away from water sources. Concentrating cemeteries may present its own problems, however the concentration would eliminate certain problems with rural area cemeteries. Further a movement to centralize cemeteries would create public awareness and likely lead to the realization by the public that this much formaldehyde in one location may be undesirable and could be a catalyst to switching over to forms of disposition that does not require formaldehyde. In other words attempting to concentrate formaldehyde could lead to the issue of why formaldehyde use is so prevalent in use to become a more publicly debated issue. A large scale public debate over formaldehyde would be beneficial as formaldehyde is a serious concern as it has been upgraded to a known human carcinogen yet is still used for the vast majority of embalmings. The issue of efficient land use will become even more relevant over the next decades as the baby boomer generation will have the potential to claim an enormous amount of land upon their deaths, in the form of burial plots in cemeteries.

The Problem of Baby Boomers

The baby boomers are now in the range of their mid-50s to late 60s, in the coming two decades they will be approaching the average life spans of most Americans. What this means is that in the next two decades there is likely to be a great need for disposal of the dead, the baby boomers are, relative to other generations, a large generation. None of this is particularly shocking information as it is rather obvious, it is not difficult to foresee that demand will increase when the supply of the dead increases. What may be surprising though is that lack of public policy planning for this inevitability. If current trends continue it is likely that half or more of the baby boomers will have a traditional burial barring a dramatic cultural change. While the cremation rates have continually increased since 1960 the increase still projects to be the minority option as the majority of this baby boomer generation will prefer to be buried. The baby boomers demise will create an increase in the demand of burial services and consequently land needed to dispose of the dead. While this problem hangs over the next few decades, there is little guidance in the law and policy of states addressing this eventual demand for land. For example urban planners rarely address cemetery development and planning. This essentially allows the process to be driven by the funeral industry that benefits from it economically. The dynamics of allowing an industry which profits most from burial and not alternative disposals means that this industry will likely not follow the best policy in regards to efficient land use and the public good. Instead it is most likely that the funeral industry will instead follow the most prudent economic policy that maximizes the value of their products and services, which would limit a sustainable approach because the more land that is in demand and used up the more valuable it becomes. The incentives of the funeral industry do not align with the public good, standard policies of efficient land use is good for the greater economy as well as in the public's best interest in maximizing efficient and sustainable use of land. This in turn means that supply and demand will unfold and it is not unrealistic to believe that an industry that profits from burial would value land for such purposes increasing in value due to increase demand. This is contrast to a more desirable model of public policy urban planning. While it can be difficult to determine how many deaths will occur in a single town or county because populations and demographics can fluctuate over time these areas. Regardless of how the more localized demands and needs may change, the overall national increase in demand makes it prudent that this shift will demands a change in how disposition of remains is performed. A challenge of addressing the issue of baby boomers comes from America's ignorance of the issues or unwillingness to address an issue so directly entwined with death.

It is appropriate to label America as a 'death-adverse' society, which is to mean that American society, as a whole, tends to avoid dealing with death in substantial ways until it is presented on an individual level. Because America has a professional and commercial enterprise dedicated to handling the dead, the lack of public interest and awareness creates problems in regards to the laws and regulations of burial practices. The main problem created is that because there is little public knowledge or interest in the area the funeral industry itself has the ability to in effect write its own laws or protect laws that the industry as a whole benefits from. Without any political pressure on burial and a lack of awareness there is no significant form of opposition to the funeral industry creating favorable laws for itself or maintaining the status quo. There is a need to challenge the status quo, and to implement laws that make economic sense.

Solutions

Change law/regulations that require a certain amount of graves in a given space. There will be approximately 76 million baby boomers whom will have a need for body disposition over the next two to three decades and if cremation rates continue to increase approximately half will be cremated and half will have traditional burials, meaning an expectation of 38 million traditional burials from baby boomers alone. Coutts in making his calculation of how much land will be needed to meet the demand of dying baby boomers used the average plot for a burial is 4 by 12 feet as his starting point. Coutts did not take into account space between given plots, while many cemeteries may be efficient on this point due to economic principles of maximization of the land a law should still be put in place that would force the average plot size to be decreased. The law should apply to all zones that are designated cemeteries by their local municipalities and the plots should be adjusted to be plots of 3 by 7 feet plots would nearly cut the land needed for burials in half. Going from 130 square miles to under approximately 80 square miles is a significant improvement, this same calculation can be roughly applied to the predicted land that will be needed of around 64 square miles, the new law would get the land required below 35 square miles. To illustrate the significance of how much land is saved, imagine the full size of Atlanta and take away nearly 75% of the city, the illustration is difference between the worse-case scenario of land usage and the best-case scenario of land usage. Just this simple kind of law could help counter act an enormous amount of inefficient land use brought about by burial.

This law of course would be met with likely ire from the funeral industry, the average width of a casket is 2.3ft while the average length is 7ft, the length of the caskets would likely have to be slightly shrunk in order to ensure the casket would fit a 7ft plot. The first and easily correctable complaint will be one of unreasonably enforcing the provision on people who are larger. This is easily correctable with an exception that burial plots are allowed to be adjusted when the person being buried requires more space than what is legally allowed, this exception has to be shown by the funeral home or parties representing the deceased's estate. That issue put aside, it is highly likely that the funeral industry would rail hard against this law as it would interfere with big ticket items such as caskets and vaults. Likely spinning the law as an infringement upon the freedom of citizens on how they want to be disposed. This argument is illogical because there are already restrictions on burial, a person cannot be buried wherever he or she may like to be buried, say in a school's playground area. This would be a sensible arrangement and if using more space than the 3 by 7ft is desired and does not meet an exception then that person can pay substantially more to have that extra space. This kind of law could be nearly impossible to institute without a serious public-relations effort, in order to get such a law the media would need to articulate the policy behind it. The funeral industry would likely fight back arguing that some aspect of people's 'burial rights' were being trampled upon, how this would play out in the public is up to debate.

A better proposition would be to encourage cremation and green burials through tax incentives and favorable zonings in desirable places to be 'laid to rest.' The most land efficient method that is widely available is cremation. The facilities used for cremation are not large, provide a needed service and the ashes created after the process of cremation takes up little space. Further cremation helps avoid any potential environmental problems that may be a result of using formaldehyde based embalming fluid for burial. Given the benefits of cremation it would appear to be the most feasible form of disposition that could help limit the amount of traditional burials that occur.

Cremation is far more affordable than traditional burial, the average cremation costs around $3,725 compare this to the $8,565 cost of a traditional burial. In response to any movements to promote cremation the funeral industry as a whole would likely push back against any legislation furthering cremations use among the public. Currently the regulations that are in place in the majority of states encouraged embalming by making funeral homes virtually the only entities that can gain embalming certifications. A drawback that will need more study is the impact of formaldehyde entering the atmosphere from cremation, this obviously only occurs when the body has been embalmed first most likely for the purposes of viewing before cremation or even done to boost revenue by a less than ethical funeral home. Luckily there are two positive indicators that cremation would not create a problem, because cremation appears to have a minimum impact on the release of formaldehyde from the cremation of an embalmed body. Further, formaldehyde does not appear to be bioaccumlative which means the release of formaldehyde would be unlikely to store itself into organic materials. Unfortunately the effect of the atmosphere does not appear to have been extensively studied at this point in time.

Realism: Netherlands

Although the best way to minimize the impact of burials on land use would be to adopt federal laws limiting the use of embalming, non-biodegradable coffins, and vaults, as well as cemetery plot size, it is unrealistic to expect that Congress would enact a more uniform system for human remain disposition in the near future. However, times change as well as attitudes, and the reasons for change can vary. Sometimes values do not change drastically but instead there is increased pressure on a natural resource, in this case land. The Netherlands are a great example of how regulations can work to better utilize land and have a uniform system. In the Netherlands there is a process in which an individual chooses to either be buried or cremated. If burial is chosen, then the individual may choose which government-designated area to be buried in and the availability of space in the designated area will be reflected in the price of burial. The individual pays 1,000 Euros for remains to stay buried for ten years, or 2,000 Euros for remains to stay buried for twenty years. Once the time expires, a trust, descendants, or other party may renew the lease. If not, the body is removed and cremated to create space for another decedent.

This is an incredible system that maximizes efficient land-use and attaches value for the use of land for burial purposes. The Netherlands was forced to adopt such a policy because of the country has limited land due to its small size, while America may never have to deal with such a lack of land, there is still an incredible amount of land being used inefficiently for traditional burials. America would benefit greatly from an adoption of more land-efficient policies in regards to the disposal of human remains.

Conclusion

Some sort of change is needed in the near future to minimize public health issues and minimize the amount of land that will be used for burials. The baby boomer generation's consumption of land for burial plots will only be the beginning of a potential large scale land use problem. The world has more people in it today than at any other point in its history and America's population will continue to grow. If burial practices do not change, then an incredible amount of land will no longer be sustainable or easily converted into efficient parcels. The statutes proposed as a solution to this problem are hardly as draconian as they might first seem, when taking other country practices such as the Netherlands into consideration. Ultimately the baby boomer generation may be the beginning of a large land use problem or the beginning of alternative disposition preferences which are sustainable and land-use efficient.

❖　❖　❖

St. Louis #1, New Orleans, Louisiana
Photo by Tanya D. Marsh

CHAPTER 10.6
THE DECAYING STATE OF NEW ORLEANS' DISTINCTIVE CEMETERIES
Shelby Roth

Millions of visitors travel to New Orleans each year to enjoy the food, music, and unique ambience. Preservation Hall, Bourbon Street, and Jackson Square draw hordes of tourists, but equally fascinating are the city's ancient cemeteries. New Orleans' distinctive cities of the dead and their crumbling, white-washed tombs have drawn the attention of artists and writers for centuries. Yet, evolving legal complications surrounding Louisiana's abandonment statute hold a certain fascination for many legal professionals in New Orleans. Louisiana's antiquated cemetery abandonment statutes keep New Orleans' historic cemeteries in a state of disrepair and make it nearly impossible for the managing cemetery authorities to afford preservation of these historic landmarks.

Notable Cemeteries

Some of the best-known cemeteries in New Orleans are St. Louis No. 1, St. Louis No. 2, and St. Louis No. 3, all located in the Vieux Carré (the French Quarter). St. Louis No. 1 opened in 1789 after the older predecessor, Saint Peter's Cemetery, was destroyed by fire. It contained sections for Catholics, Non-Catholics and "Negroes." The third section appears to have been reserved for slaves, because free people of color were buried according to their religion. St. Louis No. 2 is located three blocks away from St. Louis No. 1 and opened in 1823. St. Louis No. 3, established in 1854, is located approximately 2 miles from the French Quarter, on Esplanade Avenue. St. Louis No. 3 is the largest of the three cemeteries, containing approximately 10,000 multiple-use burial sites, including 3,000 wall vaults, 1,500 to 2,000 individual family tombs, and about twelve society tombs. All three cemeteries are owned by the Roman Catholic Diocese of New Orleans.

Another well-known cemetery in New Orleans is Lafayette No. 1, located in the Garden District. Lafayette No. 1 is the oldest of the seven municipal cemeteries in New Orleans. It is non-denominational and non-segregated. Lafayette No. 1 takes up a city block and was platted in 1832. It contains 500 wall vaults, 1,000 family tombs, and the remains of approximately 7,000 people.

Types of Tombs

While there are several different types of above-ground tombs found in New Orleans' historical cemeteries, three types dominate the landscape—family tombs, society tombs, and wall vaults. Family tombs are the most common tomb type in New Orleans. They are derivative of the family tombs used in pre-Christian Rome, later adopted throughout the Mediterranean and France. Family tombs maximize space and economy, allowing multiple generations to be entombed together. Family tombs have slots for one or more caskets at a time. A casket is placed in the tomb and then the opening is closed with brick or a stone panel. After a period of time has passed, the casket is removed and the human remains are separated from the casket. The human remains are placed in a bag and then deposited in a niche at the rear or bottom of the tomb (the "*caveau*"). The casket is disposed of as refuse. [Note: Examples of family tombs are on the first pages of Chapter 5.4, Chapter 15.3 and Chapter 15.5.]

Society tombs are larger version of family tombs and designed for the use of religious groups, clubs, fraternal organizations, and other groups. During the 1800s, joining a society group enabled the poor to pool their resources in a common fund that ensured their interment in a consecrated cemetery. [Note: Examples of society tombs, both in Lafayette #1, are on the first pages of Chapter 9.1 and Chapter 15.2.]

The final type of tomb is the wall vault. Many of the old cemeteries in New Orleans are surrounded by walls that contain individual vaults. Those individual vaults could be purchased for the permanent use of an individual who did not have a family or was not a member of a society. They were also used on a temporary basis for family members who died before a family tomb could be opened to accept another entombment. When the family tomb could be re-opened, the remains that had been entombed in the wall vault would be deposited in the family tomb's *caveau*. [Note: An example of a New Orleans wall vault follows Chapter 4.6.]

Entombed remains decomposed rapidly in New Orleans' subtropical climate. To mask the resulting odor, the managing cemetery authorities poured lime on the bodies and planted fragrant trees around graves.

Origins

There are several competing explanations for the reason that New Orleans' cemeteries are so distinctive and different from the majority of American cemeteries. Some attribute the use of above-ground tombs to the city's high water table. Located between Lake Ponchartrain and the Mississippi River, much of New Orleans, including the French Quarter, is built on marshland. As a result, the water table—a geological barrier that separates saturated soil from unsaturated soil—is abnormally high. This would appear to preclude the in-ground burial of caskets at normal depths. Although caskets may resurface following heavy periods of rain, the high water table was not a contributing factor to the structure of New Orleans cemeteries. Instead, recent excavations have found in-ground burials across New Orleans that date back to the 1700s—contemporaneous with New Orleans' famed above-ground cemetery, St. Louis No. 1.

Lafayette #1 Cemetery, New Orleans, Louisiana

Others theorize that the design of New Orleans' cemeteries may be attributed to sociological factors. They claim that above-ground tombs were utilized during New Orleans' population boom in order to more efficiently house the city's ever-increasing dead. However, above-ground tombs can be found across Louisiana in cities that did not experience population growth like New Orleans. Therefore, population theories which attempt to explain the origin of New Orleans' above-ground tombs are unlikely.

Instead, the actual reason behind the distinctive architecture of New Orleans' cemeteries is much less well-known. Unlike many American cities, early New Orleans was influenced more significantly by the French and Spanish than the English. Throughout the city's early years, the French and Spanish battled constantly for control of New Orleans. While French leaders ruled supreme, so did their customs. Likewise, when Spanish leaders controlled New Orleans, Spanish customs were adopted. As a result of this back-and-forth governance, many traditional New Orleans customs, such as the above-ground tombs, resulted from a combination of Spanish and French influences. Although the family tombs, wall vaults, and society vaults seem foreign to most modern Americans, in reality, such above-ground tombs were utilized across Europe for more than 1000 years. Examples of family tombs can be found in American cemeteries as well, particularly in New England and the Mid-Atlantic region.

A Year and a Day

Touring a historic New Orleans cemetery or speaking with locals would inevitably raise the subject of the *year and a day* rule—the idea that a corpse must remain casketed and inside a tomb for a year and a day before it can be removed and placed in the *caveau*. Although there is no legal precedent for the year and a day rule, and cemeteries may establish their own timelines, scholars believe this tradition to be attributed to either mourning customs that took hold during the French rule of New Orleans or antiquated New Orleans city ordinances. These customs gave the widow a formal mourning period of one year and a day after the death of a spouse, which allowed her the opportunity to visit her husband's gravesite before another body was placed inside the same tomb. Not only did this allow the family of the deceased to return to the grave on the anniversary of the death, it gave ample time for the body to adequately decompose. As there is no overriding statutory requirement and no current, dire shortage of cemetery space in New Orleans, managing cemetery authorities may leave a tomb untouched for as long as they deem appropriate.

Legal Ownership and Abandonment

The United States is a common law jurisdiction, based on the law derived from England. The exception is the state of Louisiana, a civil law jurisdiction governed by the 1804 Napoleonic Code. Civil law differs from common law in that more emphasis is placed on judicial interpretation, rather on precedents set by other courts. In as far as cemetery law is concerned, however, the Civil Code does not rule supreme – the Cemetery Act does. Archdiocesan, municipally-owned, and parish-owned cemeteries in Louisiana are governed by Title 8 of the Revised Statues of the State of Louisiana, commonly known as the Cemetery Act. In the absence of relevant provisions in the Cemetery Act, the state will look to general property principles in the Civil Code to serve as a gap filler.

In New Orleans, families or individuals seeking to bury a loved one in a cemetery, whether owned by a private organization, municipality, or the Archdiocese must purchase a right of interment. Historically, the written title to the cemetery space was granted to the families and was descendible for generations. This practice has been largely replaced by the purchase of interment rights. The right of interment – essentially a special kind of easement – gives the family an interest in and exclusive access to the cemetery plot, while the actual title of the cemetery plot remains with the owner of the cemetery itself.

New Orleans' historic cemeteries remain a popular tourist attraction for millions of people. However, tourists may do more harm than good to the physical state of the cemeteries. In response to vandalism, the Archdiocese decided in March 2015 to limit admission to St. Louis No. #1 to family members of the deceased and licensed tour guide companies. This recent prohibition has left many outraged as they claim the Archdiocese is infringing on their personal rights to visit a historic landmark. One of the most prominent organizations dedicated to preserving and promoting the legacy of New Orleans' historic cemeteries is Save Our Cemeteries. When cemetery owners are unable to maintain their tombs whether it be because of family indifference or vandalism, Save Our Cemeteries will contract with local masons to repair decaying headstones in hopes of restoring them to their former glory. The exorbitant cost of these projects, many costing millions of dollars, makes restoration difficult.

As a result of New Orleans' decaying graveyards, some cemeteries and nonprofits alike have begun to analyze the abandonment section in the Cemetery Act in hopes of making a profit by reselling interment rights to abandoned cemetery plots. From a historic preservation perspective, reselling rights to abandoned cemetery plots could provide a source of income which will assist in the maintenance of New Orleans' derelict cemeteries. However, these transactions are not as simple as they may seem. Whether private, public, or Archdiocesan, the cemetery space must first be considered abandoned under Louisiana law.

The appropriate cemetery authority may deem a cemetery space as abandoned under the Cemetery Act if it meets one of two conditions: (1) after a 25-year abandonment period and an additional 10-year-period where the cemetery authority attempts to locate the previous owners or heirs to the tomb; or (2) if the plot is unfit for burial and the cemetery authority has used diligent efforts to locate the previous owners or heirs of the plot to no avail.

Because of the aforementioned time delays in the existing statutes, the process of reselling interment rights is incredibly complex. As a result, few cemeteries opt to attempt the resale and, as a result, they fall further and further into a state of disrepair. Moreover, the notion of reselling interment rights to abandoned cemetery spaces becomes morally complicated when decisions have to be made regarding the remains already in the space. This process will be watched closely by cemetery law experts as judicial decisions continue to develop.

If the statutory time frames were changed and the process of selling interment rights to abandoned cemetery spaces became more feasible, it would create a slew of legal and moral dilemmas–both for families and the managing cemetery authorities alike. If interment rights to abandoned properties could be sold, what would happen to the remains of the people already interred in that space? Would the cemetery dig a mass grave and merely dump the remains of the previously interred there? It is highly unlikely that the family members of the deceased would be in favor of this option. Instead, it is more likely that the remains would be individually tagged and stored – allowing for re-interment if the family of the deceased were to purchase the rights to a different cemetery plot. Despite these possible complications, Louisiana's current abandonment statute needs revision. Revising the abandonment provisions in the Cemetery Act might lead to additional funding for cemeteries to be put toward historic preservation efforts.

As New Orleans' cemeteries become increasingly popular tourist destinations, they likewise become increasingly vulnerable to vandalism. However, the true problem lies in Louisiana's antiquated abandonment provisions. The required waiting periods specified in the abandonment statutes leave New Orleans' managing cemetery authorities without recourse to prevent further physical decay, other than to prevent admission to the public. As a result, many New Orleans' cemetery owners choose to avoid the abandonment statute altogether and not resell abandoned plots – thus, leaving untapped an enormous source of revenue for preservation efforts. As more of New Orleans' cemeteries become desperate to generate income for historic preservation, judicial decisions may result in modernized abandonment statutes with less cumbersome waiting periods.

❖   ❖   ❖

Winchester Cemetery, Winchester, Ohio
Photo by Tanya D. Marsh

CHAPTER 10.7
THE OLIVE BRANCH CEMETERY

C. Allen Shaffer, *The Standing of the Dead: Solving the Problem of Abandoned Graveyards*
32 CAP. U. L. REV. 479 (2003)

This rural Ohio cemetery is one of thousands of places in modern America where the property rights of the dead, the sentiments of the living, and economic and political reality stand in stalemate. A brief statement of the facts regarding this property and its legal status illustrates the issues facing rural communities containing early American burial sites in every jurisdiction.

Hidden now beside a freeway overpass, this acre and its sixty graves were originally the gift of a Revolutionary War soldier to his country church. In the deed of gift, the donor gave to the Olive Branch Methodist Church a fee simple, with instructions that the land "be maintained forever as a temple to Jesus Christ and a burying ground for the faithful departed."

For a hundred years, the Olive Branch Church and its cemetery was an important but unremarkable link in the life of its township. Like many of its counterparts, the Olive Branch Church did not keep records of the allocation of plots, and no deeds, contracts, or agreements are known to survive for individual burial plots. The Olive Branch Church dissolved as a consequence of the depression of the 1930s, and by that time there had been fewer and fewer burials with the passage of years—as an urbanizing America drew families from the farms.

Under Ohio law at the time (as is still the case in Ohio and many other states), the fee interest in the land comprising the abandoned Olive Branch Cemetery was transferred to the trustees of Washington Township, Ohio in 1932. Like most family and rural church burying grounds, there were no maintenance funds associated with the transfer, although Ohio law mandated then (as now) the continuing maintenance of the grounds by the trustees.

In the next seventy years, the surrounding acres of land would first be transected by one of Ohio's major North-South freeways, and the location of an important exit would pass directly next to the abandoned Olive Branch Cemetery. Oil companies and land development firms would purchase the surrounding area, but the location of the cemetery—precisely where a gas station would be located at the end of the southbound exit ramp—would remain a problem. Meanwhile, the cemetery itself sunk into complete disrepair as the Township ceased even to mow the area in the 1980s, claiming rattlesnake infestation.

The remaining monuments continue to degrade, vegetation is taking over the site, and the only sign of human attention to the site is the presence of beer cans and fast food wrappers. Those trying to preserve the site—distant relatives living in other areas—have found that they lack legal standing to challenge the trustees' performance. As collateral relatives of the third generation past the decedents, Ohio law does not provide them standing and as non-residents of the Township they would find it difficult to prove the requisite nexus of interest to file for mandamus.

Although Ohio law mandates that township trustees maintain such cemeteries, it provides no funding to do so. The Washington Township trustees would have to levy a special tax on their own initiative (which is provided for in the statute to maintain burial grounds), which would certainly guarantee their removal at the next election in this far from affluent rural area.

Like so many thousands of similar sites, the Olive Branch Cemetery and its cargo of pioneer graves continues to sink under the realities of modern society, as the living struggle to find a method of bringing the various interests to a forum of resolution. But of the many types of burial places in America, only one type presents this problem … the pioneer cemetery.

❖   ❖   ❖

Winchester Cemetery, Winchester, Ohio
Photo by Tanya D. Marsh

CHAPTER 10.8

DESERTING GOD'S ACRE: THE PROBLEM OF ABANDONED CEMETERIES IN NORTH CAROLINA

Cristine R. Dixon, 6 WAKE FOREST J.L. & POL'Y S.S. 1 (2015)

In Cameron Village, North Carolina, there is a small plot of land behind a luxury apartment building near Oberlin Road that appears to be an untouched, wooded area from the satellite view above. In this "twisted secret garden," however, there are makeshift shelters for the homeless, a massive tree branch that has fallen across the land, and tall fences erected around the property. There are also fallen, cracked, and crumbling headstones for the deceased who are fortunate enough to have some grave marker left at all.

Out of the estimated 600 people who found their final resting places in this cemetery, "in the middle of bustling semi-urban development, complete with businesses, thoroughfares and multi-family housing," only 145 graves have a formal or informal grave marker. While it is known to be one of the four historically black cemeteries in Raleigh, it remains unclear whether this cemetery was primarily dedicated to former slaves and what kind of story its inhabitants have yet to tell. What is certain is that Oberlin, a neighborhood with deep roots as a place where emancipated slaves found their homes, is missing out on a valuable piece of its history as a once sacred ground is overwhelmed by overgrowth, decay, and indifference.

I. INTRODUCTION

> The sentiment of all civilized peoples, since earliest Biblical times, has held in
> great reverence the resting places of the dead as hallowed ground.

Mills v. Carolina Cemetery Park Corp., 242 N.C. 20, 27 (1955). Cemeteries in North Carolina enjoy little in the way of statutory protection or functioning mechanisms of property law. With 31,666 cemeteries spread across the one hundred counties of North Carolina, the abandonment of these properties affects residents all over the state, if for no other reason than the public blight that a neglected, overgrown piece of property causes a community. Even the smallest county in North Carolina, which is home to just over ten thousand residents, still has sixty-six cemeteries. Old churchyards are some of the most likely sites to be neglected or abandoned and are overlooked in favor of larger, perpetual care cemeteries with open gravesites. When cemeteries become unattended or abandoned, they are not recycled back into the property system in the same way that any other property might be. In the absence of clear statutory authority to resolve these problems, "the only reasonable thing to do about the problem [of abandoned cemeteries] is to wait and hope."

II. ROADMAP

Part III addresses the various issues that arise with abandoned cemeteries, such as lack of litigation and guidance from the courts, upholding community standards, and imprecise statutory language. Part IV explains the current legal status of abandoned cemeteries in North Carolina and brings attention to the shortcomings of the relevant statutory provisions. Part V and its subsections explain the possible courses of action—whether it is through government action or through the work of individuals in the community—and identifies the issues that arise with each.

III. WHY DO WE CARE?

There is a uniquely American interest in the rights of decedents to their final resting place. According to the theory of dedication, a community as a whole shares an ownership interest in cemeteries. North Carolina courts have explicitly stated that there is a legitimate state interest in the preservation of the sanctity of the grave. *See Massey v. Hoffman*, 184 N.C. App. 731, 735 (2007) ("Our Courts have long held that preservation of the sanctity of grave sites is a proper exercise of police power by the State of North Carolina."); *Strickland v. Tant*, 41 N.C. App. 534, 537 (1979) ("It is undisputed that the State has a legitimate interest in the disposition of dead bodies and the preservation of the sanctity of the grave."). Despite this interest, there are practical problems with maintaining cemeteries that may increase the likelihood of abandonment. "For example, mowing cemeteries created in irregular patterns and the lack of local expertise in the maintenance of cemetery monuments and the options for exhumation and relocation are but two of the unique problems that add to the expense of these sites." The properties themselves can be expensive to maintain, but it remains an important interest for people in the community to be able to visit their loved ones.

One of the reasons that this issue has not received much attention from the legislature is the lack of litigation in this area. Legal channels to compel action regarding a cemetery are "often unavailable because few interested parties have or can gain standing to bring suit." Many abandoned cemeteries are in such a state because they have lacked space for new burials for some time now, and relatives of the deceased have long since moved away without notice of their standing.

It is also more difficult to ascertain when a cemetery has been abandoned than it may be for other types of properties. When a school is abandoned, there are no class sessions held, no cars parked on the property, and no sporting events played. An abandoned church will no longer be filled with a pulsating congregation. Cemeteries are unique in that they are being "used" by decedents in perpetuity. The common law has tried to create bright line characteristics to determine whether or not a cemetery has been abandoned:

> As long as a cemetery is kept and preserved as a resting place for the dead, with anything to indicate the existence of graves, or so long as it is known or recognized by the public as a cemetery, it is not abandoned. However, a cemetery may be said to be abandoned where . . . the cemetery has been so neglected as entirely to lose its identity as such, and is no longer known, recognized, and respected by the public as a cemetery.

14 C.J.S. Cemeteries § 19 (2015). There are still difficult questions that remain—what constitutes the identity of a cemetery and how can a community be defined to include decedents' loved ones—to gauge whether a community recognizes a property as a cemetery. Furthermore, vague and inadequate language compounds the many gaps in the common and statutory law. Since this law is not often challenged through litigation, its shortcomings remain unaddressed.

IV. LEGAL BACKGROUND

The North Carolina General Assembly has attempted to address the issue of abandoned cemeteries. *See* N.C. GEN. STAT. § 65-85 to -113 (2013). The Abandoned and Neglected Cemeteries statute first sets out to define terms that may otherwise be ambiguous: abandoned, cemetery, neglected, and public cemetery.

"Abandoned" is defined as "[c]eased from maintenance or use by the person with legal right to the real property with the intent of not again maintaining the real property in the foreseeable future." There are several issues that this definition raises. First, it is unclear which persons have "legal right" to own or use the property as a licensee. Second, the definition is triggered by the intent of these unidentified persons, which is difficult to measure from both a practical and a legal standpoint. Finally, the relevant time period of abandonment has been defined as "the foreseeable future," which is particularly problematic when the property at issue is one that has likely been used for dozens or hundreds of years and will presumably be used for perpetuity.

"Neglected" is defined as "unattended or uncared for through carelessness or intention and lacking a caretaker." This standard is a little more clear since it might be apparent that a piece of property has been unattended if there is overgrown grass or an excess of litter. Unfortunately, most of the statutory language refers to abandoned cemeteries, not neglected cemeteries.

Furthermore, parts of the North Carolina General Statutes authorize or give permission to individuals or entities to assume control of or enter the abandoned cemetery but do not require any action on the part of either individuals or the government. For example, a descendant who reasonably believes that a loved one's remains are in the abandoned cemetery, or "any other person who has a special personal interest," may enter in order to "discover, restore, maintain, or visit" a grave with the permission of the landowner. The county commissioners are also "authorized to oversee" abandoned public cemeteries in order to, among other things, "preserve them from encroachment." It is noteworthy that these are only authorized powers rather than duties mandated by statute. This is not an uncommon problem among states that address cemetery maintenance; such requirements are "often muddied by statutory language of permission rather than obligation." If county commissioners, in their discretion, decide to oversee an abandoned public cemetery, they are "authorized to appropriate from the general fund of the county whatever sums may be necessary from time to time" in furtherance of such oversight.

While the Act does impose duties and obligations on government actors, the statute does not cast a wide net. County commissioners are given responsibilities in reference to three types of cemeteries: rural, abandoned, and public. N.C. GEN. STAT. § 65-111 (2013). These duties and responsibilities are limited to keeping records of the properties and the "persons in possession and control" of the properties must submit records to the office of the register of deeds and to the Department and the Publications Divisions in the Department of the Secretary of State. The subsequent subsections of the article address county commissioners in their care of abandoned, public, rural cemeteries, but there are no further duties imposed. If the "local governing body of the institution which owns the cemetery" raises two-thirds of the expense of "beautifying" the property, the board of county commissioners is authorized to appropriate the remaining one-third from the general fund of the county. Without the help of the institutional owner of the cemetery (if there is one at all), the county commissioners are granted the option of overseeing "that the boundaries and lines are clearly laid out, defined, and marked" by taking "proper steps to preserve [the property] from encroachment." In such cases, the commissioners are authorized to take "whatever sums may be necessary from time to time" in order to exercise this control over an abandoned cemetery.

In short, the only duties or obligations imposed upon state actors in North Carolina appear to be limited to the recordkeeping of abandoned, public, rural cemeteries, leaving the other expressly authorized powers at the discretion of the county commissioners. The problematic statutory definition of "abandoned" aside, "rural" cemeteries are not defined for the purpose of this article.

"Public cemeteries" are defined as having "no qualification to purchase, own, or come into possession of a grave in that cemetery." Deciding which cemeteries belong in the public sphere may be difficult because a church, a non-profit organization, or a private or commercial company may have varying ownership interests in cemetery properties. While many private properties may have been set apart for burial purposes, the current laws of North Carolina do not reach any of these properties, and give neither authority nor responsibility to any persons or agencies regarding this property. It is unclear just how many of the 31,666 cemeteries in North Carolina would be considered either public or private, but the laws (or lack thereof) addressing both are inadequate. Action is discretionary and these properties may sit and become overgrown, magnets for crime, or simply just eyesores for the community.

Other states have similarly attempted statutory solutions to this problem. Looking to our neighbors to the south, South Carolina seems to share an interest in preserving the final resting places of its inhabitants. S.C. CODE ANN. § 6-1-35 (1989). However, just as the North Carolina statutes are underdeveloped and impose no real duty to maintain, South Carolina statutes similarly "authorize" counties and municipalities to expend public funds and to use inmate labor to ensure the preservation and protection of their cemeteries. However, this protection seems ineffective when there are no incentives or penalties associated with the effort to maintain them.

Several states provide detailed statutes about when exactly a cemetery is "abandoned" by its previous owner and how the process of assigning this label works. Attempts to create a bright line rule can seemingly exclude the unique factual circumstances that surround these pieces of land. Juxtaposed against this idea that a cemetery is abandoned after it has been left alone for some period of time is the American idea that the deceased are entitled to a final resting place in a grave for perpetuity.

While it is rare, some families are willing to bring legal action when the sanctity of ancestral gravesites is compromised. The importance of cultural beliefs in the sanctity of gravesites becomes apparent when courts are willing to invade the precious right to privacy to allow an interested party to maintain an existing gravesite. In *Massey v. Hoffman*, 184 N.C. App. 731 (2007), petitioner Rethea Massey sought access to respondent Doug Hoffman's property "for the purpose of restoring, maintaining, and visiting the gravesites of her relatives." The North Carolina Court of Appeals noted that even if the person seeking access cannot get the permission of the landowner, that person can get an order allowing entrance from the clerk of the superior court. In addition to being "a descendant of the deceased" or a person with "special interest" in the grave, the petitioner need only establish that entry onto the property "would not reasonably interfere with the enjoyment of the property by the landowner" in order to gain access through a court order. The court goes on to reject the argument that access to land for "discovering, restoring, maintaining, or visiting a grave" could be considered a taking without just compensation. Rather, the North Carolina statutes were interpreted to implement a "proper exercise of a police power." This case aside, the North Carolina statutes remain underdeveloped due to the lack of litigation on cemetery matters; this lack of court intervention perpetuates legislative underdevelopment.

V. TAX LIENS: REDUCE, RE-USE, RECYCLE

Generally, when the owner of a piece of real property is delinquent on real estate or property taxes, a lien will attach to the property to secure the payment. A tax lien only exists where there is a "debt or obligation secured." If taxes remain unpaid, the government can offer the property at a tax sale or auction of the property in order to recover the delinquent real property tax. In this way, abandoned property is recycled. The collection of property taxes in the form of a sale or auction of the property serves as a sort of recycling mechanism, whereby neglected property returns to the live property market. The local or state government serves as a facilitator of this recycling process and executes an important public interest in preventing valuable property from becoming a public blight.

Like some other categories of property, cemeteries are exempt from property tax. N.C.

GEN. STAT. § 105-278.2 (1987). "A cemetery, by its inherent nature, is not subject to the laws of ordinary property." 14 C.J.S. Cemeteries § 1 (2015). This means that cemeteries do not enjoy the protection of the recycling mechanism that property taxes might provide, and, once abandoned, do not have a clear channel through which they may return to the active property market. This makes abandoned cemeteries a unique problem that would be better addressed by more clearly worded statutes that impose duties on persons or government actors instead of simply authorizing discretionary powers.

VI. WHAT ARE THE ALTERNATIVES?

The statutes addressing abandoned cemeteries in North Carolina provide neither incentive for action nor consequences for inaction other than a failure to prepare and keep on record a list of all abandoned public cemeteries in the office of the register of deeds. Two schools of thought provide diametrically opposed solutions to the problem of abandoned cemeteries.

A. "People All Over The World, Join Hands, Start a Love Train"

One school of thought might suggest a departure from imposing a duty on the government in favor of allowing individuals and organizations to take on the responsibility of maintaining or otherwise making decisions about abandoned cemeteries. Oberlin Cemetery in Raleigh, described at the beginning of this article, has been lucky enough to benefit from press exposure that raised public awareness about the plot of land. Oberlin Cemetery was fortunate to be surrounded by a gracious community invested in its history, and, as a result, the Friends of Oberlin organization was born in 2011.

Friends of Oberlin was started by "descendants of Oberlin Village founders, residents of the Oberlin community, residents of the City of Raleigh and other citizens who have a passion for stewardship." The group succeeded in taking tangible steps toward protecting the cemetery, such as obtaining a designation as a historical landmark for the cemetery. In this way, the sacred grounds of ancestors have a living, breathing advocate—with no extra cost to the taxpayers of Raleigh, other than those who spend their time lending a helping hand to the community. The stated purpose of the organization is to "preserve the legacy and grounds of the Oberlin Cemetery" and to "document oral histories of persons laid to rest at the site."

In a Rousseau-ian world, communities might come together on their own—without government intervention—to protect and preserve the sanctity of cemeteries. If each person—or even a portion of the population—were willing to donate a small amount of personal time, abandoned cemeteries could be cared for in perpetuity, without imposing a monetary expense on the citizens of North Carolina. Perhaps descendants or next of kin could be charged with dedicating some of their time and efforts to maintenance of cemeteries where their loved ones are buried.

There are several issues with a proposed solution along these lines. First, the current statutory language authorizing interested persons and other parties to maintain and care for abandoned cemeteries essentially provides this option already; unfortunately, many citizens are not chomping at the bit to pay their dues in preserving history and sacred grounds. Second, there is not a black and white line that can be drawn wherein this option would not "cost" anything to

North Carolinians. There is a great cost associated with the loss of valuable and unique property, as well as the effort expended by the people who take the time to individually clean up and maintain these cemeteries. Finally, cemeteries and burial grounds often become abandoned because they are forgotten and overgrown or hidden in the back corner of an old farm. In a practical sense, leaving citizens to fend for themselves will likely result in inaction when the problem of abandoned cemeteries is weighed against the multitude of issues that individuals face in their communities on a daily basis.

B. "In This World Nothing Can Be Said To Be Certain, Except Death And Taxes"

The North Carolina General Statutes already allow for some funding of cemeteries through the current system of taxation. *See* N.C. GEN. STAT. § 160A-209 (2013). The statutes provide a fairly extensive list of purposes for which a city may levy property taxes subject to some restrictions. There are only a few exceptions that give a city the authority to levy property taxes without any restriction as to rate or amount. Unfortunately, the subsection that refers to cemeteries is—demonstrating a theme in North Carolina cemetery statutes—short and vague. The relevant statute states that a city may levy taxes "[t]o provide for cemeteries." It is unclear whether to "provide" for a cemetery is limited to the creation of new cemeteries or includes the preservation, care, and maintenance of existing cemeteries.

Even accepting the more expansive definition of this subsection, one lingering problem is that this decision is left up to individual cities in North Carolina. The number of cemeteries per county varies drastically—ranging from sixty-six cemeteries in one county to 1,200 in another. These numbers would also undoubtedly vary from city to city, which makes uniformity across the state nearly impossible. The interests of local government representatives are varied, and it would be difficult to see consistent action, particularly because the problem of abandoned cemeteries is not a highly profitable one nor does it plague the thoughts of the average North Carolina citizen.

A practical solution might be to fund the maintenance of abandoned cemeteries at the state-level, thereby spreading the cost evenly throughout counties and municipalities. In this way, larger cities like Charlotte could defray the cost that the more rural, unpopulated areas (littered with old churchyards and spread-out acreage) would be left with if taxes were raised at the county level. The arguments against this approach would likely be analogous to those raised against property tax in general: the lack of return on the investment, slow growth of the tax rate in this area, and general public resistance to the idea that property should be taxed. However, the counter-argument stresses that property tax is a "necessary evil" in order to "preserve the integrity and independence of American local government, and that might be a price worth paying." Additionally, the problem of abandoned cemeteries has more of a "bounded scope" than other problems requiring redress through state funding. Larger, perpetual care cemeteries "will not devolve into neglect" in the same way that small churchyards or back corners of old farms might.

Were the State to maintain these properties, the main cost would likely be keeping the grass and plants on the property from becoming overgrown, and preventing the area from being a public eye sore to the community. The main argument against imposing this tax—the immediate monetary cost to taxpayers in the state—is paired with a hearty counterargument. Property is unique in character and thus "warrants distinctive treatment." Its value is both innate and economic. Thus, the loss or waste of this property is also an expense that society incurs. While this expense might be less tangible, since taxpayers' wallets are none the lighter, it is just as real of an expense as a tax. Arguably, it is more serious than a tax increase because real property is a physical medium, whereas tax and currency systems can be constantly reworked. If viewed in a vacuum of short-term consequences, property tax increases may seem unnecessary, but when considering both short- and long-term consequences, the preservation of real property (and its inherent value) is of paramount importance for North Carolina and all of the states in this country.

C. Envisioning a Solution

This Comment advocates for a solution that includes three separate modifications to the current statutes addressing abandoned cemeteries in North Carolina.

First, the definition of "abandoned" should lean further toward a bright line rule than the current definition, which seeks to measure intent "in the foreseeable future." Instead, the status of abandonment should be triggered by the passing of a substantial number of years (fifty or seventy-five, for example) wherein the owner is no longer identifiable and there has been no activity at the burial site.

Second, abandonment statutes should not be limited to cemeteries that are both public and rural. Revised statutes should address "abandoned cemeteries" in general, without limiting the scope. The current limitation creates a lack of statutory guidance for cemeteries that are located in populated, urban areas, where public eye sores might be more easily viewed from crowded streets and where criminals might be looking for a secluded, tucked away piece of land in the city. Furthermore, private companies who have since dissolved or are no longer able to be found after a reasonable search and inquiry should not be exempt from these laws.

Third, abandonment should trigger an obligation that is imposed upon the counties of North Carolina to take action regarding the cemetery. This obligation should extend well past preparing and keeping on record a list of abandoned cemeteries in the office of the register of deeds. The statute should state, in part:

> Upon abandonment, the county shall provide for the maintenance and repair of the abandoned cemetery, expenses to be assessed to the county. If a county does not provide for such maintenance and repair of the property, the county shall, at its own expense, transfer the graves that are located in the abandoned cemetery to an established and currently maintained cemetery.

The statutes should give the state authority to impose a tax on its residents that will be shared equally among counties in order to defray this cost. This minimal increase in cost for taxpayers would have a dramatic impact on the protection of gravesites, the protection of future property interests, and the preservation of history in North Carolina.

VII. CONCLUSION

Throughout North Carolina, the deceased who have been laid to rest in old and forgotten cemeteries are without advocates among the living. The common law provides little protection, and few individuals are willing to spend the money to initiate court proceedings when there is very little tangible return for the petitioner. The statutes addressing abandoned cemeteries are sparse, vague, and do not impose any responsibilities, but instead only authorize parties to exercise optional powers over the properties. Improving the quality of the statutory language addressing abandoned cemeteries can provide a channel through which these uniquely valuable and historically relevant properties may be protected to preserve the sanctity of burial grounds in North Carolina.

❖   ❖   ❖

CHAPTER 11

INTERMENT RIGHTS

Cupola Cemetery, Richardson County, Nebraska
Photo by Tanya D. Marsh

CHAPTER 11.1

INTERMENT RIGHTS

Tanya D. Marsh

In Chapter 2.2, the burial practices of the ancient Romans are described. Although these practices varied over time, the centerpiece was the family tomb and the crypt underneath. Spadoni asserts in Chapter 2.2 that the tomb was controlled by the head of the family, who was responsible for its care and obligated to inter the remains of all members of the family. However, Chapter 2.4 and Chapter 2.5 introduce the concept of *res divini juris* and *res humani juris*—property subject to divine law and property subject to human law. The Commentaries of Gaius, excerpted in Chapter 2.5, note that property subject to divine law, such as burial places, are the property of no one. The doctrines of the Roman law of sepulcher, recounted in Chapter 2.6, expand upon this concept.

Roman law provided that land, once used for burial purposes, was forever dedicated to that use. If it could not be used for any other purpose, it logically follows that there is no purpose in assigning an owner to it—after all, what could an owner do with it?

A concept that worked well in pagan Rome did not translate to Christian Rome. The Church owned the buildings of worship and the surrounding churchyards. Burial was no longer based on membership in a family, but membership in a parish. Family members in pagan Rome may have had a right of sepulcher with respect to their family tomb, but only members of a parish in good standing had a right to be buried by the Church, in real estate owned by the

244

Church. There was no owner of the family tomb in pagan Rome, and the head of the family had a limited ability to make rules. In Christian Rome, Catholic Europe, and, finally, Anglican England, the Church had temporal and ecclesiastical authority over burial and the churchyard. Individuals and next of kin had little opportunity to challenge the rules imposed by the Church regarding eligibility for burial, methods of burial and memorialization, and management of the churchyard.

Before death and interment in pagan Rome or Christian Europe, there were two parties—the individual to be interred and the person or entity who controlled the place of interment. If we think about the situation using the metaphor of the "bundle of sticks:" in pagan Rome, the individual holding the right of sepulcher held nearly all of the sticks; and in Christian Europe, nearly all of the sticks were held by the entity who controlled the place of interment. In other words, the power balance was completely inverted.

The Reformation did not alter this balance of power. But Americans innovated in the location of interment from colonial times, creating municipal cemeteries, family burying grounds, and community cemeteries to complement the traditional churchyards. Increased urbanization in Europe and the United States during the 19th century accelerated this pattern of innovation, as explained by the examples of New York City in Chapters 11.3, 12.6, and 12.7, and San Francisco in Chapters 12.8, 12.9, and 12.10. The foundational assumptions of English ecclesiastical and common law regarding the balance of power between the individual to be interred and the person or entity who controlled the place of interment simply did not apply in the United States. To further complicate matters, a potential third party was added to the mix—the lot owner.

Cemeteries owned by cemetery corporations, municipalities, non-profit organizations, and even religious organizations sold property interests in particular portions of the burying ground ("lots") to individuals and families for the interment of multiple persons. This practice was more like the family tombs of pagan Rome than the Christian churchyards, but in the United States, unlike Rome, cemetery ground may be owned. Therefore, U.S. law was required to establish the relative interests of the person to be interred, the owner of the lot, and the owner of the cemetery. It did so through the creation of the common law Right of Sepulcher and the common law Right of Interment.

The Common Law Right of Interment

Chapter 1.3 introduces the common law "Right of Sepulcher." Described more fully by Samuel Ruggles in Chapter 7.3, the Right of Sepulcher actually includes two phases of rights. First, the next of kin have a common law right (which, in modern U.S. law is often trumped by express statutory law) to control the decedent's remains and to determine the place and manner of their disposition. Second, the next of kin have particular rights after remains have been interred. Again, as described more fully by Ruggles in Chapter 7.3, the common law generally recognizes the rights of the next of kin to access and (in conjunction with courts of equity) to act as a limited guardian of the interests of the interred remains.

The common law recognizes a second right with respect to the dead—the "Right of Interment." Unlike the Right of Sepulcher, the Right of Interment attaches to the burial place, not the human remains. Like the Right of Sepulcher, the Right of Interment includes two phases of rights. First, the purchaser of a lot, grave, tomb, or niche from a cemetery is entitled to certain rights before any human remains have been interred therein. The second phase begins upon interment.

As discussed in Chapter 9, the first phase of the Right of Sepulcher is not a property right—there can be no property interest in human remains. But the Right of Interment is clearly a property right, and when the Right of Sepulcher and the Right of Interment merge—following the interment of human remains—that merged right is most accurately characterized as a property right. That does not mean that the human remains themselves are transformed into property, but the common law does hold that once human remains are interred within the earth, they become part of the real estate itself. The seeming inconsistency of these doctrines has yet to be resolved by the common law courts.

The Right of Sepulcher, which arose in the common law to compensate for the lack of an established church acting as the guardian for the dead, attaches to all human remains in the United States. The Right of Interment, which arose in the common law to compensate for the unprecedented variety of burying grounds in the United States, is more limited in its application. It is used only with reference to burial places purchased by individuals or families from a third party (a cemetery corporation, municipality, religious organization or other third party that owns the surrounding land). The Right of Interment does not attach to remains buried on one's own land or in a churchyard, Potter's Field, or other burying ground if the right to a particular grave was not purchased.

Chapter 11.3 includes information regarding the sale of lots and graves in Green-Wood Cemetery, a well-known rural cemetery in Brooklyn, in 1853. The materials include the deed used at the time to convey lots, intended for the use of a family and not to be confused with single graves. The deed does not expressly convey a fee simple interest in a lot, although it does use classic conveyance language—"grant, bargain, sell and convey"—and expressly coveys no lesser interest. Indeed, the booklet including the deed form states that "purchasers of lots acquire not merely the privilege of burial, but also the fee simple of the ground which they purchase..." Those rights were limited, however, by the rules and regulations of the cemetery, which were intended to be attached to the deed. The rules, which are also restated in Chapter 11.3, strike the modern reader as similar to the aesthetic and use restrictions commonly imposed on a 21st century residential subdivision. Purchasers of single graves, or even groups of graves, did not appear to receive a fee simple interest, but only a Right of Interment (which Green-Wood refers to as the "privileges of burial").

The distinction between ownership of a fee simple interest and ownership of a Right of Interment was a central focus of the *Ruggles Report*. The families claimed that "the grants from the church were intended to convey, and did legally convey, the fee of the land occupied by the vaults and their steps: [and] that the church retained no legal estate or interest in the land so conveyed." Conversely, the church claimed that "the grants of the vaults were not intended to convey, and did not convey, any portion of the legal fee, but only a privilege or easement in the land to bury the dead; [and] that the whole legal estate in the laud remained in the church, subject only to such privilege or easement; and that the possession of such of the vault-owners." In that dispute, the resolution of the nature of the property right conveyed to the families affected the distribution of eminent domain proceeds. Ruggles acknowledged that in that case, and more broadly, the nature of the property right may be a distinction without a difference. In either event, the owners of the property interest are subject to both the dedication of the land for cemetery purposes and the rules and regulations adopted by the cemetery. The property interest is therefore so restricted that even if it were technically a fee simple, it is practically indistinguishable from a servitude. The land cannot be used for any other purpose (as in pagan Rome) and is subject to the rules of the cemetery owner (as in Christian Europe). That same discussion can be found in numerous reported cases in the United States.

The summary is this—a Right of Interment exists in U.S. common law, a right that conveys certain property rights to a burial place to living persons. That right is subject to the rules promulgated by the cemetery, the scope of which—as further discussed in Chapter 13—are given wide deference by the government. It is also subject to the interests of the deceased, which are considered and often enforced by courts of equity. Disputes over disinterment—discussed in Chapter 14—frequently highlight the clash between these three sets of interests.

❖   ❖   ❖

St. Paul's Chapel, New York City, New York
Photo by Tanya D. Marsh

CHAPTER 11.2

FAMILY, COMMUNITY, AND CHURCHYARD BURIALS IN AMERICA

C. Allen Shaffer, *The Standing of the Dead: Solving the Problem of Abandoned Graveyards,*
32 CAP. U. L. REV. 479 (2003)

> A rustic cemetery ... where the avarice of the living confines within narrow
> limits the ... dead; where the confused medley of graves seems like the wild
> arrangement of some awful convulsion of the earth.

A Rustic Cemetary, 4 LITERARY MAGAZINE AND AMERICAN REGISTER 22, 27 (Aug. 1805).
Burials in early America took place in four places: by pioneers in isolated, unorganized places on
the true frontier; on a family farm, sometimes in a multifamily burying ground; in churchyards,
perhaps open to public as well as church members; and for the poor, unknown or criminal, in
"potter's fields." Taken together, these sites are the most likely to be neglected, abandoned, or
suddenly rediscovered during construction or farming.

Modern writers (and this Comment) tend to speak of these four types of burying
grounds under the one phrase "pioneer cemeteries," although these burials actually concern
different types of land and occurred over a 200-year span of time.

A. Graves of the True "Pioneers"

The graves of the true American pioneers are often unmarked and solitary, and they can turn up
almost anywhere—reflecting the practical problem of needing to bury the dead where they died.
Sometimes, these burials were made near or within established Native American burial places,

248

creating some confusion for those attempting to follow the Native American Graves and Relics Repatriation Act.

Because of the extreme circumstances under which these deaths and burials occurred, it was not expected that true pioneer burial sites would be protected or maintained, and in fact they were often left unmarked. These sites have not been the subject of much litigation, except in states like Nebraska, where a public controversy arose over the treatment of the graves of Nebraska's first settlers. This controversy ultimately resulted in the passage of Nebraska's Unmarked Burial Sites and Skeletal Remains Protection Act (Reburial Act), which applies many of the same strict regulations to these graves that are contained in the Native American Act.

B. Domestic Burying Grounds

> Wherever there is a solitary dwelling, there is a domestic burying place, generally
> fenced with neat white pailings, and deliberately kept, however full the settler's
> hands may be, and whatever may be the aspect of the abode of the living.

Harriet Martineau, 2 RETROSPECT OF WESTERN TRAVEL 228 (1838). Harriet Martineau, traveling through the American frontier, saw this next step in the establishment of family burial grounds as "symbols of civilization and domestication." Along with former churchyards, this is one of two types of burying grounds that are most likely to be in dispute today. Family burial grounds often are found on a high part of the land of an original farm, and are often both shaded by trees planted for the purpose and ringed with a fieldstone wall or other enclosure. They are less popular in the New England States, where those settlers continued the European custom of churchyard burial.

Free African Americans in Northern states, as well as those subject to slavery in the South, were interred in separate sections or in completely segregated burial places. In an attempt to protect their fragile family and community ties, they developed and protected these areas as best they could.

Susan Cooper, the daughter of James Fenimore Cooper [wrote] that "'small family burying grounds, about the fields, are very common,'" and that "the prevalence of farm burials 'had its origin ... in the peculiar circumstances of the early population, thinly scattered over a wide country, and separated by distance and bad roads from any place of worship.'" Susan Fenimore Cooper, RURAL HOURS (1851).

C. Burials in the Churchyard

Churchyard burying grounds in early America were remarkably similar in layout, monuments, and management regardless of religious tradition. Graves were not carefully plotted, and records were not always kept and were certainly not always accurate. The sacredness of the space, which would become the norm in the latter part of the nineteenth century, had not yet developed—and using the space for fairs, markets, and other events was common. Fence and wall enclosures, as well as an increasing unwillingness to displace the dead or obliterate the cemetery, itself became more common in the nineteenth century.

D. Burial of the Poor: The "Potter's Field"

Few potter's fields existed in America before the nineteenth century, and they were more a feature of cities than rural areas. They were often moved or abandoned, especially after epidemics, and it is rare to be able to identify one of them today. Today, the principal problem of these potter's fields is their inadvertent discovery and exposure during urban construction projects. However, no legal stalemate is created by such a finding, in that all jurisdictions have statutory provisions outlining procedures for the unexpected finding of human remains and their disinterment and eventual reburial.

E. Modern Perpetual Care Cemeteries

The rise of the modern cemetery and memorial park began with the establishment of the Mount Auburn Cemetery outside Boston in 1831. With perpetual care provisions such as maintenance trusts, modern recordkeeping, state regulation, and widely agreed-upon expectations and plans, these parcels are not an issue for rural land owners or developers.

❖ ❖ ❖

Stereoscopic of Henry Ward Beecher's Grave, Green-Wood Cemetery, Brooklyn, New York
Photo by Benjamin West Kilburn (1891)

CHAPTER 11.3
SALES OF LOTS AND GRAVES
RULES AND REGULATIONS OF THE GREEN-WOOD CEMETERY (1853)

The Grounds of this Institution now comprise three hundred and sixty acres. They are more extensive than those of any similar institution in this country or Europe, and are entirely free from incumbrance.

These grounds are situated in Brooklyn, on Gowanus Heights, about two and a half miles from the Atlantic Ferry. They are beautifully undulating and diversified, presenting continual changes of surface and scenery, and are remarkably adapted to the purpose for which they are appropriated. The elevated portions of the Cemetery afford numerous and interesting views…

The various Avenues in the grounds (exclusive of paths) extend about fifteen miles. …

Sale of Lots

[P]urchasers of lots acquire not merely the privilege of burial, but also the fee simple of the ground which they purchase… [T]hey are the sole proprietors of the Cemetery …

[A]s the ground is exempt from public taxes, and from liability for debt, and is sold in lots which are not subject to assessment, or annual charge, the proprietors can never be forcibly deprived of their ground.

Purchasers may choose from all unselected ground not reserved for public monuments or other special uses. …

The price of an ordinary Burial Lot is $110, and in proportion for any additional fractional dimensions. When, however, four or more lots are taken at one time, by one or more persons, in a group, they are sold at $90 each. Smaller plots, but not less than one third of a lot, will be sold, at proportionate rates. These prices include all charges for grading and keeping in order. No charge will be made for any work unless especially ordered by lot owners.

The enlargement of families and the desire which is naturally felt to be laid with one's kindred at death often render it desirable to secure more than an ordinary lot. To facilitate this object a lower price is fixed where four or more lots are taken in one place.

Large plots also admit of superior improvements, while the expense of inclosure is proportionately reduced as the plot is enlarged. The cost of a vault under ground together with the price of a lot will about suffice to purchase four lots, to inclose which requires but fifty-six feet more of railing than is needed for a single lot. Where four lots are inclosed together in a square or oblong form, the expense for each lot is one half less than if separately inclosed. ...

The advantage of large plots compared with vaults on single lots, are now generally appreciated. Many of the beautiful hills and knolls, which are found in the Cemetery, may be separately inclosed without incurring much more expense than will be necessary to inclose a single lot. More space is thus obtained for interments, as well as for the adornment of the grounds with shrubbery and flowers. It prevents also that excessive and unsightly crowding together of monuments which prevails where single lots only are laid out, and greatly aids in preserving the rural character of the Cemetery.

The size of each lot is 12 by 25 feet, containing 300 superficial feet, in addition to which a foot is allowed on the margin all around, for purposes of inclosure, making the plot, in effect, 14 by 27 feet, and containing 378 superficial feet. Around each lot, when sold separately, and around each group of lots when sold as above, a space of three or four feet is always allowed. ...

Proprietors may dispose of their lots, and have the transfer recorded on the books of the Company, by the payment of one dollar for each transfer.

Lots are conveyed by the Institution in the following form and manner:

Know all Men by these Presents, That the Green-Wood Cemetery, in consideration of _____ dollars, paid to them by _____ of _____, the receipt of which is hereby acknowledged, Do hereby grant, bargain, sell and convey to the said _____ heirs and assigns _____ Lot _____ of Landlord in the Cemetery of the said Corporation, called "The Green-Wood Cemetery," situate in the Eighth Ward of the City of Brooklyn, in the State of New-York, which Lot __ delineated and laid down on the Register Map or Plan of the said Cemetery, in the possession of said Corporation, and _____ therein designated by the number _____ containing _____ superficial feet.

To have and to hold the herein above granted premises to the said _____ heirs and assigns forever; subject, however, to the conditions and limitations, and with the privileges specified in the rules and regulations hereto annexed. And the said The Green-Wood Cemetery, do hereby covenant to and with the said _____ heirs and assigns, that they are lawfully seized of the herein granted premises in fee simple: that they have a right to sell and convey the same for the purposes above expressed; that the said premises are free and clear of all charges and incumbrances, and that they will warrant and defend the same unto the said _____ heirs and assigns, For Ever.

[Note: The Rules and Regulations of Green-Wood Cemetery were attached to the "deed of conveyance." Excerpts from the Rules as they existed in 1853 appear below.]

I.   All lots shall be held in pursuance of "An Act to incorporate the Green-Wood Cemetery," passed April 18, 1838, and the several acts to alter and amend the same, passed April 11, 1839, May 11, 1846, April 5, 1850, and June 8, 1853, and shall not be used for any other purpose than as a place of burial for the dead, nor shall any person be allowed to be interred therein, who shall have died in any prison, or shall have been executed for any crime.

II.   The proprietor of each lot shall have a right to inclose the same with a wall not exceeding one foot in thickness, nor one foot in height above the surface, to be placed on the margin allowed for the purpose; or with a railing, (except of wood); but the Trustees request that all such railings be light, neat, and symmetrical.

III.   Proprietors shall not allow interments to be made in their lots for a renumeration, nor shall any transfer or assignment of any lot, or of any interest therein, be valid, without the consent in writing of the said company first had and endorsed upon such transfer or assignment.

IV.   No disinterment shall be allowed without permission being obtained at the office of the Corporation.

V.   The proprietor of each lot shall have the right to erect any proper stones, monuments, or sepulchral structures thereon, except that no slab shall be set in any other than a horizontal position; that no vault shall be built entirely or partially above ground, without permission of the Company, and that all monuments and all parts of vaults above ground, shall be of cut stone, granite, or marble. The proprietor of each lot shall also have the right to cultivate trees, shrubs and plants in the same; but no tree growing within the lot or border, shall be cut down or destroyed, without the consent of the Company. ...

VII.   If any monument, effigy, or inclosure, or any structure whatever, or any inscription be placed in or upon any lot, which shall be determined by a major part of the Trustees for the time being, to be offensive or improper, or injurious to the appearance of the surrounding lots or grounds, the said Trustees, or a major part of them, shall have the right, and it shall be their duty to enter upon such lot, and remove the said offensive or improper object or objects. ...

IX.   The proprietors of lots, and their families, shall be allowed access to the Grounds at all times, observing the rules which are or may be adopted for the regulation of visitors.

Public Lots

Single graves may be procured in Lots of three kinds.

First. In Lots inclosed by a hedge, at ten dollars each, for adults, and five dollars each for children under ten years of age.

Second. In Lots inclosed by an iron railing, at fifteen dollars each, for adults, and seven dollars and fifty cents for children under ten years of age.

Third. In Lots inclosed by a hedge, where any number of contiguous graves, *not less than two*, may be had at twelve dollars and fifty cents each, for adults, and one half that sum for children under ten years of age.

In all these cases the usual charge for opening the graves is included in the prices named.

In Lots of the *first* and *second* classes no monuments can be allowed excepting slabs laid upon the graves, or thick headstones, not exceeding nine inches in height above the graves.

Neither slabs nor head-stones may be more than two feet wide, for adults, and eighteen inches for children. In Lots of the *third* class, small monuments may be erected, sufficient space being provided for one monument to each plot of two graves. In all cases they must rest upon a stone foundation at least six feet deep.

Graves purchased in any of the public lots, may be used for other interments, by paying the usual cost of opening graves, as hereafter mentioned. If Lots should afterwards be purchased, the full cost of the graves vacated will be allowed, after deducting the expenses for originally opening the ground, and for the disinterment of the remains. Tickets admitting a family at all proper times are given to all who purchase graves.

Interments in Tombs

Permanent interments may be procured in Tombs erected for the purpose, at fifteen dollars each. For children under twelve years of age, seven dollars and fifty cents; under two years, five dollars.

❖ ❖ ❖

Salem Cemetery, Winston-Salem, North Carolina
Photo by Tanya D. Marsh

CHAPTER 11.4
RIGHTS AND LIABILITIES OF LOT OWNERS
Sidney Perley, MORTUARY LAW (1898)

The tenure of a lot owner depends not only upon the terms of the deed itself, but upon the act of incorporation of the cemetery from which the title is derived, and to the limitations of its powers, and the manifest intent of the parties to the instrument.

The burial of dead bodies in the land of a third person without right, and without the consent of the owner, gives no title thereto or interest therein, until a prescriptive or other right or title can be shown.

Tenure

Every owner of a burial lot must be deemed to have purchased and to hold it for the sole purpose of using it as a place of burial.

A deed of a burial lot from a cemetery association, if they have power to make such a conveyance, the habendum clause being "to have and to hold," etc., to the said, etc., "his heirs and assigns, for the uses of sepulture only, and to or for no other whatever, subject, however, to the condition and limitation and with the privileges specified in the rules and regulations now made or that may hereafter be made and adopted by the managers of the said cemetery for the government of the lot holders and visitors of the same," passes the fee and the possession, though the company is to have the general care and management of the cemetery, it not being incompatible with the rights of the lot owners to manage their own lots.

Generally, the right in the lot is an easement only, the right to use it for burial and cemetery purposes, but with no other interest in the fee. But under the peculiar nature of the subject matter, as an easement cannot be gained except by deed or by a prescription of long standing, the courts term the right of burial in lots a license only, though with one or two exceptions they have all the qualities of easements. In the case of *Conger v. Treadway*, 50 Hun (N.Y. 451 (1888), a conveyance of land having been made to ten persons, on condition that the same was conveyed "for the purpose of a cemetery or burying place for the dead, and for no other purpose," a man bought a lot therein, but did not obtain a deed, which was promised to him, and he buried his dead in the lot from time to time, and erected monuments and beautified the lot, to the knowledge of the owner, the court held that the title to the land itself did not pass, but the exclusive right of burial did, no formal deed being necessary. A certificate of a burial lot, signed by the secretary of the board of trustees of a cemetery association only, without seal or other formality, passes no interest in the land, as an easement or otherwise; it is a license only. The following is a copy of the certificate in the case of *McGuire, adm'r, v. Trustees of St. Patrick's Cathedral*, 54 Hun (N.Y. 207 (1889), which was held to convey a license only: ... "Received from John McGuire ten dollars, being the amount of purchase money of a grave two feet by eight in Calvary Cemetery, with privilege to erect a headstone thereon."

The title to the soil of Roman Catholic cemeteries is in the Bishop of the Catholic Church, in trust for the congregations and societies of the church under him, to be by them used and enjoyed according to the principles and polity of that church, to be used exclusively for the interment of those who at the time of their death were in regular standing in that church, according to its principles, usages, and doctrines; it being consecrated by religious services to that use; and according to its rules a permit must first be granted by the pastor of the church. The lot owner is bound by such doctrines and policies of the church, if he knows of them, and agrees to them, etc. But none but the church itself can rightfully declare who is a Catholic, it being a question of church government and discipline, and must be determined by the ecclesiastical authorities; and their decision is final. A person who, having a sane mind, commits suicide, is never allowed knowingly to be interred in a Catholic cemetery. In Canada an attempt was unsuccessfully made to refuse burial to a member of the "Institut Canadien," a literary society which had incurred ecclesiastical censure, the Bishop of Montreal having in his lifetime forbidden such membership on pain of being deprived of the sacrament.

It is probably true that any organization, religious or secular, may control the right of burial in its own cemetery, and declare who shall enjoy it; and that liberty must be exercised so as not to encroach upon prior rights of others, but binds those who obtain privileges after such rights are acquired, taking subject to them. To hold otherwise would leave every possessor of a lot the privilege to do as he liked, and inter whom he pleased, however much his act might disturb the consciences of others. All that a lot owner acquires in a Catholic cemetery is a privilege to use it for the purpose to which it was dedicated, and the rules in force when he acquires such privilege measure the extent of, and limit, that use.

Duration of Tenure

A license to bury in the Catholic cemeteries may be revoked upon the licensee's becoming anti-Catholic, and equity will not aid in preventing the same. In the case of *McGuire, adm'r, v. Trustees of St. Patrick's Cathedral*, when the license was obtained the purchaser was a Catholic, but before he died he had apparently opposed the faith, and was not recognized as a Catholic by the church. The permit to bury was refused, though the wife of the deceased had been buried in the lot. Justice Daniels dissented from the rest of the court, holding that no evidence of any act on the part of the deceased that was scandalous or sinful had been introduced, that he had died in the faith of the Catholic Church, and that the permit ought not to be refused without giving the lot owner a chance to be heard.

The right to inter bodies in lots in cemeteries, be it an easement or a license, cannot continue longer than the territory is used as a cemetery, or the corporation decide that the ground is no longer desirable as a place of interment, and the license is revoked, the right of future interment being thus extinguished. So of the burying ground of a church.

Interest in Proceeds of Sales of Lots

Where a town cemetery is discontinued, lots in a new cemetery being given to owners of lots in the old one, and the bodies, monuments, etc. removed, and the town voted that "all money received from the sale of lots," etc., "shall constitute a fund for the purpose of defraying the expense of repairing and · improving the avenues, walks, and public grounds of the cemetery," there is no contract with the lot owners that the money received from that source shall be applied to the use and improvement of the cemetery, nor that the fund shall be set apart as a trust fund.

Duty to Others

Every right in a cemetery lot, from an absolute ownership to an easement and license, is held subject to the restriction that it shall not be so exercised as to injure others.

Rights of the Public

Lots are always held subject to the right of the public to take them for its own use if public necessity requires, or when the abolition of the burial ground is necessary for sanitary reasons.

Removal of Bodies on Abolition of Cemetery

When it becomes necessary to vacate the ground for burial purposes, all that the lot holder can claim is notice of such vacation, that he may remove the bodies interred therein, and also the monuments, gravestones, etc., which he has placed thereon. That is his only remaining right, and after that is exercised his interest and right therein absolutely cease. On his failure to make such removal, others interested in the abolition of the cemetery can do so at their own expense. The expense of removal, when it is done by the lot owner himself, can be collected of the parties in whose interest the abolition is made. But he cannot claim compensation for monuments, vaults, etc., if he permits them to remain. He can have no claim for reimbursement of the amount he paid for his right, whether he has ever used the lot for interments or not. Interest in the Rest of the Cemetery. Lot owners and owners of graves have no control or rights in the remainder of the cemetery, except rights of way and such rights as are had by the public.

If a corporation fails to keep the walks, drives, and approaches of its cemetery in proper repair, a lot owner can compel it to do so by a bill in equity.

Where a lot is sold with reference to a plan, on which appears a certain avenue leading to or close beside the lot, affording a convenient highway to and from it, the purchaser has a right of way over it, and it cannot be legally obstructed. Equity will protect this right by injunction if necessary, whether the lot owner has an absolute or a qualified interest in the lot.

Privileges of Visitors

Persons visiting the graves of deceased relatives or friends for the purpose of testifying their respect or affection for the dead have a right to do so, and, if they are improperly interfered with by the owner of · the easement, a court of equity will interfere for their protection.

Right to Build Vaults and Tombs

Every owner of a cemetery lot or other interest in a burial place, having the right to erect and maintain vaults for the purposes of interment, is subject to the police power of the State, in the exercise of which future interments may be prohibited and remains of persons already buried caused to be removed; and the power may be delegated to municipal corporations, and enforced by appropriate ordinances. No conditions or covenants in deeds can prevent the legislature from declaring such use unlawful and causing its abandonment.

In the case of *Rosehill Cemetery Co. v. Hopkinson*, ex'x, 114 Ill. 209 (1885), the cemetery company had a rule that no vault or tomb should "be constructed in the cemetery until the designs of the same accompanying the specifications, and a diagram of location, shall have been submitted to the board of managers, and approved by them"; and the deed of the lot in question was drawn subject to the act of incorporation and the rules and regulations thereto annexed, etc., one of the rules annexed being as follows: "The proprietor of each lot shall have the right to erect any proper stone or monument or sepulchral structure therein, except that no fault shall be built entirely above ground without permission of the company, and no monument and no portion of vaults above ground shall be of other material than cut stone, granite, or marble, without the consent of the company." The owner of the lot proceeded to erect a vault upon it, when the cemetery officers prevented further work. The vault was in itself satisfactory to the board of managers, but they objected to having a vault built on that particular lot, as it was in front of the entrance, and would somewhat obstruct the view. The court granted the prayer of a bill for an injunction against the interference of the cemetery corporation.

Interest in Association

Where the charter of an incorporated association provides that the members thereof numbering from five to fifteen, for instance, shall be elected by the association, lot owners do not become members until they are so elected, and have no right to inspect the books of the company.

Where an unincorporated association owns a burial ground, and provides that, if members withdraw, they shall "have no more right or title or interest in the aforesaid society, or interest in the benefit arising from the graveyard of the said society," it is not meant that a member owning a lot in the cemetery, in which he has made interments of persons in his family, loses all rights of burial in said lot, but is confined to the interest of the association in the income from the sale of lots, etc. in the cemetery. The owner of the lot acquires the privilege and right of making interments in the lot to the exclusion of others, so long as the ground remains a cemetery, and could maintain trespass *quare clausum fregit* for breaking and entering the same by digging a grave therein, in which the defendant buried the remains of a person without the consent of the plaintiff, who is the owner of the lot. And where malice or want of good faith is shown, the plaintiff is entitled to punitive damages.

Rights in Free Cemeteries

In a free neighborhood cemetery, when one has staked out a lot and entered into possession of it, and has not abandoned it, it is trespass in another to fence a part of this lot into his own lot, or to obstruct a road way necessary for its use; and the possessor of the lot can defend his possession against such appropriation by his neighbor. A cemetery corporation is liable also to the proprietor of a grave for the negligent burial of a stranger therein. Where a man bought a lot in a cemetery of a city and interred his child therein, the city having, through the agency of the sexton, the sole control and supervision of the cemetery, and the city subsequently wrongfully sold the lot to another person, the sexton carefully removing and reinterring the remains in a common burial lot, not knowing that the lot belonged to the father of the dead child, judgment was given against the city in a civil action brought for the trespass, the damages being merely nominal.

Ornamentation

The owners of lots or graves have a right to ornament them with shrubs and flowers; and where a lot owner is given this right in the deed of the lot, he does not lose it by a rule or regulation of the cemetery association that he cannot have the work of ornamentation performed by others than himself and the cemetery employees, passed subsequently to the delivery of the deed.

Recovery of Possession

If a lot owner is ousted of his possession, his title to the lot and right of possession as licensee is insufficient to support an action of ejectment, the cemetery company having the possession legally.

Construction of Deeds as to Bounds

The deed of a lot owner which bounds his lot on an avenue does not convey any title to the middle of the avenue, as it would in ordinary conveyances. His right is only that which all the lot owners have,—a right of passage simply. If the right of way to and from a lot is not disturbed, and the owner is not injured thereby, a cemetery association, acting in good faith, can close up an avenue and an open space adjoining the lot, and apply it to purposes beautifying the grounds, in spite of the objection of the lot owner. These rights of the general owners of the cemetery are necessary in order to secure uniform taste and skill in the arrangement and care of the cemetery, and permanence and progress.

Rights of Several Owners of Lots

The purchase and use of a burial lot by several parties almost always cause disagreements and contests, and a state of things to be avoided. The only case of this kind of any importance is that of *Lewis v. Walker's ex'rs*, 165 Pa. St. 30 (1894). In this case four brothers bought a burial lot, and divided its area among themselves. In the middle of the entire lot they erected at their joint expense a monument, on each side of which they inscribed the name of one of the brothers, and set apart the space opposite each name for such brother's family. In such a case, no one of the brothers can permit the interment in his portion of any person who is not a member of the family without the consent of the other brothers; and if the executors of the widow of one of the brothers cut off the raised letters on the face of the monument next her deceased husband's portion of the lot, leaving a smooth level surface, equity will not require an entirely new monument to be erected.

❖ ❖ ❖

Salem Cemetery, Winston-Salem, North Carolina
Photo by Tanya D. Marsh

CHAPTER 11.5

THE NATURE OF THE BURIAL RIGHT

Percival Jackson, THE LAW OF CADAVERS (1950)

Manner of acquisition of burial right must be considered

In considering the nature of the right of burial we must distinguish between rights, in gross, of the inhabitants of a neighborhood to bury their dead in a cemetery, public by virtue of dedication; rights privately acquired by claim of adverse possession; and rights acquired by grant.

We have heretofore distinguished the public cemetery where the right of burial is acquired by purchase from the private cemetery, the latter classification including the family cemetery as well as those privately owned and regulated. We have seen that rights to bury in a public cemetery may be acquired by grant or by virtue of dedication and that the right of burial frequently accrues to inhabitants of a neighborhood, analogously to the English parish system. Manifestly, the nature of the right of burial is not the same where one has a mere personal right of burial because of residence in a certain neighborhood, as it is where one has acquired such a right by purchase and grant. These distinctions are bound to determine or affect the nature of the right.

Nature of right of churchyard burial in England—Analogy to Pew Owners' Rights

The barest right of burial was possessed by the parishioner in common-law England. His right to burial was personal, depending upon his place of abode, and was a common appurtenant shared with every other inhabitant of the parish. In common-law England the parishioners' right of burial in the parish churchyard was akin to the rights of the pewholder.

[Jackson cites an article entitled *Rights of Burial Lot and Church Pew Owners* and explains that "Before the Reformation in England the body of the church was common to all parishioners; but after the Reformation the practice arose of assigning particular seats or pews to individuals. This assignment of pews was a mere license, and was personal to the licensee, and all disputes concerning it were determined in the spiritual courts." He also cites a New York opinion—"The right to a pew gives no right to the soil. It gives only a limited estate. ... The sale of pews in a church is not a disposition of real estate; the grantee acquires a limited usufructory right only. He may use the property as a pew; but he has not an unlimited absolute right. He cannot use it lawfully for purposes incompatible with its nature. The right, too, is limited as to time. If the house to which it was an appurtenant be burned or destroyed by time, the right is gone. ... This would seem to be in accordance with the principles which govern the English ecclesiastical courts; and I am inclined to say these principles are also to be considered as part of the common law."]

Duration of Right—Doctrine of temporary appropriation of soil in England

Having no title to the soil beneath his pew nor to the space above it, the pew owner had no right to dig a vault under it or to erect anything over it without the express consent of the church authorities. The parishioner had an analogous right of occupancy in the soil allotted for the burial of the body, a right which terminated with the dissolution of the body.

The subject was exhaustively and learnedly discussed by Sir William Scott in *Gilbert v. Buzzard and Boyer*. In that case the court was considering the right of the plaintiff to bury his deceased wife in the churchyard in an iron coffin. The churchwardens refused to put the iron coffin in the ground on account of its durability. This refusal necessarily led to the consideration of what right was acquired by interment in a grave—whether it was an exclusive right to the spot forever, or one which terminated with the decay of the body. If the former, then it was immaterial in what manner the body was deposited; if the latter, then it was important that the ground should not be occupied with durable coffins of metal. The court, concluding that the appropriation of the ground was but temporary, found that a right to interment of a body in such a way as might retard the usual process of dissolution required the parishioner to contract for greater rights than were assured to him by the rules of the common and ecclesiastical law.

[The court said in *Gilbert v. Buzzard*: "it has been argued, that the ground once given to the interment of a body is appropriated forever to that body; that it is not only the *domus ultima*, but the *domus eterna* of that tenant, who is never to be disturbed, be the condition of that tenant himself what it may. It is his forever; and the insertion of any other body into that space at any other time, however distant, is an unwarrantable intrusion. If these positions be true, the question of comparative duration sinks into utter insignificance. "In support of them it seems to be assumed, that the tenant himself is imperishable; for, surely, there cannot be an inextinguishable title, a perpetuity of possession, belonging to a perishable thing: but obstructed in a portion of it, by public authority, the fact is, that 'man' and 'for ever' are terms quite incompatible in any state of his existence, dead or alive, in this world. The time must come when his posthumous remains must mingle with and compose a part of the soil in which they have been deposited. Precious embalmments and splendid monuments may preserve for centuries the remains of those who have filled the more commanding stations of human life: but the common lot of mankind furnishes them with no such means of conservation. With reference to men, the *domus eterna* is a mere flourish of rhetoric. The process of nature will resolve them into an intimate mixture with their kindred earth, and will furnish a place of repose for other occupants of the grave in succession. It is objected that no precise time can be fixed at which the mortal remains, and even the chest which contains them, shall undergo the complete process of dissolution; and it certainly cannot, being dependent upon circumstances that differ, upon difference of soils and exposure, of climate and seasons; but observation can ascertain it sufficiently for practical use. The experience of not many years is required to furnish a certainty sufficient for such purposes. Founded on these facts and considerations, the legal doctrine certainly is, and remains unaffected, that the common cemetery is no *res unius aetatis*, the exclusive property of one generation now departed; but is likewise the common property of the living, and of generations yet unborn, and subject only to temporary appropriation. There exists a right of succession in the whole, a right which can only be lawfully obstructed in a portion of it, by public authority, that of the ecclesiastical magistrate, who gives occasionally an exclusive title in a part of the public cemetery to the succession of a single family, or to an individual who has a claim to such a distinction: but he does not do that without just consideration of its expediency, and a due attention to the objections of those who oppose such an alienation from the common use. Even a brick grave without such authority is an aggression upon the common freehold interest, and carries the pretensions of the dead to an extent that violates the just rights of the living."]

Nature of right in United States—Duration—Permanent Appropriation the Rule

Under the English influence, the right of burial was similarly defined in *Windt v. German Reformed Church*:

"The payment of fees and charges to the corporation or its officers, upon interments, gives no title to the land occupied by the body interred. It confers the privilege of sepulture for such body, in the mode used and permitted by the corporation, and the right to have the same remain undisturbed so long as the cemetery shall continue to be used as such, and so long also, if its use continue, as such remains shall require for entire decomposition; and also the right, in case the cemetery shall be sold for secular purposes, to have such remains removed and properly deposited in a new place of sepulture." "This, I am satisfied, is the whole extent of the legal rights and privileges conferred by interment, and the payment of the customary charges, in the burying grounds of our religious corporations." The court, however, desiring to find a greater right of permanency in that case, based it upon a finding of the vault owner's interest in the soil.

But, for a number of reasons, the English rule of temporary appropriation found no foothold here. In the first place, the English rule was not itself invariable. Though the English right of burial was secured without fee by ancient canon law, it had become the later practice to make charges for rites incident to burial, and the common law recognized the validity of these charges if supported by immemorial custom. Likewise it had been the practice to grant special privileges of burial in and about churches, in vaults and other parts of the church structure, to the favored. And it grew to be not uncommon to grant such favors and privileges for compensation, so that even in earlier days permanent appropriation of the land could be secured by purchase. The issue in *Gilbert v. Buzzard* was not whether a parishioner could secure more than temporary appropriation of the ground, but whether he could obtain it as a prerogative without payment of extra fee, and the decision to the contrary was followed by burial in iron coffins upon payment of the added compensation.

Likewise, comparison with the rights of the pew owner bred in this country a different rule, since the status of the pew owner differed here. "Our church establishments ... stand upon a different footing. Here we have no parish churches. With us, they are corporations aggregate, made so by law. The temporal concerns are managed by trustees, who have power to dispose of the pews by sale, and by letting them out to hire, fixing the amount of rent so as to produce a revenue. It is all a matter of bargain, and entirely conventional between the trustees and those individuals who wish to become hearers or members of the society and to have seats in the church."

Where a right of burial in a public cemetery has been acquired otherwise than by purchase, the rule of temporary appropriation of the soil dictated by necessity in England must yield to rules of burial law dictated by sentiment in this country. The compelling reason. that the dead might crowd out the living does not exist here. Even were our disposition to follow the English rule as to churchyard burial, in principle the distinction between churchyard burial and interment in a "separate independent cemetery," and the prevailing practice of acquisition of burial rights by purchase in cemeteries owned by corporations makes the question of temporary appropriation in this country largely one of but historical interest. Generally the English rule of temporary appropriation has been superseded in this country, as indeed it has also been in England, where rights are now generally acquired by purchase under the previous burial acts.

In public cemetery conveyance of burial right does not ordinarily convey fee

When the owner of land buries his dead in that land, there is coincidence of fee ownership and the possession of burial rights. This applies, however, to a private cemetery. A grantee of a right in a public cemetery does not ordinarily take a fee in the land. In England, as we have seen, the fee of the churchyard was in the parson and the burial right in the parishioner was distinct therefrom. So, too, as we have seen, when burial rights are created by dedication, the resultant estate is, in pursuance of general rules, co-extensive with the necessity, and since only a right of burial is required, the underlying fee remains in the dedicator.

It is generally true that the possessor of a right of burial in land does not hold a fee, even where the right is acquired by purchase. Where there are no statutory restrictions, it has frequently been the custom of memorial parks, within recent years, to convey a fee by deed recorded, in accordance with ordinary real estate procedure, in the office of a county clerk or similar officer. Yet in many states a deed purporting to convey the fee has been held to convey an easement only, although there is no express statutory restriction.

The line of demarcation is plain. In states where the intention is to have cemeteries owned by a corporation organized to give to the lot owners permanent management and care, there must be a right of regulation in the corporation. In such cases every sound legal and practical reason justifies retention of the fee in the association so that it may exercise control.

This is a salutary and generally prevailing view. In states where this is the policy, it is generally held that regardless of the tenor of the deed, a conveyance of a burial right in a cemetery owned by a cemetery corporation, or other association intended by statute to be vested with management and control of the cemetery, conveys only a right of burial and does not convey the fee. And this is so though the instrument by which the lot owner in a public cemetery or cemetery owned by a cemetery corporation takes be a deed of conveyance absolute in form or purports to convey an unqualified fee.

There are declarations at variance with this rule but generally where a fee may be conveyed it is because of failure to understand the necessities, or of laxity of the statutes of the jurisdiction adequately to state or enforce necessary rules of burial law. Burial right as license or privilege Where the owner of a burial right is not the fee owner, in determining miscellaneous questions, such as the rights or privileges of such owner upon attempted abandonment of a cemetery, the courts have sought to define the burial right under rules of real property law. Though it should now be easy to enforce the rights of the dead and the living by resort to rules of burial law in spite of technical terminologies, the courts have heretofore determined ultimate rights by defining the right of burial as a license or privilege.

Or an easement

The right of burial is likewise, and has frequently been said to be, in the nature of an easement. [In a footnote, Jackson notes that "[S]ome courts deny that the right of burial in a public graveyard can be an easement, because a right of burial "is not a right 'imposed for the benefit of corporeal property' In such case there is no such thing as a dominant estate to which the easement right can attach. The mere right to bury upon a tract of land in no sense fills the general definition of the term 'easement.'" ... "Yet in England a pew right is an easement; there, in the absence of statutory definition, it is considered an interest in real property (some statutes make the pew right personal property). The right of a pew holder is limited to occupation for worship. At common law unless the right to a pew was an easement proper, by reason of attachment to a dominant estate, it was purely of ecclesiastical cognizance."]

In Any Event, an Interest in Real Property

However, whatever may be the classification given it by rules of the law of real property to meet given situations, the right of burial is an interest in real property, to be so regarded and treated, though in a restricted sense. However, the character of personal property used as an emblement to the right of burial does not change.

Real Property Rules Applicable

In consequence, title to a burial right may be acquired under real property rules, for example, by adverse possession, and a burial right passes as real property to heirs. Title to a burial right is usually acquired by deed, though a deed is not necessary where evidence otherwise establishes title. Where the Statute of Frauds required a writing to pass an interest in real property, an oral contract for the sale of a burial right was held unenforceable, though the weight of authority, for one reason or another, is to the contrary; and it has been held that an unlicensed real estate broker may not collect commissions on sale of burial plots. However, a cemetery corporation selling lots on the installment plan is not a real estate "subdivider" within the terms of a statute regulating sales of subdivided lands. Where certificates evidencing burial rights were issued and offered for resale, they were held to be securities under the state statute."

Alienability of burial right

... [D]istinction is required to exclude those rights such as exist in a public cemetery which are purely personal, like the English parishioner's. Obviously they cannot be the subject of transfer. Similarly, where the restriction is to members of a family, the right of burial is descendible but not assignable. Such rights are collective rather than individual and isolated like those of an ordinary grantee or licensee of a burial right. Where, however, one purchases the burial rights in a subdivision of a cemetery, there exists a privilege or easement which by its very nature constitutes property, and which under ordinary circumstances should be and is the subject of transfer. Good reason may exist for disposing of a burial lot before any interment has been made therein. Thus change of circumstances or removal to a distant place might dictate a change of burial place.

So long as a burial right is conveyed without injury to the remaining lot owners—i.e., not in violation of restrictions properly laid thereon in the form of regulations by the cemetery association—and so long as such conveyance violates no statutory policy of preserving to the lot owner or his next of kin a right of burial, there should be no valid objection to transfer of a burial right before the right has been exercised.

Inalienability after Interment

There is every reason in logic and sentiment for destroying the alienability of a lot once a burial has been made therein. A stranger should not be permitted to exercise any dominion over the remains. It is abhorrent and shocking to the human sense that the one buried and the survivors should be denied the solace of burial together, or that those already interred should be interred among strangers. The person to whom title to the burial lot with its remaining graves may pass, if conveyed in the absence of statutory restriction, might permit any person, perhaps a stranger to the one already interred, to be buried therein.

The law recognizes and seeks to effectuate the natural desire of man to rest with his own people by restricting alienability once an interment has been made. This is and must be the inevitable declaration of the substantive law of burial, dictated by good morals and public policy in their abhorrence of desecration of the grave. It is likewise the avowed and almost universal statutory policy. ...

Devise and succession upon death of owner

The reason for inalienability of a burial lot, once there has been interment therein, is not only to secure the grave against desecration but also to insure the common desire that members of a family be buried together. That is the primary purpose of acquiring a burial lot, and this desire not only is that of the lot owner but is shared by his wife and children. The protection of these mutual desires requires a rule of inalienability once an interment has been made, and a corollary rule that insures a place of burial to the widow and children once the lot owner dies.

The common law took no cognizance of these matters, and the common right of burial secured only a grave in which all could rest to the limit of its capacity. The right of family burial was secured to the upper classes by virtue of the maintenance of private family tombs, or the acquisition of vaults and other special privileges from the ecclesiastical authorities. These were frequently appurtenances of the estate, and along with it were so entailed and restricted by the prevalent system of land tenures as to afford all requisite protection to the members of the family. Since the modern system of burial in England and the United States is so largely statutory, the necessary protection must now be sought in the local enactments. Generally A right of burial, being an interest in real property and itself being property, passes to the heirs in the absence of specific devise or contrary statutory provision even as against general residuary legatees. The reason is obvious. The title should pass so as to concur with the right of interment of those with whom the decedent would seek to be buried and those who, conversely, would desire to rest near the decedent. Such result is however of no avail unless the heir takes subject to the rights of other members of the family to be interred with the decedent; otherwise his and their natural wishes and sentiments might be avoided. It might be said that the decedent should insure compliance with his wishes by making necessary provision in his will; but the sentiments respecting burial are so strong and so prevalent, and the reasons for failure to make a will are frequently so casual, that the former should far outweigh the latter.

Even where a specific devise is made, in the absence of statutory restriction there should be no difficulty in charging the land, once an interment has been made, with a trust permitting burial of the widow and next of kin; the trust ordinarily rising paramount over even the will of the decedent, on the theory that even a decedent's wishes must accord with the decent sentiments of the survivors and the community. Consequently it is and should be a rule of burial law that the heir should take title to the burial lot, subject to the right of burial of the widow if any, the children, or other proper descendants of the deceased.

A burial right, when passing by intestacy, vests in the heirs as tenants in common. Were it held a joint tenancy, the death of one heir would pass title to the other, and in such case it would be necessary to charge the lot with a trust in favor of the widow and next of kin of the deceased heir, in order to preserve their collective rights of burial.

In this manner, by statutory restriction upon the right to devise a burial lot, and as well by vesting a right of possession and control in widow and next of kin, the right of interment may be secured to the surviving spouse and children, so that there may not be separation after death, and so that the repose of the dead may not be disturbed by the subsequent intrusion of the bodies of strangers. ...

❖ ❖ ❖

Monticello Graveyard, Charlottesville, Virginia

CHAPTER 11.6

THE RIGHT TO ACCESS GRAVES

Alfred L. Brophy, *Grave Matters: The Ancient Rights of the Graveyard,*
2006 B.Y.U. L. Rev. 1469 (2006).

The system of property and law goes back for its origin to barbarous and sacred times; it is the fruit of the same mysterious cause as the mineral or animal world. There is a natural sentiment and prepossession in favor of age, of ancestors, of barbarous and aboriginal usages, which is a homage to the element of necessity and divinity which is in them. The respect for the old names of places, of mountains, and streams, is universal. The Indian and barbarous name can never be supplanted without loss.

—Ralph Waldo Emerson

Ralph Waldo Emerson's oration *The Conservative* recognized the power that ancient ideas and practices hold over the minds of individuals. The reverence that grows up around long-standing uses is a frequent justification for property rights. When people have used property in a way for an extended period of time they come to believe that other uses cannot interfere with theirs—that they have a claim against the entire world.

Emerson's oration also recognized the reverence we pay to ancestors. That reverence is rarely deeper than in cemeteries. In cemeteries that are located on private property, then, meet two ancient, powerful ideas: the right of property owners to exclude and the veneration of age and of ancestors. That conflict between the right to worship at our ancestors' graves and the right to exclude appears with increasing frequency these days, as landowners seek to develop land where cemeteries are located and descendants of people buried in the cemeteries seek to reclaim something of their heritage. We also see in the long-standing right to visit a cemetery, a respect for the rights of members of the community who do not own the land where the cemetery is located.

For example, the conflict appeared recently in a now generations-old dispute between the Hatfields and the McCoys in Kentucky. Descendants of the McCoys wanted access to a graveyard containing five of the six McCoys killed in feuding during the late nineteenth century. A Hatfield descendant refused them access. It is appropriate, given how important property rights have become and how important property was to the origins of the feud in the nineteenth century, that the feud once again turns on property rights. The current feud also illuminates an ancient—and rarely discussed—right of families of people interred in cemeteries, and the ways those rights limit what we think of as central rights of property owners.

This Essay explores in depth one ancient right associated with graveyards: the right to access graves of ancestors, even if they are on private property. Relatives of people buried in cemeteries on private property have a common law right to access the property to visit the cemetery. That right, which is an implied easement in gross, is recognized by statue in about a fifth of states and by case law in many others. ...[T]wo corollary rights: the prohibition against desecration of graves and the right to burial ... work in tandem to protect graves and the right to visit them. While we currently hear relatively little about these rights, they are of importance to those who choose to exercise them. Many others, if they knew their rights, might choose to exercise them as well. ...

Disputing at the Graveyard's Gate: The Right To Exclude

> I find this vast network, which you call property, extended over the whole
> planet. I cannot occupy the bleakest crag of the White Hills or the Allegheny
> Range, but some man or corporation steps up to show me that it is his.
>
> —Ralph Waldo Emerson

Emerson captures well Americans' love of property. At the center of that love are the rights to alienate, to use the property as the owner chooses, and to exclude others. There are, of course, notable limitations on those rights. Courts enforce limited restrictions on the right of an owner to alienate, and they will enjoin as nuisances—or at least require compensation for—uses of property that impose unreasonable interferences on neighbors.

Express and implied easements are also limitations on the right to exclude others. Express easements are explicit grants from one landowner to another, often a neighboring landowner, to cross the owner's property. They are the most common type of easements. However, courts also recognize implied easements. Courts imply easements in cases of estoppel, such as when the owner of the property has granted access in the past and those seeking access have made expenditures in reliance on that access; in cases of necessity, when a parcel of property is divided and sold, leaving one part landlocked; or in cases of implication by prior use, when a parcel is divided and, prior to division, one part of the parcel made use of the other part.

Courts also create easements for access after long-term, prescriptive use.

Even with respect to the right to exclude, there are occasional times when private individuals have the right of access on private property. ...

At the bottom of all of these restrictions are principles of reasonableness—reasonableness of regulations and reasonableness of use. ...

Still, and unsurprisingly, a dominant theme in American property law is that the right to exclude is "one of the most essential sticks in the bundle of rights that are commonly characterized as property." For instance, Native Americans are often restricted from accessing land owned by their ancestors. What is surprising about graveyard access is how little we hear about this ancient right, which has for generations limited the right of property owners to exclude or, phrased more positively, given some members of the public a right of access. In fact, other than a few minor mentions in legal encyclopedias, the right to access cemeteries has received virtually no commentary. ...

The Right of Access

The most important of the graveyard rights is the right of access. Some states define the right by statute, others by case law. At base, the right is an easement in gross to cross private property to access a cemetery. The easement is held by the relatives of the person buried in the cemetery, and it descends by operation of law but is neither devisable nor alienable. In a few states, other interested parties, like genealogical researchers, also have the same right of access across private property.

The right of access arises when a person is buried on property with the permission of the owners. Most commonly the deceased is a member of the family of the owners at the time of burial, but the deceased may not be related to the owners of the property. In either case, giving permission to bury the deceased carries with it an implied grant of permission for the relatives to visit the property. Sometimes the implied grant of permission for access is shown through a dedication of the cemetery, but formal dedication is not necessary. The grant of permission for access is enforced as an implied promise through estoppel or acquiescence, although courts rarely discuss the basis. The assumption is that by allowing the deceased to be buried, the owner of the property is making at least an implied promise for continued access. Moreover, courts assume that burial is made in reliance on such a promise—which is often an implied promise. In the unlikely case that the owners who granted permission for the burial still own the property, the implication of an easement to access the cemetery is relatively straightforward. The fact of burial is close to complete proof that the landowners granted permission for access.

More commonly, the claim for access is made against subsequent owners who have purchased or inherited the property, rather than against those who allowed for burial in the first place. Those wishing to visit the burial can assert an easement by estoppel against successors to the owner of the servient estate. In the case of bona fide purchases, there has to be some kind of notice of the existence of the easement—which in this case will be some kind of evidence of the cemetery. That evidence will also be necessary to show that the holders of the right of access have not abandoned the easement.

Sometimes the property containing the cemetery has also been broken into pieces, so that the people seeking to exercise the easement must cross property of several different owners to reach the cemetery. In these rare cases, courts use a second implied easement: an easement implied by necessity. In these cases, courts maintain that there was an implied reservation of the easement by the cemetery's first owner in favor of the family members of the person buried in the cemetery at the time the property was divided.

The right of access also arises when a deceased is buried in a cemetery not owned by the deceased's family. In that case, there is a two-step process. First, the easement for access is implicitly granted by the landowner to the family members of the deceased. Second, if the landowner sells, there is again an implied reservation by the seller in favor of the family members.

Sometimes there could even be a right of access over property that was never owned by the same person who owned the cemetery. That is more complex conceptually and would arise when the cemetery is landlocked. For example, Missouri provides by statute for a right of access across any privately owned land to access a cemetery. There are no cases testing the limits of the right of access in Missouri, so it is difficult to know whether a court would imply an easement across property never owned by the owner of the land where the cemetery is located.

Identifying the scope of the right from state statutes

Approximately eleven states, primarily in the South and in areas settled by Southerners, provide by statute for a right of access by relatives of people buried on private property. The statutes typically imply an easement for access. The most detailed statutory scheme is provided by Virginia, which gives family members and descendants, cemetery plot owners, and genealogical researchers a right of access across property where graves are located in order to visit and maintain the graves. The right is limited to reasonable visitation and maintenance, and motorized vehicles are not permitted unless roads are already on the property. West Virginia's statute, which is almost identical to Virginia's, also recognizes a right of access by friends.

Several other states offer a specific court procedure to obtain a permit for access to a cemetery. For instance, North Carolina provides that descendants of a deceased buried in a cemetery, as well as other people with a "special interest," may petition the superior court for an order to allow visitation and maintenance of the cemetery. As with a Missouri statute that declares a right of access across any privately owned land to reach a cemetery, the North Carolina statute contemplates the right to cross property to access a cemetery, even if the cemetery is not located on that owner's property. Thus, one might use the statute to cross the land of several different owners. The statute is not entirely a codification of common law implied reservation, because the doctrine of implied reservation would allow an easement only across property that was owned by the owner of the cemetery at the time of interment. Then, as parcels were sold off, there would be an implied reservation of the right to cross them to access the cemetery. But in the North Carolina statute, the right is broader because it allows access across other parcels. Vermont has a similar statute. ...

Perhaps the most straightforward enumeration of rights comes from Florida's statute, which provides for an easement for reasonable access to visit and maintain the cemetery. Thus, Florida deals directly with the key issue in cemetery access: the conflict between absolute exclusion and reasonable accommodation. Given the limited success of reasonableness of accommodations over the absolute of the right of exclusion, there may be a temptation to apply it in other areas of property law. In fact, the reasonableness of property rights is frequently a part of property law.

In contrast to Florida's statute, which provides access for visitation and for maintenance purposes, Indiana's statute creates the most limited rights of access. It grants a right to access cemetery land one day each year. The statute provides a legislative answer to the perplexing question of what is "reasonable use."

Arkansas has a complex and unique statutory scheme that provides for the conversion of cemeteries from private to public ownership. The legal basis for this conversion is the idea of adverse possession. The statute requires fifty years of use as a cemetery as a standard for adverse possession. The conversion to a public cemetery allows the county court to appoint public or nonprofit bodies to care for public cemeteries. However, the statutory scheme makes no provision for access; it is instead concerned with care of the cemetery.

Arizona prohibits the sale of a cemetery unless there is provision for access. The result of that statute is to provide by law for an implied easement across the cemetery's property, although the statute does not provide for access across neighboring property.

Oklahoma has two relevant statutes. One provides for establishment of streets and other ways of access to cemeteries. The statute is ambiguous, but it presumably authorizes the use of eminent domain to acquire the right of access. Another statute, of more modest scope but perhaps more use, provides relatives a right of access to abandoned cemeteries on private land. In a puzzling concluding sentence, however, the statute maintains that "[t]his section shall not be interpreted to allow the creation of an easement or claim of easement nor a right of ownership or claim of right of ownership to an abandoned cemetery." The purpose of that sentence is elusive because the statute seems to provide for an easement. However, perhaps the sentence is meant only to make clear that there is no right other than the right of reasonable access "for purposes usually associated with cemetery visits" and that it creates no rights beyond that.

Identifying the scope of the right from case law

Many of the states that do not have statutes providing for access do have case law that permits access. That permission is similar to the rights of access created by statute in states such as Florida and Texas. It provides, in essence, that the relatives of those buried in "dedicated" cemeteries on private property have the right to access that property for reasonable visits to the grave. Several states have particularly well-developed case law, including Alabama, Kentucky, and Pennsylvania. Other states have a more limited body of case law from the late nineteenth and early twentieth centuries. The following three cases illustrate how case law has defined the right of access, applied well-established property principles to the right of access, and articulated the scope of the right.

The most recent comprehensive discussion of the right of access comes from the Texas Court of Appeals case of *Davis v. May*, 135 S.W.3d 747 (Tex. App. 2003). The court interpreted the rights of Marsha May to visit the graves of her great-grandfather, James Riley Alexander, and a few other relatives. The Alexanders were buried on family-owned land, which was subsequently sold without any provision for access to the graves. Over time and after some intermediate conveyances, the property came into the hands of Emmit and Debra Davis. The Davises, as the owners of the property on which the cemetery was located, refused May access to the graves of her ancestors.

At trial, a jury concluded that May should have reasonable access, which the jury thought would be one four-hour visit per month. In affirming the judgment, the Texas Court of Appeals held that the property owner, by permitting the burials, took on the obligation of holding the property in trust for the family members of the people buried there, which included the obligation to allow access to the property, perform reasonable upkeep, and also permit further limited burials. Davis adopted the broad language of the 1911 Tennessee Supreme Court opinion in *Hines v. State*, which established that subsequent purchasers of a cemetery take it subject to the implied easement for access and further burial, stating, "The graves are there to be seen, and the purchaser is charged with notice of the fact that the particular lot has been dedicated to burial purposes, and of the rights of descendants and relatives of those there buried."

Courts have also harnessed well-established property principles, including easement by prescription and implied reservation, to permit access to a cemetery. For example, in the 1945 case *Scruggs v. Beason*, 20 So. 2d 774, 775 (Ala. 1945), the Alabama Supreme Court held that family members had the right to cross private property to visit the Choat Graveyard, which was first established in 1868 and had approximately 120 graves. There were two bases for the court's decision. First, there was an easement by prescription, as the family members had crossed the property continuously since the cemetery was first established. Second, there was an implied reservation when the private property in question was sold and divided from the land where the cemetery was located.

A 1995 case from Kentucky, *Department of Fish & Wildlife Resources v. Garner*, 896 S.W.2d 10 (Ky. 1995), is the most recent statement of the scope of the right to access a cemetery. Garner balanced the interests of relatives and the state in providing access to a cemetery in a limited-access wildlife preservation area. Jacob Garner's great-grandmother and his cousin were buried in a small cemetery of approximately three-quarters of an acre that contained approximately a dozen graves. The cemetery was located in a wildlife management area owned by the federal government and managed by the state of Kentucky. The state put up three gates, which were locked during the winter, to prevent vandalism and maintain control over the area. The court balanced Garner's right of access, which at times he exercised through self-help by breaking the gates, against the state's interest in maintaining security. It observed that "the owners of the easement and the servient estate have correlative rights and duties which neither may unreasonably exercise to the injury of the other." The court struck a balance between access and control by allowing the state to exclude the public but requiring that it provide keys to Garner and his family members so that they would have access to the cemetery whenever they would like.

There are several key steps required to create a right of access. First, there must have been a determination that the landowner initially consented to the burial on her land, which some courts refer to as dedication. The standard for dedication appears to be quite low, perhaps as little as a showing that there was some acknowledgment that people were openly buried in the cemetery. The presence of a headstone seems to be sufficient to establish dedication, but less may be sufficient. Second, there must be a determination that the cemetery has not been abandoned. The standard for abandonment is somewhat higher than dedication; courts require continuing use of the cemetery or at least some continuing recognition that bodies are buried there. Nevertheless, in some cases there are rights of access even to an abandoned cemetery. A Florida statute articulates the minority view that if the cemetery is abandoned and not being maintained, the courts will likely allow access by family members so that people who are most interested in its preservation can maintain it. Finally, although rarely discussed in case law, there likely must be a connection between those buried and those seeking access. No case articulates a requirement that those seeking access actually knew the people they are visiting. But it is possible that people who are no longer able to trace a specific connection may have no greater right of access than members of the public.

Defining the right of access

The right of access, aged as it may be, remains an amorphous right. Because the right has been litigated infrequently, there are some ambiguities. First, how close must the connection be between the person interred on the property and those claiming access? Second, how much evidence must remain of the cemetery—or how much evidence must there be about the place of burial? Finally, how broad is the right of visitation—or how frequently and how long may the visits last? In each case, courts will likely draw upon a reasonableness calculus by analogy to recent easement by implication cases and to the Restatement (Third) of Servitudes. Cemetery cases usually involve a subsequent purchaser who took with notice--constructive notice, at a minimum—of the existence of the cemetery. The question, of course, is how does one determine reasonableness for purposes of access?

In terms of the closeness of the connection between the deceased and those seeking to visit the decedent's gravesite, courts will likely allow anyone who knew the decedent to access the property. But there is also no reason to stop at the point where there is a living connection and to permit only those who knew the decedent to visit the cemetery. None of the statutes require such a direct connection, which may be a good indication of the sentiment of the common law. The statutes of Virginia, West Virginia, and North Carolina contemplate visits by people other than relatives. In fact, given the difficulty of proving family connections and the likelihood that few who are unrelated to the deceased are likely to seek out the deceased's place of burial, courts may be relatively relaxed in demanding proof of an immediate connection between the deceased and the person seeking access. If the number of people wishing to visit the cemetery becomes too burdensome, the number, time, and length of visits may be limited. Those who would impose a requirement of direct connection run the risk of limiting the right too dramatically. The legislatures that have visited this issue have not seen the need for such a strict limitation. At a minimum, those who are direct descendants of the decedent ought to have a right to visit, as long as there remains knowledge of the general area where the decedent is buried.

The final question—the number, time, and length of visits—is probably something best left to the particular equities of each case. Courts will likely take into consideration the relationship of the decedent to those wishing to visit, the hardship to the property owners caused by visitations, and the ability of the relatives to schedule visitations at other times. As our citizens' knowledge and interest in history continues to expand, courts will likely be increasingly called upon to interpret these important rights, which have up until now often been resolved through private meetings. ...

The clash between the living and the dead—between the living who want to use the property for some purpose other than memory of the dead and the living who prefer the established cemetery—has appeared since the early nineteenth century. Given the conflict between a traditional use of property and a potentially more economically efficient use of the same property, courts must balance the right of burial and access with the right to remove bodies and thus move cemeteries. Removal is sometimes necessary, especially in areas that have grown substantially since the cemetery was first established. The battle over the Trinity Church Cemetery on Wall Street in Manhattan illustrates this conflict between the long-established and not economically productive use of land and the need for making land economically productive. This is part of a vigorous debate over public versus private rights in land, which has stretched from the nineteenth century to the present. The Pennsylvania Supreme Court phrased the conflict well in 1850 when it asked whether rights of the dead would outweigh the rights of the living to use property for railroad tracks. It was a strand of the classic debate over control of property by the dead (and their relatives) or by the living.

The problem in cemeteries, however, is not just that people who are now dead are occupying the property. For preservation of cemeteries is largely about the preservation of a place for people who are alive to visit, remember, and worship their ancestors and relatives. Thus, cemeteries pose a conflict between the rights of the living to have a place of memorial for the dead and the rights of other living people to use the land in (what to them is) a more productive fashion. Yet, frequently it is spoken about as a conflict between dead and living. The Pennsylvania Supreme Court phrased the controversy as one between the abodes of the dead and the needs of the living. It said a cemetery had to be relocated so that a railroad could go through the land occupied by the cemetery. In a utilitarian fashion that is representative of antebellum judicial reasoning, the Court concluded that it could not make the railroad run through a different and more dangerous route, for that would subject the living to even more damage than relocation of the cemetery:

> The abodes of the living are not more inviolable than the abodes of the dead; yet thousands of human bones lie beneath the walks and alleys of Washington Square in Philadelphia, once its Potter's Field, now its most frequented pleasure-ground. If a cemetery cannot impede the march of improvement for purposes of recreation, how can the owner of a cottage expect that it will impede a work of necessity? The legislation of a country necessarily takes its tone from the temper and the necessities of the age. A house, a church, a grave-yard, or any thing else, may be conveniently privileged in an act to incorporate a turnpike or a canal company, because it may be avoided without lessening the usefulness of the work; but every deflexion from a right line in the bed of a railroad, is proportionately productive of danger to property and life. It is

indispensable to safety and speed that the route of it be as direct as the surface of the country will permit; but they could not be attained in a settled country if every hovel or house were privileged; and thus a quasi national work, intended for posterity, might be botched through a respect for the sacredness of temporary erections. The course of a railroad might be insuperably obstructed by the obstinacy of a proprietor in the gorge of a mountain, or the pass be made, at least, difficult and dangerous. A mangled passenger, inquiring the reason of a deflexion, when the cause of it had disappeared, might be told of our infinite respect for property at the expense of safety; but the information would neither ease his pain nor set his leg.

Brocket v. Ohio & Pa. R.R. Co., 14 Pa. 241, 244-45 (1850). ...

The Meaning of the Right of Access

... The right of access has meaning for several reasons. First, and perhaps most important, is sentimental attachment to cemeteries. The cemetery has great meaning to individuals, and sometimes, as in the case of Gettysburg and Arlington National Cemetery, they have great meaning for us as a nation. The important New York lawyer and politician Daniel D. Barnard spoke at the consecration of the Albany Cemetery in 1844 in the midst of the anti-rent movement, of which he was a strong opponent. Even Barnard, a staunch supporter of private property rights against the community, recognized the importance of cemeteries to the human spirit:

> The living cannot occupy the earth exclusively—space must be yielded for the dead. As fast as we can count men die, and their bodies must rest somewhere in the ground—such, at least, as are not consumed by fire, or swallowed up in the sea. . . . [L]and must be appropriated for their use and occupation. Where it is not thus appropriated, and appropriated liberally, the dead are defrauded. They are entitled to their share of the earth, by what seems an original and authoritative designation of the uses to which it should be subject. . . . The living must possess and subdue the earth; but a fair portion of it is the true inheritance of the dead.

Those, like Ralph Waldo Emerson, who cared less than Barnard for property rights, saw much value in cemeteries as well. But Emerson saw more precisely the value of cemeteries for what they give to us as living people. And he saw in cemeteries an opportunity to educate and improve the living. Emerson celebrated them in a speech at the dedication of Sleepy Hollow Cemetery in Concord, where he is now buried:

> I suppose all of us will readily admit the value of parks and cultivated grounds to the pleasure and education of the people, but I have heard it said here that we would gladly spend for a park for the living, but not for a cemetery; a garden for the living, a home of thought and friendship. Certainly the living need it more than the dead; indeed, to speak precisely, it is given to the dead for the reaction of benefit on the living. But if the direct regard to the living be thought expedient, that is also in your power. This ground is happily so divided by

Nature as to admit of this relation between the Past and the Present. In the valley where we stand will be the Monuments. On the other side of the ridge, towards the town, a portion of the land is in full view of the cheer of the village and is out of sight of the Monuments; it admits of being reserved for secular purposes; for games,—not such as the Greeks honored the dead with, but for games of education; . . . patriotic eloquence, the utterance of the principles of national liberty to private, social, literary or religious fraternities. Here we may establish that most agreeable of all museums, agreeable to the temper of our times,—an Arboretum . . . .

Cemeteries are, indeed, powerful places, which have received recognition by poets, by orators, by the people themselves. Visits to cemeteries remind us of the connections between the past and the present and the ways that we are dependent on the contributions made by people in the past. Cemeteries have great power to remind us of the contributions others have made; they are often the sites of celebrations, even if somber, of the past and of our debts to the people buried in them.

In a cemetery we are reminded of the connections of people to one another. Daniel Barnard spoke about these connections at the dedication of the Albany Cemetery:

This will be a common burial-place where all shall meet on terms of common fellowship and brotherhood. Every dear relation in life, severed by death, shall be found restored again in these grounds—husband and wife, parent and child, brother and sister, shall be re-united here. Friend shall meet friend here; and enemies, too, shall meet, there enmities all forgotten. Yonder city, where, as every where in life, the harmonies of society are apt to be broken by petty feuds, by ungentle rivalries, by disturbing jealousies, by party animosities, by religious dissensions, shall, one after another, as death singles them out, send up her multitudinous population to these grounds, and here they shall take their respective places, in amiable proximity to each other, peaceful, harmonious, undisturbed and undisturbing, the same shadows deepening on them, the same sun-light over them, resting in the same hope . . . .

In addition to the mystical powers of cemeteries to change the attitudes of property owners and visitors, talk of the long-standing legal rights associated with the right of access has important implications for property rights. Because the right of graveyard access existed at common law, the owners of property are not entitled to exclude or even to claim compensation for a taking. This may be part of a little-remarked trend towards humanitarian analysis of property law, which turns in part on anti-feudal sentiments existing throughout American history. Such anti-feudal sentiments provide a basis, even if dimly and incompletely recognized, for judges to protect freedom from expansive private control, as it now holds. Of course, property rights advocates may see an expansion of community rights as a form of feudalism as well. Perhaps the anti-feudal construct—that individuals should not be as dependent as they are on private property—is an analog to the new property jurisprudence, which protects from loss by excessive and arbitrary governmental changes in benefits. The parallel is that in the case of the anti-feudal construct, there are limitations on the power of property owners, just as the new property jurisprudence limits the power of the entity that bestows the property.

While we are hearing much these days about the debate about reparations for slavery and Jim Crow, there are efforts to find ways of reminding us about the past. Perhaps one of the most successful efforts to recall the past is the disclosure ordinances that require businesses to recount their connections to slavery. A few have already spoken about slave cemeteries as a place for remembering the connections to the past. Because cemeteries and monuments to the dead are important signifiers of our national identity, they remind us of the sacrifices made by people in the past and remind us, too, of both the burdens and promises of our history.

Nor has there been much talk of cemetery access, such as the descendants of slaves visiting the plantations where their ancestors labored, died, and are buried. Yet, that simple right has fewer of the problems that plague reparations lawsuits such as the statute of limitations. The Tennessee Supreme Court wrote in 1911, regarding access by descendants to a cemetery established around 1851, that the statute of limitations was not a bar to suit even though filed many years later:

> Nor is the right barred by the statute of limitations, so long as the lot is kept inclosed, or, if uninclosed, so long as the monuments and gravestones marking the graves are to be found there, or other attention is given to the graves, so as to show and perpetuate the sacred object and purpose to which the land has been devoted. No possession of the living is required in such cases, and there can be no actual ouster or adverse possession, to put in operation the statute of limitations, so long as the dead are there buried, their graves are marked, and any acts are done tending to preserve their memory and mark their last resting place.

Hines v. State, 149 S.W. 1058, 1060 (Tenn. 1911). Perhaps even less should be necessary to preserve the right of access: as long as the graves are kept alive in the memories of the community and so long as they can be located, the easement may continue.

And so one may soon see the descendants of people enslaved on southern plantations returning to those plantations to visit the graves of their ancestors and to talk about the meaning of the graves for remembering the role of slavery in our past. Cemetery visits offer something more, though. They are a metaphor for the reuniting of black and white in our common past. The master and the slave were bound together, and while there was an obscene disparity of power between them, the relationship bound both of them tightly together. In a sense, one could not exist without the other. The right to visit burial grounds is a tangible manifestation of the fact that the white and black communities are inseparable. We are tied together by our common past, our common humanity, our common nationality, and our common future. The exercise of the ancient right of the graveyard also offers the hope of recalling that common mission and of rebalancing the rights of slaves' descendants and plantation owners' descendants. And it also offers the descendants of slaves a piece of property—an easement for access—however small, that their ancestors left for them.

NOTES

The Roman jurist Ulpianus (see Chapter 2.6) wrote:

> Where anyone has a burial place but has no right of way to it, and is prevented from reaching it by his neighbor, the Emperor Antoninus and his father stated in a Rescript that it is customary to petition for a pathway to a burial place by sufferance, and it is usually granted; and, whenever there is no servitude, the privilege can be obtained from the party who owns the adjoining premises. This rescript, however, which gives the means of obtaining the right of way by petition, does not allow a civil action, but it may be applied for in extraordinary proceedings; for the governor is required to compel a pathway to be granted to the party where a reasonable price is paid, and the judge must also investigate whether the place is suitable so that the neighbor may not suffer serious injury.

How is this principle of Roman law similar to or different from the common law right of access described by Professor Brophy?

❖ ❖ ❖

Harris Cemetery, Barada, Nebraska
Photo by Tanya D. Marsh

CHAPTER 11.7

ANDERSON V. ACHESON, ET AL.

Supreme Court of Iowa, 132 Iowa 744 (1907)

LADD, J.

The city of Keokuk acquired a tract of land, and platted it for cemetery purposes. It provided by ordinance for the sale and conveyance of the lots for places of burial, "subject to such conditions and regulations and at such prices as the city council shall prescribe by ordinance or otherwise," and enacted that: "Every lot shall be used by the proprietor only for the purposes aforesaid, shall be indivisible, and shall not be conveyed by the owner out of his family after an interment has been made thereon, unless to the city, or unless the bodies have been previously removed therefrom, and shall be forever exempt from taxes by the city." Also, that "proprietors shall not allow interment to be made in their lots for remuneration, nor shall any disinterment be made without written permission by the mayor."

Sophia Whaley died in July, 1885, and her husband, Joshua Whaley, with other members of the family, selected lot 82, in block N in the cemetery, and procured the conveyance of said lot to said Joshua and his son, Mike Whaley, on the 28th of that month. The conveyance recited that "The city of Keokuk hereby sells and conveys to [grantees' names]" the lot described, and recited that it was "to be used only as a place of burial, and under and subject to the laws and ordinances of the said city of Keokuk, and to be indivisible, and not to be conveyed by the grantee out of his family after an interment has been made therein, unless to the said city, and this conveyance shall be forfeited upon failure to comply with, or the violation of, the provisions and laws and ordinances of the city in relation to the cemetery." Sophia Whaley was buried in said lot, and during the following year Joshua Whaley died, and was interred at the side of his wife. Joshua Whaley left surviving him three children, Mike Whaley, Sarah Coulson, and the plaintiff, Amanda Anderson. Prior to 1898 the defendants had acquired the lot adjoining the one mentioned, and Sue Acheson negotiated with Mike Whaley for the purchase of that in which his parents were buried. The agreed consideration was $18, the price of another lot, the cost of improving said lot and transferring the bodies of his parents, $25, and $30 for the lot in controversy. These amounts were paid to the clerk of the city council of Keokuk, $25 being given to the sexton for the removal of the bodies, and $30 being paid to Mike Whaley. Permits were secured from the cemetery committee of the city council to remove the bodies; the cemetery being under the control of such committee by virtue of an ordinance. The lot was conveyed by Mike Whaley to Sue Acheson by virtue of a permit "from the city to transfer" the same to her. Mrs. Acheson consulted plaintiff with respect to the purchase of the lot. She declined to consider the removal of the bodies of her parents, and did not ascertain until some time afterwards that the lot had been transferred to Mrs. Acheson and the bodies removed.

In February, 1903, this action was instituted, praying that defendants be ejected from the lot, and for damages for replacing the bodies of the deceased, together with the headstone which had been erected to the memory of Sophia Whaley. After the evidence had been introduced, the district court directed a verdict in plaintiff's favor, with instructions to allow the reasonable costs of restoring the bodies and the monument to the lot from which they had been taken.

1. Appellants contend that plaintiff has no such interest in or title to the lot as will sustain an action in ejectment or of right, as it is generally called in this state. Strictly speaking, there is no right of property in a dead body. After burial it becomes a part of the ground to which it is transmitted; "earth to earth, ashes to ashes, dust to dust." So, too, are the coffin, shroud, and other habiliments irrevocably consigned to the earth, as mere adjuncts to the body, which they serve to enfold while it is resolved into dust from whence it springs. With the coffined clay that they surround, "they have said to corruption, thou art my father, and to the worm, thou art my sister and my mother." They are no longer property, and their relations with the living are at an end.

But in recognition of the universal sentiment of mankind, the right to decent burial is well guarded by the law, and relatives of the deceased may insist upon legal protection to the burial place from unnecessary disturbance or wanton violation. A body once buried could not be removed in Rome except by permission of the Pontifical College, and, in the provinces, of the Governor. By the canon law, which prevailed in such matters over a large portion of Europe, a body once buried could not be removed without license from the ordinary. Because of the control of such matters by the ecclesiastical courts, the common law in its earlier period did not cover matters with relation to the burial of the dead fully, and the rules with reference thereto have been the result of gradual development, until all courts now concur in holding that the right of possession of a dead body for the purposes of burial belongs to those most intimately and closely connected with deceased by domestic ties, and this is a right which the law will recognize and protect. The authorities are equally conclusive that the last resting place of the dead, when in actual or constructive possession of a relative, will be protected from desecration at his instance.

The courts quite generally hold, however, that the purchaser of a lot in a public cemetery, though the deed be absolute in form, does not take any title thereto. The mere privilege or license to make instruments in the lot so purchased, exclusive of all others, is all that is acquired thereunder. Thus it was said in *Dwenger v. Geary* (Ind.) 14 N. E. 903: "The place where the dead are deposited all civilized nations and many barbarous ones regard in some measure, at least, as consecrated ground. In the old Saxon tongue the burial ground of the dead was 'God's Acre.' One who buys the privilege of burying his dead kinsmen or friends in the cemetery acquires no general right of property; he acquires only the right to bury the dead, for he may not use the ground for any other purpose than such as connected with the right of sepulture. Beyond this his title does not extend. He does not acquire, in strict sense, an ownership of the ground. All that he does acquire is the right to use the ground as a burial place." In *Page v. Symonds*, 63 N. H. 17, 56 Am. Rep. 481, it was said that "such right of burial is not an absolute right of property, but a privilege or license to be enjoyed so long as the place continues to be used as burial ground, subject to municipal control, and legally revocable whenever the public necessity requires it. It is a right of limited use for the purpose of interment, which gives no title to the land." In *Gowen v. Bessey* (Me.) 46 Atl. 792, the court declared that "the holder of a lot in a cemetery belonging to a municipality or religious society for burial purposes, whether his evidence of title be by deed or certificate or other means, does not acquire an absolute title to the land, but has the right or license, exclusive of any and every other person, to bury the dead upon the subdivided plot assigned to him, and a license once acquired cannot be revoked so long as the ground continues to be used as a place of sepulture. As said in *Kincaid's Appeal*, 66 Pa. 411, 5 Am. Rep. 377, "the lot owner purchases a license, nothing more, irrevocable as long as the place continue a burying ground, but giving no title to the soil." ...

In *New York Bay Cemetery Co. v. Buckmaster*, 49 N. J. Law, 449, 9 Atl. 591, the court held that an action in ejectment might be maintained by a lot owner, even though the deed recited that it was for the purposes of sepulture only. But an examination of the act of the Legislature conferring the charter discloses that the tract of land was to be held for certain specified uses, and provided that "the sublots shall be conveyed to the respective purchasers thereof when paid for in full in fee by deed, under the corporate seal of the said corporation." See Acts of 74th Legislature of New Jersey, approved March 5, 1850 (Laws 1850, p. 195), where it is expressly provided that title shall pass, as in that case there is no room for construction.

In *Buffalo City Cemetery Ass'n v. City of Buffalo*, 46 N. Y. 503, the statute, without expressly providing that the company shall retain the fee and the lot owner merely acquire a license, in effect so did by enacting that "after filing such plat the trustees may sell and convey lots or plats designated on such map, upon such terms as shall be agreed, and subject to such conditions and restrictions to be inserted in or annexed to the conveyances as the trustees shall prescribe," and that "all lots or plats of ground designated on the maps filed as aforesaid, and numbered as separate lots by the incorporation, shall be indivisible, but may be held and owned in undivided shares"; provided for exemption from taxes, and also that, after being transferred to individual holders, and an interment in a lot so transferred, "such lot or plat from the time of such first interment shall be forever thereafter inalienable, and shall upon the death of the holder or proprietor thereof descend to the heirs at law of such holder or proprietor, and to their heirs at law forever"; provided, further, that the heirs might release one to another, and that the body of no one save such as have an interest in the lot, or relative or wife of such person or relation, be buried therein except by consent of all persons having an interest in the lot. In deciding that the grounds were assessable to the company for the construction of a sidewalk, the court held that the effect of a conveyance of a lot was "no more than to confer on the holder of a lot a right to use for the purpose of interments. No such estate is granted as makes him an owner in such sense as to exclude the general proprietorship of the association. The association remains the owner in general, and holds that relation to the public and to the government. While subject to this, the individual has the right, exclusive of any other person, to bury upon the subdivided plat assigned to him. He holds a position analogous to that of a pewholder in a house of worship. It is a right exclusive of any other of the congregation, but subject to the right of the religious corporation, which represents the ownership of the property to the public, and is the legal owner of the fee of the property." It will be observed that the statute of New York contains the precise conditions incorporated in the ordinances of the city of Keokuk, and which are found in the deed to Mike and Joshua Whaley. For this reason the decision quoted is precisely in point. Nor are we inclined to think it was the purpose of the Legislature in enacting the statutes relating to public cemeteries that title should pass to those acquiring burial privileges. Section 697 of the Code confers on cities and incorporated towns the power to regulate and provide a place for the burial of the dead, and "to exercise over all cemeteries within their limits, and those without their limits established by their authority, the powers conferred on township trustees with reference to cemeteries." Turning to the statutes relating to township trustees, we find that section 583 provides for the platting of the ground for cemetery purposes, and section 584 that "all conveyances of subdivisions or lots or a cemetery thus platted shall be by deed from the proper owner." The plat is to be recorded with the county recorder, but the deed of a subdivision or lot with the township clerk. Section 587: "The trustees, board of directors, or other officers having the custody and control of any cemetery in this state, shall have power, subject to the by-laws and regulations of said cemetery, to inclose, improve and adorn the grounds of such cemetery; to construct avenues in the same; to erect proper buildings for the use of said cemetery; to prescribe rules for the improving or adorning the lots therein, or for the erection of monuments or other memorials of the dead upon such lots; and to prohibit any use, division, improvement or adornment of a lot which they may deem improper."

These are the powers over the several lots reserved under the statute by the city of Keokuk, and manifestly they are inconsistent with the acquirement of a fee under a conveyance of a lot or subdivision. The control, save merely of the bare right of burial, is retained by the municipality, and even this, under the section first quoted, is subject to regulation. The privilege or license to make interments in the lot purchased, exclusive of others, passes under the deed, but not title in or to the soil. The plaintiff was never in the actual possession of the lot, and under our statutes can only maintain the action upon proof of a valid subsisting interest in real property. A mere privilege or license is but an incorporeal hereditament, of which the sheriff cannot deliver possession, not an interest in the soil, and will not support such an action. But where the license is coupled with an interest, as where a miner, under a license to dig, search for, and take metals or minerals within a certain locality, shall open and work and be in actual possession of any mines, may, if ousted, maintain ejectment with respect to them. In *Hancock v. McAvoy*, 151 Pa. 460, 25 Atl. 47, 31 Am. St. Rep. 774, 18 L. R. A. 781, the court held that the right of sepulture was not an interest in the land such as will support an action in ejectment, in the course of the opinion saying: "As was said in *Black v. Hepbourne*, 2 Yeates (Pa.) 331, 'ejectment will only lie for things whereof possession may be delivered by the sheriff.' If a recovery in ejectment, founded on a mere right or license, such as that acquired by the grantee in the deed above referred to, were permitted, how could the sheriff, under a writ of habere facias, put the plaintiff in possession without interfering with the rights, powers, and duties of the cemetery association." In *Stewart v. Garrett* (Ga.) 100 Am. St. Rep. 179, 64 L. R. A. 99, 46 S. E. 427, a like conclusion was reached; the court observing that the action seemed inappropriate "to the ascertainment of any right in a burial lot. If any fiction is pardonable in a case of this kind, it would be fitter to hold that the fee in these sacred precincts belongs to the dead. Within these hallowed precincts no court would desire to send the sheriff with a writ of possession. The instinct of humanity is loyalty to a statute impressed upon all hearts." In *Pierce v. Proprietors of Swan Point Cemetery*, 10 R. I. 227, 14 Am. Rep. 667, the court, conceding that ejectment would not lie in such a case, considered the propriety of equitable relief at great length, and concluded that equity only can give a full and complete remedy, and that the jurisdiction is fully adequate to it. That suit was against the cemetery association, and the ruling was put on the ground that it was charged with a sacred trust for the benefit of all who may, from considerations of family or friendship, have an interest in the lots. We are of opinion that the interest of plaintiff in the lot was not such as is requisite to support an action in ejectment.

2. But no writ of ejectment was ordered in the judgment entered or subsequently issued, though prayed for in the petition. Judgment for damages alone was rendered, and these were such as might be allowed in an action for *trespass quare clausum*. Chapter 2 of title 21 of the Code, relating to the recovery of real property, has greatly modified procedure as it formerly existed in actions of ejectment, and especially in applying thereto the principles of Code pleading and proof. Particular allegations appropriate to such an action are required, and any joinder or counterclaim save as therein provided is prohibited; but in other respects the rules of pleading as found in chapter 8 of title 17 of the Code, unless inconsistent therewith, are applicable to actions of right. Damages for withholding possession or using or injuring the premises may be demanded in the petition of ejectment, and the answer may set up claim for permanent improvements. Sections 4187, 4199, Code. In the trial, as in every other, no more need be proven than is sufficient to entitle either party to recover. This appears from section 3639 of the Code, providing that: "A party shall not be compelled to prove more than is necessary to entitle him to the relief asked for, or any lower degree included therein, nor more than sufficient to sustain his defense."

3. The petition alleged damages, and if these were proven, and plaintiff may recover, the case was rightly decided. The rights of one to the burial place of his dead, in the absence of fee to the soil or right to the exclusive possession thereof, in respect to the maintenance of a civil action for its disturbance, is one of delicate, but not very satisfactory, solution. Because of the respect entertained for the final resting place of the dead, and so little temptation to disturb their

repose, disturbances of the same have rarely become the subject of litigation. The adjudications have been sufficient, however, to establish the principle that where one is permitted to bury his dead in a public cemetery, even though this be by license or privilege, he acquires such a possession of the spot of ground in which the bodies are buried as will entitle him to maintain an action against the owners of the fee or strangers, who without right so to do disturb it. In *Jacobus v. Congregation, supra*, it was held that where the purchaser of a lot continues in possession of such until his death, possession is transmitted to his heirs, and this rule was recognized in *Gardner v. Swan Point Cemetery*, 20 R. I. 646, 40 Atl. 871, 78 Am. St. Rep. 897. The nature of the interest in and the use to which a burial lot is put is such that this should be declared the rule. Appellant insists, however, that as Joshua and Mike were licensees, the death of Joshua revoked all interest in the burial lot. It may be conceded that a naked license is revoked by the death of the licensee; though this is not so as to the survivor, where the license runs to two persons. The ground is required for the purposes of the sepulture, not only of the purchaser, but of his family as well, and after these have been laid at rest the sentiment of their descendants may be relied upon to guard the last resting place of their dead as hallowed ground. The license or privilege continues so long as the land is used as a cemetery. A cemetery has been declared not to be the subject of partition. After referring to a schism in the church, the former worshipers in which now sleep in the grounds, the court said: "The only form in which the partition asked for could be made would be by a public sale, and what would these graves, of inestimable value to surviving relatives, fetch in market? They would prove a prejudice to the property, and would depreciate its price. And then, in the hands of a purchaser, they would be almost sure of desecration. Pennsylvania, with a refined and elevated sense of what is due to both the dead and the living, has forbidden by statute the opening of streets, lanes, alleys, or public roads through burial ground or cemetery, and has provided a penalty for willful injuries done to graveyards, not only to the tombstones, the fence railings, but even to the "shrub and plants" which bereaved love cultivates in such places. The sentiment is sound, and has the sanction of mankind in all ages, which regards the resting place of the dead as hallowed ground, not subject to the laws of ordinary property, nor liable to be devoted to common uses. We do but express the concurrence in this sentiment which we feel when we hold that a church and burial ground situated as these now under consideration, and owned by distinct religious societies as tenants in common, are not within the spirit and meaning of our statutes of partition, and that the court was right in denying judgment quod partitio fiat to the plaintiffs." Nor can a cemetery after dedication for burial purposes and in use therefor be mortgaged. In the former case it was said that: "We hold that the ground once given for the interment of a body is appropriated forever to that body. It is not only the *domus ultima*, but the *domus æterna*, so far as the eternal can be applied to man or terrestrial things. Nothing but the most pressing public necessity should ever cause the rest of the dead to be disturbed." Nor can it be sold under execution. And in several states it is held exempt from assessment without express statutory authority. In *Thompson v. Hickey*, 8 Abb. N. C. (N. Y.) 159, it was held that a burial lot could not be mortgaged, and in *Derby v. Derby*, 4 R. I. 414, that it was not included in a power of sale given an executor to pay debts and legacies, but passed to the heir of the testator. In *Sabin v. Harkness*, 4 N. H. 415, 17 Am. Dec. 437, it was said that those erecting a tombstone may maintain an action for its injury, and after their death the heirs of him in whose honor it was erected may prosecute such action. In *Pierce v. Swan Point Cemetery*, 10 R. I. 227, 14 Am. Rep. 667, the right of the heir thereto was sustained as against the widow of deceased, who had removed his body from the burial lot. In *Mitchell v. Thorne*, 134 N. Y. 536, 32 N. E. 10, 30 Am. St. Rep. 699, an action by the heirs for an injury to the monument of their ancestor was sustained. The peculiar use to which such property is dedicated, and the sentiment of sanctity with which mankind regard the burial place of the dead, furnish ample reason for declining to apply to it the ordinary rules of ownership and devolution. The principle of all the cases, as said in *Gardner v. Swan Point Cemetery*, seems to be that the buried body shall remain undisturbed, and that the right and duty falls to the next of kin to see that its repose is duly protected. This, however, is not to be confused with the right to the custody and control of the body before burial, when other considerations than those of kinship are involved.

4. Nor do we think appellant's contention that Joshua and Mike Whaley acquired the lot as joint tenants, and that, therefore, upon Joshua's death his interest passed to Mike as survivor, is sound. Section 2923 provides that "conveyances to two or more in their own right create a tenancy in common, unless the contrary intent is expressed." As said, the interest of Joshua was something more than an ordinary license. The right to the use of the ground as a burial place passed to his heirs, and the conveyance to him and Mike Whaley was within the rule of this statute. True, the ordinance of the city declared that the lot should be indivisible, but this, like other provisions, was enacted for the regulation and control of the lots, and not to define the nature of the interests which might be acquired therein.

5. It is urged, however, that one of the heirs of Joshua Whaley, the plaintiff, without the others, her sister, Sarah Coulson, and Mike Whaley, cannot maintain the action. Section 3463 of the Code requires that "persons having a united interest must be joined on the same side, either as plaintiffs or defendants, except as otherwise expressly provided, but when some who should be made plaintiffs refuse to join, they may be made defendants; the reason therefor being set forth in the petition." The three heirs of Joshua Whaley became tenants in common, and were each interested in the damages to the place of his burial, save that Mike Whaley had consented thereto. This may have furnished sufficient reason, without more, for making him a party defendant. But he was not made such. The petition does not allege that Sarah Coulson had been accorded an opportunity to join in the suit as party plaintiff, nor was she made a defendant. It is the universal rule that tenants in common, when jointly interested in the damages, must join in an action for trespass. But the question must be raised in the way pointed out by statute in order to be available. At the common law the nonjoinder of parties could not be taken advantage of save by a plea in abatement. The defect of parties here appeared on the face of the petition, and this is made by statute a ground of demurrer. Nonjoinder of parties is such defect; and, the defect being apparent on the face of the petition, it could not be taken advantage of by answer, save, possibly, after a demurrer had been overruled, and the omission to demurrer waived the point. The neglect to demur on the ground of nonjoinder of parties is to be given the same effect as the omission to raise that issue by plea in abatement at common law, and, as the petition was otherwise sufficient, the plaintiff was entitled to recover.

6. The bodies of plaintiff's parents were removed in November, 1898, and this action was begun in January, 1903. The petition alleged that defendants did, "in violation of the rights

of this plaintiff, exhume, dig up, and remove therefrom [the lot] the bodies of the father and mother of this plaintiff," and "had buried other bodies upon said lot, and are seeking to maintain said lot as a burial place for their own dead," and demanded damage. In January, 1904, more than five years after the cause of action had accrued, an amendment was filed, alleging that to return the bodies to the lot and restore the monument and shrubbery would cost $400, and asked that these items be included in the damage to be allowed. To this defendants pleaded the statute of limitations. The plea was not good, for no new cause of action was set up. The amendment merely specified more particularly the damages flowing from the injuries alleged in the petition.

7. The consent of Mike Whaley, in consideration of 30 pieces of silver, or their equivalent, to the desecration of his parents' graves by the removal of their bodies and the tombstone erected to their memory therefrom, can furnish no defense. Had the acts been such as he was entitled to do as a tenant in common, his consent that these might be done by another possibly would have been binding on the co-tenants; but what was done was in the nature of an ouster of possession and the commission of waste, for which he might have been held accountable to them. His consent furnished no defense.

8. Appellant insists that the bodies of the deceased, having been interred, ought not to be disturbed. This should have been given consideration by defendants before their unlawful interference with the burial place of plaintiff's parents against her protest. The authorities cited by them are in point. "To disturb the mortal remains of those endeared to us in life sometimes becomes the sad duty of the living; but, except in cases of necessity or for laudable purposes, the sanctity of the grave should be maintained, and the preventive aid of the courts may be invoked for that object." "A proper appreciation of the duty we owe to the dead, and a due regard for the feelings of their friends who survive, and the promotion of the public health and welfare, all require that the bodies of the dead should not be exhumed, except under circumstances of extreme exigency." It does not lie in the mouth of one who has committed the wrong condemned, however, to interpose this as a defense against the proper assessment of damages, or any other legal atonement for the injury suffered.

NOTES

1. What kind of property interest did Joshua and Michael Whaley acquire in Lot 82 in 1885?

2. The City ordinance prohibited division of the lot. Does this rule prohibit co-tenancies in cemetery lots?

3. Amanda Anderson asserted a property interest in the Lot 82 sufficient to eject the Acheson family from the Lot. What is the basis for her argument that she has a property interest?

4. After burial, according to the Iowa court, what is the legal status of human remains? Are they property?

5. According to this case, at common law, who has the "right of possession of a dead body"? For what purpose does this right exist?

6. According to this case, who has standing to enforce the common law "right to decent burial" after burial? What does the right protect?

7. At common law, what kind of property interest does the purchaser of a lot in a "public" cemetery [meaning, a cemetery open to the public rather than restricted to members of a particular religious faith or other group] obtain? Is the common law rule different for private cemeteries?

8. The Iowa court asserts that the reserved powers of the city of Keokuk, including the rights to "prescribe rules for the improving or adorning the lots therein, or for the erection of monuments or other memorials of the dead upon such lots; and to prohibit any use, division, improvement or adornment of a lot which they may deem improper," are inconsistent with the idea that the cemetery lot owners acquired a fee simple estate. Do you agree? Does the city of Keokuk retain rights beyond what city governments and homeowners associations retain with respect to modern residential properties in the United States?

9. If Amanda Anderson acquired a property interest in Lot 82, what is the nature of that property interest? What is she permitted to do unilaterally? What may she not do without the consent of her co-tenants?

❖ ❖ ❖

Winchester Cemetery, Winchester, Ohio
Photo by Tanya D. Marsh

CHAPTER 11.8

WILSON V. READ, ET AL.

Supreme Court of New Hampshire, 74 N.H. 322 (1907)

In the absence of any information as to the terms of the decree for the plaintiff to which exception is taken, it is presumed that the decree was drawn to effect the purpose of the bill—the restoration of the remains of Harriet A. Read to their place of original interment. The fact that no trace of the remains which the plaintiff asks to have restored was discovered in the grave where they were originally buried discloses the futility of such a decree. If none was found in the grave, it is clear none can be in the place where the earth of the grave was deposited. The law does not require that to be done which is impossible or useless. ... The court has no power to order one to do what the law will not require him to do because of its impossibility or futility. ... Not only did the body of Harriet become as matter of law after burial a part of the ground to which it was committed, but from lapse of time it has, as a physical fact, become indistinguishable from the soil in which it was placed. The body was returned to the parent earth for dissolution. That purpose has been accomplished. Whatever right the plaintiff may have to protect the burial place of her sister, no decree of the court can effect the reburial of remains no longer in existence. The plaintiff is not entitled to a decree to carry out the impossible purpose of her bill. ...

It is well settled that in this country, in the absence of ecclesiastical tribunals exercising such jurisdiction in England, courts of equity have power to settle controversies as to the burial of the dead, the care of their remains after burial, and the preservation of the place of interment from wanton violation or unnecessary disturbance. The defendants do not contest the power of the court, and the only question that can be raised is whether upon the facts the plaintiff is entitled to any relief. The cases are numerous which involve controversies as to the place of burial of a deceased relative, or as to a change of location of the remains after burial, or the diversion to other purposes of land once dedicated for use as a burial place; but none of them raises the precise question found here. This is not a controversy as to the removal of the remains of Harriet to some other location, or of the use of the burial place for other than burial purposes. The sole question appears to be whether the plaintiff can prevent the use by her sisters and brother, the owners of the burial lot, of the precise spot for the burial of their mother which was once used for the repose of their sister's remains. *Page v. Symonds*, 63 N. H. 17, 56 Am. Rep. 481, was an application to enjoin the removal of the remains of the plaintiff's relatives, by public authority, from a burial ground discontinued because of public necessity. It was then said: "Strictly speaking, there is no right of property in a dead body. ... But, while it is not property in the ordinary sense of the term, it is regarded as property so far as to entitle the relatives to legal protection from unnecessary disturbance and wanton violation or invasion of its place of burial. The plaintiff, notwithstanding he is neither the owner of the soil of the cemetery nor of the remains of his deceased relatives interred there may nevertheless be authorized to invoke protection against unnecessary desecration of their place of burial." If the action of the defendants in opening the grave of Harriet was criminal, or a wrong against the plaintiff, this proceeding is not brought to punish that action, or to recover damages for the injury to the plaintiff's right.

Is the plaintiff entitled to an order requiring the defendants to remove the remains of their mother from the place where, in accordance with her expressed wish, they now rest beside those of her husband? The question is not whether the court, in the exercise of a sound judgment, would have enjoined the opening of the grave of Harriet for the purpose of interring the remains of the defendants' mother, but is whether the court can now order the removal of the remains of Mary E. from the spot where they now rest. The plaintiff has no title to the burial lot. She is not next of kin to Mary E., and can have no voice in the selection of a resting place for her remains. Her sole interest arises from her relationship to Harriet. Under the decision in Page v. Symonds, she would be entitled to an order requiring the removal of the remains of Mary E. from their present resting place, if it could be found that their continuance there was a "wanton violation or invasion" of the place of Harriet's burial—an "unnecessary desecration" of the spot. But the reported facts are insufficient to sustain such a finding. John Read, the father of all the parties to the controversy, owned the lot, and in 1855 buried therein the remains of his daughter Harriet, who died at the age of seven months. Subsequently he buried in the same lot his wife and another daughter, the graves being so arranged as to leave a space between those of Harriet and his wife, while the other daughter, Mary A., was buried in the grave immediately on the other side of her mother's. In 1863 John married Mary E. He died in 1895, having devised the burial lot to his wife, Mary E. She buried him in the lot beside his first wife, in the vacant space between that grave and the spot where Harriet's remains were buried. Mary E. died in 1904, having expressed a wish to be buried beside her husband. The defendants, her children who now own the lot, have now buried her in accordance with her wish. The question is whether such burial is such a desecration of the spot used for the entire dissolution of Harriet's remains that the court is authorized to order the remains of Mary E. to be again dug up and buried elsewhere. When a body is once buried, courts are slow to order its removal, and will not do so except under circumstances of extreme exigency. This follows from considerations of the public health and welfare, as well as from a respect to the dead and consideration for the feelings of those who survive. Where there is controversy as to location of the grave, great weight is given to the wishes of the deceased, if known. It has even been said to be "the duty of courts to see to it that the expressed wish of one as to his final resting place shall, so far as it is possible, be carried out." The body of Mary E. now rests in the place where she desired it to lie, beside her husband. The fact that the soil in which she lies once performed for the body of her husband's infant child the same service it is now performing for hers is not a sufficient reason why her remains should again be exhumed, and her reasonable and proper wishes be defeated. No necessity probably has yet arisen in this country for holding that the right of burial is merely for the purpose of dissolution, generally requiring about a generation, and that each generation must give way to succeeding ones in the use of soil dedicated for that purpose. This case does not require such holding; for, while under the circumstances of the case as disclosed before the grave was opened a refusal to permit the opening of Harriet's grave for the burial of Mary E., or to ascertain whether it contained any remains of the former occupant, might not have been erroneous as matter of law, the fact being established that the burial made by the defendants involved no disturbance of Harriet's remains, and being one that was otherwise fit and proper to be made, and having been made, no sufficient reason appears for disturbing the existing situation. None can be suggested, except the injury to the plaintiff's feelings. In view of the relationship of the parties, an objection of this character by the plaintiff is too clearly fanciful and unreasonable to serve as a foundation for such an order. The defendants, as the owners of the lot, had not the absolute right to disturb the grave already upon the lot. Neither has the plaintiff, as next of kin, an absolute right to prevent the removal of the remains of one buried there, or other use of the land. The rights of each are bounded by rules of propriety and reasonableness determinable by a court of equity upon due application. This is the holding in effect of all the authorities. As the plaintiff has not the absolute right to require the removal of the remains of Mary E., and as the evidence has no tendency to establish the necessity, reasonableness, or propriety of their removal, no order to that effect can be made. The case does not show that such an order has been made; but, as the exceptions raise the question whether any decree can be made for the plaintiff, the power to make such an order has been considered. Some facts appear in the case as to the erection of gravestones by the plaintiff upon the lot, but it does not appear that any orders are necessary or were asked for in reference to them.

❖ ❖ ❖

CHAPTER 12

THE REGULATION OF CEMETERIES

Crown Hill Cemetery, Indianapolis, Indiana
Photo by Tanya D. Marsh

CHAPTER 12.1

THE REGULATION OF CEMETERIES

Tanya D. Marsh

"The sanctity of the dead is respected in every civilized community. Cemeteries and burying grounds are not only recognized as necessary, but are authorized, provided for and protected by humane laws." *Begein v. City of Anderson*, 28 Ind.79, 81 (1867).

Civil authorities have a number of legitimate reasons to regulate the disposition of human remains. This section will discuss four major reasons: (1) public health and safety concerns; (2) to control land use; (3) to ensure the maintenance of graveyards; and (4) to protect consumers.

Public Health

There has long been concern that the presence of human remains near the living constitute a threat to public health. In colonial days, graveyards within city limits were often overcrowded, particularly during periods of mass illness. Although modern sanitation dealt with many of these issues, on the eve of the twentieth century, cemeteries were still seen as a possible threat to public health. For example, in 1899, the Nebraska Supreme Court addressed a nuisance lawsuit brought by homeowners in Omaha who objected to the expansion of the Prospect Hill Cemetery. *Lowe v. Prospect Hill Cemetery Association*, 78 N.W. 488 (Neb. 1899). The homeowners complained that the new graves would "pollute and poison the water" of their wells. The court agreed with their concerns:

> The evidence in behalf of both parties to this controversy shows, without conflict, that contagious and infectious diseases . . . are caused by the presence in . . . the human, of infinitesimal microscopic microbes, germs, living organisms; that on the death of the human these germs multiply and reproduce themselves in countless numbers; . . . that moisture sinking and seeping into the pores of the earth will carry these germs, living and active, from graves, for considerable distances; that, if moisture containing these germs seeps into a well, the germs will communicate to persons using the water the disease of which the body died from whence the germ sprang . . . ..

Utilizing a similar reasoning, many cases holding that a cemetery may not be developed in a residential area hinge on the concern of adjoining landowners that their wells will be polluted. Although most of the cases involving objections to a cemetery based on public health and safety concerns, such as well pollution, are more than 100 years old, similar arguments are advanced today.

To Control Land Use

In 1970, the U.S. Department of Housing and Urban Development estimated that nearly two million acres of land were dedicated to cemetery purposes. No one knows how many cemeteries exist in the United States, and estimates easily top 100,000. While the volume of land dedicated to cemeteries is far less than the volume of land dedicated to other human activities, from a land use perspective, cemeteries are problematic for several reasons.

First, due largely to cultural taboos, Americans are hesitant to redevelop land previously used for cemetery purposes. A common sentiment is that the activity of burial transforms mere real estate into hallowed or sacred ground. There is little debate that the state has the power to condemn a cemetery and cause the relocation of the remains therein to another cemetery. In many states, private owners also have the right to relocate a cemetery in order to redevelop the land for commercial purposes. There are numerous examples of cemetery land being thus redeveloped, particularly in densely populated urban areas. But such decisions are often unpopular.

Second, cemeteries are necessarily located near human settlements. This is intuitively desirable. This proximity creates few problems in sparsely populated areas, but in denser urban areas, real estate dedicated to the dead is in direct competition with the needs of the living. Early American cemeteries were located within towns, next to homes and churches, woven into the fabric of the community. Beginning in the 1830s with the rural cemetery movement, new graveyards were established on the outskirts of town. Of course, as cities expanded outward, they engulfed the previously isolated cemeteries. As a result, cities and states have an interest in limiting cemeteries not only in cities, but within a buffer surrounding the present boundaries in order to plan for growth. The logical conclusion of this policy approach is that some large urban areas, such as New York City, are literally running out of burial space.

Cemetery Maintenance

When a cemetery is abandoned, most state laws permit a division of local government to take possession and maintain the graves. Determining when a cemetery has been abandoned may be a tricky business, and the definition of "abandonment" varies from state to state. Generally speaking, though, a cemetery is deemed abandoned when no living person asserts ownership of the underlying land or maintains the graves.

Abandoned cemeteries are very common in the United States. One reason is our mobile society. As time goes on, families drift apart and move away from a community. The new neighbors have no connection to those buried there and little incentive to spend resources to maintain their graves.

Abandoned cemeteries are an issue of concern for local government for a number of reasons. First, abandoned cemeteries represent a public expense with only private benefit, which many perceive as marginal at best. In America, unlike many other countries, cemeteries are generally not used as public gathering places. Instead, they are largely ignored unless a person wishes to visit a particular grave. So in the common case of an abandoned cemetery where the last internment occurred in the 1800s, few conclude that it the asset is a broad public good. For example, in 1968, the City of Pulaski, Tennessee filed a bill in the Giles County Chancery Court to authorize the city to redevelop an abandoned cemetery to a municipal cemetery park. The City explained that

> said cemetery is in a deteriorated condition; it is an eyesore to the community and contributes to the deterioration of the adjacent neighborhood. The overturned grave markers and the disorderly condition of the site makes maintenance expensive.

In the 1970s, the Pulaski example was touted as an example for other municipalities to deal with abandoned and neglected cemeteries. The federal government, through the department of Housing and Urban Development, issued a report suggesting a more radical plan to reuse cemeteries for low-income housing.

The concern that any cemetery may eventually be abandoned and become a burden on taxpayers has had a clear impact on public policy. The concept of a private pot of money designated for the perpetual care of a cemetery is a relatively new idea. It was developed in reaction to what has been described as an "attitude of indifference concerning burial places" which dates to the early parts of the Nineteenth Century. Perpetual care funds are now required in a number of states as a prerequisite to form a new cemetery. Even in circumstances where such funds are not required, some proposed cemetery projects have attracted negative attention from local government due to a failure to provide for such a fund. For example, in August 2010, the town board of Sidney, New York voted to take legal action to disinter the bodies at a private cemetery associated with an Islamic center and to prohibit future internments. The town supervisor argued that the cemetery was in violation of applicable law and that it could ultimately become the government's responsibility: "Unauthorized cemeteries have the potential of placing a financial burden on the local government ... and ... [climb] on the backs of an already overtaxed local taxpayer."

Numerous courts have stated that the government has an interest in ensuring that cemeteries are cared for out of a cultural respect for graves.

> The sentiment of all civilized peoples, since earliest Biblical times, has held in great reverence the resting places of the dead as hallowed ground. In such matters we deal with concerns that basically are spiritual. Awe toward the dead was a most powerful force in forming primitive systems for grappling with the supernatural. 'It is a sound public policy to protect the burying place[ ] of the dead.'

Massey v. Hoffman, 647 S.E.2d 457, 461 (N.C. Ct. App. 2007)

Methods of Regulation

It has long been established that municipalities may, through the exercise of their police powers, limit or even bar the internment of human remains in or near densely populated areas. However, it has also been long established that cemeteries are a necessity, and that internments may not be prohibited in places where "no possible danger to human life or health could result." For example, in the early 1900s, the California Supreme Court considered ordinances passed in San Francisco and Los Angeles, both which proposed to bar internments within city limits. The court upheld the San Francisco ordinance (later affirmed by the United States Supreme Court) but struck down the Los Angeles restriction because the county of Los Angeles "has within its limits many square miles of territory which are not only not thickly populated, but in which there are scarcely any inhabitants at all."

❖　❖　❖

Hollywood Cemetery, Richmond, Virginia
Photo by Tanya D. Marsh

CHAPTER 12.2

THE RIGHTS OF THE OWNER OF THE BURIAL PLOT

Percival Jackson, THE LAW OF CADAVERS (1950)

Grave owner and lot owner distinguished; incidents of their respective titles.

A person may acquire a right of burial by purchase of a single grave wherein he may inter one or more bodies according to prevailing custom. Single graves are usually located in what is known as a public section of the modern cemetery. In such cases the title of the owner is confined to the right to bury in the grave, with no rights in the surrounding land.

Contradistinguished from the restricted right in a single grave is the title of the lot or section owner, who possesses burial rights in a parcel of land in which more than one grave may be dug. The lot or section owner may protect his rights in the lot or section from unauthorized invasion.

Other incidents of ownership of burial rights—Rights in Roads and Paths.

In common with grave owners, lot owners possess a right of access and egress over the cemetery roads and paths established by the cemetery corporation. This right has been termed an easement, and entitles the lot owner to the reasonable and usual enjoyment thereof in view of the existing circumstances.

Under settled rules of law the lot owner may enjoin interference with these rights, and though a burial in a path in which an adjoining lot owner has an easement of passage works no physical obstruction, the existing sentiment that land should not be used for burial purposes and also as a highway makes the passageway as impassable as though there had been a physical obstruction, and gives the lot owner a consequent right to relief.

The right of access and egress likewise accrues to the next of kin of those interred in the grave.

The fee and the management of the paths and roads remain in the cemetery corporation for the common good, and the lot owners are entitled to have the funds of the corporation available therefor used to keep the roads and paths accessible and in good condition.

Rights in Undeveloped Portion of Cemetery.

The lot and grave owners take no rights in the undeveloped portion of the cemetery, except that they have an instinctive right that the unity and integrity of the cemetery be preserved as a whole, and that funds available for that purpose be not devoted to an improper use.

Other Rights.

The lot owner, subject to the reasonable regulation of the exercise of his rights, may enclose the plot or section of ground in which he possesses the burial rights; he may improve and embellish it and may exclude other persons therefrom.

The lot owner's "right to bury carries with it the right to do so by the usual custom in the neighborhood and undoubtedly includes the right of making mounds over and erecting stones and monuments at the graves" subject to the reasonable rules and regulations of the cemetery. ...

Rights subject to restriction and regulation—Generally.

[T]he exercise of the right of burial is so effectually a matter of public concern that its conduct is subject to regulation by the state in the exercise of its police power, before which all claim of vested rights must fail. So ... the right to bury may be denied the cemetery and the individual, where good reason or legislative policy dictates.

[T]he cemetery corporation exercises its chartered powers subject to the now usual reservation by the state of the power to alter, amend, or repeal the charter; and through that reserved power the state may restrict and regulate the corporation's conduct of the cemetery.

Manifestly the derivative rights of the lot owner, whether as a member of the corporation or as the holder of a burial right, being carved from the whole, are subject to its infirmities. In consequence, there can be no doubt of the right of the state and its political subdivisions, under proper authority, to regulate and restrict the right of burial of the lot owner after the acquisition by him of such rights.

The rights of the lot owner are subject to restriction and regulation; first, by statute regulating *(a)* the conduct and maintenance of the cemetery, *(b)* the conduct and management of the entity owning and operating the cemetery; second, by statute directly restricting or regulating the exercise of the rights of burial; third, by substantive rules based on reasons of instinctive policy flowing from the nature of burial rights and their proper exercise; fourth, by the lot owner's contract with the cemetery corporation, which may be evidenced by *(a)* its charter and by-laws, *(b)* the conditions contained in the deed or other evidence of title, or *(c)* the rules and regulations which the corporation may properly make. ...

Restriction and regulation of rights for reasons of instinctive policy, flowing from nature of burial rights and their proper exercise.

When we deal with restriction and regulation of the lot owner's rights, as prescribed by statute, we deal with questions of constitutional law in determining their validity. At the other extreme, when dealing with the matter of regulation by the cemetery corporation, we consider the rights of lot owners as limited by rules of contract. Between lies a field for the conception and enforcement of rules applicable to burial places, so that proper burial may be given and maintained, in accordance with proper human sentiments, even in the absence of statutory basis or common law precedent. A notion of elasticity in this field must appeal to modern legal thought as a sensible combination of a recognition of the necessity of certainty and a willingness to conform with changing mores.

While we know now that the bases of rules of burial law are found in human rather than in property values, no more recognition of human values as determinative factors is to be found in the cases on these questions than in those on most phases of the subject of burial. Generally it is the safety of property rights that has been made the *sine qua non* of these controversies, and the courts have sought rules of contract upon which to base their decisions. Consequently, only dicta can be pointed to as authority for these rules of law applicable to burial places, rather than the technical reasons advanced by the courts for their determinations. But it must not be denied that added security can be afforded the rules of burial law when a foundation can also be laid in established rules of other branches of the law.

Application of rules of burial law alone should suffice where the act sought to be denied is repugnant and does violence to normal human sentiments. The rules so evolved must necessarily be bounded by the practical and expedient within reasonable limits, but such doctrines may find themselves part of the law of burial and be supported without vestige of contractual or statutory authority. Such matters must reckon with existent sentiment, moral values, and even concurrent prejudices. ...

❖ ❖ ❖

Salem Cemetery, Winston-Salem, North Carolina
Photo by Tanya D. Marsh

CHAPTER 12.3
DANGER DOESN'T END AT THE GRAVE:
Brett Becker

Headstones falling on people and causing them injury or even death is ironic. Headstones are primarily intended to mark the life of a deceased, not to mark the place death might occur. Even though unlikely, the fact exists that this occurrence happens and is not even as rare as one would expect. In December 2013, a seventy-five year old man visiting Holy Cross Cemetery, in Brooklyn, New York, found himself pinned beneath a headstone weighing over three hundred pounds. The elderly man was paying his respects at his mother's grave when suddenly an old headstone fell on him after he attempted to brace his own fall by holding himself against the headstone. His legs were trapped and he was severely injured. About a year prior to the accident in New York, a four-year-old boy in Florida was killed when a headstone fell on him. The Florida headstone, which weighed over two hundred pounds, belonged to the grave of a man who had died in 1889, making the marker over one hundred years old. This event spurred the Florida cemetery to identify fifty headstones in need of repair and reinforcement. Working under an assumption that as graveyards become older they will consequentially fall under a greater position of disrepair, there is a need to assess the risks of falling tombstones and the liability that falls with them.

The Law and Liability

This issue is not new, but has fallen before courts many times in the past. The cases of injury or even death resulting from falling headstones have been before American courts for over a hundred years. Because falling headstones are heavy objects and injuries can be extensive, substantial awards may be available to plaintiffs—if a liable party can be identified.

Negligence is the primary route by which claims are brought against cemeteries and others in control over headstones. The negligence theory has been utilized and successfully argued in many cases. For over a hundred years courts have recognized the general duty of maintenance a cemetery assumes to its visitors and patrons. In *Dutton v. Greenwood Cemetery*, 80 A.D. 352, 356, 80 N.Y.S. 780, 782, New York's Appellate Division, Second Department, stated the principle that "[t]he [cemetery] owning the property, and lawfully assuming to supervise and control its care and maintenance, including the keeping of the monuments and tombstones ... of the grounds in safe and proper condition, the application to it of the general rule of liability for negligence necessarily follow[s]." Some states have enacted legislation imposing the duty of maintenance upon the owner of the cemetery. For example, Kentucky § 381.697(1) mandates that:

> Every cemetery in Kentucky except private family cemeteries shall be maintained by its legal owner or owners, without respect to the individual owners of burial plots in the cemetery, in such a manner so as to keep the burial grounds or cemetery free of growth of weeds, free from accumulated debris, displaced tombstones, or other signs and indication of vandalism or gross neglect.

Whether by statute or by common law, persons entering cemetery properties are typically owed some duty of care.

Typically, the establishment of such a duty coincides with the classification of those harmed on cemetery grounds as invitees. Once established as an invitee, there is a duty upon the owner of the cemetery to exercise ordinary care with respect to the land in keeping the premises safe. For the injured party to recover as an invitee for injuries sustained on cemetery property, he or she must typically prove that "(1) the owner or proprietor had actual or constructive knowledge of the hazard and (2) the plaintiff lacked knowledge of the hazard despite the exercise of ordinary care." Essentially, if there is some knowledge by the cemetery of a hidden danger, then the cemetery will breach a duty if the condition causes an injury. Conversely, knowledge on behalf of the injured party, or if the danger is open and obvious, can destroy the plaintiff's case. The lack of structural soundness of a headstone, especially one that has not been maintained for many years, is precisely the type of hazard that can lead to a successful claim against a cemetery for injuries caused by the headstone.

An injured party might lose his status as an invitee while at a cemetery and therefore is demoted to the classification of licensee. In this situation, the case may become moot, as no affirmative duty would attach to the cemetery. In *Nesterovich v. Mt. Olivet Cemetery*, 212 A.D. 286 (N.Y. App. Div. 1st Dept. 1925), a falling headstone injured a child, but the court found he was no longer an invitee because he engaged in activities on the property, which were unrelated to the purposes or uses of a cemetery. (The injured child was directed by his mother, who did not want to leave a funeral service, to go to the bathroom near a fence even though the cemetery had lavatories on the premises). Because the court held that the boy was only a licensee, the cemetery's duty was lessened and the court found no negligence. Another important factual determination is whether or not the duty has been delegated. Maintenance of burial grounds is typically a delegable duty whether by common law or specifically by statute.

One of the greatest factors that stand in an injured party's way to recovery is whether the cemetery is owned by the government or a private entity or individual. If owned by the government, then those injured on the property may be barred from recovery by the state's tort immunity statute. Even though there may be a "purchase" of a cemetery lot, the transaction involving the land typically does not give the purchaser land in fee simple and therefore make the land private. Instead, the land remains part of public property and the immunity is still applicable. In *Brock v. Richmond-Berea Cemetery Dist.*, 264 Kan. 613, 617-18, the Kansas Supreme Court recognized this principle and declined to impose any duty to inspect the grave plots absent any statutory mandate, even though the grave plots were purchased. Besides simple tort immunity, some states have enacted even more protection within their tort immunity statutes that may impact any claim resulting from falling headstones. Plan or design immunity, if enacted, might sufficiently wipe out any possible claims that might normally surpass the barriers of basic tort immunity.

At least seven states have enacted some form of plan or design immunity, which effectively bars recovery for any injury caused by a condition of government property that has been approved of by a government authority. For example, New Jersey § 59:4-6 provides:

> Neither a public entity nor a public employee is liable for an injury caused by the plan or design of public property, either in its original construction or any improvement thereto, where such plan or design has been approved in advance of the construction or improvement by the Legislature or the governing body of a public entity or some other body or a public employee exercising discretionary authority to give such approval or where such plan or design is prepared in conformity with standards previously so approved.

In order for a public entity to succeed in claiming the immunity, it only needs to show "that an approved feature of the plan sufficiently addressed the condition that is causally related to the accident." This immunity, if enacted in the jurisdiction, might allow a public cemetery to claim the design of its headstones (their placements, sizes, construction, installation, etc.) was approved and therefore is entitled to the immunity.

Preventative Laws

Some states have enacted legislation imposing duties to prevent accidents within their cemeteries. The most obvious prevention route is to legislatively ensure that old headstones are inspected and still in a safe condition rendering it safe for persons to pass through cemetery grounds. Further, legislation ensuring the proper maintenance and repairs should coincide the duty of inspection. In a more proactive approach, some states have imposed duties to not only inspect or repair, but to also require stricter standards for new headstones to ensure stability for a greater number of years. Still, some states have no laws requiring that anyone maintain cemetery property.

New York Not-for-Profit Corp. Law §1510-a mandates the owners of cemeteries to remove or repair headstones. The statutory duty allows cemeteries to remove and repair headstones, even if not owned by the cemetery, and only requires notice of the removal to the last known owners, or else posted notice if the last owners are not known. When removing a tombstone that has been deemed unsafe, Not-for-Profit Corp. Law §1510-a(c) provides:

Any monument or other marker that is removed as provided for in this section shall be replaced with a flush bronze or granite marker suitably inscribed if replacement is appropriate for identification purposes.

This method provides for a safe replacement. Interestingly, this method might suffice as the necessary approval of a plan or design as discussed above if New York were to enact a plan or design immunity statute.

The State of Maine has imposed duties upon its localities to maintain certain gravesites. Municipalities are required to keep headstones in ancient burial grounds in "good condition" and may designate a caretaker to perform such responsibilities. Me. Rev. Stat. tit. 13, § 1101. Municipalities in Maine are required to keep the headstones of any veteran of the Armed Forces of the United States within the municipality in "good condition." Specifically, the municipality must ensure: (1) that the veteran's headstone is maintained at a proper vertical and horizontal height and orientation, and (2) that after a gravesite has sunk three or more inches as compared to the ground surrounding the grave, the gravesite must be regraded.

Pennsylvania, rather than imposing a duty to replace or remove unsafe headstones, has attempted to spur maintenance of cemeteries by specifically providing immunity for such actions. 9 Pa. Stat. Ann. § 202. Pennsylvania limits the liability of owners of land that is deemed a "historical" burial ground under the "Cemetery Companies: Interment rights, restore, and maintain Act." Stated as the "general rule," the Pennsylvania act provides that "a caretaker organization or a landowner owes no duty of care to keep a historic burial place safe for entry or use by others or to give any warning of a dangerous condition, use, structure or activity on the premises of the historic burial place to persons who enter the premises." Although the statute limits duties, the stated purpose of the act is to actually encourage maintenance of such burial grounds.

Sometimes, local governmental bodies are best suited to regulate and control the installation of new headstones to ensure safety for future generations of cemetery visitors. In Bartow, Florida, city commissions took localized action by approving regulations concerning the safety of new gravesites. The new regulations mandate concrete pads beneath any new headstones placed at either of the two cemeteries owned by the city to prevent the stones from progressive leaning. The regulations go even further and regulate what may be placed around or upon the headstones. Items placed on the property by patrons must be affixed to the headstone rather than laid sporadically about the grounds. Even though some of the regulations are aimed only at reducing the accidental falls of persons rather than falling headstones, many times people lose their balance, fall into a headstone, and cause the headstone to topple.

The city of Monett, Missouri has imposed simple yet comprehensive precautions for the installation of monuments within the city's many cemeteries. Monett requires that every new grave marker be re-enforced by an eighteen-inch concrete footing. Interestingly, Monett decided that the concrete footings were sufficient and does not require any pads as required in Bartow, Florida. The monuments themselves may not exceed twenty-four inches in width or length. This limitation is based on the idea that limiting the size of the headstones will help to reduce the natural tendencies for the markers to tilt as well as the damage caused if they do fall. When the memorials are installed, Monett requires that they must be at ground level and be in a straight line with other monuments. Mandating that the original setting be at ground level helps to ensure proper installation and stability from the beginning. Requiring that monuments be placed in a straight line does nothing to increase the strength of the foundations, but it does help to reduce human error in bumping into the headstones. Such a reduction will seem to reasonably correlate to less falling headstones. Although not a perfect model, Monett, Missouri has initiated precautions that might be used as an example for other localities hoping to limit injuries occuring on cemetery grounds.

Prohibitive Laws

Some laws may actually stand as a hindrance toward ensuring safety on cemetery grounds. In Pennsylvania, for example, the Historic Burial Places Preservation Act has actually made a fairly lengthy process to remove and repair old headstones in graves declared a "historical burial place." If a cemetery has been in existence for one hundred years and no new burials have occurred in the last fifty years, Pennsylvania deems the grave a historical burial place. 9 Pa. Stat. Ann. § 212. Once deemed a historic burial place, Pennsylvania prohibits the removal or replacement of headstones unless there is either consent by a lineal descendant of the deceased, or if they are unknown, then consent of the "burial ground authority." 9 Pa. Stat. Ann. § 214(b). Presumably, the burial ground authority would be the most likely party to seek to repair or replace a headstone. The real issue lies in the next step the Historic Burial Places Preservation Act requires before any removal or repair of a headstone may commence. To remove or repair the headstone, a court order is required after a written application and hearing with notice to interested parties. The Act provides that an order must only be given upon a finding that the removal is necessary or desirable for the protection and preservation of the gravestone or memorial. Although permission might be obtained, this process complicates the ability for a structural issue to be timely addressed and prevent an accident from occurring. This Act seems to be a hindrance by placing historical sentiment over the ability to prevent harm.

Pennsylvania is not the only state with legislation that impedes the repair and removal of dangerous headstones in a timely manner. Maine has a similar statute mandating that the authorization of the headstone's owner or lineal descendant of the deceased, or if unable to be reasonably located, the authorization of the municipality or county before any repair, maintenance, or removal may be performed. Me. Rev. Stat. Ann. tit. 13, §1371(1). Simply, the requirement to receive authorization delays the ability for safety issues to be addressed. The language of these similarly situated statutes might be revised and become either: (1) inapplicable to headstones deemed unsafe by owners or keepers of cemeteries, or (2) less stringent when the headstone is removed for purposes of structural maintenance. These revisions would not only allow the protections to the historical cemetery plots to be kept in place, but would also permit proper maintenance and safety to be realized.

Connecticut enacted legislation, which on its face, seems to address this issue. Conn. Gen. Stat. Ann. § 19a-315c. As a general rule, Connecticut prohibits the removal of headstones, but permits burial ground authorities to maintain such headstones. There is a long process, requiring a minimum of ninety days posted notice, for any "renovations" of ancient burial places. If a probate court assumes jurisdiction over the "renovation" to order a hearing, the burial ground authority must wait to commence the renovation until a written order is granted. Like the statutes discussed above, this is a lengthy process that limits the ability for burial ground authorities to maintain headstones, but Connecticut makes an important distinction in maintenance practices. Connecticut, unlike the other states, seems to apply this process to burial ground authorities only in their abilities to "renovat[e] [an] ancient burial place, cemetery or burial place as a whole" as opposed to their abilities to "[r]epair, rehabilitat[e], reposition[] or reset … ancient grave markers." No lengthy process is added to this power to maintain individual headstones. It seems as though Connecticut has recognized the need to timely maintain headstones, but is also willing to put lengthy processes in place if major renovations are planned.

New Jersey further addresses the issue of maintaining the safety of cemeteries while respecting the rights of headstone owners and their memorials to loved ones. Unlike most statutes, New Jersey's statutes clearly put a greater emphasis on safety concerns. New Jersey provides a process for notification of the removal of headstones to the owners, but unlike most other jurisdictions' statutes, the removal is permitted before notification. N.J. Stat. Ann. §45:27-24(a). The ability to remove a headstone prior to notification only occurs when the removal is for "safety reasons." The only required steps before removal are for the cemetery to take photographs of the headstone and to retain them in their permanent records. After removal, the cemetery must then notify the owners within thirty days that the removal has occurred. Although the removal prior to notification might seem intrusive, precautionary measures are mandated. New Jersey requires the cemetery to store the removed headstone in a "reasonably secure manner" for one year so that the owners may come and claim possession. New Jersey's statute, like Connecticut's, provides that more notice must be given in advance of any planned renovation. Unlike Connecticut's statute, New Jersey provides that "[s]ite work necessary to repair or restore any part of a cemetery as an emergency response to vandalism, damage by weather conditions or other acts of God shall not constitute planned renovation work." New Jersey has enacted one of the most comprehensive statutes enabling safety to be a priority while still acknowledging and caring for the respect of the loved ones of the deceased and the care of their headstones.

Not only do some statutes create lengthy processes that inhibit the removal of potentially dangerous headstones, but other statutes might make the removal of such illegal. Most states prohibit the removal of headstones, but then provide exceptions for burial authorities. The competing policies at issue are: (1) the sanctity of the burial places of loved ones and their families, and (2) maintaining land and ensuring the safety of the living traversing on such land. Sometimes, legislation providing for these concerns can create unanticipated issues in application. For example, North Carolina seems to make removal of headstones illegal in certain factual scenarios even when a safety issue arises. The relevant language comes from N.C. Gen. Stat. § 14-149(a)(2), which reads:

It is a Class I felony, without authorization of law or the consent of the surviving spouse or next of kin of the deceased, to knowingly and willfully . . . Take away, disturb, vandalize, destroy, tamper with, or deface any tombstone, headstone, monument, grave marker . . . placed within any cemetery to designate the place where human remains are interred or to preserve and perpetuate the memory and the name of any person.

As it stands, the plain meaning of the statute makes the removal of any dangerous headstone for safety purposes a felony without authorization of law or consent of the headstone owners. Although the authorization of law makes a removal legal, "authorization of law" in regard to the removal of headstones is muddled in North Carolina's statutes.

Reading the previous sections of North Carolina's statutes, the legislature provided situations where punishment for defacement would not be applicable. N.C. Gen. Stat. § 14-148(b)(1) excludes "[o]rdinary maintenance and care of a cemetery by the owner, caretaker, or other person acting to facilitate cemetery operation by keeping the cemetery free from accumulated debris or other signs of neglect" from applicability to the illegal actions of defacing a gravesite. If read in conjunction, an interpretation might render that the legislature purposely did not provide such an area of inapplicability in § 14-149 when it is included in § 14-148. Further, only § 14-149 specifically utilizes the language "take away," in connection with headstones, while § 14-148 only provides for general maintenance to a gravesite in general. Because § 14-149 specifically makes it illegal to "take away" a tombstone and provides no language excluding the taking away of headstones for particular reasons, the legal actions of maintaining a grave site due to neglect provided for in § 14-148 would not encompass the removal of headstones. Essentially, the permitted actions under § 148(b) are not extended to the removal of headstones, which is a felony under § 14-149. Perhaps, the language of § 14-149 might be amended to include language like § 14-148 allowing removal of headstones when the cause is for maintenance. Other states, such as New Jersey, also make it unlawful to take a headstone, and also impose criminal liability, however, the relevant New Jersey statute does provide the language for what a lawful removal requires.

Conclusion

The failure to maintain headstones, especially those that are heavy and aging on continuously moving ground, is an issue. Although there are duties imposed upon cemetery owners by the common law, it is better to ensure the issue never gets to court. This issue appearing in court means someone has been injured or even killed. Some jurisdictions have addressed the issue and imposed duties and even methods by which the maintenance or removal process must proceed. Other jurisdictions have failed to address the issue. More worrisome, some jurisdictions have legislatively impeded those who would take on the task of maintaining headstones to ensure the safety of the property containing such headstones. In retrospect, it would be a valuable use of resources for lawmaking bodies to consider the spectrum of what has been discussed in this paper. Jurisdictions should observe what measures have been taken in other jurisdictions and what competing interests may inhibit safety, and should create a plan on how to best solve this issue and prevent future accidents.

Primarily, I would advocate that legislatures look to New Jersey's balancing of interests in regards to allowing an expedited process for the removal of dangerous headstones, while still providing measures to respect the families of the deceased. Legislatures should permit immediate removal, and only then mandate the measures necessary to notify relatives of the deceased and make the property removed available for the family to claim. Following New York's example, the best replacement method might be to replace the headstone with a flush marker, allowing the grave to be identifiable. The best solution would be to legislatively impose stricter duties upon cemeteries and municipalities to maintain the headstones, but realities make this solution cost prohibitive. Ultimately, state legislatures should grant authority to remove headstones for safety reasons, and then local governments should analyze the cost-benefit analysis and decide the process that must be followed.

❖   ❖   ❖

Hollywood Cemetery, Richmond, Virginia
Photo by Tanya D. Marsh

CHAPTER 12.4

CEMETERIES MAY NOT BE SUBJECT OF ABSOLUTE PROHIBITION

Percival Jackson, THE LAW OF CADAVERS (1950)

Public health and sentiment require cemeteries.

There is such a necessity for cemeteries from the standpoint of the protection of the public health, as well as for sentimental reasons, that an attempt absolutely to prohibit the creation and maintenance of cemeteries would be invalid. The public need for interment of the bodies of the dead is such that the legislature may not prohibit such interments in places where no possible danger to human life or health could result.

"Where...the place in which it is proposed to bury the dead is remote from human habitations, or is close to but few dwellings, the absolute prohibition of interments is an unreasonable restriction of a lawful business, not fairly justified or required for the preservation of the public health, and will not be sustained by the courts."

Cemeteries may be prohibited when prohibition is reasonable.

But short of absolute prohibition, cemeteries may be regulated and, within certain restrictions, their further creation and future maintenance may be prohibited. Whether, under the guise of the privilege under the police power to regulate cemeteries, the legislature may prohibit burials, depends upon whether under general rules the prohibition is confiscation under cover of regulation. The question does not involve judicial review of legislative discretion (which may not be permitted); it is a question of whether the subject of the prohibition bears a reasonable relation to the power of regulation.

Prohibition in cities reasonable.

The power to prohibit burial in cities cannot and should not be challenged. The experiences of large urban centers during the eighteenth century, and the consequent investigation and agitation that finally resulted in the expulsion of burial grounds from crowded places of human habitation, proved the conclusive need for regulation of places of burial by the public authorities in the interest of the public health, aside from any question of *bonos mores*. The legislative restrictions imposed upon cemeteries "indicate clearly that the legislature contemplated that they [cemeteries] were, in a measure at least, a menace to the health and property rights of the community." That the interment of bodies in the midst of thickly populated districts is likely to prove dangerous to the health of the surrounding population, and as such may properly be prohibited, is settled by a number of well-considered cases.

"Ordinarily, cities are thickly populated, whereas the portions of counties lying outside of cities are not. In view of this, it may be properly said as a general rule, that interments in cities may be prohibited...." The regulation of the cemetery under the legislative power includes the right to prohibit all future interments within the limits of towns or cities. In ancient times, in Greece and Rome, such was the universal rule. It was one of the laws of the twelve tables *'hominem mortuum in urbe ne sepelite neve vicinitate.'* It is much to be regretted that it was not adopted as our policy at an early period." Outside of a city lies a field for legislative determination and expression. "The question is whether, in the exercise of a reasonable discretion, the board may conclude that the thing prohibited is dangerous to the public health. The views already expressed make .it clear that this decision may properly be reached with regard to the interment of dead bodies in thickly settled communities. Whether the danger to be apprehended from such interment is to be best averted by a prohibition of further burials is a question of policy, to be decided by the legislative body. The court is not to substitute its judgment for that of the board of supervisors. Any evidence that might be introduced tending to show that, as a matter of fact, a particular cemetery had not proven, or might not prove, detrimental to the public health, would not alter the fact, of which courts take judicial notice, that cemeteries situated as this one is are likely to cause such injury."

Property rights subject to power to prohibit.

As, under general rules, no claim of vested right can deny the encroachment of the police power, so the prohibition of further interment involves "no invasion of any right of property. Every right, from an absolute ownership down to a mere easement, is purchased and held subject to the restriction that it shall be so exercised as not to injure others. Though at the time it may be remote and inoffensive, the purchaser is bound to know at his peril that it may become otherwise, by the residence of many people in its vicinity, and that it must yield to laws for the suppression of nuisances. If conditions or covenants appropriating land to some particular use, could prevent the legislature from afterwards declaring that use unlawful, legislative powers necessary to the comfort and preservation of populous communities might be frittered away into perfect insignificance."

And as the right of burial is exercised subject to the reserved paramount sovereign right of the legislature to protect all the people, so it has frequently been said to be a mere privilege or license, subject to regulation, control, and revocation, in the public interest; and the need of control may be present or merely anticipated. Similarly, the exercise of corporate power by a religious society or a cemetery corporation is subject to the reserved power of the state, and such society or corporation may not deny the right of the state to regulate its cemetery by claim of a vested charter right.

Thus, while application for permission to use lands for burial purposes is pending, the legislature may amend the requirements or prohibit the use of such lands.

Prohibition of future burials.

The legislature may also prohibit future burials in existing cemeteries/o the enlargement of existing cemeteries, and the creation of new cemeteries. The fact that a cemetery has already been set out yields to an ordinance thereafter adopted.

Prohibition may include compulsory disinterment.

The right to prohibit further interment in existing cemeteries includes the power to require discontinuance of such cemeteries and the disinterment of bodies theretofore interred therein, because of growth of the city, neglect and disuse or to make room for church buildings—generally, because of the encroachment of the living.

Prohibition by statute.

Interment in cities and other congested centers has been prohibited by statute.

❖　❖　❖

Dunn's Chapel Cemetery, Highland County, Ohio
Photo by Tanya D. Marsh

CHAPTER 12.5

WILLIAM J. ELLISON V. COMMISSIONERS OF WASHINGTON

Supreme Court of North Carolina, 5 Jones Eq. 57 (1859)

MANLY, J.

... [A] place of interment of the dead, is not necessarily a nuisance, but that this must depend upon the position and extent of the grounds, and especially upon the manner in which the burials are effected. The cemeteries, which have been established near the principal cities and towns of our country, ... have sprung from the idea that open space, free ventilation, and careful sepulture, not only prevent such places from becoming nuisances, but make them attractive and agreeable places of resort. The dead must be disposed of in some way, and burial in the earth, suggested by the received revelation of man's origin and destiny, is that most generally resorted to. The commissioners of the town of Washton [sic] have selected a spot outside of the town, in obedience to the act of Assembly, and the vote of the citizens, and, so far as we can perceive, it is fitting and appropriate for that purpose.

If the grounds be arranged and drained, and the burial of the dead be conducted as elsewhere in such establishments, we incline decidedly to the opinion, it will not be a nuisance, either public or private. The word nuisance is, of course, used here in its legal sense, and is confined to such matters of annoyance, as the law recognizes and gives a remedy for. The *unpleasant reflections* suggested by having before one's eyes, constantly recurring memorials of death, is not one of these nuisances. Mankind would, by no means, agree upon a point of that sort, but many would insist that suggestions thus occasioned would, in the end, be of salutary influence. The death-head is kept in the cell of the anchorite, perpetually before his eyes as a needful and salutary monitor. The nuisance, which the law takes cognizance of, is such matter as, admitting it to exist, all men, having ordinary senses and instincts, will decide to be injurious. …

Public cemeteries, for the orderly and decent sepulture of the dead, are necessary requirements for all populous towns. In fixing sites for them private must yield to public convenience, and the courts will be particularly careful and not interfere to prevent such establishments, unless the mischief be undoubted and irreparable. Our conclusion is, that *burying the dead* in public cemeteries, is not necessarily a nuisance, but might become so by careless and improvident modes of interment. It is, at most, a doubtful or contingent nuisance, and in such cases, the courts of equity will not interfere to prevent, but will leave complainants to establish the nuisance by an action at law, when it shall arise. …

And, therefore, the Court will not interfere to restrain defendants in the use of their grounds for the purpose intended, unless the nuisance be clear, or unless, as stated before, it shall be established at law. …

PER CURIAM, Decretal order reversed.

❖ ❖ ❖

St. Paul's Chapel, New York City, New York
Photo by Tanya D. Marsh

CHAPTER 12.6

A LAW RESPECTING THE INTERMENT OF THE DEAD IN MANHATTAN

Minutes of the Common Council of the City of New York 1784 – 1831 (1917)

[In 1822 there were 23 separate burying grounds south of the City Hall in Manhattan. City Hall sits at the intersection of Chambers Street on the north and Broadway on the west. St. Paul's Chapel (Trinity Church) sits two blocks south of City Hall on Broadway. Chambers Street is approximately nine blocks south of Canal Street. The Brick Presbyterian Church at the corner of Beekman Street and Nassau Street, the subject of the dispute in the *Ruggles Report*, was approximately a block southeast of City Hall and two blocks east of St. Paul's Chapel.]

In Common Council August 22nd 1822

… The Board of Health having upon the report of a Committee of their body agreed to recommend to the Common Council to pass a law interdicting at the present time the interment of Dead bodies in the Grave yard of Trinity Church the Counsel at the request of the Board of Health presented a law agreeably thereto entitled "a Law respecting Interments in Trinity Church Yard" which was passed.

In Common Council November 25th 1822

…It has been the opinion of several members of the board of Health, founded on the experience they have acquired during the late calamitous season, that the Present Health law may be so amended, and that such internal regulations may be adopted by the Common Council as to produce a reasonable hope that the occurrence of malignant disease may hereafter be arrested.

Although there is a great diversity of opinion among medical men on the subject of the origin of Yellow fever, it is nevertheless pretty generally agreed that ... the most scrupulous attention should be given to the prompt removal of every vestige of nuisance calculated to injure the atmosphere of the city. ...

It appears to be the opinion of Medical Men that the great number of the dead interred in the several cemeteries within the bounds of this City, is attended with injurious consequences to the health of the inhabitants. This subject is therefore worthy of consideration and if the effects are in reality such as some of the faculty declare them to be, ought not future interments be prohibited at least during a part of the year. ...

In Common Council February 4th 1823

...A Memorial of the Minister Elders & Deacons of the Reformed protestant Dutch Church remonstrating against the passage of the Law forbidding the interment of the Dead excepting in Private Vaults South of Canal Street was read and laid on the table.

In Common Council February 17th 1823

... A Memorial from the trustees of the First Presbyterian church remonstrating against the passing of the law now before the Common Council respecting the interment of the dead.

A Similar remonstrance from the vestry of Grace Church

A Similar remonstrance from the vestry of St. Georges Church

A Similar Remonstrance from the vestry of Christs Church

And A Similar remonstrance from the Vestry of Zion Church were severally read and laid on the table.

They were afterwards referred to the [Committee] upon the communication of the Mayor respecting the health of the city.

In Common Council March 31st 1823

... A Memorial was received from a number of inhabitants of Lumber Rector Greenwich Street & Broad Way in the Vicinity of trinity church stating that Vaults for the interment of the dead were erecting in the yard of Trinity church by order of the Vestry of said church said Memorial remonstrating against the same as offensive & injurious to the health of the inhabitants was read, & laid on the table to be taken up when the law prohibiting Interments in the City was under consideration. When the said law was under discussion it was called up and read. ...

The Remonstrance presented this evening against Vaults erecting by Trinity church was called up & read. The Board then took into consideration the law respecting interments reported by the Committee. A Motion to postpone the further Consideration was negative. After some discussion & amendments the Law was agreed to & passed in the Words following

A Law respecting the interment of the Dead

Passed March 31st 1823

Be it ordained by the Mayor Aldermen & Commonalty of the City of

New York in Common Council Convened. That if any Person or Persons shall after the first day of June next dig up or open any grave or cause or procure any grave to be opened in any burying ground cemetery or church yard or in any other part or place in this City which lies to the Southward of a line commencing at the centre of Canal Street on the North River and running through the centre of Canal Street to Sullivan Street thence through Sullivan st. to Grand Street thence through Grand St. to the East river or shall inter or deposit or cause or procure to be interred or deposited in any such grave any dead body every such person shall forfeit and pay for every such offence the sum of Two hundred and fifty dollars.

And be it further Ordained that no dead body shall after the first day of June aforesaid be interred or deposited in any vault or tomb south of the aforesaid line under the penalty of Two hundred and fifty dollars for each and every offence.

Ald. Taylor having required that the Ayes & Noes be taken on the passing of the Law The Members voted as follows … [Affirmative 15, Negative 3]. …

Resolved that a Special Committee be appointed to Select a Suitable Site for a public Burial Place to be called the City Burying ground & that the said Committee make a particular report to the end that the same may be fully considered & decided upon by this Board.

Special Meeting in Common Council April 21st 1823

… A Memorial from the Rector Wardens & Vestrymen of St. George Church praying for a modification of the late law respecting the Interment of the Dead so as to admit the interments in private Vaults and Individual Interments in the earth.

A Memorial of similar import from the trustees of the Brick Presbyterian Church.

Also one from the Rector Churchwardens & Vestrymen of Trinity Church.

Also a petition from a Considerable number of Freeholders and inhabitants of the City and one from the Corporation of the first Presbyterian church in Wall Street were presented and referred to the Board of Health. …

Special Meeting in Common Council May 19th 1823

…The Board of Health to whom as referred the Law on the subject of Interring the dead beg leave to report.

That they have again had the subject under consideration and are still of opinion that the Ordinance which they had the honour Of presenting to the Common Council and which was referred to them under the restriction that the report must Receive the Sanction of the majority of the Whole Board of Health ought to be passed and they therefore now present it to the Board for their consideration. …

Viz A Law to amend a Law passed March 31, 1823, respecting the interment of the Dead.

Be it ordained. By the Mayor Aldermen & Commonalty of the City of New York in Common Council Convened That if any person or persons Shall between the 1st day of June next and the 1st day of November thereafter inter or cause to be interred or deposited any dead body or Corpse in any Vault or tomb to the South of a line designated by the Act hereby Amended Every Person shall forfeit and Pay for every such offence the Sum of two hundred and fifty dollars.

And be it further ordained That no Corpse or Dead body shall between the 1st day of april and the 1st day of November in any year hereafter be interred or deposited in any Vault or tomb South of the aforesaid line under the penalty of Two hundred and fifty dollars for each offence.

And be it further Ordained that no Corpse or dead body Shall be interred or deposited in any Vault or tomb which may be built or constructed south of the aforesaid lien after the passage of this ordinance under the penalty of two hundred and fifty dollars for each and every offence. And be it further ordained that every Sexton or person having charge of any burying ground Cemetery or Church yard in this City shall cause the vaults or tombs which may be opened to be securely and well closed and covered with earth not less than two feet deep within twenty four hours after the deposit of any corpse or dead body therein under the penalty of twenty five dollars for each and every offence.

And be it further ordained that the Second Section of the Law hereby amended be and the same is hereby repealed.

Mr. Thorn moved that the Consideration be postponed until November next. This motion was negative. After Considerable debate had thereon—the question was taken on the first Clause and the Ayes & Noes having been called thereon, the members Voted as follows. ... So it passed in the Negative.

Special Meeting in Common Council June 2nd 1823

... The Committee on Lands & Places to whom was referred the Subject of a scite for a City Burial ground presented the following report which [was] adopted and directed to be published in the Papers employed by the Board.

The Committee on Lands & Places to whom was referred the Selection of a suitable place for a Public Burying ground

Respectfully Report.

That they have attended to the duties of their appointment and after full Consultation have selected the piece of Ground belonging to the Corporation lying between the fifth & Sixth Avenues and between Fortieth and Forty fifty Streets a plan whereof accompanies this report, as a place well calculated for a Public burying ground. The Committee, do not think it necessary to add their testimony to the many others that are accumulating in favour of a measure so vitally important to the safety and health of the Citizens at large as to the burial of the Dead at a suitable distance from the habitations of the living. They will only remark that this City is destined at no great distance of time to rival some of the Capitals of the Old world and whatever can be done to promote its Commercial and local advantages ought to engage the attention and exertions of every inhabitant as the dictate no less of interest than of Patriotism And whatever measure shall tend to security and comfort of human life and render our situation a place of safe and agreeable resort for strangers and of habitation for our resident citizens must in the nature of things advance the solid and permanent interest of all.

The ground your Committee have selected contains upwards of twenty six acres and is at the distance of three miles and a quarter from the City Hall. Its situation is high and pleasant and well calculated as to Soil for the Purpose in view. If the Corporation should approve of the Selection made by the Committee it is recommended that the whole be declared by a resolution of the Board to be reserved for a burying ground and that so much of it as shall be deemed necessary be immediately enclosed by a permanent wall properly secured at the top to prevent all intrusions, with two gates one on the fifth Avenue the other on the cross road leading from the Bloomingdale to the Middle road. Much if not the whole of this work might be done by the Convicts. The whole to be surrounded and intersected with rows of trees of a proper description. The different religious congregations of the City might be here accommodated with ground for the interment of their deceased members and stated hearers. Individuals who may choose to select particular Spots for their families might also be accommodated and a Sufficiency of Ground be still remaining for the numerous poor whose necessities in the Solemn business of interment will thus be provided for and the ground called Potters field can still be used until the Wisdom of the Board shall otherwise it being understood from some gentlemen that the neighbourhood of Potters field is beginning to be too numerously inhabited for the continuance of that ground as a place of Interment. ...

It was ... directed that the subject be referred to the Same Committee with a request that they would report in detail what further would be necessary to be done to carry the object of said Report into execution.

Special Meeting in Common Council May 10th 1824

... A Petition of the trustees of the African Methodist Church in Church St. Stating that the Burial ground assigned to them in Potters field is nearly filled & praying additional ground may be granted them in Potters field for the interment of their dead being read was referred to the Committee on Lands & Places.

NOTES

1. Trinity Church appears to have been singled out by the Common Council—a law that specifically targeted interments in the Trinity churchyard was proposed in August 1822. The churchyard, however, appears to have reached capacity during the Revolution. New interments that occurred during the 1780s were often made within three feet of the surface of the earth. A history of the church refers to this situation as "a manifest menace to the health of the city." In response, the Vestry of the church passed a resolution on May 27, 1784 that prohibited further interments in the "Burying Ground of Trinity Church, except where families have used particular Burial Places therein for some time past and except in the different vaults already built." Unless the Church's rules changed, and there is no evidence that they did, forty years later, the Common Council appeared to be concerned solely about the continuing practice of burial in the existing family vaults at Trinity Church.

2. The phrase "Potter's Field" comes from Matthew 27:7—"And they took counsel,

and bought with them the potter's field, to bury strangers in." In the United States, no established church was obligated to bury ever member of the parish. It therefore became the obligation of the government to provide for the burial of those without means to pay for it themselves. Burial grounds dedicated to paupers, or sections of larger cemeteries used for the burial of paupers, were therefore referred to as "Potter's Fields." The Potter's Field referred to by the New York Common Council in 1822-1823 was located where Washington Square park is currently situated. Approximately 125,000 burials were packed into the nine and a half acre plot. In 1823, the Common Council ordered the relocation of the Potter's Field to the corner of 49th Street and Fourth Avenue. In the 1840s it was again relocated to Randall's Island and Ward's Island. In 1851, the City widened Fourth Avenue, disinterring thousands of bodies.

3. As the population of Manhattan grew, the Common Council moved the line prohibiting new burials northward. In 1832, burials south of 14th Street were banned. In 1851, burials south of 86th Street were banned. In the mid-19th century, large new cemeteries were established in the Bronx, Queens, and Brooklyn to absorb the Manhattan dead. The next chapter includes an 1853 report on the success of Green-Wood Cemetery in Brooklyn and suggests that, by the early 1850s, public health arguments had largely overcome the protests of the Manhattan churches.

❖   ❖   ❖

St. Paul's Chapel, New York City, New York
Photo by Tanya D. Marsh

CHAPTER 12.7

REPORT ON THE SUCCESS OF GREEN-WOOD CEMETERY

RULES AND REGULATIONS OF THE GREEN-WOOD CEMETERY (1853)

Green-Wood Cemetery in Brooklyn became a Chartered Institution in 1838. Its location was the result of a careful and extensive survey of the entire vicinity of New-York. The enterprise, after four years of hard struggle, was at length placed upon a firm foundation, and the Cemetery was thrown open for interments in 1842. From that time, its history has been one of uninterrupted progress. ...

[S]even thousand lots [have] already [been] sold. Nearly five thousand plots have been surrounded with fences of iron. About three hundred tombs have been constructed—and their vaults, whether placed in side-hills or sunk in the ground, are generally of massive stone-work and durable masonry. ... In addition to a great number of horizontal tablets and small head-stones, the Cemetery contains about seven hundred monuments of marble, of sienite, or of sandstone. ... Twenty-six thousand interments have been made in the grounds. ...

Since the time when, amid alterations of home and discouragement, the foundations of this institution were laid, a great change has taken place in the public sentiment of our community. It is not now necessary to urge the manifold evils of intra-mural interment, or to present and portray the immense superiority of rural sepulture; for the former are no longer denied or doubted—and the latter has been practically demonstrated. The question may be looked upon as settled. Cities will soon cease to endure within their limits the offensive and pestilential danger. The prejudices of early association, and even the ties of love and kindred, cannot much longer reconcile the minds of any to the crowded church-yard vault.

Those very feelings, so natural and strong, which have long bound thousands to an objectionable practice, are now fast settling in another and better direction. Beneath the verdant and flowery sod—beneath green and waving foliage—amid tranquil shades, where Nature weeps in all her dews, and sighs in every breeze, and chants a requiem by each warbling bird—the dying generations of this great metropolis will henceforth be seupulchred.

Already, round our own Green-wood, cling the strong affections of many thousand hearts. Here lie the parent, the wife, the husband, the child, the lover, and the friend, once dearer to the surviving mourner than all else on earth. Hither often those survivors come, to weep and meditate unseen. And here, by the mouldering relics of what was once so dear, do they hope, at least, to lie down themselves. … What tender associations, what kindling memories, what inspiring thoughts, what Christian hopes, will be awakened in the breasts of those who, at some coming and not distant day, shall explore this silent city of the dead!

Long may this fair enclosure be preserved, unmarred by mistaken taste—undesecrated by rude hands. Let the worn and weary citizens still find here a momentary but soothing retreat from bustle and toil. Here may Sorrow and pensive Meditation ever find a home. And hither, let even the idle and the thoughtless come, to learn the lesson of their own mortality from the eloquent but unobtrusive teachings of the tomb.

❖   ❖   ❖

Holy Cross Cemetery, San Francisco, California
Photo by Andrew C. Lawson (1906)

CHAPTER 12.8

LAUREL HILL CEMETERY V. CITY & COUNTY OF SAN FRANCISCO

Supreme Court of California, 152 Cal. 464 (1907)

This action was brought to restrain the city and county of San Francisco and its officers from enforcing an ordinance prohibiting the interment of dead bodies within said city and county, and to obtain a decree declaring the ordinance void. The defendants answered and moved for judgment on the pleadings. Their motion was granted, and the plaintiff appeals from the judgment entered upon the order so made.

The complaint in the case at bar is very voluminous. ... Briefly stated, it alleges the incorporation of plaintiff in 1867 as a cemetery association pursuant to the provisions of an act approved April 18, 1859, and entitled, 'An act authorizing the incorporation of rural cemetery associations.' It is averred that in 1853 one Nathaniel Gray, and others associated with him, were the owners of a tract of land then lying beyond the corporate limits of the city of San Francisco, containing about 160 acres, which said Gray and his associates determined to appropriate and devote to the purposes of a rural cemetery. They prepared the land for such purposes, clearing it of brush and laying out roads, and doing other work. On the 30th of May, 1854, said lands were publicly dedicated to the purposes aforesaid by the name of the Lone Mountain Cemetery; the dedication being made the occasion of a 'solemn and impressive ceremony' in which the mayor of the city participated. The Lone Mountain Cemetery continued to be occupied by said association as a cemetery. In May, 1868, Gray and his associates conveyed to the plaintiff so much of the tract as had been appropriated for the purposes of a cemetery. The plaintiff entered into possession of the land, and has since continuously carried on and conducted there the business of a cemetery, under the name of Laurel Hill Cemetery. On June 23, 1871, the mayor of the city and county made a grant to plaintiff of said tract of land, in consideration of the sum of $24,139.79, paid by plaintiff to the treasurer of said city and county. Since the establishment of the cemetery and its dedication in the year 1854, plaintiff and its predecessors have sold and conveyed 40,000 lots or plots, a large proportion of which have been used for the purposes of burial, but many of them are capable of receiving a number of interments in addition to those already made therein. Over $2,000,000 have been expended by the owners of said lots and plots in preparing them for the burial of bodies and in the construction of monuments and tombs and the embellishment of monuments and tombs and the embellishment plaintiff association has also expended large sums of money in constructing roads, avenues, and paths through said cemetery, in constructing a system of waterworks, and erecting a lodge and walls. Of the area included in said cemetery the plaintiff has about seven acres unsold and ready for sale.

At the time of the establishment of the said cemetery, it was wholly outside the corporate limits of the then city of San Francisco, and was distant more than two miles in a direct line from the business part thereof, and at least one mile from the residence part thereof. No residence had then been built to the west of said cemetery, and the whole country between it and the Pacific Ocean was practically unoccupied. Plaintiff avers 'that at no time since the establishment of said cemetery has it or any part thereof been, nor has it or any part thereof, or will it or any part thereof, become injurious the senses, or an offensive to the senses, or an obstruction to the free use to health, indecent, or offensive to enjoyment of life or property, or unlawfully obstruct the free passage or use in the customary manner of any public park, square, street, or highway; that the soil of said cemetery is sand, and the natural condition and character thereof is such that no dangerous or disease-breeding elements can be transmitted through the same from the decaying remains of bodies buried therein; that since the establishment of said cemetery many residences have been built in its neighborhood, and the same have been and are now occupied with families, and yet it has not been proven that the district embracing said cemetery and said residences was unhealthy and subject to epidemics, but, on the contrary, said district has always been, and is now regarded, as particularly healthy and free from the diseases which prevail in other parts of said city and county.' There have never been any wells excavated in the neighborhood of said cemetery 'for the purpose of supplying water to any residences of families residing therein, or for any consumption of human beings.' It is further alleged that there are within the corporate limits of the city and county of San Francisco several large tracts of land, some of which consist of barren sand hills and are entirely unoccupied, and some of which are used solely for farming purposes; that some of said tracts of land contain several hundred acres, and interments of dead bodies could be made on several of said tracts of land, and within the corporate limits of the city and county of San Francisco, which would be more than a mile distant from any human inhabitant or public thoroughfare.

The ordinance complained of was passed on the 26th day of March, 1900, and provides that after the 1st day of August, 1901, it shall be unlawful for any person, association, or corporation to bury, or inter, or cause to be interred or buried, the dead body of any person in any cemetery, graveyard, or other place within the city and county of San Francisco, exclusive of those portions thereof which belong to the United States, or are within its exclusive jurisdiction.

The violation of the ordinance is made a misdemeanor. This ordinance is assailed by plaintiff upon the grounds that it deprives plaintiff of its property without due process of law, and impairs the obligation of a contract; and that it is unreasonable, in that it prohibits acts which are in no way dangerous to life, or detrimental to the public health. It is also claimed that the city and county is estopped by its acts and conduct to assert or exercise the right of making it unlawful to continue to bury the dead bodies of persons in the cemetery of the plaintiff. The ordinance contains a recital that 'the burial of the dead within the city and county of San Francisco is dangerous to life and detrimental to public health.' It purports to be passed in pursuance of what is generally known as the 'police power' of the state. ... Such ordinances must, of course, bear a rational relation to the object sought to be attained. They may not be arbitrary or unreasonable. ... But, while the action of a legislative body in assuming to exercise the police power is always subject to review by the courts, the question of the expediency or necessity of a proposed restriction is primarily for the Legislature, and the courts will not interfere with the exercise of the legislative discretion unless it clearly appears that such discretion has been arbitrarily or unreasonably exercised.

There is ample authority defining the limits of the power of legislative bodies in restricting the right of interment of dead bodies. That the interment of such bodies in the midst of thickly populated districts is likely to prove a danger to the health of the surrounding population, and as such may properly be prohibited, seems to be settled by a number of well-considered cases, cited in the opinion in the Odd Fellows' Cemetery Case. On the other hand, it is equally well settled that the interment of the bodies of the dead is proper, indeed necessary, and that the Legislature may not prohibit such interments in places where no possible danger to human life or health could result. ... The right to prohibit interments in a given territory rests upon the conditions existing in that territory. Where a cemetery in which it is proposed to make interments is located in a thickly settled community, further interments there may be prohibited because the burial of dead bodies in close proximity to the habitations of the living has a tendency to endanger the health of large numbers of persons. Where, however, the place in which it is proposed to bury the dead is remote from human habitations, or is close to but few dwellings, the absolute prohibition of interments is an unreasonable restriction of a lawful business, not fairly justified or required for the preservation of the public health, and will not be sustained by the courts. ... Where a city includes considerable tracts of this character, it will not be said that interments anywhere within the corporate limits may be prohibited merely because the territory involved is all included within the boundaries of a city. ... In the case at bar it is true that the complaint alleges that there are within the corporate limits of the city and county several large tracts of land, some of which contain several hundred acres, and that interment of dead bodies could be made on several of said tracts of land at points which would be more than a mile distant from any human inhabitant or public thoroughfare. If the ordinance did in effect prohibit the interment of dead bodies upon any such tracts of land, it may be that it would be to that extent unreasonable, or at least that this allegation would tender an issue which would require the trial court to take proof to determine whether or not under all the circumstances the ordinance was unreasonable. But at the time this ordinance was adopted, and for many years theretofore, the Penal Code of this state contained a provision (section 297) making it a misdemeanor to bury or inter, or cause to be buried, any human remains in any place within the corporate limits of any city or town in this state, or within the corporate limits of the city and county of San Francisco, 'except in a cemetery or place of burial now existing under the laws of this state and in which interments have been made, or that is now or may hereafter be established or organized by the board of supervisors of the county or city and county in which such city or town or city and county is situate.' By reason of the existence of this statute, it was already, at the time of the passage of the ordinance in question, a misdemeanor to inter any dead body in any place within the city and county of San Francisco outside of the existing cemeteries, or those to be authorized by the supervisors. There is no suggestion that the establishment of new cemeteries was contemplated. The ordinance, therefore, in effect merely prohibited the interment of bodies in existing cemeteries. It is not alleged that any such cemeteries did, in fact, exist upon any of the vacant tracts of land referred to in the complaint. Indeed, the only cemetery described by the plaintiff is its own, and that, as is shown by the allegations of the complaint itself, is situated in the midst of a thickly settled district. As is alleged, 'many residences have been built in its neighborhood, and the same have been and are now occupied with families.' As no presumptions are to be indulged in support of the pleading, it may be assumed that all the cemeteries existing in San Francisco at the date of the passage of the ordinance were similarly situated. The effect of the prohibition, therefore, was merely to prevent further interments in cemeteries situated within densely populated portions of the municipality. That such prohibition is a reasonable exercise of the police power vested in the board of supervisors clearly appears from the authorities above cited.

It is, however, claimed that the ordinance is unreasonable in its operation upon plaintiff's cemetery, considered by itself, and this contention is based upon the allegations of the complaint to the effect that the soil of the cemetery is of such character that no disease-breeding elements can be transmitted through the same, that the district in which it is has not been proven to be unhealthy or subject to epidemics, and that the cemetery does not possess the characteristics necessary to constitute it a nuisance within the definition of the Code. Civ. Code, § 3479. It is argued that no legislative body can by its mere assertion make that a nuisance which is not in fact a nuisance. This is undoubtedly true, but the ordinance in question does not proceed upon the basis that further interments are to be prohibited because the cemeteries in which such interments are sought to be made are in fact nuisances under the general law. The police power granted by the Constitution is not restricted to the suppression of nuisances. It includes the regulation of the conduct of business, or the use of property, to the end that the public health or morals may not be impaired or endangered. As was said by this court in the Odd Fellows' Cemetery Case, at page 231 of 140 Cal., page 988 of 73 Pac.: 'Whenever a thing or act is of such a nature that it may become a nuisance, or may be injurious to the public health if not suppressed or regulated, the legislative body may, in the exercise of its police powers, make and enforce ordinances to regulate or prohibit such act or thing, although it may never have been offensive or injurious in the past.' 'The exercise of this power is not limited to the regulation of such things as have already become nuisances or have been declared to be such by the judgment of a court.' The question is whether in the exercise of a reasonable discretion the board may conclude that the thing prohibited is dangerous to the public health. The views already expressed make it clear that this decision may properly be reached with regard to the interment of dead bodies in thickly settled communities. Whether the danger to be apprehended from such interment is to be best averted by a prohibition of further burials is a question of policy to be decided by the legislative body. The court is not to substitute its judgment for that of the board of supervisors. Any evidence that might be introduced tending to show that, as a matter of fact, a particular cemetery had not proven or might not prove detrimental to the public health, would not alter the fact, of which courts take judicial notice, that cemeteries situated as this one is are likely to cause such injury, and are therefore, as to further use, within the control of the legislative authority. ...

Even if the city and county had made an express contract granting to the plaintiff the right to make interments in this ground in perpetuity, such contract would have no force as against a future exercise by the legislative branch of the government of its police power. This power cannot be bargained or contracted away, and all rights and property are held subject to it. The alleged estoppel relied on can have no greater force than would a contract such as the one supposed. ... There is no ground for the claim that, because the city in 1854 considered the location in question a proper one for a cemetery, it was bound to continue to so regard it half a century later, when the situation of the cemetery with relation to the city had entirely changed. ...

It is claimed, further, that the decision of the Supreme Court of the United States in *Dobbins v. Los Angeles*, 195 U. S. 223, 25 Sup. Ct. 18, 49 L. Ed. 169, compels the conclusion that the ordinance in question is void, as depriving the plaintiff of property without due process of law. In any case, we should feel strongly inclined to follow the decision of this high tribunal, and, in a case involving a claim of right under the Constitution of the United States, we should, if that decision had been rendered in a parallel case, be bound to follow it. But we think the Dobbins Case is very different from the one before us. ... It was held that the ordinance was void upon the ground that the facts as to the situation and conditions were such as to establish the exercise of the police power in such manner as to comprise a discrimination against the plaintiff, the court saying; 'We think the allegations of the bill disclose such character of territory, such sudden and unexplained change of its limits after the plaintiff in error had purchased the property and gone forward with the erection of the works, as to bring it within that class of cases wherein the court may restrain the arbitrary and discriminatory exercise of the police power, which amounts to the taking of property without due process of law, and an impairment of property rights protected by the fourteenth amendment of the federal Constitution. ...

But these considerations do not apply to the case at bar. Here there was no change that was either sudden or unexplained. By the ordinance itself a period of almost 18 months was given to those affected by it to prepare for the change. The ordinance, passed in March, 1900, was not to be effective until August, 1901. Furthermore, ample cause for the change was shown. The land affected by it was, when originally dedicated as a cemetery, one mile from any habitation. At the time the ordinance was adopted it had become the center of a thickly populated residence district. These circumstances, which appear from the complaint itself, afford at once the justification for the exercise of the police power, and the refutation of the claim that the exercise of that power was a mere pretense for the spoliation of private rights. ...

We think the appellant has shown no reason why the ordinance in question was not a valid exercise of the legislative power of the city and county.

The judgment is affirmed.

❖ ❖ ❖

Laurel Hill Cemetery, San Francisco, California
Photo by Roy D. Graves (1935)

CHAPTER 12.9
LAUREL HILL CEMETERY V.
CITY AND COUNTY OF SAN FRANCISCO

Supreme Court of the United States, 30 S.Ct. 301 (1910)

This is an action to restrain the city and county of San Francisco and its officers from enforcing an ordinance forbidding the burial of the dead within the city and county limits. ... The plaintiff was incorporated in 1867 as a rural cemetery under a general act. The land in question had been dedicated as a burying ground, being at that time outside the city limits, and a mile or two away from dwellings and business. It was conveyed to the plaintiff, and later a grant of the same was obtained from the city in consideration of $24,139.79, which sum the city retains. The land has been used as a cemetery ever since; forty thousand lots have been sold, and over two million dollars have been spent by the lot owners, and other large sums by the plaintiff, in preparing and embellishing the grounds. By the terms of the abovementioned general statute the lots, after a burial in them, are inalienable, and descend to the heirs of the owner, and the plaintiff is bound to apply the proceeds of sales to the improvement, embellishment, and preservation of the grounds. There is land still unsold, estimated to be worth $75,000. There now are many dwellings near the cemetery, but it is alleged to be in no way injurious to health, or offensive, or otherwise an interference with the enjoyment of property or life. There also is an allegation that there are within the city large tracts, some of them vacant and some of them containing several hundred acres, in several of which interments could be made more than a mile distant from any inhabitants or highway. The ordinance in question begins with a recital that 'the burial of the dead within the city and county of San Francisco is dangerous to life and detrimental to the public health,' and goes on to forbid such burial under a penalty of fine, imprisonment, or both.

The complaint sets up that it violates article 1, § 8, and the 14th Amendment of the Constitution of the United States. ...

The only question that needs to be answered, if not the only one before us, is whether the plaintiff's property is taken contrary to the 14th Amendment. ... [I]t is said by the supreme court of the state that burial within the San Francisco city or county limits already was forbidden by statute, except in existing cemeteries or such as might be established by the board of supervisors. The board of supervisors passed the ordinance now complained of; so that, as pointed out by the court, the ordinance in effect merely prohibited burials in existing cemeteries. It was, therefore, a specific determination by the lawmaking authority as to the relation of those cemeteries to their respective neighborhoods, and the question is whether the court can say that it was wrong.

To aid its contention, and in support of the averment that its cemetery, although now bordered by many dwellings, is in no way harmful, the plaintiff refers to opinions of scientific men who have maintained that the popular belief is a superstition. Of these we are asked, by implication, to take judicial notice, to adopt, them, and, on the strength of our acceptance, to declare the foundation of the ordinance a mistake and the ordinance void. It may be, in a matter of this kind, were the finding of fact is merely a premise to laying down a rule of law, that this court has power to form its own judgment without the aid of a jury. ...

If every member of this bench clearly agreed that burying grounds were centers of safety, and thought the board of supervisors and the supreme court of California wholly wrong, it would not dispose of the case. There are other things to be considered. Opinion still may be divided, and if, on the hypothesis that the danger is real, the ordinance would be valid, we should not overthrow it merely because of our adherence to the other belief. ... Again, there may have been other grounds fortifying the ordinance besides those recited in the preamble. And yet again, the extent to which legislation may modify and restrict the uses of property consistently with the Constitution is not a question for pure abstract theory alone. Tradition and the habits of the community count for more than logic. Since, as before the making of constitutions, regulation of burial and prohibition of it in certain spots, especially in crowded cities, have been familiar to the Western world. This is shown sufficiently by the cases cited by the court below. The plaintiff must wait until there is a change of practice, or at least an established consensus of civilized opinion, before it can expect this court to overthrow the rules that the lawmakers and the court of his own state uphold.

❖ ❖ ❖

Odd Fellows Cemetery, San Francisco, California
Photo by James W. Plachek (1906)

CHAPTER 12.10

LOCATION, REGULATION, AND REMOVAL OF CEMETERIES
IN THE CITY AND COUNTY OF SAN FRANCISCO

William A. Proctor, Department of City Planning,
City and County of San Francisco (1950)

No Cemeteries, Burials, or Cremations in San Francisco

Since San Francisco's earliest days, the location, regulation and removal of cemeteries has been an important problem, one which has caused much public discussion, controversy, litigation, and even a vigorous referendum election campaign.

At present, no cemeteries are located within the limits of the City and County of San Francisco, with the exception of a small churchyard cemetery in the grounds of Mission Dolores, where the remains of early Franciscan Fathers, Spanish ranchers, and Yerba Buena pioneers repose. A military cemetery also exists in the Presidio, an Army reservation. Since 1922, the four other cemeteries then in existence have been removed, two in 1923-1925, and two in 1939-41. The vacated cemetery areas have been developed for residential use and for a university. Burials and cremations within the limits of the City and County are prohibited in the Health Code.

Most burials and cremations of San Franciscans now are conducted in the adjoining "cemetery town" of Colma, formerly called the Town of Lawndale, and located in San Mateo County immediately to the south of San Francisco. Colma was founded and incorporated by cemetery associations' representatives (the cemeteries owning three-fourths of the land within the town's limits) expressly to maintain the town as a "memorial city". Most of its 264 inhabitants (1950 Census—there were 354 in 1940) live on cemetery property, and its government is financed through business license taxes and burial permit charges. There is no municipal property tax.

Early San Francisco Cemeteries

In 1850, a cemetery known as Yerba Buena Cemetery existed on the present-day site of the Civic Center. This fifteen-acre tract was then in the middle of a sand-dune area, and cemetery maintenance was difficult because coffins were often exposed as the sand was blown away. In 1860, Yerba Buena Cemetery was abandoned, its bodies removed, and the tract acquired by the City and County as a public park. The area was never landscaped or developed, however, and much of it was sold off for commercial frontage on Market Street. The remainder provided the site of the pre-earthquake City Hall, which was destroyed in the 1906 disaster. A new city hall was started in 1912 with a $12,000,000 Civic Center bond issue, on an adjacent site, and at present the old cemetery boundaries would include commercial buildings on Market Street, the Federal Office Building, the City Public Library, Marshall Square Monument, and a block being reserved for future construction of a Courts Building.

After the demise of Yerba Buena Cemetery, four main cemeteries (known as the "Big Four") developed in the Richmond residential district, west of Van Ness Avenue, and northeast of Golden Gate Park. These were Odd Fellows Cemetery and Masonic Cemetery (originally fraternal organizations, but their successors are non-profit associations), Laurel Hill Cemetery (a non-profit association), and Calvary Cemetery, a Catholic cemetery administered as part of the property of the Archdiocese of San Francisco.

Early Efforts to Remove the Cemeteries

As early as 1880, the cry, "Remove the Cemeteries," began to he heard in San Francisco, spearheaded by owners of residential property (often right across the street from cemeteries, or with backyards abutting them), and those who thought the cemeteries' presence discouraged settlement of nearby subdivisions. Many of the cemetery lots were sold with no perpetual-care arrangements, and graves, markers, picket-fences, monuments and cemetery grounds deteriorated, became weed-filled and, despite efforts to establish adequate police and watchman guard, became havens for pranksters, juvenile delinquents, and ghouls. Some were anxious to subdivide and develop the 160 or so acres of land involved.

By 1900, most of the existing graveyards in San Francisco were nearly filled up, and rather than dedicate further cemetery land within the City and County, the Board of Supervisors decided in 1902 (Ordinance Number 8108) to prohibit burials within the city, and to forbid the sale of cemetery lots in Odd Fellows, Masonic, Laurel Hill, and Calvary cemeteries. Cremation and burial of cremation remains, however, were permitted,

Much data concerning this ordinance was lost in the earthquake and fire of 1906. At present, however, the Health Code (Chapter Five of the San Francisco Municipal Code) contains the following provisions:

> "Sec. 195. <u>Cremation of Human Remains in City and County Limits Prohibited</u>.
> It shall be unlawful for any person, association or corporation, to cremate, or cause to be cremated, the dead body of any human being within the City and County of San Francisco, exclusive of those portions of said city and county belonging to or under the exclusive jurisdiction of the United States.
> "Sec. 200. <u>Burials Within City and County Limits Prohibited</u>. It shall be unlawful for any person, association or corporation to bury or inter, or cause to be interred or buried, the dead body of any person in any cemetery, graveyard, or other place within the City and County of San Francisco, exclusive of those

portions thereof which belong to the United States, or are within its exclusive jurisdiction.

"Sec. 201. <u>Penalty</u>. Any person, association or corporation violating any of the provisions of Section 200 of this Article shall be deemed guilty of a misdemeanor, and upon conviction thereof, shall be punished by a fine of not less than One Hundred ($100.00) Dollars, nor more than Five Hundred ($500) Dollars, or by imprisonment not exceeding six (6) months, or by both such fine and imprisonment."

Cemeteries' Deterioration After Burials were Prohibited.

The cemeteries had obtained some revenue from burial charges and sale of lots, which enabled them to give some general grounds care (weeding, watering), but with the lot-sale prohibition, only the perpetual-care lots could be maintained. The "Big Four" established alternate cemetery properties in Colma (Lawndale). The Archdiocese established Holy Cross Cemetery; Greenlawn Cemetery was established by the Odd Fellows group; and Masonic was succeeded by Woodlawn Cemetery; but the Laurel Hill association did not establish a new Colma cemetery, A new Colma organization, Cypress Lawn Cemetery, a non-profit association, succeeded to most of the family plots formerly held by Laurel Hill.

Thus the Richmond District cemeteries continued to deteriorate, which encouraged further vandalism, grave-robbing, malicious mischief and delinquency,.

An article in the San Francisco NEWS summarizing the "cemeteries problem" at the time Calvary Cemetery was being moved from San Francisco, stated (Tuesday, June 20, 1939):

"Here, during the cemetery's (Calvary) abandoned years—the last burials were made in the early 1900's—ghouls held vandalish orgies.

"On moonless, foggy nights, shadowy forms have slunk into vaults. Clanking sounds, the muffled crash of a sledge-hammer, have echoed forth as vandals looted the vaults of bronze flower urns, of silver coffin handles.

"Tramps piled up their pots and pans, set up their cooking utensils for a macabre type of housekeeping, even. Some say these dank vaults were hideouts for bootleggers, during the prohibition years.

"A police guard was posted several years ago, after ghouls, apparently with a knowledge of early San Francisco history, had desecrated the musty vaults of the Donahues. This was the same Peter Donahue who rose from blacksmith— he wore a leather apron and banged away on his anvil under a buckeye tree at Market and Montgomery Streets—to be the founder of the Union Iron Works and the Northwestern Pacific Railway . . . ."

"Other ghouls have wreaked havoc. Bronze and iron grilled doors of other ornate marble and granite above-ground vaults have been pried open. Inside all is shambles. Flower urns have been ripped from wall braces, coffins hacked open, bones strewn about . . . ."

An official of Cypress Lawn Cemetery, who had participated in the Laurel Hill Cemetery removal project, in an informal interview with the writer stated that the cemeteries were well known as lovers' lanes. In the Richmond District, high school groups sometimes held "bonfire rallies" in the old cemeteries prior to athletic contests, using fence-stakes from grave borders for fuel, and high school fraternity initiations sometimes were held in the cemeteries. Richmond residents were afraid of the cemeteries as places where possible rapists, child-molesters, and other unsavory characters could hide out.

The lack of care caused natural deterioration. As stated in the aforementioned San Francisco NEWS article:

> In the years that followed, time, weather and vandals assumed control. Weeds choked the gravel paths, over-ran the graves. Tombstones fell. Monuments, such as brooding angels, became bedraggled—wings, arms, and legs fell off.

As early as 1913, strong agitation developed among Richmond District residents to have the cemeteries removed as menaces to health, eyesores, and obstacles to community progress. But the cemetery associations were generally opposed to wholesale evacuations, and the Catholic Archdiocese was strongly opposed to disturbing the pioneers' repose. It was felt that faith in the sanctity of consecrated ground would be reduced by any wholesale body-moving. Non-Catholic groups felt that the cemeteries had historical significance, and should not be wiped out. Various San Francisco pioneers, such as Senator Broderick (of duelling fame), Hallidie, the inventor of the cable car, the Crockers, and many others, were buried in the old Cemeteries.

First Cemetery Removals in 1923

In 1921, State legislation was passed in California enabling cemetery associations to abandon a cemetery (if the proposal was ratified by a majority of the lot owners) remove the remains, and dispose of the land ("'Morris Act"). Masonic Cemetery started to take action to abandon its cemetery and remove the remains under the provisions of this act,. Lot-owners not in accord with majority vote instituted legal proceedings, and the movement was soon tied up by court litigation. In the case of *Hornblower v. Masonic Cemetery Assn.*, (191 Cal. 83, 214 Pac. 978 (1923), the courts held that the right of individual lot-owners to maintain remains in dedicated cemetery land was not abolished by a decision of a cemetery association to abandon and remove. The courts enjoined the association from further removal where such action was not desired by cemetery lot-owners.

In 1923, deficiencies in the Morris Act pointed up by the court decisions were corrected in the "Second Morris Act" (Statutes of California 1923, Chap. 312). Here, the State was authorized to delegate to legislative bodies of municipalities the power to pass ordinances <u>requiring</u> the removal of bodies under the "police power" in cemeteries where burials had been prohibited by law for a certain number of years. Shortly after the passage of the Second Morris Act, the San Francisco Board of Supervisors passed an ordinance requiring the removal of bodies from Masonic and Odd Fellows cemeteries, but no mention was made in the ordinance of Laurel Hill or Calvary cemeteries.

Again, proceedings were tied up in litigation. Complainants charged that the ordinance was discriminatory in abating only two of San Francisco's four cemeteries. Finally appealed to a higher Federal court, the litigation resulted in a precedent that municipalities could abate nuisances one at a time if they so desired and if the degree of "nuisance value" required more immediate action in one case than in another. (*Gamage et al. v. Masonic Cemetery Assn.*, et al. 31 Fed. (2d) 308 (D.C., N.D. Cal. 1929) and *Masonic Cemetery Assn. et al. v. Gamage* et al. 38 Fed. (2d) 950, 71 A.L.R. 1027, Anno. 1040 (C.C.A. 9th 1930).

"The court held that merely because the board did not act affirmatively in declaring all cemeteries to be nuisances, there is no reason why the legislation should be declared invalid. The removal of any one of the cemeteries would greatly relieve the situation. It would be different if the board had permitted interments in one and not in another. Being public nuisances, the cemeteries may be abated one at a time. The board may proceed cautiously, step by step. The court further held that all zoning ordinances are discriminatory in the sense that some property holders are permitted to do and others prohibited from doing the same things in localities which are not dissimilar in actual fact, but that such laws are valid. The court said (at p. 954) that it has been generally, if not universally, held that cemeteries are subject to the police power of the state. Laws which do not directly appropriate private property, even though they in effect destroy private rights, are not, inhibited by the United States Constitution." Annotation on Chapter Four of the California Health Code contained in *California Law Governing Funeral Directors, Cemeteries, and Coroners.* Compiled by Raymond Louis Brennan. Published by the Interment Association of California, Los Angeles.

With the settlement of the complex legal tangle, Odd Fellows and Masonic cemeteries were removed in the early 1920's. In Odd Fellows Cemetery, a small section (less than five acres) was retained as a memorial park containing a mausoleum in which vaults were established for the retention of remains of many of the bodies contained in the cemetery. Some of the former cemetery was established as a commercial zone, but most of the cemetery lands were subdivided and sold for homesites, the subdivision being known as "Franciscan Heights."

When Masonic Cemetery was removed, it was purchased by the University of San Francisco (formerly St. Ignatius College) and used for an expansion of the campus of that Catholic institution of higher learning.

Controversy over Removal of Laurel Hill and Calvary Cemeteries.

Although opposition to cemetery removals in the Odd Fellows and Masonic projects stemmed mainly from individual plot-owners, a much stronger opposition existed in the case of Calvary and Laurel Hill Cemeteries. As stated above, the Catholic Archdiocese opposed in principle the idea of picking up a cemetery and moving it, to the distress of survivors of those buried there, and to the apprehension of future plot-owners in other cemeteries to the effect that "nothing is sacred or permanent—not even the place where you are laid to rest."

In Laurel Hill, the opposition was centered to a large extent on the idea of disturbing famous San Francisco pioneers buried there. Discussion at first centered around establishing streets through the cemetery to "break the bottleneck" and provide access from the downtown area to the Richmond District. The cemetery's location made dead-end streets of several important streets leading to the main business district and extensions through the cemetery would have made it more accessible to the Richmond District. Little came of this when the City Attorney found that consent of all plot-owners involved would be necessary to remove graves to provide right-of-way for the street through the cemetery (right of eminent domain not applying to cemeteries in the usual fashion).

In the late 1930's discussion centered around the idea of leaving all bodies in the cemetery and having the city take it over as a public park, removing all monuments except a few of the most famous pioneers' and letting it serve as a recreational open space. although the City Planning Commission was receptive to this idea, other city officials were cold, and most San Francisco officials apparently preferred to promote the removal of most of the cemetery and open its land up for residential subdivision. No strong support from cemetery plot-owners could be rallied to this plan, either.

The next plan proposed was the preservation of a five-acre Pioneers' Memorial Park, in one corner of the existing cemetery, in which most of the famous pioneers were buried. A mausoleum and Pioneers Memorial Museum would be constructed on this land, with bodies taken from the remainder of the cemetery area to be placed in crypts or vaults in the mausoleum. The five-acre park was to be given to the city, and administered and maintained by it.

In 1937, the Catholic Archdiocese ceased its opposition to disturbing Calvary Cemetery, and in that year the City and County Board of Supervisors passed ordinances ratified by the electorate at the November general election, requiring the removal of Laurel Hill Cemetery and Calvary Cemetery, as authorized under the Second Morris Act of 1923. Under the ordinances, cemetery associations can reserve ten percent of the area of the original cemetery for a memorial park in which monuments of historical interest, graves of important persons, and a mausoleum or columbarium containing remains removed from the balance of the cemetery can be placed. This allows about five acres for each cemetery. In the November election the ordinances were approved by a majority of the voters and the removal of Laurel Hill and Calvary Cemeteries was thus required to be started within three years.

In 1939 and 1940, considerable momentum gathered behind the idea of preserving one-tenth of Laurel Hill Cemetery as a Memorial Pioneers Park, as allowed by the removal ordinances. This was spearheaded by the historical Monuments Committee of the National Recreation Association, and backed by the California Pioneers Society and the Native Sons of the Golden West. A five and a half acre tract was outlined, which would not interfere with projected new streets to be put through the property after body removals had taken place, and this area would contain existing graves, vaults, and monuments …

The Board of Trustees of the Laurel Hill Association, however, (after a letter poll of as many plot owners as could be contacted) in August of 1940 decided not to try to retain any of the existing cemetery for a memorial park to be maintained by it. Instead, it decided to send all disinterred bodies to a receiving vault at Cypress Lawn Cemetery in Colma, San Mateo County, and then construct vaults for the Laurel Hill bodies, and construct a Pioneers Memorial Building at Colma which would embody the ideas originally proposed for Pioneers Memorial on the original cemetery site.

Operation of the Cemetery Removal Projects—Laurel Hill and Calvary

The entire removal program for Calvary and Laurel Hill involved over 90,000 bodies mostly buried between 1860 and 1900. Calvary Cemetery removal was handled directly by the Archdiocese of San Francisco, with lay personnel employed by Holy Cross Cemetery doing the actual work of disinterring at Calvary, transporting the bodies by hearse to Colma and reinterring at Holy Cross. All bodies disinterred at Calvary on any particular day were reinterred on the same day at Holy Cross.

Extensive record-searches had been undertaken in the Office of the Archbishop by lay workers working under clerical direction, to ascertain addresses of relatives, survivors, lot-owners, and others having an interest in the interred remains. This record-searching took years to complete. Individuals desiring to have remains disinterred privately were given an opportunity to have them separately removed to lots or vaults in Holy Cross or other cemeteries, only the expense of the cemetery lot being borne by the relatives. Extensive records are now maintained at Holy Cross and cross-indexed so that the location of any remains transferred from Calvary can be readily located. Calvary remains were placed in a large five-acre burial mound in one of the choice locations of the Cemetery, but no individual markers were erected.

Disinterring was done carefully, by hand labor, at Calvary and remains placed in redwood boxes of varying sizes, depending on whether they consisted of "dust," skeletons, or well-preserved remains. Family groups were placed together as far as was possible. The fact that Catholic cemetery rules prescribe an eight-foot depth for earth graves made both disinterring and reinterring an expensive job. A priest was always in attendance for all phases of the operation, and an inspector of the San Francisco Department of Public Health was also always present on the cemetery while disinterring was being undertaken. Screens were erected to prevent intrusion of curious onlookers, and work was carried on in a "careful and reverent manner." Relatives, heirs, survivors, plot-owners, or others properly interested, could witness the disinterment of particular person's remains, and their reinterment. Approximately 55,000 bodies were removed from Calvary in the project, most of them being transferred to the "Calvary Mound" in Holy Cross, although in many cases, families had individual remains transferred to family vaults or graves on privately-owned lots in Holy Cross. Careful records had to be maintained, and daily reports submitted to the Director of Public Health of San Francisco as to the number of bodies transferred, identity, conditions of remains, name of receiving cemetery, and the like. Similar reports were submitted to the Public Health Officer of Lawndale, and burial permits filed. Cemetery officials in both Calvary and Laurel Hill removal projects could immediately answer an interested relative as to whether or not their great-aunt had been transferred yet.

Bodies in Laurel Hill Cemetery were removed through a contract made by the Board of Trustees of the Laurel Hill Cemetery Association with Cypress Lawn Cemetery Association and the Cypress Abbey Company, of Colma. Approximately 35,000 bodies were removed in this operation, taking about sixteen months to complete. Every effort was made (as in the case of Calvary) to contact heirs, relatives, or plot-owners, so that they could make private removals and reinterments under their own arrangements, if possible. "Careful and reverent" handling of the remains was also the watchword here, and the view of curious passers-by was screened by six-foot cloth windscreens; jewelry found in graves and caskets was inventoried and placed in envelopes and sealed inside reinterment boxes. These boxes (made of redwood) were of varying sizes depending on conditions of the remains, and were all affixed with metal identification tags.

All bodies disinterred during a day were carried by hearse that day to Colma, where they were placed for storage in the Cypress Abbey Company's mausoleum, where they were to be kept, pending the construction of the Laurel Hill Association's memorial mausoleum and Pioneers mausoleum in Colma. Construction of the Laurel Hill mausoleum was delayed by the advent of World War II in 1941, and for six years the bodies were kept in Cypress Abbey's mausoleum. After the war, construction costs had risen so high that the Laurel Hill Association's proceeds from sale of the cemetery lands was insufficient—after cost of body-removals from Laurel Hill and storage in Cypress Abbey had been paid—to follow original plans for a mausoleum, and construction of a memorial or monument was decided on instead. A large "Burial Mound" plot was purchased within "Cypress Lawn Cemetery (and endowed with a perpetual-care fund) and underground concrete vaults were constructed to house the 35,000 Laurel Hill bodies. 'Each of the vaults holds several bodies, depending on the size of the removal-boxes in which they were placed, (some vaults holding fifty bodies), and family groups were placed together as far as possible. The "Burial Mound" covers about five acres.

Over 1,000 bodies were disinterred privately by relatives, heirs, family friends, or others, and moved to private plots in Cypress Lawn or other cemeteries. In some cases, the monuments which had been placed in Laurel Hill were likewise moved and placed over the new graves. Bodies were removed at the expense of the Cypress Lawn organization, but relatives paid the cost of reinterment and the cost of the new grave plot.

Total cost of removing bodies from Laurel Hill to Cypress Lawn, and reinterring them in the underground concrete vault was $535,125, which is itemized as follows:

Removal of bodies from Laurel Hill	$121,544
Purchase of burial mound in Cypress Lawn	$85,230
Construction of underground vaults	$86,194
Reinterment of bodies in vaults	$37,606
Endowment for perpetual-care fund	$204,552
Total	$535,125

From the sale of the Laurel Hill site, about $100,000 to $125,111 remains to finance the construction of a monument or memorial structure of some sort to be placed on the Cypress Lawn burial mound. Plans for this memorial are now being considered by the Laurel Hill Association Board of Trustees and plans are being drawn up by Thomas D. Church, one of the West' s foremost landscape architects.

Interesting details of the Laurel Hill cemetery removal project were found by the author in looking over some files made available to him by the management of Cypress Lawn Cemetery.

The plan of operation followed was to fence off a particular section of the cemetery (i.e., an area surrounded by cemetery drives) and remove all the bodies in it before moving to the next. The general movement was from west to east, getting the older, smaller, non-perpetual-care graves first, with the better-maintained family plots in the eastern end being moved last. This allowed more time for private removals. Three gangs of grave-diggers (nine men to a gang) were used, each under a bonded foreman. A general foreman, or superintendent, had charge of the entire operation, including clerical work at the cemetery office (keeping "inventory" of bodies removed and still in the cemetery up to date, filling out Health Department forms, making identification tags for removal boxes, etc.).

Sizes of removal boxes varied from six by six by twelve inches to two by three by six feet, and their cost varied from $.08 to $2.75 apiece.

A watchman was employed to act as gatekeeper during daytime operations (to prevent entry by persons not having a proper interest in the disinterments, relatives, etc.), and a night watchman was employed to prevent vandalism and malicious mischief.

After operations had been completed, the entire cemetery tract was retrenched to insure that all bodies had been removed. In this search, 189 additional bodies were located and removed.

The City and county removal ordnance of 1937 had specified that grave markers, headstones, and monuments, should remain for a period of ninety days after bodies were removed, so that interested parties could make prior disposition of them. Although some relatives, friends, historical societies and others did take over removal of these monuments (many of great historical value), the response was disappointing to the cemetery officials. In some cases, special appeals were made to the historical societies and pioneer groups, sometimes with a favorable response, other times not. Unclaimed headstones and monuments were turned over to the City and County Department of Public Works, which hauled them away in its own trucks for use in making sea-walls at Aquatic Park, and at the municipal yacht harbor.

Condition of remains disinterred varied from "dust" to almost perfectly embalmed bodies, the latter resulting from filling of cast-iron caskets with groundwater acting as a preservative. The superintendent of the disinterment proceedings told the author that his was an interesting job, but that in some cases it was not "pretty". The smell of death was often present, even though the remains had been laid to rest from thirty to seventy years previously. An interesting sidelight was the great number of infants buried, compared to present day frequencies of infant burials. The old cemetery records showed more daily infant burials than is true today in the Colma cemeteries, despite the larger population served today. Thus, a tangible evidence of reduced infant mortality rates.'

Laws, Rules, and Regulations Affecting the Cemetery Removals.

The general legal authority setting the pattern for the procedures followed in the removal of Laurel Hill and Calvary cemeteries was established in the "Second Morris Act" passed in 1923 (Statutes of California, 1923, Chap. 312) which has been incorporated with few changes into the Health and Safety Code of California as Chapter 4. under the provisions of this act, the Board of Supervisors passed Ordinances Numbers 17.193 and 17.194 "Ordering and Demanding the Disinterring and removal of Human Bodies Therefrom (Calvary and Laurel Hill) and Fixing a Time within which such Disinterring and Removal must be Performed" on April 26, 1937, approved by the voters November 2, 1937. The actual removals were carried out under rules and regulations established by the City and County director of Public Health, as required by the ordinances.

The State Health Code provides that "the governing body of any city, or city and county, having a population of more than 100,000 ..." (Chapter 3 has provisions for cities of less than 100,000 population)" may order the disinterment and removal of human remains interred in all or any part of any cemetery of more than five acres in extent, situated within its limits, where the right of interment in the cemetery has been prohibited by law for a period of fifteen years or more, whenever the governing body by ordinance declares that the further maintenance of all or any part of the cemetery as a burial place for the human dead threatens the health, safety, comfort, or welfare of the public and demands the disinterment and removal beyond the limits of the City or City and County of the human remains interred therein."

The State Code provides that a reasonable time of not less than two years may be set as a deadline for body removals. If the cemetery association or lot-owners do not undertake the removals in the period specified, the city itself may proceed to remove the remains and reinter them in another cemetery outside the City or City and County limits.

Likewise, the Code states that the "cemetery authority" (Association, board of trustees, church or other body operating the cemetery) may, after a period wherein plot-owners, relatives, heirs or others interested, are notified to remove the bodies in the cemetery, proceed itself to undertake the removals. (This is to prevent suits, as occurred in the case of Masonic and Odd Fellows cemetery-removal projects in 1923 here a majority of plot-owners had voted to abandon the cemeteries, but the courts held that the legislation then in force did not give authority to remove bodies against the wishes of the plot-owner or heir, inasmuch as the ownership-interest in the plot had not been wiped out by such majority vote.)

Other sections of the chapter provide for notices to friends or relatives prior to removal of remains, for removal of remains privately by relatives or friends; for requiring that monuments or memorials be left on the cemetery plot ninety days subsequent to the removal of the body; for reinterment in separate and suitable receptacle and respectful interment in another cemetery in a county or city where burials are permitted; for reservation of sufficient of the original cemetery site for the erection of a mausoleum or columbarium, and/or preservation of monuments or vaults of historical interest, and preservation of remains in the mausoleum or columbarium where it is desired that they not be removed from the cemetery location; for hearing before a superior court in the county in which the original cemetery was located to determine: (a) that all bodies had been removed from the cemetery land proposed for removal of dedication, and (b) that the property was no longer used or required for interment purposes. The Code also provided that funds received for the sale of cemetery lands could be used for:

(a) Acquisition of lands and improvements for cemetery purposes.

(b) Disinterment, removal, and reinterment of bodies.

(c) Perpetual care of graves, markers, and cemetery embellishments.

(d) The payment of expenses incidental to the disinterment, removal, and reinterment.

(e) "Any other purpose consistent with the objects for which the cemetery authority owning the cemetery is created or organized."

San Francisco's removal ordinances were merely implementations of the State Code, and in them it was noted that the two cemeteries were larger than five acres and that "health, welfare, and safety" factors required their removal, allowed the cemetery authorities three years in which to accomplish the task, provided that not more than ten per cent of the cemetery area could be retained for a memorial park, columbarium and mausoleum, and provided that the work should proceed under rules and regulations established by the Director of Public Health. The ordinance said that if the bodies were not removed by the cemetery association during the time limit specified, that the City and County itself would proceed with the disinterment of the bodies in the cemeteries and their reinterment in cemeteries outside the limits of the City and County.

The Director of Public Health of the City and County of San Francisco adopted rules and regulations to be followed in the cemetery removals shortly after the removal ordinances were approved by the electorate in 1937.

These rules and regulations required the cemeteries to maintain in their offices and to file with the Director a Register of Names (alphabetically arranged) of all interments remaining in the cemetery. Every thirty days, a list of disinterments made during the preceding thirty days was to be submitted showing name and identity of remains removed, section disinterred from, and cemetery, mausoleum or columbarium to which removal was made, these lists to be certified by the proper cemetery official. These monthly certificates and to contain the following statements:

(a) That disinterments were made in a decent and respectful manner.

(b) That each of the human remains as found was enclosed in a separate and suitable receptacle, properly marked, registered and recorded (all in a manner prescribed by law—i.e., the State Health Code).

(c) This certification was to be concurred in by an inspector of the Director of Public Health.

Mechanical appliances were allowed by the Director's rules and regulations to "remove the surface in order to insure accurate location of interments, and to remove surface earth, stone curbs, monuments, trees, vaults, slabs, headstones, drains, gutters, pipes, concrete work and the like." This was limited to a depth of within two feet of human remains' resting places. Remaining work of disinterment was prescribed to be done by individual hand labor, with each human remains separately and carefully disinterred by hand.

Individual disinterment permits were required where relatives or friends desired private or individual removals. The cemeteries were authorized to exclude from the area of disinterments all persons except those actually engaged in the work, or with a proper interest in the activities. The Director of Public Health appointed inspectors (full-time) to be on hand at all times at the cemetery to insure compliance with the regulations, make reports to the Director, and the like.

The provision in the regulations allowing mechanical appliances to be used to de-mount monuments and gravestones caused sane protests and concern on the part of some Laurel Hill plot-owners, and those interested in preserving the pioneers' monuments. "They are going to demolish our beloved Pioneers' monuments and vaults with Bulldozers.'" In actuality, hand labor was used as far as possible in the demounting of the monuments, with block-and-tackle and other mechanical aids used on a careful and individually-controlled basis so that the monuments and headstones could be preserved. This careful preservation increased the operating cost of the removal process considerably, and in some cases was not followed by a similar concern on the part of relatives, friends, historical or Pioneer societies in the actual preservation of the monuments.

The cemetery authorities not only followed all the regulations, but took all possible precautions to insure a proper and reverent handling of the remains removed and reinterred. It was realized that the entire cemetery-removal program would decrease people's faith in the sanctity of dedicated cemetery ground, and as a matter of fact, an increase in cremations was noted by officials of cemetery associations in Colma during and subsequent to the San Francisco cemetery-removal programs. Considerable "sales-resistance" was also noted on the sale of cemetery lots, inasmuch as prospective purchasers would cite the cemetery-removals as an example, and say, "'What assurance do you have to give us that my plot will not, fifty years from now, be picked up and moved to make way for more densely built-up residential development's?'"

Colma (Lawndale)—"The Cemetery City"

As was stated above in Section IV., cemeteries were established in Colma (then called Lawndale) in San Mateo County in the early 1900's, at about the same time that the San Francisco Board of Supervisors passed its ordinances prohibiting further burials inside the limits of the City and County. Great blocks of agricultural land were purchased by the various associations and church groups to insure an adequate expansion factor". After the first San Francisco cemetery-removals (Odd Fellows and Masonic) had been completed in the early 1920's, it was decided to incorporate the area in which the cemeteries were located, so that the "memorial character" of the area could be preserved against encroachments of inconsistent uses, and so that adjacent cities or towns could not secure removal of cemeteries from their sites by annexing the area and passing ordinances requiring the removal of the cemeteries.

Thus, Lawndale was incorporated in 1924 as an 'Incorporated Town" (now known in the California Code as "Cities of the Sixth Class"). The name was changed recently from Lawndale to Colma because: (a) it was found that a post office of Lawndale existed in Southern California, in an unincorporated community of about 3,500 persons, and (b) the unincorporated town of Colma, adjacent to Lawndale, had been annexed to Daly City, thus leaving the name unused, so to speak. The City of Colma was listed in the 1950 Census as having 264 inhabitants. In 1940, the Census counted 354 persons in the town.

The City has no municipal property tax, and its small budget is paid out of burial fees (at $1.00 per burial), and from business license taxes. Government activities are centered in a beautiful little Spanish Mission style City Hall, located on El Camino Real, a six-lane divided state highway which bisects the city, where monthly meetings of the unpaid City Council take place, and where the Municipal Judge holds court on automobile speeders caught within the city limits on the state highway. The City Council appoints the various city officials, such as City Clerk, City Treasurer, City Attorney, Police Chief, Fire Chief, and Public Health Officer. Most of these officials receive a small monthly stipend, typically $25 a month, and their municipal duties require only a few hours a day of their time. The police department, and several clerical personnel at the city hall complete the full-time municipal personnel.

Policy problems are studied by standing committees of the City Council (Judiciary, Police and Health; Finance and Municipal Affairs; Highways, Buildings and Drainage; Lights and Water).

Cemetery associations own about three-fourths of the land located within the city limits. Highway frontage on El Camino Real (U.S. Route Number 101-Seattle-San Francisco-San

Diego) which is not given over to cemetery use is used for florists' shops, nurseries, monument works, stonecutters' shops, and other businesses allied to cemetery activities.

Most of the residents and voters of Colma are connected with cemeteries, or allied activities, in some way. They are either proprietors or employees of the flower shops, nurseries, stonecutters and monument works, or they are employees of the cemetery associations, or their tenants. There are some residents who are not connected with the cemetery business (who own their own homes and work outside the city limits), but they are in the minority.

The cemeteries have established an association which is influential in establishing joint policies, and in formulating a unified front as to measures to be undertaken to protect their common interests. Interestingly enough, few of the officers of this association, or of the cemetery organizations themselves, are residents of Colma.

Just as the original intent of the incorporation was to preserve the "memorial character" of the area, as stated to the author by cemetery officials, so many of the ordinances enacted by the City Council are designed, directly or indirectly, to preserve the city's memorial character.

Not until March of 1950, however, was machinery for city planning and zoning established within the city. Ordinance Number 81, March 2, 1950, provided for the establishment of a City Planning Commission, established an interim zoning ordinance, and provided for the drawing up of a Master Plan and Zoning Ordinance. Only three zones were established in the interim zoning ordinance:

(1) "C—1" Cemeteries and accessory uses (stonecutters, nurseries , monument works, florists, etc.)

(2) "G—1" Residential

(3) "G—2" Agricultural

In this ordinance's preamble, it is stated:

"Whereas a majority of the lands located within the incorporated area are devoted to cemetery and accessory uses and

"Whereas. . .to protect the character and stability of both cemetery and residential land uses as an essential matter of public health and welfare. . . the establishment of the ordinance is necessary."

The ordinance provides that no land use, other than cemeteries and accessory residential or agriculture can be established without permit from the City Council. The memorial character of the city is outlined in this paragraph from the ordinance:

The City of Colma is a Memorial City, the great majority of the buildings and lands located therein being dedicated to cemetery and accessory uses, making it essential to properly designate certain areas in order that compatibility may be obtained between cemetery uses and residential uses for the public health and welfare, and that certain uses be recognized as incompatible to the use presently served by the major areas within the incorporated limits of the city.

An immediate reason for establishing zoning in Colma was the projected move on the part of a non-cemetery property owner to sell off his farm land for use as a "Drive-In" theater, which would have been located immediately adjacent to one of the largest cemeteries. The act was adopted prior to initiation of any official action for the establishment of the theater (application for building permit), so that the City Council had sufficient legal basis for refusing the permit on the ground that the area was zoned for cemeteries.

Another important ordinance on Colma's books is one passed in 1948 (Number 76, November 12, 1948) which prohibits defacement or breaking of monuments, destroying of planting, depositing of rubbish, and the like in cemeteries, and prohibits "loitering or remaining on the grounds of a cemetery without the express permission of the superintendent after closing hours." (The loiterer then has the burden of proof to show that he was on a "lawful errand" in the cemetery.) This type of ordinance was cited to the author by a cemetery official as being one of the definite advantages of incorporation as a municipality. Where no such ordinance exists, "loiterers" can only be ordered off the land and cited for trespass. With the ordinance, the City Police Department can be notified, and the loiterer arrested for violation of the ordinance, and cited to appear before the municipal judge. "Controls of this sort are necessary, as there always appear to be a certain group of individuals who seem to get pleasure out of perpetrating malicious mischief in graveyards, skylarking, or even grave-robbing, and they are a very hard group to catch up with. It is important to our plot-owners, and to the relatives of those buried here, that adequate protection be established to guard against disrupting the memorial and reverent atmosphere that should surround a cemetery,"

Others of the city's ordinances are not particularly different from those of other cities, but they are, no doubt, useful in aiding in preserving Colma, as a "Memorial City". For instance, a 1937 ordinance (Number 49) prohibits bill-boards within the city limits. Dumping of refuse along public highways is prohibited. The keeping of animals and fowl is regulated; licenses are required for hog ranches (issued by the Public Health Officer after approval by the City Council). An ordinance passed in 1929 prohibits operation of vehicles in such a manner as to "cut in" on funeral processions. Ordinances affecting building permits, business licenses ("can be revoked if the business is not conducted in an orderly manner"), abatement of dilapidated buildings are also on the books. Discharge of firearms within the city limits is prohibited.

The Public Health Officer is one of the most important officers of the city. He is charged with the supervision of all "interment, cremation and disposal of human bodies in the Town, and issuance of burial permits." Interestingly enough, this ordinance regulating burial procedures was amended 1929 to permit cemeteries' receiving of human remains exhumed from other cemeteries, with proof of twenty-five years' burial to be substituted for the death certificate usually required (i.e., to care for the San Francisco cemetery-removal project).

New cemeteries cannot be established in Colma without approval by the City Council of the site location by written permit. The application for such cemetery establishment must include statements as to:

(a) The qualifications and experience of the officers of the proposed cemetery organization.

(b) Whether it is to be a profit or non-profit corporation.

(c) Statement of fiscal plans for perpetual care.

(d) Statement as to extent of perpetual care.

In general, officials of cemetery associations in Colma regard the incorporation of the city as an essential protection against the intrusion of businesses and land uses which might be proper in normal circumstances, but not in keeping with the proper environment for good cemeteries, They also regard it as their strongest weapon against being -- like Laurel Hill and Calvary cemeteries in San Francisco—"picked up and moved further out into the country" when the pressure of land for further subdivision ad urbanization causes sentiment that "land for the living be substituted for land for the dead".

Cemetery officials with whom the author conferred expressed the feeling that the pressure to send cemeteries further and further out into the countryside could work hardships on some people. For many people, visits to loved ones' graves, placing of flowers on headstones on Sundays, holy days, Memorial Day, and so on, is an essential part of their religious life. Although Colma is situated within a few miles of the southern borders of San Francisco, and can be reached by public transit in about forty-five minutes from most of San Francisco's residential sections, they did not believe that cemeteries in metropolitan areas should be placed in more remote locations where they were inaccessible to the mass of people from the city's densely populated sections. Such remoteness would, in a manner of speaking, interfere with the exercise of what they consider to be a part of their religious rights and religious liberty.

Cremation is increasing in proportion to the total number of remains handled. Catholic church law does not permit the burial of cremated remains (except in certain circumstances and exceptions) in consecrated Catholic cemeteries.

Use Made of Land Vacated in San Francisco by the Removal of the Cemeteries

The abandonment of the four cemeteries in San Francisco (Masonic, Odd Fellows, Laurel Hill and Calvary) resulted in the addition of about 162 acres of developed area to the city's land use pattern, as follows:

Disposition of the land acquired for "live" uses was as follows:

Odd Fellows (1923)	27 acres (approximately)
Masonic (1923)	30 acres (approximately)
Calvary (1939-41)	49.2 acres
Laurel Hill (1939-41)	55.4 acres

(a) Odd Fellows Cemetery: A five acre tract was retained for a mausoleum and memorial park. About three additional acres now are used for commercial purposes. Approximately seven acres are in use in the Angelo Rossi Playground under the Jurisdiction of the San Francisco Recreation Commission. Most of the balance (excluding street area) is in single family row-house development,

(b) Masonic Cemetery: The entire thirty acres has been taken over for the campus of the University of San Francisco, a Catholic institution for higher learning,

(c) Calvary Cemetery and Laurel Hill Cemetery sites were developed residentially together with shopping centers.

Originally, extensive plans were developed for the construction of a 1,000 unit low-cost public housing project on Calvary Cemetery property, but a strong battle was waged against this on the part of real estate men in the city, the Downtown Association, and other business groups and neighborhood groups in the Richmond District. The San Francisco Housing Authority found another site for the project (Sunnydale near the San Mateo County Line), and with the advent of the war, public housing on both Laurel Hill and Calvary was forgotten.

As the area involving the cemeteries had wisely been restricted to uses permitted in "First Residential" districts, the City Planning Commission had a definite voice in determining the type of subdivision which could be developed in this "frontier in the middle of the city." Through stipulations, the type of "Second Residential" (any multiple-family dwelling) could be controlled. Ten-foot set-back lines were established, a forty-foot height limit was established, a building coverage lit of 65 per cent was included in the stipulations for zone change. Lot subdivision followed the standards in the new minimum lot size ordinance calling for a minimum frontage width of thirty-three feet and 2500 square foot minimum area per lot. These restrictions encouraged emphasis on "flats"—two to three "flats" per house—and most of the buildings are attached row-houses. Suggestions that these two areas be built at low coverage with tall apartment buildings were rejected in favor of flats.

The shopping centers in the areas are required to provide parking space adequate for the size of the store areas, and signs not flush with the buildings are prohibited. A height limit is established for the commercial buildings.

❖   ❖   ❖

CHAPTER 13

RACIAL AND RELIGIOUS DISCRIMINATION IN CEMETERIES

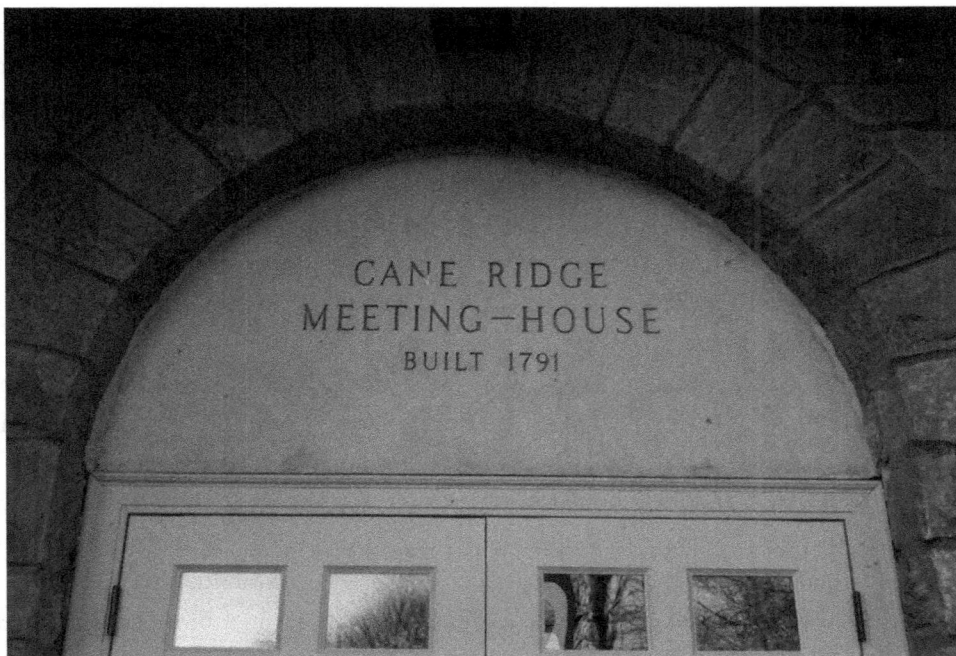

Cane Ridge Meeting House, Paris, Kentucky
Photo by Tanya D. Marsh

CHAPTER 13.1

RACIAL AND RELIGIOUS DISCRIMINATION IN CEMETERIES

Daniel Gibson

A member of the negro race well buried, is, from the standpoint of physical nuisance, no more so than the body of one of the Caucasian race; yet no one will deny that, if the privilege of burial in it were extended to the negro race, the value of Cave Hill as a cemetery for white people would be at once entirely destroyed.

> *Hertle v. Riddell*, 127 Ky. L. Rprt. 623, 635 (1907)

I cannot believe that a man's mortal remains will disintegrate any less peaceable because of the close proximity of the body of a member of another race, and in that inevitable disintegration I am sure that the pigmentation of the skin cannot long endure.

> *Long v. Mountain View Cemetery Ass'n*, 130 Cal.App.2d 328
> (1955) (J. Dooling, concurring)

We have desired, since at least Biblical times, to be buried with our ancestors. In Chapter 6.4, Justice Joseph Story references this desire in his dedication of the cemetery at Mount Auburn. This desire has often motivated racial separation in burial. Different religious rites or beliefs often necessitate further separation between the faithful and those of other faiths, even within cemeteries open to those of more than one faith. Catholic canon law and English ecclesiastical law both limited church burial to baptized or communing members of the faith. Municipal and privately-owned cemeteries, like Vienna's *Zentralfriedhof*, Europe's largest cemetery, and Green-Wood Cemetery in Brooklyn, include separated sections for Catholics, Protestants, Jews, and other religious groups.

In the United States, cemeteries were segregated on the basis of race as well as religion. For example, in 1790, the Vestry of Trinity Church in New York City passed a resolution "forbidding the indiscriminate burial of negroes" in the churchyards at St. Paul's Chapel and Trinity Chapel. Slaves were routinely buried in separate cemeteries while the practice of slavery continued. Even otherwise comparatively egalitarian people, such as the Moravians of Winston-Salem, North Carolina, separated the dead by race. The practice continued well into the 20th century. In the United States, cemeteries have traditionally been granted broad power to create and enforce rules, including discriminatory rules.

The Civil Rights Act of 1866, 42 U.S.C. § 1982, provides that

All citizens of the United States shall have the same right, in every State and Territory, as is enjoyed by white citizens thereof to inherit, purchase, lease, sell, hold, and convey real and personal property.

Until June 1968, the courts did not consider the Civil Rights Act of 1866 to apply to private discrimination, only to state action. That changed with the decision of the Supreme Court in *Jones v. Alfred H. Mayer Co.*, 392 U.S. 409 (1968), which held that: "§ 1982 bars all racial discrimination, private as well as public, in the sale or rental of property..."

If the Civil Rights Act of 1866 applies to private discrimination, then it would forbid racial discrimination in cemeteries only if the Right of Interment were understood to be a right to purchase, hold or convey real or personal property. Given the confusion about the nature of the Right of Interment, as discussed in Chapter 11.1, it is not surprising that cemeteries wishing to enforce racial restrictions, argued that the Right of Interment is not a property interest. A federal district court soundly rejected such reasoning from Elmwood Cemetery in the *Terry* case included as Chapter 13.4 and it now seems clear that racial discrimination in cemeteries is illegal.

❖ ❖ ❖

Arlington National Cemetery, Arlington, Virginia
Photo by Tanya D. Marsh

CHAPTER 13.2

RELIGIOUS AND RACIAL DISCRIMINATION

Percival Jackson, THE LAW OF CADAVERS (1950)

Where one is dealing with a public cemetery in which there are rights of burial in all persons who reside in a particular neighborhood, as where free education or hospitalization is furnished at community expense to the members of a community, there is no room or necessity for implication of contract. The respective rights and relations of the members of the community are governed by the rules of the social order, and in this country, except where statutes to the contrary enacted under the guise of the police power have been tacitly permitted, no discrimination based upon race, color, or religion may be recognized. Those who choose to exercise their common rights may do so, and the rights are exercised subject to the similar rights of others. So there may not be exclusion of a suicide from a public burial ground. But where there are communal activities, voluntarily segregated along religious and racial lines, the natural desire for such segregation after death, which is as strong in races deemed inferior as in others, justifies resort to implication of contract, where the right to violate the sentiments of the majority is based on claim of vested property rights unaffected by express contract.

Religious discrimination

We are not now discussing the restrictive effect of express contract; but inherent implications arise from the necessity of protecting the mutual purposes of those who associate for the burial of the dead. Because the genesis of our law of burial was in the churchyard, it is easy to recognize the necessity of respecting the rule and doctrines of the church where the line of demarcation is spiritual. Therefore, under general rules of burial law, almost universal sentiment will sustain a refusal to permit burial of a heretic in a strictly religious cemetery.

Racial discrimination

Without aid of settled rules of law, it is more difficult to justify similar conclusion where the question is one of racial discrimination, but there again the question is one of actual sentiment and the effect of its violation. In the absence of contract or statute, attempts to enforce racial discrimination touch springs of social discontent and meet with greater resistance. In parts of the country where racial feeling is as strong as religious feeling, one finds a ready tendency to prevent the introduction of bodies of members of the colored race in cemeteries used by the whites.

"A member of the negro race well buried, is, from the standpoint of physical nuisance, no more so than the body of one of the Caucasian race; yet no one will deny that, if the privilege of burial in it were extended to the negro race, the value of Cave Hill as a cemetery for white people would be at once entirely destroyed. A lot which is now worth in money as much as $500 would not, after such a change in the by-laws, be worth $50. Property which in the aggregate may now be worth millions, would then be rendered practically worthless." *Hertle v. Riddell*, 127 Ky.L.Rptr. 623, 635 (1907).

But in *Richmond Cemetery Co. v. Walker*, 97 S.W. 34 (Ky. 1906), the court said:

"The appellant does not present a single legal reason why the judgment of the lower court should be reversed. Its theory and theme is one of sentiment—that the peace and good order of the community requires that the two races have separate burial places; that this is the policy of the state, as shown by it requiring separate coaches on railroads, and separate schools for the white and colored people. This was accomplished by statutes, but the General Assembly has never enacted any statute requiring separate burial places for the two races, and this court is powerless to prevent any person, either white or black, from any legitimate and legal use of his property, and it has no power to force him to accept any price that may be offered for his property."

Thus, in the absence of express restriction, the courts in general will refuse to recognize or enforce any implied or tacit racial restriction.

❖ ❖ ❖

Hollywood Cemetery, Richmond, Virginia
Photo by Tanya D. Marsh

CHAPTER 13.3

CLARA MAE LONG V. MOUNTAIN VIEW CEMETERY ASS'N

District Court of Appeal, First District, Division 2, California,
130 Cal.App.2d 328 (1955)

NOURSE, Presiding Justice.

... These facts are: The defendant maintained a cemetery in which were burial plots, a crematorium, and three mausoleums, one of which was set aside for the exclusive use of members of the Caucasian race. The plaintiff demanded that her husband's remains be deposited in this restricted mausoleum. There is no contention that the other two were not just as suitable and as properly maintained as the third. There is no evidence of any kind showing why the plaintiff rejected this offer.

The only question of law involved here is whether section 51 of the Civil Code applies to this case. That section reads: "All citizens within the jurisdiction of this state are entitled to the full and equal accommodations, advantages, facilities and privileges of inns, restaurants, hotels, eating houses, places where ice cream or soft drinks of any kind are sold for consumption on the premises, barber shops, bath houses, theaters, skating rinks, public conveyances and all other places of public accommodation or amusement, subject only to the conditions and limitations established by law, and applicable alike to all citizens."

The settled rule of law is that the expression "all other places" means all other places of a like nature to those enumerated, i.e., "restaurants, hotels" etc. In a similar case involving a like statute the Supreme Court of Illinois held that the expression "all other places of public accommodation and amusement" did not include cemeteries. Directly in point is the recent case of *Rice v. Sioux City Memorial Park Cemetery*, Iowa, 60 N.W.2d 110, where the same rule was applied to the refusal of the cemetery to accept for burial the remains of an Indian in a plot of land restricted to the use of members of the Caucasian race.

There is no merit in any of the arguments of appellant.

Judgment affirmed.

KAUFMAN, Justice (concurring).

I concur on the authority of *Rice v. Sioux City Memorial Park Cemetery*, 60 N.W.2d 110, where the Supreme Court of Iowa construed the Iowa Civil Rights Statute which is very similar to Sections 51 and 52 of the Civil Code of California and determined questions of constitutional law involved.

The court held that a provision in a contract for the purchase of a burial lot in a private cemetery permitting only members of the Caucasian race to be buried therein was not void as being violative of equal protection clauses of either Federal or State Constitutions and is not void as being violative of public policy. Further, that Iowa's Civil Rights Statute was not violated.

I also agree with the view that Sections 51 and 52 of our Civil Code only apply to living citizens of this state. Plaintiff was not denied the right to enter the cemetery but was merely refused permission to bury her husband in the cemetery. Accordingly no rights given to plaintiff by Sections 51 and 52 of the Civil Code have been violated by defendant.

DOOLING, Justice.

I concur, but I cannot resist a word of protest. I cannot believe that a man's mortal remains will disintegrate any less peaceably because of the close proximity of the body of a member of another race, and in that inevitable disintegration I am sure that the pigmentation of the skin cannot long endure. It strikes me that the carrying of racial discrimination into the burial grounds is a particularly stupid form of human arrogance and intolerance. If life does not do so, the universal fellowship of death should teach humility. The good people who insist on the racial segregation of what is mortal in man may be shocked to learn when their own lives end that God has reserved no racially exclusive position for them in the hereafter.

❖ ❖ ❖

God's Acre, Salem, North Carolina
Photo by Tanya D. Marsh

CHAPTER 13.4

MRS. MARGARET TERRY V. THE ELMWOOD CEMETERY

Northern District of Alabama, 307 F.Supp. 369 (1969)

LYNNE, Chief Judge.

This class action for damages, injunctive and/or declaratory relief was brought by Negro plaintiffs, Mrs. Margaret Faye Terry, Mrs. Jimmie Lee Terry and Mr. Blevin Stout, who were not allowed to purchase burial lots in the public cemetery owned and operated by defendant, The Elmwood Cemetery Corporation. [The court notes in a footnote: "The law contemplates two classes of cemeteries, public and private. The former class is used by the general community or neighborhood or church, while the latter is used only by a family or a small portion of a community. … The test is public user." Under this test, Elmwood Cemetery is a public cemetery.] The facts are not disputed and consequently the action has been submitted to the court for a judgment on the pleadings pursuant to Federal Rules of Civil Procedure 12(c).

Bill Henry Terry, Jr., a Negro citizen of the United States and of the State of Alabama, volunteered to serve his country as a soldier on September 22, 1968, was sent to Fort Gordon, then to Japan, and arrived in View Nam on March 8, 1969. Having a premonition that he might be killed while in Viet Nam, he told his mother and young wife, two of the plaintiffs in this action, that he wished to be buried in Elmwood Cemetery in Birmingham, Alabama, in the event of his death. On July 3, 1969, Bill Terry was mortally wounded by the enemy while he was participating in a search and destroy mission. His body was sent back to the United States with the customary military escort, and upon arrival in Alabama was taken by the military authorities, in the company of the plaintiff mother and the plaintiff wife, to the Elmwood Cemetery, where the two mentioned plaintiffs attempted to purchase a burial plot. A man who identified himself as the manager of Elmwood refused to sell a cemetery lot for interment of Bill Terry's remains to these plaintiffs solely because they were Negroes. Elmwood has attempted to justify this action by answering that it has a policy of refusing burial in its cemetery to persons other than Caucasians which is based on the fact that all lot deeds for grave sites at the cemetery contain a provision limiting interment in Elmwood Cemetery to members of the Caucasian race, and that rules and regulations promulgated by Elmwood in 1954 provide in part:

"Cemetery lots shall be owned only by human beings of the white and/or Caucasian race and the said lots shall be used only for burial of human bodies of the white and/or Caucasian race, and such ownership and use shall at all times be subject to the Rules and Regulations and By-Laws of Elmwood now or hereafter in force. Any attempted transfer of a lot or interest in a lot to one not authorized to own same shall be invalid and of no force and effect and the corporation shall not be obligated to honor such transfer."

Since Bill Terry's wife and mother had already arranged for a funeral, when they were refused the right to purchase a burial lot from Elmwood, they had no alternative on July 19, 1969, but to have his body interred in a Negro cemetery.

On July 25, 1969, the wife and mother of Bill Terry, along with Belvin Stout, a Negro citizen of the United States who resides in Hueytown, Alabama, who also was not allowed to purchase a grave site from Elmwood because he was a Negro, filed this suit, alleging, inter alia, unlawful discrimination against Negroes as a class by Elmwood, which discrimination constitutes a badge or incident of slavery contrary to the thirteenth amendment of the Constitution of the United States and the 1866 Civil Rights Act, 42 U.S.C. § 1982 (1964). Jurisdiction of the court was invoked pursuant to 28 U.S.C. §§ 1343(3) & (4), 2201 (1964).

The Terry plaintiffs have offered to exhume the remains of Bill Henry Terry, Jr., and to transfer them to the Elmwood Cemetery if the court declares that the defendant wrongfully abridged plaintiffs' rights in refusing to sell them lots in the cemetery solely because they were Negroes.

Elmwood, through its attorneys, has indicated that it will comply with any declaration of rights the court shall make in this matter, and therefore the court will simply declare the rights of the parties, as authorized by 28 U.S.C. § 2201 (1964), and shall decline to issue an injunction at this time.

[1] It is the opinion of the court that the 1866 Civil Rights Act, now embodied in 42 U.S.C. § 1982 (1964), requires that Negroes and other non-Caucasians be extended the same rights to purchase cemetery lots as whites are given. That Act provides:

> All citizens of the United States shall have the same right, in every State and
> Territory, as is enjoyed by white citizens thereof to inherit, purchase, lease, sell,
> hold, and convey real and personal property.

Prior to June 17, 1968, it had long been assumed that this Act did not proscribe private discrimination, but was enacted by Congress under the authority of the fourteenth amendment of the United States Constitution, and thereby was circumscribed by the "state action" limitations of that amendment. At least one of the reasons for this erroneous assumption was the tortured legislative history of the 1866 Civil Rights Act. It was enacted by an angry and punitive Congress, over the veto of President Andrew Johnson, shortly after the close of the War Between the States. Because many legislators at the time were of the opinion that it was perhaps unconstitutional, after the fourteenth amendment was ratified in 1868, the 1866 Civil Rights Act was reenacted in 1870. Because of its restricted interpretation, it was seldom invoked by the courts.

However, in June, 1968, the Supreme Court of the United States in the landmark case of *Jones v. Alfred H. Mayer Co.*, 392 U.S. 409, 88 S.Ct. 2186, 20 L.Ed.2d 1189 (1968), resurrected this statute from the catacombs of desuetude, and held that: "§ 1982 bars all racial discrimination, private as well as public, in the sale or rental of property, and that the statute, thus construed, is a valid exercise of the power of Congress to enforce the Thirteenth Amendment."

The defendant has vigorously contended that interests in cemetery lots fall without the scope of § 1982. The court is not persuaded. Basically, there are two strings to defendant's bow: (1) § 1982 can only be supported by the thirteenth amendment if the section is considered a fair housing law, and Jones should therefore be limited to its precise facts; (2) the rights of a purchaser of a cemetery lot, because of its unique nature, do not fall within the meaning of the phrase 'real and personal property' as used in § 1982. The first aspect of the argument may be disposed of quickly, but the second point requires more detailed consideration.

Since the famous case of *Marbury v. Madison*, the doctrine of judicial review by the federal courts has been firmly established, and pronouncements by the United States Supreme Court concerning the scope of constitutional provisions and the breadth and validity of statutes are considered the law of the land, binding on this and all other federal and state courts. It is true that the facts in Jones involved the refusal of the defendants to sell the plaintiffs in that case a home in a Missouri community solely because the plaintiffs were Negroes. However, the statements concerning the scope of § 1982 were broad, and the effect of the decision was to reactivate a statute which had fallen into disuse. Nowhere did the Court indicate that § 1982 could only be sustained under the thirteenth amendment if construed as a fair housing law. To the contrary, its "badge of slavery" rationale indicates that it considers that § 1982 is valid and applicable in any situation involving racial barriers to the acquisition of real and personal property. In holding that the thirteenth amendment authorized § 1982, the Court stated:

"Thus, the fact that §1982 operates upon the unofficial acts of private individuals, whether or not sanctioned by state law, presents no constitutional problem. If Congress has power under the Thirteenth Amendment to eradicate conditions that prevent Negroes from buying and renting property because of their race or color, then no federal statute calculated to achieve that objective can be thought to exceed the constitutional power of Congress simply because it reaches beyond state action to regulate the conduct of private individuals. The constitutional question in this case, therefore, comes to this: Does the authority of Congress to enforce the Thirteenth Amendment 'by appropriate legislation' include the power to eliminate all racial barriers to the acquisition of real and personal property? We think the answer to that question is plainly yes. "By its own unaided force and effect," the Thirteenth Amendment "abolished slavery, and established universal freedom." ... Whether or not the Amendment itself did any more than that— a question not involved in this case—it is at least clear that the Enabling Clause of that Amendment empowered Congress to do much more. For that clause clothed "Congress with power to pass all laws necessary and proper for abolishing all badges and incidents of slavery in the United States."

Cases subsequent to Jones construing §1982 conclusively demonstrate that this court is on sound constitutional ground in recognizing the broad construction of the reactivated statute. Several recent cases have emphasized the broad language in Jones, three of them holding that whites as well as Negroes are protected by §1982, and another construing the section to protect Negroes from exploitation by white real estate entrepreneurs. In addition, since Jones, courts have awarded damages, both actual and exemplary, and attorneys' fees, to parties whose rights under §1982 have been violated, in spite of the fact that the statute does not mention the availability of these remedies. Finally, the Supreme Court itself, on December 15, 1969, focused upon §1982 to hold that Negroes may not be barred from acquiring membership shares in and thereby becoming members of community recreational organizations.

Considering these authorities, this court, while recognizing that Jones has been strongly criticized by some commentators and was perhaps an exercise in judicial activism, is of the opinion that its real effect is to reactivate §1982 generally. It therefore becomes the duty of this court to determine whether a cemetery lot is "property" within the meaning of the 1866 Civil Rights Act, 42 U.S.C. §1982 (1964).

In any case, the concept of "property" is an elusive one. Property law is replete with semantic problems. It is possible for the same court in the same jurisdiction within the span of a few years to give the same general type of interest in property several different labels. Frequently too, the narrow line between contract rights and property rights is vague. The problems inherent in the area are compounded when interests in land are incorporeal in nature. However, if a functional rather than a conceptual approach is used toward property law and interests in land, it is clear that a purchaser's interest in a burial lot is a "property right" whether it be called an easement, license, right of sepulture or whatnot. Tiffany [in The Law of Real Property (3d ed. 1939) has stated:

"The privilege of interring bodies in a burial ground belonging to a corporation or association has been referred to as an easement, as a usufructuary right, and as a license. However characterized, the lot holder, as he is frequently termed, even if not owner of the fee, has an interest in the lot which is such a property right as the law recognizes and protects from invasion. In the final analysis, a "property right" of any nature may be defined as "that type of relationship which is entitled to protection from a decision maker."

Tested against this standard, it may be conclusively established that interests in cemetery lots are property rights. It has been held in Alabama, and this is evidently in accord with the common law in many states, that owners of cemetery lots may maintain actions of trespass against persons who wrongfully interfere with their grave sites, that title to a cemetery lot may be obtained by prescription or adverse possession, and that actions equitable in nature may be maintained by a lot owner's heirs to prevent interference with a dedicated alleyway adjacent to the burial plot. Moreover, cemetery lots may be specifically devised or pass by intestate succession. In addition, the Alabama Legislature has recognized that a cemetery lot is some type of property interest, because it has exempted cemetery lots from "levy and sale, under execution or other process."

The conclusion that the owners of burial rights have a property interest in their lots is further supported by a recent Michigan case, *Spencer v. Flint Memorial Park Ass'n*, 4 Mich.App. 157, 144 N.W.2d 622 (1966), which held that it is a denial of equal protection of the law in contravention of the fourteenth amendment "for a state to enforce a restrictive agreement of a cemetery association which would deny the owner of a cemetery plot, who is a Negro, the right to bury a non-Caucasian therein." The Michigan court recognized the semantic problems in this area, but concluded that an interest in a cemetery lot is a property right:

"As pointed out by the defendant, the interest of the plaintiff herein is a burial right or right of sepulture. There is no question but that such burial right is a peculiar interest incapable of being pushed into the convenient pigeonhole lawyers and judges are so wont to place difficult concepts. It is not a fee interest, but rather a right of burial which is transferable and the rights of holders thereof are legally enforceable. … Regardless of what label we hang on this interest, it is a property right."

To establish that cemetery lot owners do not have "property rights" in cemetery lots, the defendant relies primarily on several general statements from legal encyclopedias, and some observations made by the Alabama Supreme Court in a 1955 case. However, these pronouncements may be explained away by noting that later in the same authorities, statements are made to the effect that burial rights are property interests, and by recognizing that the writers of these conclusions were struggling with the semantic problems inherent in the area.

Assuming then, that the owners of cemetery lots, or burial privileges therein, have a "property right" in such lots because their interests will be recognized, protected and effectuated by the courts, it is clear that cemetery lots are "property" within the meaning of §1982, because the words "real and personal property" as used in the statute exhaust all the possibilities of types of property. …

Furthermore, in *Walker v. Pointer*, 304 F.Supp. 56 (N.D.Tex.1969), the Northern District of Texas held that implied easements of ingress and egress, and licenses, are "property" within the scope of §1982. In that case, white plaintiffs were allowed both actual and exemplary damages, where the manager of an apartment house had evicted them with malice solely because they had entertained Negroes in their apartment. Under this authority, it is clear that cemetery lots, or rights of burial therein, even if considered "easements" or "licenses," are "property" within the meaning of §1982.

The court is also of the opinion that because of the new interpretation of §1982, the racial covenants and regulations of Elmwood restricting burial in its cemetery to Caucasians are void and of no legal effect, because now, under Jones, even private discrimination is unlawful in the sale or purchase of real or personal property. The court is, of course, aware of the decisions in *Shelley v. Kraemer*, 334 U.S. 1, 68 S.Ct. 836, 92 L.Ed. 1161 (1948), and *Hurd v. Hodge*, 334 U.S. 24, 68 S.Ct. 847, 92 L.Ed. 1187 (1948), and their progeny, which held in effect that neither state courts nor the federal courts in the District of Columbia could enforce racial restrictive covenants without contravention of the equal protection clause of the fourteenth amendment or the public policy of the United States. It was generally assumed under these decisions that private discrimination was still constitutionally allowable, even though under expanded concepts of 'state action' and other judicial techniques, courts more and more reached out to strike down discriminatory practices. However, the day has passed when even private discrimination in the lease or sale of property will be allowed by the United States Supreme Court.

In all fairness to Elmwood, it should be noted that covenants restricting burial in cemeteries to Caucasians are not a Southern or Alabama phenomenon. As recently as 1953, it was estimated that there were racial restrictive covenants in ninety per cent of all public cemetery deeds and regulations in the United States, because "people, like animals, prefer to be with their own kind." *Rice v. Sioux City Memorial Park*, 245 Iowa 147, 60 N.W.2d 110 (1953), aff'd mem. 438 U.S. 880, 75 S.Ct. 122, 99 L.Ed. 693 (1954), vacated, petition for cert. dismissed, 349 U.S. 70, 75 S.Ct. 614, 99 L.Ed. 897 (1955).

Also, the court is aware of and has examined the several decisions that have upheld racial restrictive covenants or regulations with regard to cemetery lots. However, it suffices to observe that this authority is obsolete, all of it antedating *Jones*.

Applying the principles enunciated herein to the facts of the instant case, the court holds that under §1982, defendant Elmwood is legally obligated to sell burial plots in its public cemetery to all United States citizens, on equal terms, without regard to race or color, and has unlawfully abridged plaintiffs' rights under such statute by refusing to sell them cemetery lots solely because they are Negroes. Further, the court declares that the provisions in all existing Elmwood Cemetery lot deeds limiting interment in such cemetery to members of the Caucasian race, and similar provisions in the Elmwood rules and regulations, are void and of no legal effect.

Since the court has concluded that §1982 is dispositive of the rights and duties of the parties to this case, it will not consider the contention of the plaintiffs that the action of defendant Elmwood in refusing to sell cemetery lots to plaintiffs was also violative of 42 U.S.C. §1981 (1964). Furthermore, because compensatory damages cannot yet be accurately ascertained, the court will pretermit consideration at this time of plaintiffs' claim for damages, both compensatory and punitive, and for attorneys' fees. Consequently, jurisdiction of this cause will be retained, pending voluntary compliance with the principles enunciated and rights declared in this opinion, and reapplication to this court by the plaintiffs for an award of damages.

Judgment in conformity with the foregoing opinion will accordingly be entered.

❖ ❖ ❖

CHAPTER 14

DISINTERMENT

Crown Hill Cemetery, Indianapolis, Indiana
Photo by Cass Pyatt

CHAPTER 14.1
THE COMMON LAW OF DISINTERMENT
Tanya D. Marsh

The American law regarding the status, treatment, and disposition of human remains is essentially state law. There is little federal statutory law, and none of it is relevant to disinterment (other than the disinterment of the remains of Native Americans). There is a significant base of common law rooted in English common and ecclesiastical precedents. Beginning in the early 20th century, state legislatures began passing statutes that supplemented and formalized aspects of the common law, but which did not completely replace it. Most of these modern statutes focus on the regulation of the funeral and cemetery industries. There has been little uniform law activity in this area, so while the common law is fairly coherent and consistent, state statutes vary widely.

The American common law regarding burial rights and disinterment is derived from English common and ecclesiastical law. For approximately 900 years, jurisdiction over burials in England was the sole dominion of ecclesiastical, rather than civil authorities. At English common law, an individual had the right to be buried in the parish churchyard, so long as the individual was not ineligible, under ecclesiastical law, to receive burial in consecrated ground. The common law obligated the next of kin of the decedent to take possession of the remains prior to interment and to make arrangements to ensure that the decedent received a decent burial. Once a decedent had been buried in the parish churchyard, ecclesiastical law provided that the Church of England held the remains "in trust" until the Second Coming of Christ, when the dead would be resurrected. If remains were buried in unconsecrated ground, they came under the protection of the public rather than the Church. English common and ecclesiastical law held that the surviving kin of the decedent had no rights to the remains following interment and could bring no civil action against those who disturbed interred remains.

American common law obviously could not completely adhere to these precedents because we lack a universal church and body of ecclesiastical law. But the general approach in the American common law regarding the disposition of human remains has been to adhere to the cultural and legal precedents of the English system as closely as possible. Therefore, it is a foundational principle of American common law that a surviving spouse or next of kin has the right "to control and direct the burial of a corpse and arrange for its preservation." *Whitney v. Cervantes*, 328 P.3d 957, 960 (Wash. Ct. App. 2014), citing *Guilliume v. McCulloch*, 24 P.2d 93 (Wash. 1933). This common law right, however, ends upon interment. *See, e.g. Pierce v. Proprietors of Swan Point Cemetery*, 10 R.I. 227, 234 (1872) (holding that "any and all rights which [the respondent] may have claimed as widow ceased and determined, if they ever had an existence, on the burial of the body in 1856."); *Friedman v. Agudath Achim N. Shore Congregation*, 115 N.E.2d 553, 555 (Ill. App. Ct. 1953) ("The wishes of wife and next of kin are not always supreme and final though the body is yet unburied … Still less are they supreme and final when the body has been laid at rest and the aid of equity is invoked to disturb the quiet of the grave.")

Once a body has been interred, the owner of the cemetery may have superior rights to next of kin to determine whether disinterment is permissible, particularly if the cemetery owner is a religious organization and the decedent adhered to that faith during life. The reported cases that examine this doctrine mainly pertain to persons interred in cemeteries owned by the Roman Catholic Church or Jewish congregations. *See, e.g. Raisler v. Krakauer Simon Screiber Congregation*, 47 N.Y.S.2d 938 (1944); *Mitty v. Oliveira*, 244 P.2d 921 (Cal. Dist. Ct. App. 1952). In those cases, courts differentiated between circumstances where a written contract prohibiting disinterment existed or did not exist. *See, e.g. Wolf v. Rose Hill Cemetery Ass'n*, 832 P.2d 1007, 1009 (Colo. App. 1991) (holding that when considering a petition for disinterment, a court should take into account "whether a written contract between the cemetery and decedent or next of kin exists that discusses rights of removal."). A leading case arose where the children of a deceased couple petitioned the court to permit the disinterment of their parents from a Jewish cemetery. Citing Jewish law, the cemetery refused to permit the disinterment. The court discussed the role of a court of equity in resolving such disputes:

> The cemetery of the defendant is maintained pursuant to the authority of the laws of this state, and, in the absence of a regulation adopted by the defendant as to who shall determine the right of removal, such right must be determined, when presented to a court of equity, upon equitable grounds, and not by the Jewish law. Ecclesiastical law is not a part of the law of this state, nor are equitable rights to be determined by it; on the contrary, when a court of equity exercises its powers, it does so only upon equitable principles, irrespective of ecclesiastical or any other law. … It may be that if an agreement were made with a cemetery association that remains there interred could not thereafter be

disinterred, a court of equity would enforce the agreement; or, if a religious corporation had a rule, to which a member subscribed, that if his remains were interred in a cemetery controlled by it they could not thereafter be removed, that a court of equity would refuse to exercise its powers to decree removal. But that is not this case. There was no agreement that the remains of Adela would not, after interment, be disinterred. Nor had she subscribed to any rule of the defendant which prevented such removal, unless that fact be inferred from her membership alone, which is insufficient. That the court had the power, under the findings of the referee and the facts developed by the evidence, to decree a removal is sustained by numerous authorities.

Cohen v. Congregation Shearith Israel in City of New York, 114 A.D. 117, 119-20, 99 N.Y.S. 732, 734 (App. Div. 1906) aff'd, 189 N.Y. 528, 82 N.E. 1125 (1907).

Courts Have Equitable Jurisdiction Over Interred Remains

American common law followed English precedent in holding that the next of kin do not control human remains following interment. Given the absence of an established church, it was therefore necessary to designate a civil authority that could serve as the post-interment guardian of remains. In 1829, the United States Supreme Court declared that American courts have the equitable power and obligation to exercise jurisdiction over the dead. *Beatty et al v. Kurtz et al.*, 27 U.S. 566 (1829) ("[In the event of an interference with the sepulchers of the dead], [t]he remedy must be sought, if at all, in the protecting power of a court of chancery; operating by its injunction to preserve the repose of the ashes of the dead, and the religious sensibilities of the living."). *See also Pierce v. Proprietors of Swan Point Cemetery*, 10 R.I. 227, 232 (1872) ("Courts of equity have full jurisdiction, and such jurisdiction has been frequently exercised, to protect and preserve the repose of the dead…").

The equitable jurisdiction of the courts over graves and cemeteries remains a strong principle in the modern common law. *See, e.g. Harris v. Borough of Fair Haven*, 721 A.2d 758, 762 (N.J.Super.Ch. 1998) ("It is true, also, that the Superior Court possesses equitable jurisdiction, as a general matter, over the dead. This means, without the need for further delineation, that once a body is buried it is deemed to be in the custody of the law and the removal or disturbance of those remains lies, when not otherwise provided by legislation, within the court's equitable powers the invocation of which infrequently occurs.")

❖ ❖ ❖

Crown Hill Cemetery, Indianapolis, Indiana
Photo by Cass Pyatt

CHAPTER 14.2
WILLIAM G. PIERCE & WIFE
V.
PROPRIETORS OF SWAN POINT CEMETERY & ALMIRA T. METCALF
Supreme Court of Rhode Island, 10 R.I. 227 (1872)

In this case one of the respondents, Mrs. Metcalf, has removed the body of her husband from its former place of burial in Swan Point Cemetery, and claims that she had the right to do so, being, as his widow, entitled to the charge of it. The claim is resisted by his only child, the complainant.

It seems strange that controversies of this sort have not arisen often before. In Europe burials were matters of ecclesiastical cognizance, and the practice of burial in churches and churchyards common. In many parts of New England the parish system prevailed, and every family was considered to have a right of burial in the churchyard of the parish in which they lived, until they removed to another parish. In Rhode Island, from the scattered nature of the population in most parts of the state, it was early the practice to bury upon the family estate, and when the estate was sold the right was generally reserved. Burial grounds of this sort have remained to families for many generations, in many cases from the first settlement, and the dead are brought from a great distance to be buried among their ancestors and kindred. By the civil law of ancient Rome, the charge of burial was first upon the person to whom it was delegated by the deceased; second, upon the *scripti haeredes* (to whom the property was given), and if none, then upon the *haeredes legitimi* or *cognati* in order. But a body once buried could not be removed except by the permission, in Rome, of the Pontifical College, and in the provinces, of the

Governor. And by the Roman law there was a distinction of tombs into *familiaria* into which any member of the family might be admitted, and *hersditaria* for one's self and his heirs. The heirs might be compelled to comply with the provisions of the will in regard to burial. And the Pontifical College had the power of providing for the burial of those who had no place of burial in their own right.

By the canon law, which prevailed in such matters over so large a part of Europe, every one was to be buried in the parish churchyard, or in his ancestral sepulchre (if any), or in such place as he might select. A wife was to be buried with her last husband, if more than one. If a person permanently changed his residence, then he was to be buried in the parish churchyard of his new residence.

In England, by their ecclesiastical law, by which this subject was regulated, every person (with exception of traitors, &c.) had a right to be buried in the parish churchyard. And a claim of right by custom to bury as near relatives as possible, was held bad. The whole was under the direction of the ordinary, and was of ecclesiastical cognizance. And once buried, the body could not be removed without license from the ordinary. And the person who set up a monument, or on his death, the heir of the deceased, might have an action for injury to it. And the husband was bound to bury his wife. See for a full account, Bingham's Christian Antiquities, from which much of the historical matter in legal arguments and in reports has probably been taken without acknowledgment.

Rex v. Stewart, 12 A. & E. 773, was an application for a mandamus to compel overseers, &c., to bury a person. The court: "It should seem that the individual under whose roof a poor person dies is bound to carry the body decently covered to the place of burial; he cannot keep him unburied, or do anything which prevents Christian burial; he cannot therefore cast him out, so as to expose the body to violation, or to offend the feelings or endanger the health of the living; and for the same reason he cannot carry him uncovered to the grave." The mandamus was refused for other reasons.

The question is new in this state; and we do not know that it has ever occurred in our mother country, and but seldom in the United States. That there is no right or property in a dead body, using the word in its ordinary sense, may well be admitted. Yet the burial of the dead is a subject which interests the feelings of mankind to a much greater degree than many matters of actual property. There is a duty imposed by the universal feelings of mankind to be discharged by some one towards the dead; a duty, and we may also say a right, to protect from violation; and a duty on the part of others to abstain from violation; it may therefore be considered as a sort of quasi property, and it would be discreditable to any system of law not to provide a remedy in such a case.

It is common to speak of the right of burial, of a person's right to be buried, &c. In the case *Rex v. Stewart*, before quoted, the court say: "Every person dying in this country ... has a right to Christian burial; and that implies the right to be carried from the place where the body lies to the parish cemetery."

In *Gilbert v. Buzzard*, 1 Hagg. Con. 348, and S. C. 3 Phill. 335, Lord Stowell (Sir William Scott) says: "The rule of law which says that a man has a right to be buried in his own churchyard is to be found most certainly in many of our authoritative text writers; but it is not quite so easy to find the rule which gives him the right of burying a large chest or trunk in company with himself. That is no part of his original and absolute right, nor is it necessarily involved in it. That right, strictly taken, is to be returned to his parent earth for dissolution, and to be carried thither in a decent and inoffensive manner. When these purposes are answered, his rights are perhaps fully satisfied in the strict sense in which any claim in the nature of an absolute right can be deemed to extend." So Dr. Burn, quoting Gibson's *Codex Juris. Ecclesiae Anglicanae*, says: "Every parishioner hath and had always a right to be buried in" the parish burial ground.

Most people look forward to the proper disposition of their remains, and it is natural that they should feel an anxiety on the subject. And the right of a person to provide by will for the disposition of his body has been generally recognized. We have seen that by the canon law a person had a right to direct his place of sepulture. Now, strictly speaking, according to the strict rules of the old common law, a dead man cannot be said to have rights. Yet it is common so to speak, and the very fact of the common use of such language, and of its being used in such cases as we have quoted, justifies us in speaking of it as a right in a certain qualified sense, and a right which ought to be protected. And a sort of right of custody over, or interest in the dead body, in the relatives of the deceased, is recognized in the statutes of many of our states. The laws of Indiana, R. S. ch. 7, § 37, prohibit the removal of a dead body without the consent of the near relatives, or without the consent of the deceased, given in his lifetime. The laws of Louisiana and California recognize the interest of the relatives of the deceased in the body. And see also the late English Statute of Burials, 15 & 16 Victoria, ch. 85, §§ 32 and 33; *Baker's Laws relating to Burials*.

… When a case, not affected by any statute, arises in any of our courts of justice, and the facts are established, the first question is, whether there is any clear and unequivocal principle of the common law, which directly and immediately governs it, and fixes the rights of the parties. If there be no such principle, the next question is, whether there is any principle of the common law, which, by analogy or parity of reasoning, ought to govern it. If neither of these sources furnishes a positive solution of the controversy, resort is next had (as in a case confessedly new) to the principles of natural justice, which constitute the basis of much of the common law; and if these principles can be ascertained to apply in a full and determinate manner to all the circumstances, they are adopted, and decide the rights of the parties. If all these sources fail, the case is treated as remediless at the common law, and the only relief which remains is by some new legislation by statute, to operate upon future cases of the like nature."

…In *Kurtz v. Beatty & Ritchie*, 2 Pet. 566, 584, which was to obtain an injunction to prevent the removal of tombs and graves, Judge Story, in giving the opinion of the United States Supreme Court, says: "It is a case where no action at law. … could afford an adequate and complete remedy. …. The remedy must be sought, if at all, in the protecting power of a court of chancery,—operating by its injunction to preserve the repose of the ashes of the dead and the religious sensibilities of the living."

In cases like the present no common law action could avail much. The owner of the lot might have *trespass quare clausum*, &c., but he could only recover damages in money. He might have an action of detinue for the body, or so much earth, &c., taken away; or perhaps might have replevin; if buried by permission on another's land, it might perhaps be considered a license or easement, for disturbance of which the person who procured the burial might have an action;

but it is easy to see that neither form of action affords a sufficient remedy, or could with any certainty restore the body to the proper custody.

Equity only can give a full and complete remedy, and we think the jurisdiction is fully adequate to it.

It seems the deceased Mr. Metcalf purchased a burial lot, and was, on his decease, with the consent of his widow, one of the respondents, and the complainants say they believe according to his own wishes, buried in it. The respondent, Mrs. Metcalf, has demurred to the bill, thus admitting these alleged facts, for the purposes of the present hearing. Taking these allegations as uncontradicted and true, as the body was removed by the widow, without the consent of the child, from a place where it was deposited by his own wishes and her consent, we think it should be restored to the place whence it came.

It is not necessary to decide at present what might have been done if the child had assented, or what the child might do of herself. And from the view we take of the case it is of less consequence to whom the custody is given.

Although, as we have said, the body is not property in the usually recognized sense of the word, yet we may consider it as a sort of quasi property, to which certain persons may have rights, as they have duties to perform towards it arising out of our common humanity. But the person having charge of it cannot be considered as the owner of it in any sense whatever; he holds it only as a sacred trust for the benefit of all who may from family or friendship have an interest in it, and we think that a court of equity may well regulate it as such, and change the custody if improperly managed. So in the case of custody of children, certain persons are prima facie entitled to their custody, yet the court will interfere and regulate it. We think these analogies furnish a rule for such a case, and one which will probably do most complete justice, as the court could always interfere in case of improper conduct, e. g. preventing other relatives from visiting the place for the purpose of indulgence of feeling, or testifying their respect or affection for the deceased.

The complainants further charge that after the body had been surreptitiously disinterred by Mrs. Metcalf, and had been surreptitiously removed by her to the newly prepared grave, the superintendent of the defendant corporation, upon his attention being then for the first time called to the matter while the body was thus exposed, did not direct its immediate reinterment in the lot from which it had been taken, but permitted and allowed it to be interred in the new grave which Mrs. Metcalf had had prepared for it in the lot to which it had been removed; and therefore pray that said corporation may be directed to restore the remains to the lot from which they were removed, and that said Mrs. Metcalf be enjoined from interfering therewith. The defendant cemetery corporation has answered admitting the statements of the bill, and while denying the jurisdiction of the court to direct or control the management of the internal affairs of the corporation, submitting to execute or permit to be executed such decree as the court may make in the premises.

Consent of course cannot give jurisdiction. But we think there is no doubt of the jurisdiction of the court in this case. This corporation holds these lands for certain purposes, and for those only. They have no doubt a certain control over the property, but that control is to be exercised in such manner as to carry out, at least not to interfere with, the legal rights of those who hold burial lots under them. They are in fact trustees for certain purposes, and when the trust is not properly executed, this court has the same jurisdiction to compel its execution as in case of any other trust. ...

❖   ❖   ❖

Lynchburg Cemetery, near Humboldt, Nebraska
Photo by Tanya D. Marsh

CHAPTER 14.3
THOMPSON V. HICKEY
Supreme Court, New York County, New York
8 Abb. N. Cas. 159 (1880)

The evidence clearly enough shows that the conveyance made by the plaintiff to the defendant Hickey, of the burial plot, was intended as security only for the repayment of the moneys loaned; and although it is absolute in form, it was a mortgage security only, which character it has not lost, and as such it must be considered.

The right of the plaintiff as mortgagor could not be divested by the private sale made by Hickey to Farnham, and by the latter to Clark. Neither Hickey nor his immediate grantee could give any better right or interest than they really took. Besides, Clark, when he was asked on the trial as to his knowledge of the original transaction between plaintiff and Hickey, and as to its being a loan of money, replied, "in writing I never heard of it." A fair implication arises from the qualification, that he had otherwise heard of it, and that would be sufficient to put him upon inquiry. Hickey conveyed to Farnham for the nominal consideration of $1, and on the same day Farnham conveyed to Clark for the consideration of $225, but Clark held back part of the price until the bodies of the plaintiff's children should be removed. The whole transaction between Hickey and the other defendants wears a suspicious appearance, which the evidence does not remove, and suggests a plan to deprive the plaintiff of the burial plot unjustly and without notice. But I apprehend that there are sufficient reasons in law and equity to prevent the consummation of the wrong.

The Greenwood Cemetery Association was incorporated for the purpose of establishing a burial ground, and for this purpose it was authorized to acquire a tract of land within the limits of the city of Brooklyn. The corporation was authorized to sell the grounds in lots or plots, to be used exclusively as a place of burial of the dead. There does not appear in the charter of this corporation, in terms, any absolute restraint upon the power of voluntary alienation of a cemetery lot by an owner. Yet I am persuaded that when a person has taken a conveyance of a burial lot, and has made interments therein of the dead of his family, it is in such condition that it cannot be mortgaged to secure the payment of a debt or the return of money borrowed. Such an act is prohibited by the equity and true spirit of the statute. For, observe how careful the legislature has been to secure the sleep of the dead from disturbance. The cemetery itself is exempted from public taxation, and the lots or plots of ground when conveyed are declared to be exempt from assessment, and cannot be sold on execution, or be applied to the payment of debts under any insolvent law. And as no public road, street or avenue shall be laid out or opened over the land, the same would seem to be absolutely secured against invasion. A mortgage, equally with an execution upon a judgment, might in the end expose the lot for sale. And although the letter of the charter under consideration is not so full, yet the legislature has clearly expressed its mind upon this precise subject in the provisions contained in chapter 133 of the Laws of 1847, entitled an act authorizing the incorporation of "rural cemeteries." By section 11 of that act, it is provided that when plots or lots shall be transferred to individual holders, and after there shall have been an interment in a lot or plot so transferred to individual owners, such lot or plot, from the time of such interment, shall be forever thereafter inalienable, and shall, upon the death of the holder or proprietor thereof, descend to the heirs-at-law of such holder or proprietor, and to their heirs-at-law forever; and chapter 310 of the Laws of 1879 declares that it shall not be lawful to mortgage land used for cemetery purposes, or to apply it in payment of debts.

Legislation upon this subject has been in accord with the sentiments of humanity, and with the spirit of our civilization, and has shown a considerate regard for the sanctity of the burial-places of the dead. By the incorporation of cemeteries, and their preservation as such, it has secured an immunity from disturbance for the dead which could not be obtained through burials in church-yards, which were liable to be unsettled by the sale of the church property.

When the case of *Lautz v. Buckingham* was before Mr. Justice BRADY at special term, he distinctly pronounced against the legality of a mortgage executed upon a cemetery lot by the proprietor thereof. He says, "regarding it in the light of a mortgage security, I think it is not to be sustained. It is against good morals, and therefore against the policy of the law, to encourage such instruments." It is true that the judgment of the special term was reversed at the general term. But it is to be borne in mind that in that case no interment had been made in the lot at the time the mortgage was given, and it may be that it might not be considered an offense, either against good morals, public policy, or against the spirit of the statute, to convey or mortgage a cemetery lot before an interment had been actually made therein. For such a sale or conveyance satisfactory reasons might possibly exist. A man might desire to change his lot for one larger or more eligible. I do not regard the act of April 5, 1850, as affecting the question we are now considering. It declares under what circumstances a lot is inalienable. It does not authorize a mortgage or a sale thereunder by implication even.

But that it is an offense against good morals to mortgage a small isolated plot of ground in a cemetery, dedicated exclusively, under the sanctions of the law, as a sanctuary for the dead of one's family, and already consecrated by the ashes of one's kindred, I am sure cannot be well questioned. Such a transaction is clearly a breach of the policy of the statute, is contrary to its equity, and is within the evils it was designed to cure, and our moral nature protests against it. As a consequence of such a transaction, we have here a stranger calling upon a father to disinter his three children, who have been buried for a period of ten years in a cemetery lot, with a threat that if the parent will not, he himself will do it. And suppose he carries his threat into execution, what then? Sepulture must, in the end, be had, and that, it is believed, the statute was intended to secure permanently, against disturbance from any such cause as is indicated by the mortgage in question.

The sentiments and feelings which people in a Christian State have for the dead, the law regards and respects, and however it may have been anterior to our legislation on the subject of cemeteries, the dead themselves now have rights, which are committed to the living to protect, and in doing which they obtain security for the undisturbed rest of their own remains.

In any view which may be taken of this subject I am sure that the defendant should be restrained from interfering with the children's graves. If the conveyance executed by the plaintiff to Hickey, although it be in form absolute, is supposed to confer any present right, it must yield to the easement of the bodies already buried there, which should in no event be disturbed.

But, as has been already decided, the conveyance to Hickey was a mortgage security only, and until the plaintiff's rights have been judicially ended through a proceeding in court his complete possession and control of the lot cannot be interfered with, and for that reason also the threatened acts should be restrained. And a suit in equity is a proper proceeding to secure such restraint.

In *Kurtz v. Beatty* (2 Pet. 566, 584) Judge STORY says: "It is a case where no action at law could afford an adequate and complete remedy. The remedy must be sought, if at all, in the protecting power of a court of chancery, operating, by its injunction, to preserve the repose of the ashes of the dead and the religious sensibility of the living."

Taking up dead bodies from the place where they have been interred, without authority, is a misdemeanor at common law.

But, in addition to relief by injunction, I am of opinion that it should be adjudged, for the reasons above stated, that the transfer made by the plaintiff to Hickey of the cemetery lot, as security for a loan of money, was and is void, and that the subsequent transfers to the other defendants are also void, and that they should severally be delivered up to be canceled, and that the plaintiff's name should be restored to the records of Greenwood Cemetery as the owner of the lot.

The loan of money made by Hickey to the plaintiff, it is urged on behalf of the plaintiff, was usurious and void, but the relief granted is not put upon that ground. And if Hickey or his assigns conclude that they have any legal claim for the recovery of the money loaned they are at liberty to institute and prosecute an action for its recovery, to which the plaintiff, notwithstanding this determination, may interpose any defense he may have.

❖   ❖   ❖

Lafayette Cemetery #1, New Orleans, Louisiana
Photo by Tanya D. Marsh

CHAPTER 14.4

HOWARD COHEN AND OTHERS

V.

CONGREGATION SHEARITH ISRAEL IN THE CITY OF NEW YORK

Supreme Court of New York, Appellate Division, First Department
114 A.D. 117, 99 N.Y.S. 732 (1906)

The plaintiffs are the eight children of Daniel S. and Adela Cohen, deceased, and the defendant is a congregation of the Hebrew faith, incorporated in 1805 under the Religious Incorporation Act of 1784. Adela Cohen died on the 28th of February, 1890, and on the application of her husband Daniel S., permission was granted to, and she was buried in the row in defendant's cemetery at Cypress Hills, for which a nominal charge was made, and the next space in the row reserved for the grave of Daniel, which space remained vacant until after his death, April 3, 1901.

Adela Cohen, during her life, expressed to Daniel and their children her regret that they did not possess a family plot in which they could all be buried, and subsequent to her death Daniel expressed a wish that the whole family, including Adela, should be buried together, and he requested that his children obtain a plot, if possible, for that purpose. Two days before his death, and while he was very ill, his son Howard purchased a lot in Mount Neboh Cemetery, a short distance from the defendant's cemetery, and the plaintiff caused his remains to be interred in that plot. No other interments have there been made, but it was purchased by Howard for the purpose of being used as a family burying plot--his intent being to carry out the wish of his father in that respect. About the time this plot was purchased, and before the death of Daniel, application was made to the defendant for leave to disinter the remains of Adela for the purpose of reinterring them in this plot, but it was refused upon the ground that such disinterment was forbidden by the Jewish law. Subsequently this action was brought to procure a judgment establishing the right of the plaintiffs to disinter the remains of their mother for the purpose of reinterring them in the family plot in Mount Neboh Cemetery and enjoining the defendant from interfering with such disinterment. The issues raised by the pleadings were sent to a referee to hear and determine, and upon his report the plaintiffs had a judgment, from which defendant appeals.

Much evidence was given at the trial bearing upon the question as to whether it was permissible to disinter the remains under the Jewish law—that of the plaintiffs tending to show it was, and that of the defendant that it was not. ... Having found, as a fact, that an expressed intent that a body interred may, perhaps, be removed, entitled the proper parties thereafter to remove it, under the practice adopted by the defendant corporation, and that Daniel S., at the time the remains of Adela were interred, had this intent, was all that was necessary to entitle the plaintiffs, when applying to a court of equity, to the relief asked. Especially is this so when such finding is read in connection with the other facts developed at the trial, and there is no finding that he did not express this intent to the proper authorities of the defendant or the person having charge of the cemetery. The finding that he had this intent, and that Adela had, previous to her death, expressed a wish that all of the family should be buried in one plot, and the unanimous feeling of all the children to the same effect, coupled with the purchase of another lot and the request made of the defendant prior to the death of Daniel, we think would have justified a finding that the interment of Adela was conditional, and, therefore, the disinterment was not contrary to the Jewish law.

The cemetery of the defendant is maintained pursuant to the authority of the laws of this State, and in the absence of a regulation adopted by the defendant as to who shall determine the right of removal, such right must be determined, when presented to a court of equity, upon equitable grounds and not by the Jewish law. Ecclesiastical law is not a part of the law of this State, nor are equitable rights to be determined by it; on the contrary, when a court of equity exercises its powers, it does so only upon equitable principles, irrespective of ecclesiastical or any other law. As was said in *Matter of Donn* (14 N. Y. Supp. 189): 'When an ecclesiastical body assumes jurisdiction and control over a corpse, its acts are of a temporal and juridical character and not in any sense spiritual; and, under our laws and institutions, when it attempts so to do it is acting outside of its proper jurisdiction and domain.'

It may be that if an agreement were made with a cemetery association that remains there interred could not thereafter be disinterred, a court of equity would enforce the agreement; or if a religious corporation had a rule, to which a member subscribed, that if his remains were interred in a cemetery controlled by it they could not thereafter be removed, that a court of equity would refuse to exercise its powers to decree removal. But that is not this case. There was no agreement that the remains of Adela would not, after interment, be disinterred. Nor had she subscribed to any rule of the defendant which prevented such removal, unless that fact be inferred from her membership alone, which is insufficient.

That the court had the power, under the findings of the referee and the facts developed by the evidence, to decree a removal is sustained by numerous authorities.

I am of the opinion that the judgment is right and should be affirmed, with costs.

❖   ❖   ❖

Arlington National Cemetery, Arlington, Virginia
Photo by Tanya D. Marsh

CHAPTER 14.5

YOME V. GORMAN, ET AL.

Court of Appeals of New York, 242 N.Y. 395 (1926)

The controversy has its origin in an attempted disinterment of the bodies of the dead.

John D. Yome and the plaintiff, Anna Yome, his wife, bought an eight-grave plot in Holy Cross Cemetery, Brooklyn. They had buried two infant children in the same cemetery many years before. The approach of old age seems to have warned them of the need of providing a resting place for themselves and for others who were close to them. There is a statement by the plaintiff that the plot was taken with the thought of supplying a place of merely temporary burial. Its size, however, the number of its graves, and the use thereafter made of it, suggest a purpose more enduring. Holy Cross Cemetery is maintained by the Roman Catholic Diocese of Brooklyn. Burial within the cemetery is a privilege reserved to those who have died in communion with the Roman Catholic Church. The certificate of ownership delivered to the purchasers of plots expressly so provides, and provides also that the right of burial shall be subject to the rules and regulations of the Bishop of the Diocese. In the faith of the Church, plaintiff's mother and brother were buried in the plot so purchased. This was done some years ago while Mr. Yome was yet alive. The end came for him in February, 1925. On his deathbed he received the sacraments of his church, and he was laid in his grave in accordance with its rites. A rule of the Church forbids the removal of a body from consecrated ground to ground that is unconsecrated, or consecrated to another faith.

There was swiftly a change of heart. Plaintiff, though baptized a Roman Catholic, became the owner of a plot in a non-Catholic cemetery, where it is now her purpose to be buried. She made demand upon the defendants, the Roman Catholic Diocese and the Supervisor of Cemeteries, for permission to remove the bodies. They refused to yield to the demand on the ground that disinterment for the purpose of removal to a cemetery of another faith would be an act of desecration. Plaintiff, seeking to justify her position, insists that her husband was without devotion to the tenets of the Church, and did not care where he was buried if only he was close to her. Defendants remind us on the other hand that he was reared in the faith of the Church, and died in it, sending for a priest upon his deathbed to gain the privilege of burial in consecrated ground. What the plaintiff says of her husband, she says in substance also of her mother and her brother. The infant children, buried long before, were too young to have religious convictions or wishes of their own. The surviving next of kin support the plaintiff in her request that the bodies be removed.

This action is brought to restrain the defendants from preventing the removal. A temporary injunction to that effect was granted at Special Term. The Appellate Division, affirming the injunction order, has certified an appeal to us. The questions framed are not free from ambiguity. We interpret them as propounding the inquiry whether the privilege of removal is to be accorded as a matter of right. If less than this was meant, an injunction so drastic would not have issued in advance of judgment. The order restrains the defendants from interfering with the removal of the bodies by the plaintiff during the pendency of the action. If it stands, there will be nothing left to try, for the bodies will be removed before the cause is brought to hearing. Such an injunction, if ever permissible in advance of final judgment, is plainly inappropriate unless the undisputed facts are such that a trial is a futility. If there are motives to be probed and opposing equities to be weighed, there must be the searching scrutiny of a trial and the sanction of a judgment.

Upon the record before us, one may draw conflicting inferences of duty and propriety. The wishes of wife and next of kin are not always supreme and final though the body is yet unburied. Still less are they supreme and final when the body has been laid at rest and the aid of equity is invoked to disturb the quiet of the grave. There will then be 'due regard to the interests of the public, the wishes of the decedent, and the rights and feelings of those entitled to be heard by reason of relationship or association.' A benevolent discretion, giving heed to all those promptings and emotions that men and women hold for sacred in the disposition of their dead, must render judgment as it appraises the worth of the competing forces.

To the making of that appraisal many factors will contribute. One may not fix their values in advance, for in so doing one would overlook the varying force of circumstance. One can do little more than offer the suggestion of example. The wish of the deceased, even though legal compulsion may not attach to it, has at least a large significance. Especially is this so when the wish has its origin in intense religious feeling.

Only some rare emergency could move a court of equity to take a body from its grave in consecrated ground and put it in ground unhallowed if there was good reason to suppose that the conscience of the deceased, were he alive, would be outraged by the change. Subordinate in importance, and yet at times not wholly to be disregarded, are the sentiments and usages of the religious body which confers the right of burial. We do not interpret the terms of this certificate of purchase as importing a contract between the cemetery and the owners of the plot that there shall be no disinterment at any time if forbidden by the tenets of the Church or the orders of the Bishop. How far such a contract, if made, would call for enforcement by injunction there is no occasion to determine. Even without contract, sentiments and usages, devoutly held as sacred, may not be flouted for caprice. They must be weighed in the balance with the motives and feelings that sway the acts of the survivors. Removal at the instance of a wife or of kinsmen near in blood to satisfy a longing that those united during life shall not be divided after death may seem praiseworthy and decorous when removal at the instance of distant relatives or strangers would be arbitrary or cruel. The dead are to rest where they have been laid unless reason of substance is brought forward for disturbing their repose.

We have sought, not to declare a rule, but to exemplify a process. The considerations we have instanced and others of like order may move a court of equity to keep a grave inviolate against the will of the survivors. They are none of them so absolute, however, that they may not be neutralized by other. The wish expressed during life may have been declared casually or lightly. The bond of religion may have been weak, and the bond of marriage or of kinship may have been strong. Separation after death from the resting place of wife or child may have seemed an evil more poignant than separation after death from the faithful of the church. We are told by Mrs. Yome that so her husband would have felt. Her statement does not control us. To some extent, though not at all conclusively, it is contradicted by his acts. The trier of the facts must probe his state of mind. With this, when it is ascertained and the intensity of his feelings measured, must be compared the sentiments and wishes of wife and kin surviving. A like process must be followed before the other graves may be disturbed. Right must then be done as right would be conceived of by men of character and feeling.

The order of the Appellate Division and that of the Special Term should be reversed without costs; the first, second, and third questions are not answered since they contain recitals that are inappropriate and to some extent erroneous; and the fourth question, which is construed as an inquiry whether a case for an injunction has been made out as a matter of right upon uncontroverted facts, is answered in the negative.

CRANE, J. I concur. I see no reason why interment may not be a matter of contract. If so, I am of the opinion that a contract was made here which prevents removal contrary to the rules of the Church.

❖ ❖ ❖

CHAPTER 15

DESECRATION

Zentralfriedhof [Central Cemetery], Vienna, Austria
Photo by Tanya D. Marsh

CHAPTER 15.1

DESECRATION

Tanya D. Marsh, THE LAW OF HUMAN REMAINS (2015)

After interment, human remains are considered to become a part of the ground in which they are committed. As Lord Coke and William Blackstone explained, disturbance of desecration of interred human remains would not entitle the heirs to damages. However, the owner of the real estate in which the remains were interred could maintain an action for trespass. In addition to the right to sue for trespass, it was a crime in England to damage any monument or fence in a churchyard, punishable by a fine or imprisonment.

Some U.S. courts have held as a matter of common law that when a grave is disturbed, "the real basis of injury is the violation of the feelings of the living by the indignity to the dead, rather than the invasion of the right of property." *Larson v. Chase*, 50 N.W. 238 (Minn. 1891). Grave desecration can be accomplished through variety of means, including burying strangers in a family plot, unlawful disinterment, vandalism to the tombstone or monument, burial of animals in a cemetery dedicated to humans, drilling oil wells in a cemetery, and plowing over graves. At common law, "the disturbance of a grave is an indictable offense as highly indecent and contrary to good morals." *King v. Elrod*, 268 S.W.2d 103, 105 (Tenn. 1953).

These common law protections of the interred dead, however, are less effective as time passes and the living no longer have any connection to the dead. Many states have therefore adopted statutes that criminalize grave desecration in various ways. For example, in North Carolina, it is a felony to knowingly and willfully, without authorization of law:

(1) Open, disturb, destroy, remove, vandalize or desecrate any casket or other repository of any human remains, by any means including plowing under, tearing up, covering over or otherwise obliterating or removing any grave or any portion thereof.

(2) Take away, disturb, vandalize, destroy, tamper with, or deface any tombstone, headstone, monument, grave marker, grave ornamentation, or grave artifacts erected or placed within any cemetery to designate the place where human remains are interred or to preserve and perpetuate the memory and the name of any person. This subdivision shall not apply to the ordinary maintenance and care of a cemetery.

N.C. Gen. Stat. Ann. § 14-149.

In Kentucky, an individual commits the crime of "violating graves" if he:

(a) Mutilates the graves, monuments, fences, shrubbery, ornaments, grounds, or buildings in or enclosing any cemetery or place of sepulture; or

(b) Violates the grave of any person by destroying, removing, or damaging the headstone or footstone, or the tomb over the enclosure protecting any grave; or

(c) Digs into or plows over or removes any ornament, shrubbery, or flower placed upon any grave or lot.

Ky. Rev. Stat. Ann. § 525.115.

There is no uniform law on this subject and state statutes vary widely, both in terms of the specific behavior that is prohibited, and in the criminal penalties attached to that behavior.

❖ ❖ ❖

Lafayette Cemetery #1, New Orleans, Louisiana
Photo by Tanya D. Marsh

CHAPTER 15.2

DESECRATION OF CEMETERIES

Sidney Perley, MORTUARY LAW (1898)

The last resting places of the dead are regarded in a certain sense as sacred. They are universally considered as being hallowed. No one, other than the owners of the soil and those who have easements or other rights therein, has a right to, or can with impunity, disturb the soil, or anything in it or attached to it. Both the civil and criminal branches of the law, as well as equity, rise to their protection; and even attempts to injure or in any way desecrate such places are punished, and the guilty parties prohibited from carrying out their designs.

The Soil

All suits for the disturbance of the soil can be brought by its general owners. If the soil is that of English churchyards, they must be in the name of the parson, of cemetery associations in their corporate name, of public cemeteries in the name of the town or city owning them, of denominational cemeteries in the name of the church, and of private cemeteries in the names of the owners of them, as the freehold, which is the tenure disturbed, is in these several parties only. An action generally lies in favor of either the owners of the freehold or the owners of the easement of burial, or both, when both have been injured, though it was early held in England that for the disturbance of human remains in churchyards only the parson bad a right of action, the right of the heir of the deceased in the easement apparently being overlooked.

Fixtures.

If gravestones or other things that have been placed on or attached to lots in cemeteries are injured or taken away in the lifetime of the person or persons who erected them, such person or persons must be the plaintiffs in suits for damages therefor at common law; but if those persons have died before the injury is wrought, all subsequent suits must be brought by the heir of the deceased, and not his executor or administrator. The same is true of a bill for an injunction, when injury is threatened; and if it is desired that the injunction should apply to the whole yard, all the parties having such interests must be joined. The reason of these rules is that those who erect monuments, etc., have a greater interest in their preservation than any other person, and this interest the law aims to protect. No one is so likely to care for them after their erectors have passed away as the descendants or heirs of those whose memory they preserve, and to them the law gives the right of action. The fact that the ancestor died intestate makes no difference.

Private Cemeteries

In the case of *Mitchell et al. v. Thorne,* a private burial place on the ancestor's own land, with a right of way thereto, was reserved to him and his heirs forever in a deed of the premises. The defendant, who held the estate under the grantee, proceeded to level off the graves, tear down the headstones, and destroy the enclosing fence, and threatened to continue the desecration. One of the heirs of the deceased original grantor brought suit for damages, and for an injunction restraining the threatened desecration. The court sustained the bill, and held that the fact that whether the ancestor had died testate or intestate had no effect upon the case, and that the fact of intestacy need not be stated in the bill.

Public Cemeteries

In the case of *Commonwealth* v. *Viall,* an ancient burial ground had been pastured by the owner of the fee, and otherwise treated as his own, except that he did not disturb the graves or their fixtures. It was taken by the town as a public cemetery, and subsequently he undertook to cut down some of the trees and cultivate a portion of the ground, but was restrained by the court from further demolition or use as the owner of the title to the soil.

Practice

As the law can give only pecuniary damages for the desecration of a burial place, it is inadequate as a means of protection. The equity court should be sought, and an injunction obtained to stop further desecration without delay. In a civil action brought by an heir for the desecration of a cemetery lot for the recovery of damages, it is not necessary that all other parties having interests similar to that of the plaintiff should join with him, as he can only recover to the extent of his individual damage.

Relatives or friends of the deceased persons buried there may enjoin the owner of the fee of a cemetery from desecrating their graves, or meddling with the monuments, etc., and all parties interested need not be joined as plaintiffs.

The form of the action to be brought at law for damages is trespass, and not case.

Where a cemetery is unnecessarily described, in an indictment for desecrating and disfiguring it, by metes and bounds, with minuteness and particularity, it must be proved exactly as set forth.

❖   ❖   ❖

Metairie Cemetery, Metairie, Louisiana
Photo by Tanya D. Marsh

CHAPTER 15.3

FEDERAL LEGAL PROTECTION FOR CEMETERIES

Ryan M. Seidemann and Rachel L. Moss,

Places Worth Saving: A Legal Guide to the Protection of Historic Cemeteries in Louisiana and Recommendations for Additional Protection, 55 Loy. L. Rev. 449 (2009)

Significant evidence of our shared cultural heritage is fading before our eyes, a victim to development and various forms of destruction. Historic cemeteries are among the many historical and archaeological sites threatened today. The issues facing historical and archaeological sites are a product of poorly understood state law and the virtual absence of federal law protecting historic cemeteries.

Most cultures consider cemeteries sacred spaces. These spaces contain the physical remains of human beings—generally the ancestors of a community—and are held to be inviolate in nature by many. However, the inviolate nature of cemeteries is becoming less paramount in the Western world, and preservation of human remains does not always win out in the "march of progress" when cemeteries are in the way of the living's expansion plans. It is precisely this "march of progress" that now threatens these sacred and historically important sites; the protection of these sites is the subject of this Article.

With the constant growth of Western society, many cemeteries are seen as nothing more than valuable property, wasting away beneath concrete blocks and fading superstitions. Too often, developers resort to demolishing cemeteries altogether or simply removing what they can before they build on top of the remains. Additionally, looters cause other forms of destruction and desecration. Further, even well-intentioned preservationists cause substantial damage to cemeteries because they are unaware of proper conservation methods and lack any regulatory control. On a national level, cemeteries are destroyed due to disrepair and abandonment, when the owners of the land simply overlook the needs of cemeteries and leave them to the hands of time and Mother Nature, resulting in vandalism and erosion.

Although developers, looters, and careless owners are greatly to blame for the problems that our historical cemeteries face, they are not alone. Lawmakers have generally, though likely inadvertently, ignored cemeteries, leaving such sites without adequate protection and regulation to safeguard against destruction. Such protection could come, as it should and occasionally does in Louisiana, in the form of permitting requirements, laws, and other regulations to keep developers at bay and looters away, while giving landowners guidelines to properly restore the history that rests on and under their property. While protection does exist for cemeteries falling into specified categories, many traditional historic cemeteries remain under-protected. Nonetheless, in American culture in general and in Louisiana in particular, there is currently a generally-held sanctity for cemeteries. ...

National Environmental Policy Act

... In a broad sense, the National Environmental Policy Act (NEPA) is the gateway legislation for virtually all federal environmental and historic preservation legislation. The National Historic Preservation Act (NHPA) and other laws like it find their authority through NEPA's required environmental analyses. However, NEPA only applies to federal actions, permits, and expenditures. Thus, if a project only involves state, local, or private actions, and requires only permits or funding, NEPA (and thus, NHPA) does not apply. Regardless, as triggering legislation for NHPA, NEPA does play an important role in cemetery protection at the federal level.

National Historic Preservation Act

In 1966, Congress enacted NHPA to bolster protections of important historic properties. Unfortunately, NHPA, while creating a significant amount of paperwork for federal and state agencies, does little to actually protect historic properties. The reason for this lack of protection largely stems from the following language in Section 106 of the NHPA, which provides:

Prior to the approval of the expenditure of any Federal funds on the undertaking or prior to the issuance of any license, as the case may be, take into account the effect of the undertaking on any district, site, building, structure, or object that is included in or eligible for inclusion in the National Register.

NHPA provides that when federal funding (or via NEPA, federal permitting or actions) is involved in a project, National Register-listed and eligible properties must be "considered" before the project goes forward. There is no requirement that the project be redesigned to ensure the protection of such sites or even to mandate mitigation of such activities' impacts on sites. Admittedly, these protections may be bolstered by federal agencies permitting various activities by mandating mitigation or avoidance as a requirement of another permit, but this leaves the protection of sites in the discretion of the federal government, a potentially disappointing prospect.

In practice, eligible and listed sites are often avoided or mitigated during the course of such projects. However, cemeteries occupy a unique position of disregard under the NHPA, making it more difficult for those interested in protecting them to actually do so. Under the NHPA, "ordinarily cemeteries ... or graves of historical figures ... shall not be considered eligible for the National Register." While discussing numerous arguments for how cemeteries may be considered eligible for National Register listing, Thomas King notes that "if you want a cemetery to be regarded as eligible, you have to be pretty slow to be unable to find a way to make it so." In fact, however, there are very few "traditional" cemeteries listed on the National Register. What, then, is to be done with the isolated, abandoned cemetery that does not gain protection from federal laws? This is where the lacuna exists under the federal law that [state law may address]. In addition to this lacuna, the minimal protections that actually do exist under federal law are not very helpful.

The Native American Graves Protection and Repatriation Act

In 1990, Congress passed the Native American Graves Protection and Repatriation Act (NAGPRA).

NAGPRA sets forth a mechanism for the return and reburial of certain Native American skeletal remains and sacred objects from museum and university collections across the United States, as well as providing for the protection of in situ remains. NAGPRA applies to Native American human remains in two contexts: one, curated remains housed in museums or other institutional collections that receive federal funding and, two, remains found on federal or tribal lands.

As mentioned, NAGPRA applies to Native American remains discovered on federal and tribal lands; it also applies to objects of cultural patrimony discovered on those lands. The Act applies if such remains are found after NAGPRA's enactment date; further, NAGPRA prioritizes the order of such items' right of possession. If lineal descendants can be associated with the items, those individuals hold the primary position of possession. However, where direct lineal descendants cannot be identified, a tripartite scheme of possession determination is employed:

(A) the ownership shall be "in the Indian tribe ... on whose tribal land such objects or remains were discovered;"

(B) the ownership shall be "in the Indian tribe ... which has the closest cultural affiliation with such remains or objects

and which, upon notice, states a claim for such remains or objects; or"

(C) "if the cultural affiliation ... cannot be reasonably ascertained and if the objects were discovered on Federal land that is recognized by a final judgment of the Indian Claims Commission or the United States Court of Claims as the aboriginal land of some Indian tribe," then

(1) the ownership shall be "in the Indian tribe that is recognized as aboriginally occupying the area in which the objects were discovered, if upon such

notice, such tribe states a claim for such remains or objects... ."

(2) ownership shall be "in the Indian tribe that has the strongest demonstrated relationship" if it can be shown "by a preponderance of the evidence that a different tribe has a stronger cultural relationship with the remains or objects... ."

Importantly, these provisions and the means for identifying affiliation only apply to remains or objects discovered after November 16, 1990, and not to remains and objects already curated by that date. Additionally, this scheme does not restrict the excavation of remains or the disturbance of Native American cemeteries after November 16, 1990; it just sets in place a mechanism for determining who ultimately controls the remains. Finally, for remains that are not claimed by a group identified under *25 U.S.C. § 3002,* NAGPRA provides no guidance as to disposition.

The Archaeological Resources Protection Act of 1979 (ARPA)

The stated purpose of ARPA is, in pertinent part, to "secure ... the protection of archaeological resources and sites which are on public lands... ." Many cemeteries are also considered to be archaeological sites to which ARPA would apply. ARPA is intended to protect against one thing: pothunting. Congress has identified the threats to such archaeological materials and sites as "their commercial attractiveness" and inadequate protection from destruction due to "uncontrolled excavations and pillage." Thus, although this law may provide some protection for certain cemeteries, its main aim was not to protect cemeteries.

The regulations promulgated under ARPA require that activities impacting archaeological sites on federal lands are undertaken pursuant to a permit process. The regulations for ARPA are limited, however, in their potential application to historic cemeteries: the archaeological site to be protected must be older than 100 years in order to trigger ARPA. Although this stipulation will likely catch many historic cemetery sites, it is possible that some such cemeteries are less than 100 years old or that portions of older cemeteries are not yet 100 years old, thus calling into question the applicability of ARPA to the entire site. Nonetheless, what protections may exist under ARPA are subject to the federal government permitting and do not necessitate further discussion here.

Section 4(f)

In addition to NEPA and the NHPA, Congress has enacted special preservation legislation for situations when federal road construction is involved. Known as "Section 4(f)," the parks and historic preservation provisions of the Federal-Aid Highways Act has been famously used to prevent the federal government from developing a highway through a beloved Memphis park. However, no reported case exists on the effectiveness of this Act in cemetery preservation. Despite this lack of a judicial test, the plain language of Section 4(f), codified at *23 U.S.C. 138,* does provide some hope that cemeteries may be protected from federal projects by the law, to wit:

> ... the Secretary [of the U.S. Department of Transportation] shall not approve
> any program or project ... which requires the use of any publicly owned land
> from a public park, recreation area, or wildlife and waterfowl refuge of national,

State, or local significance as determined by the Federal, State, or local officials having jurisdiction thereof, or any land from an historic site of national, State, or local significance as so determined by such officials unless (1) there is no feasible and prudent alternative to the use of such land, and (2) such program includes all possible planning to minimize harm to such park, recreational area, wildlife and waterfowl refuge, or historic site resulting from such use.

As noted by Olesh, Section 4(f), as enacted, provides a strong mandate to the federal government to minimize impacts to historic sites (which presumably would include cemeteries). Indeed, Yahr notes that Section 4(f) is even more useful in the preservation of historic sites than NEPA, because:

While NEPA dictates the procedure for federally funded construction projects affecting public resources, section 4(f) is substantive. It provides the Secretary of Transportation with explicit instruction of what considerations to make when the projected impacts use certain public resources. If a project fails to meet section 4(f)'s requirements, it is ineligible to receive federal funding.

Unfortunately, Section 4(f) is of limited utility for cemetery protection and preservation. As Olesh correctly notes, the courts and the federal agencies have undermined and weakened the strong language of Section 4(f). Further complicating the utility of Section 4(f) for cemetery preservation is the reality that it only applies to federal road projects. Thus, state and local projects do not trigger the protections of Section 4(f), nor do the emerging threats from private development.

❖   ❖   ❖

Glasnevin Cemetery, Dublin, Ireland
Photo by Tanya D. Marsh

CHAPTER 15.4

MICHELS V. CROUCH

Court of Civil Appeals of Texas, Eastland, 122 S.W.2d 211 (1938)

GRISSOM, Justice.

Lige Crouch sued Henry M. Michels for damages alleged to have been caused by the desecration of the graves of his children. Plaintiff's petition contained allegations that his two children were buried in a public cemetery known as the "old Goree Cemetery." Plaintiff's petition further contained allegations describing the place of burial of his children, alleging that the spot for more than thirty years had been segregated from other lands by substantial fences and the graves therein marked, and that the place described had, for such length of time, been recognized and cared for as the last resting place of departed members of plaintiff's family, and other citizens of the community, and sufficiently alleged facts showing the designation of the spot and its continued existence as a cemetery. Plaintiff further alleged: "That although said cemetery, graveyard and burial ground was segregated, designated and set apart from surrounding lands the defendant on or about the 15th day of January, 1937, unlawfully entered into and upon said sacred enclosure and burial place and unlawfully, wrongfully, wickedly, wantonly and maliciously and with a heart bent on mischief and in total disregard of either legal or moral duty to his fellowman or to society, broke, tore down and removed the fences surrounding the said cemetery, graveyard and burial ground and caused the fences around the same to be torn down and removed and thereby permitted and allowed a large number of cattle which defendant was then pasturing for other persons for hire, to graze in and upon and over the graves of the departed children of this plaintiff and other persons who were buried in said cemetery and burial ground and to trample upon, obliterate and destroy the markings of the last resting places of the loved ones of these plaintiffs *and said defendant further wrongfully, illegally, wickedly, wantonly, and maliciously caused his agents and employees to plow into, over and across the said cemetery, graveyard and burial ground and into, over and across the graves of the departed loved [ones] of these plaintiffs in total disregard of the rights of these plaintiffs and thereby caused these plaintiffs to suffer great and agonizing mental pain and anguish,* all to plaintiff's damage in the sum of Twenty Five Thousand Dollars for which plaintiffs sue herein." [Italics added.] …

We think it evident that the allegations in plaintiff's petition show the suit to be one for willful trespass, for which plaintiff claims damages (1) for mental anguish, and (2) exemplary damages. The petition contains no allegation of actual damage, other than for mental anguish, and is not a suit for damages based on negligence.

In answer to special issues submitted to it the jury found, in substance: "(1) That Henry J. Michels plowed across the unmarked grave of plaintiff's child. (2) That in doing so, he was the agent, servant, or employee of the defendant and acting within the scope or apparent scope of his authority. (3) That said act was the willful act of Henry J. Michels. (4) That Henry J. Michels struck the tombstone of the grave of the plaintiff's child. (5) That in doing so he was acting within the scope or apparent scope of his authority as agent, servant, or employee of the defendant. (6) That the above act was negligence. (7) That the above negligent act was the proximate cause of the injury to the tombstone. (8) That Henry M. Michels tore down the fence enclosing the cemetery. (9) That the taking down of the fence was negligence. (10) That the negligence in taking down the fence was the proximate cause of the injury to the tombstone. (11) That the negligence in taking down the fence was the proximate cause of the injury to the unmarked grave. (12) That ten dollars would reasonably compensate Lige Crouch for the injury to the tombstone. (13) That $5,000 would reasonably compensate Lige Crouch for the damages caused by plowing over the unmarked grave, as a direct result of the willful act of Henry M. Michels, his agents, servants, or employees, including mental pain and anguish. (14) That the agents, servants, or employees of the defendant were guilty of gross negligence in injuring the tombstone. (15) That Henry M. Michels, the defendant, was guilty of gross negligence in tearing down and removing all or any portion of the fence. (16) That $2,500 should be allowed as exemplary damages for the gross negligence and willful acts of the defendant."

Judgment was entered for plaintiff for $7,510 and defendant appealed.

In support of our conclusion that plaintiff's petition discloses an action for a willful trespass, but is insufficient to authorize recovery for damages resulting from defendant's negligence we call attention to the following authorities: "For the purpose of determining the relationship of the subject in hand to other branches of the law, it may be observed at the outset that 'negligence' cases are those which involve liability for injury to person or property, the injury not having been the consequence of conduct which was premeditated, or accompanied by the intention or volition of the actor. If the injury or damage is shown to have been the … intended result of the wrongdoer's act, the legal situation is described in the terminology of the common law by the words 'assault,' 'defamation', 'nuisance', 'trespass', and many others." 30 Tex.Jur. 647.

Trespass is a willful or intentional wrong, and liability therefor is not dependent upon negligence. Where the suit is for damages resulting from a willful trespass only, it is erroneous to submit to the jury the question of a defendant's negligence. A judgment based on findings of negligence is not supported by mere allegations of a willful trespass.

It is fundamental that a plaintiff must recover, if at all, upon the cause of action alleged. The case, at least in so far as it was submitted to the jury on the issues of negligence and the judgment based on findings of negligence, was tried upon a wrong theory, and must be reversed. Plaintiff, of course, recognizes the rules that a plaintiff must recover on the cause of action alleged, and that the allegations and proof must correspond, but contends that his pleadings are sufficient to state a cause of action for either negligence or willful trespass. We think that neither the legal conclusion that defendant was negligent in the matters complained of, or that his negligence was the proximate cause of plaintiff's injury, nor facts from which such conclusions may reasonably be drawn are contained in the petition.

The evidence disclosed that more than forty years prior to the trial of this case a man by the name of Dick Keys died and was buried on a hill west of Goree, Texas. The owner of the land on which he was buried offered to give 2 1/2 acres of land out of a different portion of the tract for use as a cemetery if the relatives of the deceased would remove his remains to the designated spot. Apparently this was done. Dr. Smith, owner of the tract adjoining that designated by Mr. Parks, who gave the first 2 1/2 acres for such purpose, donated an equal amount of land for the purpose of establishing a community burial ground. Thereafter the tract was fenced. About ten white persons were buried there, and monuments and markers erected. No white person has been buried there for many years. On one side of this cemetery negroes were buried, and continued to be buried there occasionally up to the year of the trial of this case. The evidence is sufficient to show a designation of a tract for a cemetery and its continued existence as such. The fact that the remains of the dead buried there have not been disinterred, and that tombstones still mark the places of their burial, although the grounds may not have been cared for, is sufficient alone to show that there has been no abandonment of the tract as a cemetery.

Though defendant purchased the land on which the cemetery was located, without reservation of such tract as a cemetery shown in either his deed or chain of title, nevertheless the physical presence there of the fence, tombstones and graves, was adequate notice of the use of the spot, and, so acquiring title, defendant obtained no right to use the burial ground in any manner inconsistent with or inappropriate to the designation and use of it as a cemetery.

Viewing the evidence, as we must, in the light most favorable to plaintiff, we find the following additional facts disclosed by the evidence: The cemetery was located on land which defendant owned in 1936. According to the testimony of defendant and his son they entered into a contract in December, 1936, for the sale of the land on which the cemetery was located by the father to the son. They testified, in effect, that the son, Henry J. Michels, took exclusive possession and control of this land about January 1, 1937, prior to the alleged desecration of the graves. This testimony is disputed only by proof of the fact that defendant removed some of the fence surrounding the cemetery in the early part of 1937, and, perhaps by inconsistencies in their testimony relative to the asserted sale. Defendant's deed conveying the land to his son was not actually delivered and the cash consideration paid, according to their testimony, until May, 1937. There is much conflict in the testimony as to the actual condition of the fence, or portion thereof, removed by the defendant. The most that can be said is that there was a fence surrounding all, or a major portion of the cemetery. That it was dilapidated; that most of it had fallen to the ground, and it was of little practical value, except to mark the boundaries of the cemetery plot. Under the facts disclosed by the entire record since the fence was insufficient to protect the cemetery from the invasion of livestock, but, if it were sufficient for such purpose, since it was not proved that livestock entered the cemetery after the removal of the fence by defendant (although the proof shows that they did prior to its removal), we think the removal of such cemetery fence under the circumstances disclosed, taken alone, would not authorize a recovery, if any, of more than nominal damages. True, the record shows that the cemetery grounds were entered and the land between the burial places of the white and negro people plowed. No connection is shown between the removal of the fence and the plowing and damage to the tombstone. It is not shown that the removal of the fence by defendant was in furtherance of a plan for the plowing; the evidence is that Henry J. Michels did not know that defendant removed the fence. It is further shown by the record that the land was plowed close to the grave of one of plaintiff's children, and there was evidence that such tombstone was struck and tilted to an angle of 45 degrees; that the unmarked grave of another of plaintiff's children, immediately south of the grave marked by the tombstone had a furrow plowed down the center of the grave. All the evidence with reference to anyone plowing in the cemetery is that it was done by Henry J. Michels, defendant's son, about 36 years of age, who says he owned the land at the time he plowed there, and had exclusive control thereof. Perhaps the circumstances are sufficient to justify the conclusion, or inference, that Henry J. Michels, while plowing in the cemetery, which act he admits, struck and damaged the tombstone, and plowed a furrow down the middle of the unmarked grave. If so, we find no evidence that at the time Henry J. Michels did such things, if he did, that he was an agent, employee or servant of Henry M. Michels, or was "caused" by Henry M. Michels to do such things. Having so concluded, after a painstaking study of the record, it naturally results that we find as to the acts proved, other than the removal of the fence, a willful trespass by defendant was not shown. The jury in answer to special issue No. 14 found that $5,000 would compensate plaintiff for mental anguish suffered by him "as a direct result of the willful act of Henry M. Michels, his agents, servants, or employees ... *for damages caused by plowing over the unmarked grave.*" [Italics added] The award of $5,000 was restricted solely to one act, that is, "plowing over the unmarked grave." There is no evidence that defendant plowed over the grave. The evidence shows that Henry J. Michels plowed in the cemetery. If the evidence is sufficient to justify the conclusion that defendant's son plowed over the grave, still it is insufficient to show that at such time he was acting as the servant, agent or employee of the defendant, or was "caused" by the defendant to plow over the unmarked grave. The same issue, based on defendant's negligence, was submitted to the jury by special issue No. 13. It was not answered.

Appellant contends that the judgment for $5,000 for mental anguish resulting solely from plowing a furrow across the unmarked grave is excessive. Many facts and authorities are cited by defendant lending support to that contention, notwithstanding the fact that juries are allowed much latitude in cases of mental anguish. But, since defendant's liability for the act for which $5,000 was awarded plaintiff as compensation for mental anguish cannot, for other reasons, be sustained, we think it is unnecessary to pass upon that question.

The jury found and the judgment awarded plaintiff $2500 as exemplary damages. The reason therefor is readily apparent when defendant's testimony is read. The defendant testified:

"Q. Now, Mr. Michels, when you tore the fence down on the east side of that grave yard you didn't care who had people buried there, did you? A. Well, I didn't have anything to do with it.

"Q. With taking the fence down? A. No, with the people that is buried there.

"Q. You didn't care about the people that was buried there, did you? A. No, why should I. * * *

"Q. But you didn't care what happened to them, did you? A. No, why should I be responsible."

Because, under our view and understanding of the case, the judgment for actual damages cannot be sustained we find it necessary for that reason to reverse the judgment in so far as a recovery of exemplary damages is awarded.

The answer of the jury to special issue No. 12, fixed the amount of damage to the tombstone at $10 and found such damage to be "a direct result of the *negligence*" of defendant, his agents, servants or employees. There were no allegations of damage to a tombstone. The finding that the damage to the tombstone resulted from the negligence of defendant, his agents, servants or employees, we think, is not sustained by either pleading or proof.

Plaintiff attempted to prove a willful trespass by defendant causing actual injury and damage to plaintiff's property and mental anguish. Actual damages resulting from mental anguish may be recovered, as a separate or independent element, when caused by a willful trespass in which actual damage to plaintiff's property is sustained. But only such damages caused by mental anguish are recoverable as results directly and proximately from such trespass.

For the reasons stated the judgment of the district court is reversed, but it appearing that the cause, in part, was submitted upon a wrong theory; it not appearing that the case has been fully developed; and it appearing that justice will best be served by a remand of the cause, the judgment will not be rendered.

The judgment is reversed and the cause remanded.

❖ ❖ ❖

Lafayette Cemetery #1, New Orleans, Louisiana
Photo by Tanya D. Marsh

CHAPTER 15.5

R.B. TYLER COMPANY V. KINSER

Court of Appeals of Kentucky, 346 S.W.2d 306 (1961)

STANLEY, Commissioner.

The children and a grandchild of Mrs. Maggie Edwards, deceased, recovered a judgment of $3,000 against the appellant, R. B. Tyler Company, for desecration of her grave.

Mrs. Edwards was buried in 1944 in St. Stephens cemetery in Louisville close to a fence line in the back part of the cemetery. Her grave was then, and continued to be, marked by a temporary iron stake and a plastic card. In constructing the North and South Expressway along the edge of the cemetery, the appellant, the contractor, had sheet piling driven at the boundary line. There was some slipping of the earth, and a crack or large hole was caused at the place where Mrs. Edwards was buried. A large quantity of dirt and debris were thrown on and over her burial place and destroyed the grave marker. Several pictures made at the time graphically show the obliteration of the grave and despoiling of the burial lot. The caretaker of the cemetery did not believe the body had been moved except perhaps several inches with the entire ground.

A low retaining wall with a wire fence on it was placed on the boundary line after the completion of the new highway, and the surface inside was graded. The burial plot was put in a better and cleaner condition than it was before. But the grave cannot be exactly located. By reference to the cemetery plat the location can be done only with approximation. There is no dispute about the essential facts.

The daughter and son testified to their great devotion and frequent visits and tender care of their mother's grave and to their emotional distress over its condition during the construction work and over their present inability to locate her burial spot exactly.

The instructions authorized a verdict for the plaintiffs upon the jury's belief that there was damage or interference with the grave and obliteration of the marker thereon caused by the defendant's employees if their acts were malicious or grossly negligent or wantonly done. The jury was further instructed that the plaintiffs were not entitled to recover for any damage caused by cracks or openings in the ground or throwing of dirt upon the grave if they further believed that the openings or cracks or damage to the surface had been remedied by the defendant. The terms 'malicious,' 'grossly negligent' and 'wantonly' were defined in the usual way.

The appellant contends the court should have instructed the jury that 'unless the jury believe from the evidence that the coffin or the body of Maggie Edwards was exposed to view or was removed from its burial place in St. Stephens cemetery or there was physical injury done to her remains and that said acts were done either (a) maliciously, (b) by gross negligence, or (c) wantonly, i.e., with a reckless disregard for the rights of another, then the law is for Tyler and the jury should so find.' Another instruction offered and refused was to find for the defendant if Mrs. Edwards' remains and their container were uninterrupted and undisturbed and sustained no hurt or injury.

The instructions were properly refused. There was no evidence upon which they could have been based, and the submitted law was too restricted or limited as to the basis of liability for damages.

… [T]he right of next of kin to recover damages for the desecration of a grave is generally recognized as being for a common law tort. It is based upon the reality of an intrusion into tender feelings. The resting places of the dead have been revered and regarded as hallowed ground from the earliest days.

It is the law of this jurisdiction that next of kin have a right to recover damages for mental anguish for 'unwarranted interference with the grave of a deceased person' as well as for an act which affected the body interred therein if either act was done maliciously or wantonly or by gross negligence.

In the instant case there was a violation of the grave not materially different from the desecration in *Codell Construction Co. v. Miller, supra*, by dynamite blasts set off in the course of highway construction along a graveyard.

We may add that in this connection malice is imputed where the wrongful act evidenced the entire want of care or great indifference to the consequences and the rights of others.

The judgment is affirmed.

❖ ❖ ❖

King's Chapel Burying Ground, Boston, Massachusetts
Photo by Tanya D. Marsh

CHAPTER 15.6

RHODES MUTUAL LIFE INSURANCE COMPANY, INC. V. MOORE

Supreme Court of Alabama, 586 So.2d 866 (1991)

Rhodes Mutual Life Insurance Company, Inc. ("Rhodes"), appeals from the judgment entered on a $75,000 jury verdict in favor of Robert Moore and George Moore, Jr., in this action to recover damages for the negligent desecration of a grave. We affirm.

Robert Moore and George Moore, Jr., are the great-grandson and the great-great-grandson, respectively, of the late Bob Moore, who died in 1975 and was buried at St. Austin's Cemetery in Mobile. Rhodes was the owner of the cemetery at the time of the incident made the basis of this action. George Moore, Sr., who is the brother of Robert Moore and the father of George Moore, Jr., chose not to participate in this action, and, although he was present during the trial of the case, he was never made a party.

The material evidence, viewed in the light most favorable to the plaintiffs, as our standard of review requires us to view it, *Deupree v. Butner,* 522 So.2d 242 (Ala.1988), is aptly summarized in the plaintiff's brief:

> "On Easter Sunday of 1987, George Moore Jr., went to St. Austin's to visit the grave of his great, great grandfather. He was accompanied by ... Mr. Charles Davis. George Moore Jr., was raised in the same house with his great, great grandfather and consequently was very close to him. On this occasion, George Moore Jr., and Charles Davis went to the grave of the late Bob Moore

and attempted to pull some weeds that had grown up around the headstone. George Moore described the headstone as being a vertical headstone placed on the ground that stood about eighteen inches high. He further stated that the family, including himself and Robert Moore, all contributed to the initial cost of the headstone.

"Mr. George Moore went on to say that he had the opportunity to return to the cemetery on Mother's Day, approximately two weeks later. His uncle, Robert Moore, accompanied him. At one point, the men went to the site where the late Bob Moore's grave and headstone had been two weeks prior, however, it was nowhere to be found, and instead, two fresh graves were in its place. The cemetery owner/Rhodes Life Insurance [was] contacted and a search for the grave site and headstone was conducted, but no traces were found. The search was visual only, as the Defendant kept no records of the location of any particular individuals.

"The only individual having any knowledge of grave locations was a gravedigger named Lyles. Neither he nor anyone else was able to locate Mr. Bob Moore's grave site. Mr. Ronald Ali, the vice president of Rhodes Life Insurance, when asked if he thought it was a prudent practice to run a cemetery without keeping records of where the people are buried, answered that 'he didn't think so.' The only person who claimed to know where Mr. Bob Moore was buried was Mrs. Lillian Lovett, a one-time owner of the cemetery. She stated on direct exam that Mr. Bob Moore was buried next to a Mr. Woodrow Jones. A cross-examination of Mrs. Lovett revealed that she was unclear as to why she happened to be able to remember where Mr. Bob Moore was buried, and further revealed that she could not remember the names of anyone else buried in the alleged vicinity of Mr. Bob Moore's grave site. To this date, the Defendant cannot tell the Plaintiffs where the grave or headstone of Bob Moore is located."

Rhodes contends that the trial court erred in denying its motion for a judgment notwithstanding the verdict or, in the alternative, a new trial. It argues (1) that because George Moore, Sr., was alive at the time this action was filed, George Moore, Jr., had no standing to prosecute an action for damages; (2) that George Moore, Sr., who, as previously noted, was not made a party to this action, was an indispensable party under Rule 19, Ala.R.Civ.P.; and (3) that the evidence was insufficient to warrant submitting the negligence claim to the jury.

The plaintiffs argue (1) that George Moore, Jr., had standing to join in this action because of his close relationship to the deceased; (2) that the trial court did not err in determining that George Moore, Sr., was not an indispensable party under Rule 19; and (3) that the evidence was sufficient to create a fact question as to whether Rhodes had negligently caused the desecration of Bob Moore's grave. We agree.

In *Hogan v. Woodward Iron Co.*, 263 Ala. 513, 83 So.2d 248 (1955), this Court held that the deceased's daughter could not prosecute an action for damages allegedly resulting from the desecration of the deceased's grave, where the widow was still alive. The following rule was stated:

"Upon thorough examination of our decisions concerning interference with burial sites, we note that in every case before us the proper parties plaintiff have been the surviving spouse or the next of kin, in order (or the question of proper parties was not raised). ... From the foregoing cases and from our consideration of the ties that bind the survivors to the deceased, we conclude the rule applicable to parties plaintiff in a case of this kind to be: In the event of damage to the grave of a deceased person, the right of action, if any, accrues first to the surviving spouse unless, of course, there are special circumstances, such as a failure of the surviving spouse to act, or the couple was separated at the time of death and an heir or next of kin had the deceased interred. If there is no surviving spouse, the right is in the next of kin in the order of their relation to the deceased. The logic of this rule is well stated in a similar New York case wherein the Court of Appeals, through Chief [Judge] Pound, held:

" 'As to the son's case, we conceive the rule to be that the surviving spouse whose duty it is to bury the deceased has the sole right to sue, during his or her lifetime, for damages due to interference with the dead body. To such a one is intrusted the duty to guard the dead. True it may be that he may neglect to exercise such right. Others may then act. Possibly the surviving members of the deceased's family might join as plaintiffs, but it is inconceivable that each member of the family could maintain a separate action to recover for mental pain and anguish. In the multitude of such actions there is injustice. The son, therefore, had no cause of action. The complaint was properly dismissed. Const. art. VI, § 8.'

"This rule also prevails in Kentucky." ... "The rule above stated is consonant with this court's expressions as to the right of action for unlawful interference with the burial of deceased relatives." 263 Ala. at 515, 83 So.2d at 249.

The rule stated in *Hogan* clearly contemplates that when there is no surviving spouse, as in this case, the right to bring an action for the desecration of a grave vests in the next of kin in the order of their relation to the deceased; and that all individuals occupying the same degree of kin should join in the action so as not to subject the defendant to the risk of a multitude of different actions. However, we do not think that this rule should be applied so narrowly as to automatically preclude a more distant relative of the deceased, who had had a very close and intimate relationship with the deceased, from joining in an action with a member of the deceased's family closer in relation to the deceased. In *Levite Undertakers Co. v. Griggs*, 495 So.2d 63, 65 (Ala.1986), this Court, rejecting the defendants' contention that only the closest living relative could maintain an action for the wrongful detention of remains, noted that the plaintiffs (the widow and two children) were not fighting among themselves for possession of the remains, but, instead, stood "united against their common antagonists—each equally suffering injury under their hands." We note that other courts have also recognized that the rule of priority enunciated in *Hogan* should be applied with reason. Those courts have stressed that the particular circumstances of the case should be examined to see whether there had been a special intimacy or association between the plaintiff and the defendant. ...

We hold that under the facts of this case, the trial court did not err in allowing George Moore, Jr., to join his uncle in this action. The amount of damages (i.e., for mental suffering and distress) actually suffered by George Moore, Jr., was a question for the jury. ...

For the foregoing reasons, the judgment is affirmed.

❖　❖　❖

Salem Cemetery, Winston-Salem, North Carolina
Photo by Tanya D. Marsh

CHAPTER 15.7

CORA PHILLIPS HAIRSTON, ET AL.

V.

GENERAL PIPELINE CONSTRUCTION, INC., ET AL.

V.

MOUNTAIN STATE INSURANCE COMPANY

Supreme Court of Appeals of West Virginia, 226 W.Va. 663 (2010)

McHUGH, Justice:

This matter comes before this Court upon a request from the Circuit Court of Logan County to answer five certified questions regarding the law of grave desecration in West Virginia and the effect of West Virginia Code § 29--1–8a (1993) on the common law of grave desecration. Upon thorough review of the briefs, arguments, record, and applicable precedent, this Court answers the certified questions, as reformulated, and remands this matter for further proceedings consistent with this opinion.

I. Factual and Procedural History

In the action underlying these certified questions, Equitable Production Company (hereinafter "Equitable") hired General Pipeline Company (hereinafter "General Pipeline") in 2004 to relocate a gas pipeline on a large tract of wooded, unimproved land in Crystal Block Hollow in Logan County, West Virginia. At several different locations along the pipeline, General Pipeline used a small bulldozer to pull a truck loaded with pipe through wooded sections to the pipeline. On August 7, 2004, at the location which has become the subject of the underlying litigation, the bulldozer was driven, with its blade raised off the ground, through an area containing grave sites. This wooded area contained graves that allegedly were not indicated on any map, reserved or otherwise identified in a deed, identified by any obvious sign, included on a list of grave sites maintained by any State agency, or otherwise reasonably identifiable as an area containing graves. The defendants contend that the area was significantly overgrown with vegetation and contained mostly unmarked grave sites. Some actual grave markers were buried in forest debris. When the operator of the bulldozer realized that the bulldozer had passed through the grave site area, he immediately blocked off the area and relocated the route to connect with the pipeline at a different location.

The fifteen plaintiffs, as relatives of the decedents buried in the graves, filed complaints in the Circuit Court of Logan County, seeking recovery of damages for grave desecration. General Pipeline and Equitable were the original defendants in this litigation, and General Pipeline later filed a third-party complaint against Mountain State Insurance Agency, Inc., asserting a claim of negligence in the procurement of General Pipeline's insurance policy. Subsequent to the exchange of written discovery, General Pipeline filed a Motion for Summary Judgment. Based upon the issues raised in the litigation, the lower court entered an order on November 16, 2009, certifying the following five questions to this Court.

1. *Does W.Va.Code § 29-1-8a preempt a common law cause of action for direct or indirect desecration of a grave?*

Answer of the lower court: Yes, except as to claims for the desecration of graves and related items in a publicly or privately maintained cemetery or of graves less than fifty years old.

2. *What are the elements of a common law action for desecration of a grave, grave site, cemetery or burial ground?*

Answer of the lower court: The elements of a common law cause of action for the desecration of a grave in a publicly or privately maintained cemetery are:

> 1. that it is shown that a cemetery, with identifiable boundaries and limits, exists at the place alleged;
>
> 2. that it is shown that the area was dedicated to the purpose of providing a place of burial by the owner of the property or that the owner acquiesced in its use for burial;
>
> 3. that it is shown that the area was identifiable as a cemetery by its appearance prior to the defendant's entry onto the area or it is shown that the defendant had prior knowledge of the existence of the cemetery;
>
> 4. that it is shown that the decedent in question is interred in the area;
>
> 5. that it is shown that the decedent in question was interred by license or right;
>
> 6. that it is shown that the plaintiff is the next of kin of the decedent in question with the right to assert a claim for desecration;
>
> 7. that it is shown that the person charged with the desecration defaced, damaged or

otherwise mistreated the physical area or the contents of the cemetery in a way that a reasonable person knows will outrage the sensibilities of others.

3. *What are the recoverable damages in a common law action for desecration of a grave, grave site, cemetery or burial ground?*

Answer of the lower court: Nominal damages at least, are awardable, and compensatory damages may be recovered if actual damage is shown; damages for mental distress may be awarded; and punitive damages may be awarded if a plaintiff can prove that the defendants' conduct was willful, wanton, reckless or malicious.

4. *Does West Virginia recognize a common law cause of action for indirect desecration of a grave, grave site, cemetery or burial ground? If so, what are the elements of such a cause of action and what are the recoverable damages?*

Answer of the lower court: A cause of action for the indirect desecration of a grave site located in a publicly or privately maintained cemetery is permitted in West Virginia. The elements of such a cause of action are the same as those identified in the Answer to Question 2, above, plus: It must be shown that the indirect desecration has, in some manner, affected the specific grave site made the subject of the claim in such a manner as to outrage the sensibilities of others.

5. *Who are the "next of kin" who possess the right to recover in a common law cause of action for direct or indirect desecration of a grave?*

Answer of the lower court: The decedent's surviving spouse or, if not now living, then the now living person or persons of closest and equal degree of kinship in the order provided by West Virginia Code § 42–1–1, et seq.

By order entered March 30, 2010, this Court accepted the certified questions for review. …

III. Discussion

… In order to clearly address the legal issues of statutory preemption and common law cause of action presented herein, this Court finds it necessary to reformulate the questions as follows:

1. Does West Virginia Code § 29–1–8a preempt a common law cause of action for direct or indirect desecration of a grave?

2. Does a common law cause of action for direct and/or indirect grave desecration exist, and, if so, what are the elements of such actions and the damages recoverable?

3. Who are the "next of kin" who possess the right to recover in a common law cause of action for grave desecration?

A. Statutory Preemption of State Common Law

West Virginia Code § 29–1–8a (1993), enacted within legislation regarding the administration of the Division of Culture and History, recognizes "a real and growing threat to the safety and sanctity of unmarked human graves in West Virginia..." The statute specifies that "the existing laws of the state do not provide equal or adequate protection for all such graves" and observes as follows: "As evident by the numerous incidents in West Virginia which have resulted in the desecration of human remains and vandalism to grave markers, there is an immediate need to protect the graves of earlier West Virginians from such desecration."

The legislature provided that the statute was "not intended to interfere with the normal activities of private property owners, farmers, or those engaged in the development, mining or improvement of real property." The prohibitions provided by the statute include, in pertinent part, as follows:

No person may excavate, remove, destroy, or otherwise disturb any historic or prehistoric ruins, burial grounds, archaeological site, or human skeletal remains, unmarked grave, grave artifact or grave marker of historical significance unless such person has a valid permit issued to him or her by the Director of the Historic Preservation Section...

Of the various definitions provided by the statute, it is necessary to recognize particular attributes which provide the essential framework for an understanding of the scope of the statute. For instance, the definition of an "unmarked grave" is limited and is specified as "any grave or location where a human body or bodies have been buried or deposited *for at least fifty years and the grave or location is not in a publicly or privately maintained cemetery or in the care of a cemetery association, or is located within such cemetery or in such care and is not commonly marked* [.]" Likewise, the definition of "disturb" is listed as "excavating, removing, exposing, defacing, mutilating, destroying, molesting, or desecrating in any way of human skeletal remains, unmarked graves, grave artifacts or grave markers[.]

The statute also provides certain other penalties for violation...

This Court's review of the statute discloses a clear legislative intent to preempt common law desecration claims with respect to the narrowly-defined matters identified and covered by the statutory protection. The statutory language, as referenced above, specifically states the legislature's intention, as follows: "The Legislature finds that there is a real and growing threat to the safety and sanctity of unmarked human graves in West Virginia and the existing laws of the State do not provide equal or adequate protection for all such graves." ...

The particularized statement of purpose adequately indicates the legislature's intentions, and this Court holds that West Virginia Code § 29–1–8a preempts common law with respect to the matters specifically addressed in the statute. The statute preempts all common law claims involving "historic or prehistoric ruins, burial grounds, archaeological site, or human skeletal remains, unmarked grave, grave artifact or grave marker of historical significance." The statute clearly provides that any unmarked grave, defined as a grave over fifty years old *not* in a publicly or privately maintained cemetery *or* a "not commonly marked" grave over fifty years old in a maintained cemetery, will be encompassed within the statutory coverage. Grave markers are included in the statutory protection only if they are "of historical significance."

The preemptive effect of the statute applies only to the narrowly-defined categories of graves and other related items that the statute delineates. Thus, common law is not preempted by the statute where the legislature has not specified statutory protection in West Virginia Code § 29–1–8a. Common law civil remedies remain available in grave desecration cases where the grave is not subject to this statutory protection. Criminal penalties are also available under West Virginia Code § 61–8–14 (2010). Interestingly, West Virginia Code § 61–8–14(b)(3) provides that desecration "means destroying, cutting, mutilating, effacing, injuring, tearing down, removing, defacing, damaging or otherwise physically mistreating *in a way that a reasonable person knows will outrage the sensibilities of persons likely to observe or discover his or her actions.*" West Virginia Code § 29–

1–8a does not provide a definition of desecration.

B. Common Law Cause of Action for Grave Desecration and Damages Available

The common law cause of action available for desecration of those graves not encompassed within West Virginia Code § 29-1-8a remains viable. The parameters of such a common law cause of action have developed in distinct contexts as this Court has addressed specific situations. A primary paradigm for a common law grave desecration cause of action emerges through an analysis of those prior cases.

In *Ritter v. Couch*, 71 W.Va. 221, 76 S.E. 428 (1912), this Court addressed the issue of a common law action for grave desecration and recognized that an action in equity lies for desecration of a grave which has been dedicated for cemetery purposes. The sanctity of a cemetery and the need for a cause of action to recover damages for desecration were succinctly observed by the *Ritter* Court, as follows:

If relatives of blood may not defend the graves of their departed[,] who may? Always the human heart has rebelled against the invasion of the cemetery precincts; always has the human mind contemplated the grave as the last and enduring resting place after the struggles and sorrows of this world.

A more specific analysis was accomplished in *England v. Central Pocahontas Coal Co.*, 86 W.Va. 575, 104 S.E. 46 (1920), wherein this Court held that near relatives of a decedent may maintain a cause of action for damages for desecration of a grave or body because the bodily remains are accorded a type of property right. The *England* Court also noted that, "[g]enerally, a cemetery lot in the country is a notable object and has well defined boundaries and is easily identified." In syllabus point one of England, this Court held:

While strictly considered there is no right of property in a dead body, nevertheless the right to bury a corpse and preserve the remains is a legal right, which in this country is regarded as a quasi right in property, the violation of which is cognizable in and may be redressed at the suit of near relatives by an action on the case against the wrongdoer.

In pertinent part of syllabus point two of *England*, this Court explained: "Whether such right of burial exists by deed or by mere license, so long as it exists and is not lawfully revoked or destroyed, it may be ... redressed and protected in our courts[.]"

In *Whitehair v. Highland Memory Gardens, Inc.*, 174 W.Va. 458, 327 S.E.2d 438 (1985), this Court addressed a situation in which the defendant had obtained permission to disinter and rebury certain bodies due to highway construction. The defendant was eventually accused of negligence in the handling of the bodies. In syllabus point three of *Whitehair*, this Court stated that "[a] cause of action for negligent or intentional mishandling of a dead body does not require a showing of physical injury or pecuniary loss. Mental anguish is a sufficient basis for recovery of damages."

In syllabus point three of *In re Hillcrest Memorial Gardens*, 146 W.Va. 337, 119 S.E.2d 753 (1961), this Court enunciated a defining characteristic of a cemetery as an area "set apart," explaining as follows:

A cemetery is a place where dead bodies of human beings are buried; an area of ground *set apart* for the burial of the dead, *either by public authority or private enterprise.* It includes not only lots for depositing the bodies of the dead, but also such avenues, walks and grounds as may be necessary for its use, or for shrubbery and ornamental purposes.

In *Bennett v. 3 C Coal Co.*, 180 W.Va. 665, 379 S.E.2d 388 (1989), the plaintiff had sought damages for surface cracks in grave sites allegedly incurred through mine subsidence. The *Bennett* Court found that "a cause of action will lie for the unlawful desecration of a grave site even though no disturbance of the body interred therein can be shown." Further, the *Bennett* Court found that "damages for mental distress may be recovered by the next of kin for the disturbance or desecration of a relative's grave." The Court rejected the contention that damages for mental distress were not available for the unlawful disturbance of a grave site where no physical disturbance of the body could be demonstrated, recognizing that family members will generally suffer mental distress if either the bodies or the grave sites are desecrated. The potential for punitive damages was also discussed, and the *Bennett* Court applied the traditional rule that punitive damages would be available upon proof that the defendant engaged in "a wilful, wanton, reckless or malicious act."

This Court thereafter addressed allegations of grave desecration in connection with logging and strip mining in *Concerned Loved Ones and Lot Owners Association of Beverly Hills Memorial Gardens v. Pence*, 181 W.Va. 649, 383 S.E.2d 831 (1989). In *Pence*, this Court reiterated the established principle that a cemetery is properly characterized as a land set aside and dedicated for the specific purpose of a cemetery. The *Pence* Court explained that "[t]he intention of the owner of the land to dedicate it for a public cemetery, together with the acceptance and use of the same by the public, or the consent and acquiescence of the owner in the long-continued use of his lands for such purpose" is sufficient to evidence a proper dedication.

The *Pence* Court also discussed damages potentially available to the plaintiffs, explaining that the plaintiffs may be entitled to "compensatory or only nominal [damages], depending upon the nature of the harmful acts as the evidence at trial demonstrates." The *Pence* Court noted as follows: "It has been held that in this type of action, nominal damages at least, are awardable, and compensatory damages may be recovered if actual damage is shown." As in *Bennett*, the *Pence* Court found that "punitive damages may be recovered in this case if the plaintiffs can prove that the defendants' conduct was willful, wanton, reckless, or malicious." The potential for recovery of damages for mental distress for the disturbance or desecration of the graves was again recognized.

In its order certifying questions to this Court in the present case, the lower court accurately recognized that the gradual development of the common law of West Virginia on the issue of grave desecration has not generated precise elements of the tort, focusing instead upon the rights of a plaintiff in a specific factual scenario. In the situation of these certified questions, we are faced with a much broader request than has previously been addressed in more fact-specific inquiries. As the Court of Appeals of New York aptly recognized when confronted with an issue requiring evaluation of historic development of common law regarding improper use of body parts of a deceased person, "this inquiry cannot possibly yield answers with perfect congruity considering the different context in which common-law courts dealt with this subject. Although the case before us is unprecedented, the common law offers enough guidance for us to answer the question confidently."

Throughout this Court's evaluation of grave desecration matters, certain intrinsic principles have emerged. A prerequisite to common law recovery has consistently been a showing that the land upon which the decedents are buried is an actual cemetery, with identifiable boundaries or limits. Moreover, it must be recognized that in order to prove a claim of negligence, the defendant's violation of a duty owed to the plaintiff must be demonstrated. ...

This Court holds that the elements of a common law cause of action for grave desecration are: (1) the grave site in question must be within a publicly or privately maintained cemetery, clearly marked in a manner which will indicate its use as a cemetery, with identifiable boundaries and limits; (2) dedication of the area to the purpose of providing a place of burial by the owner of the property or that the owner acquiesced in its use for burial; (3) the area was identifiable as a cemetery by its appearance prior to the defendant's entry or that the defendant had prior knowledge of the existence of the cemetery; (4) the decedent in question is interred in the cemetery by license or right; (5) the plaintiff is the next of kin of the decedent with the right to assert a claim for desecration; and (6) the defendant proximately caused, either directly or indirectly, defacement, damage, or other mistreatment of the physical area of the decedent's grave site or common areas of the cemetery in a manner that a reasonable person knows will outrage the sensibilities of others.

As the lower court recognized, this Court has permitted recovery where the act of desecration was committed indirectly. ... Although a grave can certainly be subjected to grave desecration indirectly, the indirect manner of harm is an evidentiary issue encompassed within a cause of action for grave desecration, rather than a matter of pleading a separate cause of action. The cause of action remains grave desecration whether it was accomplished through direct or indirect means, and actual grave desecration is required. Thus, this Court disagrees with the manner in which the lower court answered the question regarding a cause of action for indirect desecration. ...

[T]he damages available in a common law cause of action for grave desecration include nominal damages; compensatory damages if actual damage has occurred; mental distress; and punitive damages if the defendant's conduct is determined to be willful, wanton, reckless, or malicious.

C. Next of Kin Possessing Right of Recovery Under Common Law

This Court has consistently specified that the next of kin are entitled to recover damages in a common law cause of action for grave desecration. In *Whitehair*, this Court stated as follows:

"[T]he cause of action ordinarily belongs to the party with the right to possession of the body ... provided that he or she was living with the decedent at the time of death ... and has not waived his or her right.... If the spouse is deceased, the cause of action passes to the next of kin, *in order of relation established by the statute governing intestate succession.*"

West Virginia Code § 42–1–1 (1995) (Repl.Vol.2010), *et seq.*, governs intestate succession and will provide a framework for a determination of the next of kin entitled to recovery in grave desecration claims. However, as the lower court and the parties to the underlying action have emphasized, the individuals entitled to recovery in a grave desecration case must necessarily be limited in some fashion, rather than requiring an exhaustive search of all living relatives and permitting every living descendant of the decedent to maintain or join a cause of action.

This single cause of action principle was explained by this Court in *Warner v. Hedrick* ... as follows: "The Courts in a substantial majority of jurisdictions consistently have held that a single wrongful act causing damage to the property and injury to the person of one individual gives rise to only one cause of action against the wrongdoer." ...

Although this Court has not taken the opportunity to apply this single wrongful act concept to a claim of grave desecration, other courts have utilized this principle in explanation for limiting the number of claims available in a grave desecration case. In *North East Coal Co. v. Pickelsimer*, 253 Ky. 11, 68 S.W.2d 760 (1934), for instance, the court held that "[i]t is universally agreed that the right of action of the 'next of kin' is a family right, and daughters and sons or brothers and sisters may maintain one action and not a separate action by each one of them."

Similarly, in *Holleman v. Elmwood Cemetery Corp.*, 295 Ala. 267, 327 So.2d 716 (1976), the Alabama court found that all persons who occupy the same degree of kinship to the decedent should join in the same suit. To require otherwise "would subject the defendant to numerous suits by different parties for the same cause of action which should be settled in one suit." In *Hogan v. Woodward Iron Co.*, 263 Ala. 513, 83 So.2d 248 (1955), the court held that "[i]n the event of damage to the grave of a deceased person, the right of action, if any, accrues first to the surviving spouse, unless, of course, there are special circumstances.... If there is no surviving spouse the right is in the next of kin in the order of their relation to the deceased." ...

Based upon the foregoing analysis, this Court agrees with the answer to the certified question provided by the lower court on the issue of those entitled to recover and holds that the next of kin who possess the right to recover in a common law cause of action for grave desecration shall be the decedent's surviving spouse or, if such spouse is deceased, the person or persons of closest and equal degree of kinship in the order provided by West Virginia Code § 42–1–1, et seq.

D. Conclusion

Subsequent to this Court's reformulation of the certified questions from the Circuit Court of Logan County, we respond as follows:

Question No. 1: *Does West Virginia Code § 29–1–8a preempt a common law cause of action for direct or indirect desecration of a grave?*

This Court's Answer: Yes, to the extent that West Virginia Code § 29–1–8a specifically designates protection for certain narrowly-defined categories of graves and other related items.

Question No. 2: *Does a common law cause of action for direct and/or indirect grave desecration exist, and, if so, what are the elements of such actions and the damages recoverable?*

This Court's Answer: A common law cause of action for grave desecration does exist, and the elements of such cause of action are: (1) the grave site in question must be within a publicly or privately maintained cemetery, clearly marked in a manner which will indicate its use as a cemetery, with identifiable boundaries and limits; (2) dedication of the area to the purpose of providing a place of burial by the owner of the property or that the owner acquiesced in its use for burial; (3) the area was identifiable as a cemetery by its appearance prior to the defendant's entry or that the defendant had prior knowledge of the existence of the cemetery; (4) the decedent in question is interred in the cemetery by license or right; (5) the plaintiff is the next of kin of the decedent with the right to assert a claim for desecration; and (6) the defendant proximately caused, either directly or indirectly, defacement, damage, or other mistreatment of the physical area of the decedent's grave site or common areas of the cemetery in a manner that a reasonable person knows will outrage the sensibilities of others. A separate and distinct cause of action for indirect grave desecration does not exist; grave desecration accomplished through indirect means is encompassed within the elements of a common law cause of action for grave desecration.

The damages available in a common law cause of action for grave desecration include nominal damages; compensatory damages if actual damage has occurred; mental distress; and punitive damages if the defendant's conduct is determined to be willful, wanton, reckless, or malicious.

Question No. 3. *Who are the "next of kin" who possess the right to recover in a common law cause of action for grave desecration?*

This Court's Answer: The "next of kin" who possess the right to recover in a common law cause of action for grave desecration include the decedent's surviving spouse or, if such spouse is deceased, the person or persons of closest and equal degree of kinship in the order provided by West Virginia Code § 42–1–1, et seq.

Having answered the foregoing certified questions, as reformulated, we remand this matter to the Circuit Court of Logan County for further proceedings consistent with this opinion.

Certified Questions Answered and Case Remanded.

❖ ❖ ❖

SELECTED BIBLIOGRAPHY

William Blackstone, COMMENTARIES ON THE LAWS OF ENGLAND, VOLUME II 429.

Norman L. Cantor, AFTER WE DIE: THE LIFE AND TIMES OF THE HUMAN CADAVER (2010)

E. Coke, THIRD PART OF THE INSTITUTES OF THE LAWS OF ENGLAND 203 (1809)

Douglas Davies & Alastair Shaw, REUSING OLD GRAVES: A REPORT ON POPULAR BRITISH ATTITUDES (1995)

James J. Farrell, INVENTING THE AMERICAN WAY OF DEATH, 1830-1920 (1980)

Drew Gilpin Faust, THIS REPUBLIC OF SUFFERING: DEATH AND THE AMERICAN CIVIL WAR (2012)

David H. Getches, *Special Treatment of Cemeteries*, 40 S. CAL. L. REV. 716 (1967)

Richard Grey, A SYSTEM OF ENGLISH ECCLESIASTICAL LAW: EXTRACTED FROM THE CODEX JURIS ECCLESIASTICAL ANGLICANI OF THE RIGHT REVEREND THE LORD BISHOP OF LONDON (1732)

Mark Harris, GRAVE MATTERS: A JOURNEY THROUGH THE MODERN FUNERAL INDUSTRY TO A NATURAL WAY OF BURIAL (2008)

Percival E. Jackson, THE LAW OF CADAVERS AND OF BURIAL AND BURIAL PLACES (2nd ed. 1950).

Michael Kerrigan, THE HISTORY OF DEATH: BURIAL CUSTOMS AND FUNERAL RITES, FROM THE ANCIENT WORLD TO MODERN TIMES (2007)

Doron Kornbluth, CREMATION OR BURIAL: A JEWISH VIEW (2012)

Paul Koudounaris, THE EMPIRE OF DEATH: A CULTURAL HISTORY OF OSSUARIES AND CHARNEL HOUSES (2011)

Gary Leaderman, THE SACRED REMAINS: AMERICAN ATTITUDES TOWARDS DEATH, 1799-1883 (1996)

J. Brooke Little, THE LAW OF BURIAL: INCLUDING ALL THE BURIAL ACTS AND OFFICIAL REGULATIONS, WITH NOTES AND CASES (1888)

John Claudius Loudon, ON THE LAYING OUT, PLANTING, AND MANAGING OF CEMETERIES; AND ON THE IMPROVEMENT OF CHURCHYARDS (1843)

Tanya D. Marsh, THE LAW OF HUMAN REMAINS (2015)

Alfred George Marten, THE BURIAL QUESTION (1877)

Sidney Perley, MORTUARY LAW (1896).

Robert M. Poole, ON HALLOWED GROUND: THE STORY OF ARLINGTON NATIONAL CEMETERY (2009)

PRESERVING SACRED GROUND: SHOULD CAPITAL OFFENDERS BE BURIED IN AMERICA'S NATIONAL CEMETERIES: HEARING BEFORE THE COMMITTEE ON VETERAN'S AFFAIRS, 109TH CONGRESS, 1ST SESSION, 9-22 (2005)

Samuel B. Ruggles, AN EXAMINATION OF THE LAW OF BURIAL IN A REPORT TO THE SUPREME COURT OF NEW YORK (1856)

C. Allen Shaffer, *The Standing of the Dead: Solving the Problem of Abandoned Graveyards*, CAP. UNIV. L. REV. 479 (2003)

Robert Shay, *The Cemetery Lot: Rights and Restrictions*, 109 U. PA. L. REV. 378 (1961)

David Charles Sloane, THE LAST GREAT NECESSITY: CEMETERIES IN AMERICAN HISTORY (1991)

David E. Stannard, DEATH IN AMERICA (1975)

Joseph Story, AN ADDRESS DELIVERED ON THE DEDICATION OF THE CEMETERY AT MOUNT AUBURN SEPTEMBER 24, 1831 (1831)

E. Lewis Thomas, BAKER'S LAW RELATING TO BURIALS (6th ed. 1901)

Howard Evarts Weed, MODERN PARK CEMETERIES (1912)

Stephen Wickes, SEPULTURE (1884)

14 Am. Jur. 2d Cemeteries §§1-48

3 Am. Law. Zoning §18:19. Cemeteries (5th Ed.)

14 C.J.S. Cemeteries §§1-34

ABOUT THE AUTHORS

Tanya D. Marsh is a graduate of Indiana University—Bloomington (B.A. in history and political science) and Harvard Law School. She practiced law in Indianapolis for ten years before joining the faculty at the Wake Forest University School of Law in 2010. Marsh developed and began teaching the first course on funeral and cemetery law in an American law school in 2013. She has been elected to the membership of the American Law Institute and the American College of Real Estate Lawyers, and is an active leader in the American Bar Association—Real Property Trust and Estate Law Section and the Association of American Law Schools. Marsh is nationally recognized for her work in the law of human remains and cemetery law. She is the author of articles on the subject that have been published in the WAKE FOREST LAW REVIEW, the REAL PROPERTY TRUST AND ESTATE LAW JOURNAL, and THE HUFFINGTON POST.

Marsh is the author of the first treatise on funeral and cemetery law since 1950—THE LAW OF HUMAN REMAINS (2015). She is also the author of the forthcoming DISPOSITION OF HUMAN REMAINS—A LEGAL RESEARCH GUIDE (2015) and REGULATION OF THE FUNERAL INDUSTRY—A LEGAL RESEARCH GUIDE (2016) and the editor and primary author of GRAVE NEW WORLD: READINGS IN AMERICAN FUNERAL AND CEMETERY LAW (2015).

Marsh is a licensed funeral director in the State of California.

Daniel Gibson is a graduate of Campbell University (B.A. in government) and a 2015 graduate of Wake Forest University School of Law. Gibson has worked in a civil and criminal litigation, judicial chambers, and state government. Since 2013, he has researched funeral and cemetery law with Marsh. His research and input aided Marsh's funeral and cemetery law course and publications. Gibson contributed to Marsh's treatise on funeral and cemetery law. He hopes to use the skills he has learned from Marsh and Wake Forest to continue to serve his home state of North Carolina.

Català: El Cementiri Vell de Poble Nou (Barcelona)
Photo by David Chacobo

The painting on the cover of the book, "The Kiss of Death," was created by Dub Lee. It was inspired by the marble statute in Poblenou Cemetery in Barcelona, Spain. The sculpture, depicting death as a winged skeleton, is located at the grave of Josep Llaudet Soler. His epitaph reads:

> His young heart is thus extinguished. The blood in his veins grows cold. And all strength has gone. Faith has been extolled by his fall into the arms of death. Amen.

www.ingramcontent.com/pod-product-compliance
Lightning Source LLC
Chambersburg PA
CBHW082126210326
41599CB00031B/5883